Creation and Transcendence

Creation and Transcendence

Theological Essays on the Divine Sublime

Paul J. DeHart

LONDON • NEW YORK • OXFORD • NEW DELHI • SYDNEY

T&T CLARK

Bloomsbury Publishing Plc

50 Bedford Square, London, WC1B 3DP, UK
1385 Broadway, New York, NY 10018, USA
29 Earlsfort Terrace, Dublin 2, Ireland

BLOOMSBURY, T&T CLARK and the T&T Clark logo are trademarks of Bloomsbury Publishing Plc

First published in Great Britain 2021
Paperback edition published 2023

Copyright © Paul J. DeHart, 2021

Paul J. DeHart has asserted his right under the Copyright, Designs and Patents Act, 1988, to be identified as Author of this work.

For legal purposes the Acknowledgments on p. xi constitute an extension of this copyright page.

Cover design: Terry Woodley
Cover image: Oleg Romanko / Alamy Stock Photo

All rights reserved. No part of this publication may be reproduced or transmitted in any form or by any means, electronic or mechanical, including photocopying, recording, or any information storage or retrieval system, without prior permission in writing from the publishers.

Bloomsbury Publishing Plc does not have any control over, or responsibility for, any third-party websites referred to or in this book. All internet addresses given in this book were correct at the time of going to press. The author and publisher regret any inconvenience caused if addresses have changed or sites have ceased to exist, but can accept no responsibility for any such changes.

A catalogue record for this book is available from the British Library.

Library of Congress Cataloging-in-Publication Data
Names: DeHart, Paul J., 1964– author.
Title: Creation and transcendence : theological essays on the divine sublime / Paul DeHart.
Description: London ; New York : T&T Clark, 2021. |
Includes bibliographical references and index. |
Identifiers: LCCN 2020044057 (print) | LCCN 2020044058 (ebook) |
ISBN 9780567698704 (hardback) | ISBN 9780567698735 (epub) |
ISBN 9780567698711 (pdf)
Subjects: LCSH: Creation. | Transcendence of God. | Christianity–Philosophy. |
Philosophical theology. Classification: LCC BT695 .D44 2021 (print) |
LCC BT695 (ebook) | DDC 231.7/65–dc23
LC record available at https://lccn.loc.gov/2020044057
LC ebook record available at https://lccn.loc.gov/2020044058

ISBN: HB: 978-0-5676-9870-4
PB: 978-0-5676-9874-2
ePDF: 978-0-5676-9871-1
ePUB: 9780-5676-9873-5

Typeset by Newgen KnowledgeWorks Pvt. Ltd., Chennai, India

To find out more about our authors and books visit www.bloomsbury.com and sign up for our newsletters.

And the highest and most perfect degree of our knowledge in this life, as Dionysius says in his book on mystical theology, is when we are conjoined to God as to one unknown. ... Whence in order to indicate the unknowing in this most sublime of all knowing, it is said of Moses in Exodus 20-21 that he approached the darkness in which God is.

Thomas Aquinas
Summa Contra Gentiles III 49

Nothing finite can satisfy the desire of the intellect.

Thomas Aquinas
Summa Contra Gentiles III 50

Whoever desires the infinite does not know what he wants. But the inverse does not hold.

Friedrich Schlegel
Lyceum Fragments

Contents

Note on Aquinas Citations and on Pronouns for God — ix
Acknowledgments — xi

Introduction — 1

Part One *Cultus Mentis*: Accommodating the Endless Object — 19

1 Can Pascal Forgive Descartes? God's Ambiguous Infinity — 21

2 Absolute Dependence or Infinite Desire: Subjective Alignment with God in Schleiermacher and Kierkegaard — 41

3 "The Passage from Mind to Heart Is So Long …" Kierkegaard's *Repetition* and the Ontology of Agency — 55

4 $f(S)\frac{1}{3}$: The Instance of Pattern in Kathryn Tanner's Theology — 85

Part Two Dogma and the Infinite God: Trinity, Christology, Grace — 103

5 On the Contrary: Thomistic Second Thoughts on Eberhard Jüngel — 105

6 John Milbank's Divine Comedy: Not Funny Enough — 123

Part Three Aquinas and God's Ideas: The Impossible Mind of the Creator — 183

7 "Nothing in This Book is True, But It's Exactly How Things Are" — 185

8 Eclipse of the Divine Mind: The Divine Ideas as Anti-Platonic Epistemology — 195

9 The Creature Makes Itself: The Divine Ideas as Anti-Platonic Soteriology — 219

10 Improvising the Paradigms: The Divine Ideas as Anti-Platonic Ontology — 241

Works Cited — 271
Index — 281

Note on Aquinas Citations and on Pronouns for God

References to the *Summa Theologiae* are to part, question, article, and (where relevant) answer to objection. Example: *STh* I/II q. 93 a. 1 ad 2 would be the first part of the second part, the ninety-third question, first article, answer to the second objection. References to the *Summa contra Gentiles* are to book, chapter, and paragraph number, thus: *ScG* II 45 no. 10.

I have found no fully satisfying way of solving the problems surrounding gendered pronouns for God. In this book, I have employed a little strategy I learned from some of the later essays of Herbert McCabe: a regular alternation between male and female. If it brings readers up short just a bit, without distracting from the actual points I seek to make, then I will be happy. It is intended as just such a destabilizing or mildly discomfiting reminder, akin to Heidegger's "crossing" of being. It is vulnerable to criticisms from different directions, and some readers will surely be unhappy with it, but it does have some advantages. Why use "she"? The painfully slow (and still globally contested) ascent of women to fully recognized humanity and genuine partnership with men in voice, dignity, and social co-responsibility is one of the defining adventures of contemporary history. As a tiny gesture in the direction of that great and necessary project, I decided to tamper with pronouns. I intend reference to God as "she" to serve, not as a promotion of female deity, but rather as a minor but insistent disruption of the potentially suffocating hegemony of male grammatical markers. Feminist theologians have given good reason to suspect that this hegemony functions, in spite of all caveats and good intentions, to augment a covert imaginative gendering of God as male. But then why still use "he" at all? One justification of its continued presence might be precisely the exposure of its arbitrariness and the disorientation of its pseudo-naturalness through the repeated interruption of its historical monologue by feminine pronouns. I have more in mind, though. I do not maintain the use primarily as a comfort to those who cherish traditional language's male gendering as such, though I am glad if it keeps them on board long enough to become aware of its ambiguity. But I wish to maintain a subdued or "crossed" use of male language for God precisely in the interest of those who are becoming increasingly allergic to it. I do not pursue a complete purge, that is, because I have no desire to contribute to (justly) sensitive contemporary readers being cut off from the enormous and indispensable heritage of traditional doctrine, woven as the latter is into a web of androcentric language. Without seeking to mask the sexist cultural assumptions informing the standard grammar, I hope to sustain among readers the continued appropriation (critically faithful) of the great stream of doctrine by providing practice in gently removing the sting from the male vocabulary. Only by learning to bracket the traditional discourse's gendered language for God in the right way (not at all denying the accompanying penetration, the degree debatable in each case, of patriarchal modes of thought) will it be possible to prevent male God-language from becoming, for a growing number of readers, a cloud obscuring every element of argument, insight, and wisdom that has arisen prior to the feminist awakening. Just as I want my theology students, all of them, to think of the entire Christian tradition as *belonging to them* (and they to it), a usable, indeed transformative, past in spite of its alienating and dangerous elements, so I want to work against the formation of a generation of readers who are so sensitized to male language for the deity that they cannot listen past it. Hardly a widespread problem, one might respond, but I have seen enough from my own students to make me think my concern is not misplaced. Finally, what might be gained from oscillating between both? First, both sets of goals just outlined (for "she" and "he" usages, respectively) are promoted by having the different pronouns arise in a deliberately equal yet random fashion. (The accidental nature of any particular use means that no gendering intention lies behind any instance in a given phrase or sentence.) Second, the slightly subversive shifting between masculine and feminine codings for God seems not unfitting in a time of intense reflection on the culturally constructed elements elaborated upon the biological sexual dyad. Finally, the very strangeness of the usage might have the advantage of problematizing easy reading, thereby problematizing as well easy, "natural" language for God. After all, making talk about God harder, in the right ways, is a deeply traditional and perfectly orthodox thing to do (see Sebastian Moore's essay cited in the introduction below and Nicholas Lash, *Voices of Authority* [London: Sheed &Ward, 1976], 105–6).

Acknowledgments

I am grateful to the editors and publishers for permission to reprint several of the chapters of this book.

Chapter 1 was first printed in *The Journal of Religion*, 82 (2002): 75–96. Reprinted by permission of the University of Chicago Press.

Chapter 2 was first printed in *Schleiermacher und Kierkegaard: Subjektivität und Wahrheit. Akten des Schleiermacher-Kierkegaard-Kongresses in Kopenhagen, Oktober 2003*, ed. Niels Jørgen Cappelørn, Richard Crouter, Theodor Jørgensen, and Claus Osthövener (Berlin: Walter de Gruyter, 2006), 561–76. Reprinted by permission of Walter de Gruyter.

Chapter 3 was first printed in *Modern Theology*, 31 (2015): 91–122. Reprinted by permission of John Wiley & Sons, Ltd.

Chapter 4 was first printed in *The Gift of Theology: The Contribution of Kathryn Tanner*, ed. Rosemary P. Carbine and Hilda P. Koster (Minneapolis: Fortress Press, 2015), 29–55. Reprinted by permission of Fortress Press.

Chapter 5 was first printed in *Indicative of Grace – Imperative of Freedom: Essays in Honour of Eberhard Jüngel in His 80th Year*, ed. R. David Nelson (London: Bloomsbury T&T Clark, 2014), 51–70. Reprinted by permission of Bloomsbury Publishing Plc.

Chapter 6 has not previously been published. Portions of the first half were delivered as a talk and discussed at a faculty colloquium hosted by the Lumen Christi Institute in Chicago (February 2019). My thanks are due to Thomas Levergood, director of the Institute, for his invitation; the Theology Club of the University of Chicago Divinity School for its support; and especially to Jeremy Wilkins and Jordan Wales for their insightful comments on the material, prompting a number of revisions from which the chapter has greatly benefited.

Chapter 7 has not previously been published.

Chapter 8 was first printed in *Ephemerides Theologiae Lovanienses*, 93 (2017): 1–27. Reprinted by permission of Peeters Publishers.

Chapter 9 was first printed in *Theological Studies*, 78 (2017): 412–34. Reprinted by permission of Sage Publications.

Chapter 10 was first printed in *Modern Theology*, 32 (2016): 594–621. Reprinted by permission of John Wiley & Sons, Ltd.

I am also grateful for the following publishers or copyright holders for permission to use several excerpts as epigraphs.

To E.J. Brill Publishers for the quote on p. 123 from Jonathan Z. Smith, and to Wm. B. Eerdmans Publishing Co. for the quote on the same page from Maurice Blondel, both used as epigraphs for Chapter 6. To Fergus Kerr for the quote on p. 128 used as the epigraph for Section I of Chapter 6. To the University of Toronto Press for the quote on p. 144 by Bernard Lonergan used as the epigraph of Section III of Chapter 6.

To Wayne State University Press for the translated quote on p. 172 by Jean Paul, and to Broadway Video for the line from *Mr. Mike's Mondo Video* on the same page, both used as epigraphs for Section V of Chapter 6.

Finally, the title of Chapter 7 quotes the title of an already published book:

Nothing in This Book Is True, But It's Exactly How Things Are, 25th Anniversary Edition by Bob Frissell, published by North Atlantic Books, copyright © 1994, 2009, 2019 by Bob Frissell. Reprinted by permission of North Atlantic Books. I thank the publisher for this permission.

Introduction

I.

The chapters assembled in this volume are contributions toward a Christian theology of creation *ex nihilo*. "Christian" here delimits the intellectual history and religious tradition explored; the term also indicates the book's authorial perspective: embedded within a particular history of communal life and teaching, convinced of its access to truth, and committed to its continued flourishing. Not that the elaboration of such a theology is relevant to Christianity alone. In fact, the connected ideas of an absolute and transcendent creator, an intelligent and voluntary act of creation, and an utterly spontaneous origination of all finite reality, all essence, actuality, and possibility— these are the common heritage of Judaism and Islam as much as Christianity, as the magisterial comparative work of David Burrell has shown.[1] This tradition took centuries to elaborate and perfect, reaching an initial peak of sophistication with the great medieval theologians (in each of the great monotheisms) but still philosophically viable today. It is at any rate the most natural construal of "maker of heaven and earth," the creedal language on the lips of millions of worshipping Christians across the globe.

Many thinkers, in philosophy and theology, continue to test and enhance the conceptual coherence of what can be called "creational monotheism." Others establish its articulation with, and demands upon, the other elements of the Christian confession. Still others, such as Rowan Williams, have meditated on the spiritual or existential dimension of the doctrine.[2] And few have reflected as powerfully on the revolutionary impact (cultural, political, and religious) of this gift of the Hebrews as the British Dominican Herbert McCabe, for whom it was a charter of human freedom: the proclamation of the death of all gods, in the name of the radical proximity of the mystery that originates all.[3] But the reception among Christians of creational monotheism is today far from universal. Beyond the failure not uncommon among many theologians even to notice the deep implications of creation *ex nihilo*, head-on challenges from various directions have been made.

Some objections are raised on ethical grounds. For example, the classical doctrine of creation is sometimes thought to be inimical to ecological thought and practice;

---

[1] See, e.g., David Burrell, *Freedom and Creation in Three Traditions* (Notre Dame: University of Notre Dame Press, 1993).
[2] Rowan Williams, "On Being Creatures," in *On Christian Theology* (Oxford: Blackwell, 2000), 63–78.
[3] Herbert McCabe, *God Matters* (London: Geoffrey Chapman, 1987), especially Part I.

ecotheologians like Sallie McFague decry the implied picture of a natural order deprived of sanctity and divine presence in its own right, contrasted with a disembodied and otherworldly source of all value.[4] Feminist critiques often follow similar lines, as in the case of Catherine Keller's poetic and highly original speculations in the tradition of process metaphysics; some of the power of her evocative reimagining of creation lies in its contrast with a supposedly traditional model of a distant and dominating "male" deity "controlling" a passive and material "other."[5] The thoughtfulness and moral passion often evidenced in these critiques demand their serious consideration. But it must be asked whether the deleterious ethical consequences rightly of concern to such critics really follow from the classical doctrine with the necessity that is usually alleged. Much depends, in fact, upon the quite varied ways in which traditional creation is pictured, or upon the metaphors used to clothe its austere metaphysical armature. Defenders of the older doctrine against its frequent caricature have reason to echo Newman's lament concerning the supposed incompatibility of Christian faith with modern science: "It is not reason that is against us, but imagination."[6] It is at least to be hoped that the way creation *ex nihilo* in all its rigor is imaginatively evoked in the chapters that follow might suggest that the pictures that so readily occur to many of a domineering deity and an inert, devalued cosmos are in fact arbitrary, if not directly contrary to the actual sense of the doctrine.

There are also (sometimes joined to ethical criticisms, sometimes not) challenges to the strictly intellectual viability of the traditional account of God's relation to the world, often in the name of a better scheme. One of the great counter-traditions of this sort originated in the Kantian epistemological attack on metaphysical reason. Accepting the premises of this critique, the idealist systems of the early nineteenth century sought to articulate "the Absolute" as the ultimate principle grounding the transcendental subject or finite determinacy as such; various "speculative theisms" persisted in German philosophy for some time after. The other great theistic lineage intended to replace classical accounts had its heyday in the early twentieth century, rejecting as outdated the Aristotelian metaphysical conceptualization of natural interaction and change and extrapolating instead from the findings of modern physical and life sciences. Whitehead's metaphysics of process was by far the most influential system of the latter type, particularly among Christian theologians searching for an alternative to the classic account.

Today the real rivals to classical creative monotheism, especially among Christian theologians, are to be found in theological extensions of these two philosophical traditions. True, the sweeping dismissal on epistemological grounds of metaphysical reflection (whether in the name of Kantian transcendentalism, Humean empiricism, or logical positivism) is no longer the automatic consensus within philosophy. Sophisticated and compelling explorations in large-scale realist ontology have been and continue to be achieved; some of them extend the insights and trajectories of

---

[4] Sallie McFague, *The Body of God: An Ecological Theology* (Minneapolis: Augsburg Fortress, 1993).
[5] Catherine Keller, *The Face of the Deep: A Theology of Becoming* (New York: Routledge, 2001).
[6] Nicholas Lash, *The Beginning and the End of 'Religion'* (Cambridge: Cambridge University Press, 1996), 82.

Aristotelian and scholastic metaphysical reflection, but all of them give the lie to any lingering prejudice concerning the modern impossibility of theistic metaphysics. Such a prejudice informed the luxuriant speculative growth in Kant's wake, where the ultimate principle was understood not as the transcendent creator but rather as the transcendental ego or as the primal absolute unity generating yet overcoming the subject/object and nature/spirit divisions.

It is not the Kantian starting point but the speculative culmination in Hegel that is the persistent, half-hidden scheme informing most of the still-influential theological system-builders of the latter part of the previous century. Hegel's fervent conviction was that his philosophy, where the absolute eternally actualizes itself through the incorporation of the negativity and death of history into its own identity, is the true meaning of the cruciform theologies of Paul and Luther. Amid the upheavals and disillusionment of the twentieth century, a series of theologians tried to outbid the cultural "death of God" by repeating this Hegelian gesture of a "speculative Good Friday," using radical rereadings of the doctrines of incarnation and Trinity to justify situating negation, suffering, death, and/or quasi-temporal actualization as necessary elements of theistic discourse. Variations on this theme are central to Protestant heavyweights like the later Barth, Moltmann, Pannenberg, Jüngel, and Jenson, and are arguably present (if somewhat tempered) in Catholic thinkers like Kasper and Balthasar.

The other systematized theological approach to the God-world relation, equally hostile to classical theism, lies in more or less faithful appropriations of process metaphysics. Again, philosophical winds have shifted. Whitehead's decision that the only philosophically respectable theistic function is to ground (and instantiate!) the principles of organic constitution and physical interaction is connected with no longer reigning scientistic assumptions (i.e., that the valid role for ontological reflection must be that of securing natural scientific investigation as the exclusive cognitive paradigm, or at least that of theoretically coordinating its findings). It is instead the grand speculative picture he devised, where God and world form a perpetual dyad, proceeding together on an open-ended journey into mutual creative enrichment, that has captured the imaginations of some Christian theologians dissatisfied with what is perceived to be a static, abstract, substance-based, and relationless scheme of God and world. It is not at all as evident today as it was to many moderns, including Whitehead, that scientific theorizations of the natural world have obviously discredited pre-modern metaphysical concepts. But the appeal of his theism no longer lies in its modernism or scientism but in its perceived advantages for the promotion of a more chastened, responsible, and humane version of Christian belief.[7]

---

[7] Perhaps the biggest obstacle to the reception of classical creationism in all its ramifications lies not in the theological adoption of these Whiteheadian and Hegelian alternatives but rather in the radical subordination of creation to Christology. In the wake of Barth there are many theologians who ground all theological claims in special revelation and Christology and who are consequently uncomfortable with the very idea of a relatively free-standing treatment of creation as a central doctrine in its own right. Whether acknowledged or implicit, such Barthian prejudgments are typically in play when the radical asymmetry between creator and creature as classically conceived is diluted or abandoned, usually in the name of privileging putatively more primal modes of divine act (grace, love, election, suffering), and often worked out through the incorporation of the

Whatever the authentic ethical, psychological, and cultural impulses that lie behind their adoption (and the insight, integrity, and urgency of such impulses is not here denied), these great rival schematizations of the doctrine of creation are finally incompatible with the creative monotheism assumed and developed in this book. The goal here is certainly not a comprehensive refutation of these alternatives, if that were even possible for such all-encompassing conceptual frameworks, but rather the commendation of creational monotheism (as inspired especially by Thomas Aquinas) by exhibiting its scope and coherence, working out in greater detail some of its implications, and (hopefully) reimagining it in less alienating and more seductive terms. This commendation is all the more necessary today given the negative role so often assigned to creational monotheism as the great foil, a self-evidently damaging legacy from the past that needs to be abandoned.

Still, where (as here) its viability is granted, creational monotheism will naturally confront the rivals with critical sallies of its own. In regard to process thought, the counter-position assumed and elaborated upon in the present volume should be referred back, at least generally, to ideas already well expounded by David Burrell, Robert Sokolowski, and Austin Farrer, whose magnificent *Finite and Infinite* still stands as a vital resource for present and future work on creational monotheism.[8] As for the speculative *theologia crucis* that has subsumed the doctrine of creation among so many of the Protestant systematizers, the point at issue really lies with the prior Hegelian elevation of negation into the absolute. He blazed a trail that many, directly indebted to him or not, continue to follow. All that will be said here is that classical theism is a standing rebuke to the famous Spinozist dictum: "All determination is negation." This is a perfectly acceptable description of created or finite being masquerading as an absolute metaphysical axiom. It is a fallacy both of Platonist theology and of German idealism and romanticism (Schleiermacher excepted) that it allowed this subordinate proposition to stray into definitions of the highest principle. Creational theism insists that the divine is determinate (i.e., not indeterminate) precisely as limitless positivity. It was the gift of Aquinas to fashion the most useful conceptual tools for the rational apprehension of limitless positivity, though largely (inevitably) in the shape of regulations for our ideas (disqualifications, torsions, analogical prolongations) and clamps upon our anthropomorphic imaginings. So creational theism will refuse from the outset the still common maneuver that

---

God-world relation into a speculative Trinitarian scheme. The epistemology of revelation hereby assumed, as well as the Christomonist reduction of God's ways with the world to outworkings of the incarnation, should both be directly and energetically challenged, but, apart from the critical remarks on Tanner and Jüngel below, that is not the task here. In lieu of such detailed engagement, this volume's constructive counter-project as a whole can be regarded as an implicit identification and questioning of these still widely shared theological biases.

[8] David Burrell, *Aquinas: God and Action* (Notre Dame: University of Notre Dame Press, 1979); David Burrell, *Faith and Freedom: An Interfaith Perspective* (Oxford: Blackwell, 2004); Robert Sokolowski, *The God of Faith and Reason* (Notre Dame: University of Notre Dame Press, 1982); Austin Farrer, *Finite and Infinite: A Philosophical Essay*, 2nd ed. (London: Dacre Press, 1959). Many scholars of Aquinas could also be mentioned here. For a concise analysis of Farrer's book, see Paul DeHart, "Farrer's Theism: *Finite and Infinite*," in *Austin Farrer for Today: A Prophetic Agenda*, ed. Richard Harries and Stephen Platten (London: SCM Press, 2020), 98–110.

employs variants of Hegel's Trinitarianism to involve negativity, whether necessary or freely undertaken, in the absolute being.

So then, the position on creation under discussion in the following chapters is not given a comprehensive exposition, nor is it developed systematically from basic principles. That work has already been done by superior predecessors. What, then, is the particular approach of the volume? What does it contribute to this already old and extensively elaborated tradition of creational monotheism? The theme that animates all of these chapters is that of the infinity of God, its meaning and implications. The note of divine infinity is sometimes associated with Duns Scotus in contrast to Aquinas; the latter, though certainly not denying its truth in application to God (he accepts without demurral an objector's statement that "God is infinite and his effects are finite"), employs the term with restraint and does not grant it a central metaphysical role. But if we employ the term in a broad sense, that of utter freedom from the bounds or limits of the created order, several of the implications of creational monotheism that will be explored in what follows can fruitfully be cast as modes of God's infinity. And unlike the terms "transcendent" or "absolute," the adjective "infinite" injects a useful note of extravagance or immeasurable elevation. The former terms seem to connote too readily the limit (the immanent or relative) that is exceeded, allowing it to enter surreptitiously into the definition of God; "infinite," on the other hand, suggests something more satisfyingly (if disturbingly) unrestrained. In short, the term "infinite" (and the related "immense") serve as shorthand for the kind of transcendence associated with a strict doctrine of creation from nothing.

God is infinite as unbounded actuality; whatever is real, active, effective, or beautiful in the countless limited forms that make up the world is only a feeble echo, a cramped suggestion or murky reflection of the complete and immediate actuality of God's being. As unbounded actuality God contains unbounded possibility; not only whatever is not God, but also whatever could ever not be God in any way is virtually resident within the divine power. Finally, God is unbounded intention; God knows and wills not only the immeasurable reality that God is but also every tiniest detail of the actual created world along with the numberless shadow-beings in the domain of the unactualized. But another note must be added here. God's infinity has so far been described in terms of a lack of any outward bound or limit in being, knowledge, or power; the same term should also suggest that God lacks any inward bound or limit. God is not composite, theoretically resolvable into metaphysical elements or constituted by prior moments; if God is without bounds, God is also without seams or joints. This is the note, closely related to theistic infinity, of God's simplicity. This additional consideration conditions our grasp of the divine infinity, lest the totality of God's being be conceived in any way as the aggregate of created realities or perfections, and lest the divine power and knowledge and will be theorized in their untrammeled extension over and involvement with created beings as somehow, really or intentionally, defined by their multiplicity and difference.

"Nothing is simpler than God. Just for that reason, nothing is more difficult than to think God."[9] The deep truth of Ingolf Dalferth's pronouncement is borne out by the

---

[9] Ingolf Dalferth, *Gott: Philosophisch-theologische Denkversuche* (Tübingen: Mohr Siebeck, 1992), 1.

following chapters, their successes and failures. For if the general background theme of the book is provided by divine infinity and simplicity in their unity as implications of creational monotheism, the specific accounts and arguments are concerned with three sorts of problem that arise in thinking through them. First, it is impossible to think the infinite God without reflection upon the relation of the thinker, the human subject, to God. But how could the subject dispose itself properly to this uniquely unmanageable object, this (one is tempted to say) non-object? Part One is concerned with this issue of subjective alignment with the creator. Second, these are Christian theoretical explorations, shaped by the assertion of Jesus of Nazareth as the perfect individual enactment of the human, divinely operated and extendable through history. Part Two concerns those difficult junctures where the infinite God of creational monotheism must be integrated with other basic Christian claims: Trinity, incarnation, grace. Finally, Part Three explores a particularly subtle but fateful issue: how the infinite-yet-simple God can possibly know perfectly and create willingly a world of staggering intricacy and multiplicity, without becoming "infected" in any way, metaphysically (as creator) or intentionally (as knower) by that multiplicity. This abstruse, seemingly marginal issue, which originates in debates over the interpretation of Aquinas, turns out to be rich in implications for philosophy and theology.

II.

Before giving an overview of the ordering and thematic linkages of the individual chapters, a word might be prefaced concerning the prominent role theological anthropology plays in this book. Why should a book about creational monotheism spend so much time talking about the human self? The answer, generally speaking, is that any talk about God, the source and meaning of all existence, including human existence, must inevitably be talk about us as well. Intellectually responsible talk about God will involve at some point talk about talk (what are the ultimate possibilities of language?), talk about knowledge (how are thoughts about God cognitively informed?), talk about the good (how does the unique final value relate to the moral universe of values?), and talk about the future (what are we for?). Even the more specialized topics outlined above cannot avoid bringing in anthropological reflection. Part One, obviously, is directly concerned with the problem presented by divine infinity to the rational human subject. Part Two must likewise discuss anthropological matters insofar as they are implicated in the central Christian mysteries of incarnation and grace. Even Part Three, directly focused as it is on rethinking the problem of divine ideas, quickly leads into a dispute over their human significance; once Christian Platonic theories are called in question, the ideas as epistemic illumination and salvific telos are problematized.

Intelligence (understanding and will) as a peculiar human capacity plays a special role in all such considerations. An interesting link between the intellectual act as God's image in creation and the already indicated principle of divine simplicity can be suggested here, though it cannot be developed. Any theistic model (Whitehead's is no exception) appeals to some implicit stratification of value within the created order, some hierarchy of entities or acts, in order to articulate the projected excellences of the divine. From the perspective of creational monotheism, one error of process theism is the unconfined conceptual extension granted to analysis of natural processes; even God as the highest principle is defined as that agent sufficient to supply boundary conditions and attractive orientation for all organization and development. As Whitehead in effect transforms the laws of cosmic ordering into principles of being itself, God must be the highest exemplification of these laws; God's transcendence is limited to that of the grandest natural entity.

This contrasts sharply with the radical simplicity that controls analogical thinking in classical theism. Alerted by Aquinas' teaching, one might suspect that the process approach to the divine suffers from a perspectival illusion due to the peculiar location of the human observer within the cosmic order. For the Thomist, human beings are located at that last point in the upward scale of being where creaturely excellence coincides with organizational complexity. Surprisingly, the systematic postulation of a realm of disembodied intelligences, that is, angels (interpreting scriptural accounts but conceptually elaborated as Aristotelian simple substances), performs a crucial function in breaking off or relativizing this connection. Humanity is thereby rendered a threshold phenomenon; ascent in the scale of being beyond that level is marked by increasing metaphysical simplicity, that is, greater formal unification integrating enhanced richness of content. Hence, the prime analogical model for higher levels of existence is no longer the intensified complexification of physical systems but the subsumption of greater masses of information under simpler but more powerful conceptual formulations. The angelic possibility need not be actually affirmed in theorizing the divine; it stands simply as a sign problematizing any straightforward extrapolation of organic systematics by suggesting an alternative scale of value: the increasing scope of intelligent unification, an ordered reduction of proliferating data to higher eminent integrations.[10]

After this aside, attention can now be directed to the overall shape of this collection. How do the different chapters connect with one another to develop the themes of the work as a whole? The first chapter introduces the basic ambiguity, from a theological perspective, of the idea of divine infinity. On the one hand, it can represent that abstract intensification of transcendence that leaves the very idea of God alien and hostile to the constraint and fragility that a saving God is supposed to take on and transfigure: *menschenfeindlich*, in Nietzsche's parlance. On the other hand, it can represent the intractability of the idea of God within the empire of human reason, the impossibility of God as a concept among others. This duality of possibilities points to the twofold problem or challenge involved in any attempt on the part of theology to employ the philosophy of the infinite (Descartes's *l'être infini*) as a tool for theologically articulating the scriptural God of creation and salvation (Pascal's *Dieu d'Abraham*,

---

[10] In Aquinas, the constant factor at every level is the Aristotelian formal cause. At first, the increasing power of forms is marked by the ability to unify and command ever more intricate systematic arrangements of the material substrate; the animating forms of human beings are the pivot point beyond which increased formal power is marked by the ability to persist and perform living and intentional functions independently of any bodily instrument.

d'Isaac, et de Jacob). Pascal accused Descartes of substituting the former for the latter, an unforgiveable offense in theological eyes. Yet if the doctrine of creation ultimately demands an infinite God, the dual problem is that of reconciling the approaches, in two senses. On the one hand, the challenge will be to properly affirm the conceptual elusiveness of the divine infinite without rendering unintelligible God's covenantal engagement with fallen humanity, especially as codified in the doctrines of incarnation and Trinity. On the other hand, the challenge will be to safeguard the radical conceptual transcendence of the creator without defining God as the opposite of the world, hence as antihuman.

The second chapter indicates two possible subjective postures that can bring together the infinite deity with an anthropological account of faith, which must involve an appropriate receptivity to that infinity. Schleiermacher and Kierkegaard mount a common front in their intent to protect the limitless divine against the pretensions of speculative reason; pursuant to this end, however, they promote two quite distinct subjective orientations.[11] The properly receptive personal stance for Schleiermacher lies in the permeation of consciousness by that dimension of immediate (i.e., nonobjective) self-awareness referencing the always-prior derivation from a transcendent source of one's own existence and its total interactive context ("absolute dependence"). Kierkegaard, for his part, renders the divine presence to the conscious self in terms of volition rather than feeling; the particular individual must continually will its chosen forms of existence as a renunciation of the finality of any limited good (an "infinite negative resolution"), actualizing in each emerging situation a desire for the infinite good. Taken as ultimate the two stances indicated might well be incompatible, but each one preserves a genuine insight into the divine infinity. Schleiermacher correctly affirms the radical asymmetry between creator and creature, with the resulting barriers against the literal application to God of anthropomorphic attributes.[12] Kierkegaard's

---

[11] Kierkegaard's strong anti-idealist emphasis on God's transcendence of human reason is well known. Much less noted, at least among theologians, has been the parallel stance of Schleiermacher. His determined removal of God or the absolute from theory's grasp was not just a marker of his resistance to idealism's pretensions. It singled him out even among the early romantic thinkers (Hölderlin, Novalis, Schlegel) whose basic philosophical orientation he shared. For a useful (albeit wary) discussion that highlights a number of revealing passages, see Manfred Frank's introduction to Friedrich Schleiermacher, *Dialektik*, vol. 1, ed. Manfred Frank (Frankfurt: Suhrkamp, 2001), 91–7 and 109–12.

[12] Schleiermacher's theorization of the Trinity in its own way addresses the first challenge of divine infinity. See Paul DeHart, "*Ter mundus accipit infinitum*: the Dogmatic Coordinates of Schleiermacher's Trinitarian Treatise," *Neue Zeitschrift für Systematische Theologie und Religionsphilosophie* 52 (2010): 17–39. He insists upon an almost classically rigorous model of the creator's transcendence yet deftly combines this with a promising (if not fully satisfying) account of the economic engagements of God, present within the immanent realm as Son and Spirit. Insisting upon the role of intelligent intentionality ("rational consciousness") as the site of this presence allows him to give a structural function within the doctrine of the Trinity to the divine infinity. God takes authentic shape within the world as covenantal counterpart, and this not in spite of the absolute power of creativity but because of it. Yet in elaborating these differentiated receptivities of God's power within the world, Schleiermacher maintains the strictest vigilance against the smuggling into God's eternal identity of human relations or modes of being. This danger, particularly the temptation to import Christ's human suffering into the deity, is vividly discussed from a Thomist standpoint in McCabe, *God Matters*, 39–51. A book-length treatment of this issue is Thomas Weinandy, *Does God Suffer?* (Edinburgh: T&T Clark, 2000). The same anti-anthropomorphic position, now in regard to gender roles and sexual relations, is carefully argued in Linn Tonstad's

conception likewise recalls the divine grounding of every worldly moment, but in a volitional context this points to the limitless desire to keep freely affirming myself or my own createdness within a developing, providential history.

Chapter 3 thoroughly explores this via Kierkegaard's concept of "repetition," showing how (when mediated by Aquinas' metaphysical framework) it supplies the elements of an ontology of human agency in face of the absolute God of creation and providence. The Kierkegaardian ethic envisions the penetration of each moment of an individual's existence with freedom's desire to continually construct the self in correspondence to the creator's successive shaping of its situation. In effect, as opposed to the Greek ideal of "living the life of the ideas" (to be revisited in Chapter 9), Kierkegaard proposes the eternal meaning of oneself as a pursuit in and through historical existence. The infinite dimension of human desire is thereby unveiled: the boundless, constitutively unfinished willing of an unanticipatible self, at last propelled via its restless historical unfolding into the abyss of the creator's idea. This is, in a way, a post-romantic version of Aquinas' Aristotelian claim that the intelligent soul is "in some sense everything," which logically should present the will with the endless desire to be one with everything, only satisfied in union with God. Moreover, even though Schleiermacher likewise incorporates the creator's infinity into his account of the Christian gospel, Kierkegaard's foray has the advantage of moving beyond the negative (anti-anthropomorphic) function of the concept; he shows how the infinite is not just the unfathomable "whence" that causes or "places" the self but also the ultimate telos that drives the forward thrust of free existence. Thus, Kierkegaard offers a possible answer not only to the first but also to the second challenge of divine infinity: the latter no longer confronts the human as dangerously alien once infinity has been unveiled as the essence of the human as well. Indeed, one infinite draws out the other: "The greater the conception of God, the more self there is."[13]

Chapter 4 amounts to a confrontation between this kind of subject-defining desire for God and the neo-Barthian objections raised in Kathryn Tanner's powerful forays into systematic theology. Her suspicion of created grace and denial of any human "possession" of the divine gifts dispenses with the supernatural virtues and indeed with any innate orientation to God; her excellent critique of social Trinitarianism tends toward an excessive prioritization of relational networks over individual agency, and her eschatology foresees no consummation of our deepest inherent capacities. The cumulative result, where divine grace appears to find no natural point of connection with our humanizing operations, seems unduly confrontational and "unnatural." For Aquinas, ultimate happiness can only truly be mine if it consists in my unfettered performance of my highest function. But on Tanner's model the highest divine benediction upon the human takes a puzzlingly arbitrary form, connecting only accidentally with our innermost orienting drive and its performances. Besides, Aquinas' approach joins with Kierkegaard's to answer Nietzsche, since for them

---

formidably intelligent book *God and Difference: The Trinity, Sexuality, and the Transformation of Finitude* (New York: Routledge, 2016).

[13] Søren Kierkegaard, *The Sickness Unto Death*, ed. and trans. Howard V. Hong and Edna H. Hong, vol. 19 of *Kierkegaard's Writings* (Princeton: Princeton University Press, 1980), 80.

divine being donates itself to the innate infinity exercised by the human self's defining potencies. Graced nature thereby inoculates the human against the metaphysical virulence of divine infinity.

These first four chapters, comprising Part One, share a common theme: thinking the possible existential appropriation of the limitless creator-from-nothing highlights certain radical structures within human selfhood. Part Two enters more explicitly into the complex of Christian doctrine, applying some of the principles sketched in the first part to throw a critical light on two influential contemporaries; in each case the systematic appeal to the theology of Aquinas emerging in the latter chapters of Part One is extended.

Behind Tanner's preference for an anthropology of almost formless receptivity over one of infinite performance lies Barth's suspicion of the human appropriation of grace (itself a variant on Luther's forensic account of justification). Similarly, it is Barth's internalization of Jesus' human death within the Trinitarian constitution of God (amplifying Luther's theology of the cross) that orients Eberhard Jüngel's thought, the focus of Chapter 5. Driven by the perceived demands of post-Shoah theodicy and employing a Heideggerian event-based ontology, Jüngel's profound essay in anti-theistic Trinitarian reconstruction openly rejects Aquinas' negative theology, logic of analogy, and classical creationism. In response, critical questions are again raised in the name of divine infinity. Grasped in its true radicality, this infinity cannot exclude or oppose creaturely, including human, finitude. Not acknowledging this, Jüngel puts forth an account of Trinitarian relations that falls foul of the implications of classical creationism: the limitlessness of the creator forbids the incorporation into the divine being of the dynamic of finite relations and the play of human interpersonality. Persisting in this direction leaves Jüngel with a deity self-mediated by its own negativity, and a structural account of divine self-disclosure that splits the Trinity into an historical economy and its postulated eternal double.[14]

The lengthy sixth chapter outlines a Thomistic ontology of grace using as a foil the theology of John Milbank. Now it is not Barth but Balthasar who appears the seminal influence (with the latter drawing classical inspiration not from Luther's vision but, arguably, from Bonaventure's).[15] While Jüngel's construal of the Trinity presses the "theology of the cross" to an extreme, Milbank's account of nature and grace does the same with the "theology of glory." Taking up Balthasar's project of reconfiguring the entire metaphysical structure of creation around the descents of Christ and the Spirit, Milbank radicalizes the result into a kind of monism of grace via an extended application of de Lubac's critique of extrinsicism. Though ostensibly preserved, nature in Milbank's scheme is so subsumed by grace as to be rendered idle in its own right

---

[14] The chapters on Tanner and Jüngel sprang from occasional pieces; strict limits of space made for curtailed discussion. Readers must be left to decide if the brevity here vitiates the critique; Tanner herself has strongly contested my reading of her anthropology. But regardless of the points on which their respective portrayals might be challenged, the constructive counter-positions outlined in these chapters retain their significance for developing this book's approach to the infinite creator.

[15] A convincing argument for Bonaventure as the presiding spirit within Balthasar's metaphysical edifice is made in Junius Johnson, *Christ and Analogy: The Christocentric Metaphysics of Hans Urs von Balthasar* (Minneapolis: Fortress Press, 2013), especially the first two chapters.

("evacuated"). Moreover, the totalizing impulse of Balthasar's massive Christianization of metaphysics feeds Milbank's claim of theology as "metadiscourse."

The alternative model presented in the chapter assumes that the immensity of God's self-donation to the world is not ultimately defined on the structural level of ontology, but must unfold on the plane of historical event.[16] To quote some of the summative remarks:

> God's gracious act in and toward the world, the self-gift of the infinite Being, cannot be ontologized (i.e. made ingredient within the universal structure of created being), nor can it be naturalized (i.e. made into a definitive component of essential humanity). To be sure, created being and human nature are constitutively open to this infinite gift, but on their own terms they maintain a structurally ambiguous relation to it. … On the alternative model outlined here, God's self-gift involves, first, an interplay across a gap or interval of difference between defined, subsistent entities and a moving pattern of relations and operations, including contingent ones, in accord with an overall order; it also demands a similar interplay across a gap between nature and grace, habitual forms distributed via contingent motions by actual grace; and, third, it at least implies an interplay across a gap between (culturally speaking) "the world" as the total enterprise of human meaning-making and faith's critical collaboration-through-interrogation, undertaken while "on the way" through history, on pilgrimage.

The last point is where the doctrinal arguments about grace and nature find their methodological application in the critique of Milbank's triumphalist theory of theological discourse.

So far this introduction has offered brief comments on each chapter in order to show how they can be read as contributions to a single project: exploring the consequences of God's infinite transcendence in light of creation *ex nihilo*. The four chapters remaining to be discussed, making up Part Three of the book, do not require individual summary in order to be situated within this volume. For unlike the previous entries, these were conceived and written in close connection with each other; it will be sufficient to identify the topic that unites them. That topic is the mind of the creator: granted both the infinity and the radical simplicity of God's being, how must the intelligence of God in the act of creation, God's eternal knowledge of the temporally extended order, be conceived?

The first two parts concerned how the infinite creator is received by finitude: into the finite subject as its transformative object and into the finite order of creation as incarnate Word and as divinizing grace. But (as already suggested in the critique of Jüngel) the fundamental asymmetry defining the relation between creating God and created world forbids the opposite reception: finitude *qua finite* cannot be "received"

---

[16] This point that the infinite self-gift of God cannot be effected ontologically without actualization as history is also important for the theology of the incarnation. I have developed the implications in a book-length essay on Jesus's divinity as a pneumatic-cultural construction, *Unspeakable Cults* (forthcoming 2021 from Baylor University Press).

into the infinite. This is the other side to the logic of creation from nothing. This creates a deep problem where God's knowledge of the world is concerned: God's being is one, simple, eternal, while the world is multiple, differentiated, temporal. How can God's timeless act of knowledge perfectly intend worldly objects without incorporating multiplicity and difference into the divine being? Aquinas' account of the "divine ideas" can, on a certain reading, be seen to offer a brilliant solution to this problem; this solution and its important implications for theology form the substance of Part Three.[17] The four chapters of this part collectively present a speculative description of the divine mind as *immense*. Divine infinity and simplicity, in other words, demand a rendition of God's perfect knowledge of creation as incommensurable with the reasoning or ideation of any created intellect. This means that the intentional content of God's knowledge cannot be in any sense a replication of created formalities, along the lines of Plato's ideas, but instead an eminent pre-containment.

Aquinas is central to the way these chapters develop this issue of the immensity of God's knowledge or intelligence. As already discussed, he avoided making specifically human modes of understanding the paradigm case for the intellectual act. It was the ingenious Pierre Rousselot who drew attention to the critical limitations of human intellectual exercise due to its embodied dependence upon sensual data.[18] Angels symbolically indicate the barrier to any extension of human intelligence to God via an extrapolating inference simply in terms of enhanced scope or degree of resolution; the very mode of understanding itself must be different. Aquinas may be said to have warned later thinkers against conceptualizing God's intellectual engagement with the finite reality on the model of human *thinking*. From such a standpoint, Whitehead's absolutization of a model of ideation as necessarily implicated with organic embodiment is bound to be unsatisfactory.

But more important for these chapters is the way Aquinas' account of the achieved intellectual act as identity, not confrontation of subject and object, provides the basic scheme for understanding the unique intentional presence of created realities in the divine mind (the "*modus eminentior*").[19] God attains in perfect unity a complete grasp of multiplicity. The determinacy of finitude, determinacy-as-negation, has no natural place in God's mind. That is, it is "present" only as the exterior reflex of God's creative decision. It plays no role in the divine essence, nor in the hypostatic relations. Instead, finite determinacy is known by God only as a function of the willing of actual finitude,

---

[17] The contested reading of Aquinas upon the basis of which these chapters develop their model of divine knowledge is only given cursory treatment in the chapters themselves. A fully elaborated investigation of the Aquinas material can be found in Paul DeHart, "What Is Not, Was Not, and Will Never Be: Creaturely Possibility, Divine Ideas and the Creator's Will in Thomas Aquinas," *Nova et Vetera* 13 (2015): 1009–58. Its length and specialist orientation precluded this piece's inclusion in the present volume, but those seeking the detailed interpretations of Aquinas which undergird Part Three are directed to it.

[18] Pierre Rousselot, *Intelligence: Sense of Being, Faculty of God*, trans. Andrew Tallon (Milwaukee: Marquette University Press, 1999). Originally published as *L'Intellectualisme de saint Thomas* in 1908.

[19] The inspiration of Lonergan for my arguments here should be obvious. One of his great themes was the superiority (epistemologically, metaphysically, and even theologically) of the Aristotelian model of cognition as identity of knower and known to the Platonic model of confrontation between them.

the created order; such a will in God is not abstract, it is always a concrete will to create "this" world. Hence, God's knowledge of the world ("ideas" *sensu stricto*, as defined by Aquinas) is definite only vis-à-vis that world. God's infallible and complete knowing of all possible creatures is otherwise identical with knowing the divine essence and power: it is virtual or implicit. This is no cognitive lack because only the actual "is," the possible simply *qua* possible (i.e., as not stabilized by any actual created entity) "is" not, so there is nothing to know.

Hegel, indeed the idealist tradition generally, accepts the already mentioned Spinozist axiom that all determination is negation; creational theism just denies it. True determinacy lies first in the infinite actuality of God (which cannot be supplemented or completed and is perfectly self-identified), second in the created actuality. Finite possibility is found in God either virtually only, in God's omnipotence, or else in the creature willed and known as willed. Even in the finite order generally, possibility is only a shadow cast by actual determinacy. If for the Hegelian system, premised upon the ultimacy of negation, the key concept that must be defended is that of *Aufhebung* (the successive process of conceptual sublation, removal-through-higher-integration), then for creational theism, premised upon an ultimate positivity or perfect fullness, the absolutely essential concept is eminence (eternal prior containment as a virtual partial resolution within an utterly simple but infinite richness of content). The four final chapters attempt to theorize this eminence via Aquinas' doctrine of divine ideas.

They also try and suggest the problems that have arisen for any doctrine of creation that is not on its guard against the various intellectual traditions that have failed to maintain their grip on these stipulations. On the one hand, there is the confusion that knowledge increases as a function of the accumulation of random detail rather than of intensified simplicity; on the other, there is the entertainment of counterfactual possibility as equaling the actual in determinacy rather than seeing it as the indistinct haze of virtuality that only borrows determinacy from its relative proximity to the actual. From the perspective of creational monotheism, both of these must be regarded as disorders of imagination triumphing over reason. All sorts of dubious speculative ventures have resulted, from the late medieval explosion of "ground" mysticism (where God's creative idea of me is granted the wrong priority over my created actuality), to Molinist "middle knowledge," to Leibniz's monadology and on to German Idealism (with its continuing echo in theology) where God's engagement with the world becomes a moment of theogonic self-actualization.

God's knowledge of the possible is certainly not "indeterminate" in the defective sense, as if failing to obtain the determinacy of the object of knowledge. The point is rather that the possible attains exactly, and only, the determinacy that God wills it to have. Hence, the *modus eminentior* does not lie in the mere duplication within God of finite determinations in their multiplicity and distinction. But this in turn means that the limitlessness of God's knowledge makes it different from ours not quantitatively but in kind. God's knowing is not "infinite" as if it were an unbounded increase of apprehended detail, as Leibniz seemed to think. God does not know infinitely *more* items of information but rather knows in an infinite *manner*. The way God knows, the mode of created actuality's intentional presence in the divine intelligence, is utterly unlike even the greatest conceivable grasp of the same actuality by the most exalted created intelligence. In this consists the immensity of God as intellectual act.

All that remains is the working out of these claims in some detail in the four chapters. Chapter 7 is a brief transitional chapter that introduces the final three chapters as a group. It points out their common conceptual orientation as outworkings of a voluntarist and "anti-Platonic" reading of Aquinas on divine ideas; the latter's rethinking of the tradition disqualified God's ideas for the traditional functions assigned them within the Christian Platonist tradition.[20] Chapter 8 discusses the sequestration of the ideas from their former role as truth-makers or "illuminators" of human cognition. Chapter 9 argues that the ideas can no longer be approximated to or approached as human ideals or objects of attainment. Chapter 10, finally, explores the consequences for the doctrine of God once the ideas are no longer thought of as fixed distinctions within the divine self-understanding that root finite differentiation in the divine essence.

III.

The chapters of this book were written separately over a period of fifteen years. Looking back on the specific circumstances in my intellectual development that led to the emergence of these pieces with their dominant themes, I am struck by the contrast between the thematic unity of this book and the contingent nature of its varied origins. But I am also deeply grateful for the specific teachers, authors, and colleagues who, without realizing it, were instrumental in initiating or furthering this project by their questions, insights, and example. While I was still a student, David Tracy first pointed me in the direction I have travelled ever since; his encouragement, and his own continued labor in thinking the infinite God, have sustained me. I still remember, too, the kindness to me of the now sadly departed Edward Farley who, upon my being hired at Vanderbilt in 1997, read unasked my dissertation and tendered his comments (an intimidating experience!). One typically discerning little query he made in response to a claim about Descartes forced me to do some more thinking. He thereby planted the seed that resulted in the initial version of Chapter 1, the starting point for my continued engagement with the idea of divine infinity.

The next stage was my first encounter with the thought of Rowan Williams, one of whose essays appeared in a volume I assigned for a class on postliberalism in 2000. I was so taken with the essay that soon after I eagerly bought and read *On Christian Theology*, which had appeared the same year. Generally, the original yet profoundly "catholic" theological vision of this book made a deep and permanent impression; specifically the remarkable chapter on creation *ex nihilo* gave a decisive impetus to

---

[20] Interpreters of Aquinas who are uncomfortable with the phrase "anti-Platonic" should not mistake what it refers to: a highly focused elimination of Platonic idea-theory rather than an (impossible) general "de-Platonification" of Aquinas. See Benjamin DeSpain's concerns on this point and my response. Benjamin DeSpain, "Quaestio Disputata: Aquinas's Virtuous Vision of the Divine Ideas," *Theological Studies* 81 (2020): 453–66. Paul DeHart, "Quaestio Disputata: Divine Virtues and Divine Ideas of Virtues," *Theological Studies* 81 (2020): 467–77.

my developing concern with that doctrine in its classic form. Shortly after, in the spring of 2001, my colleague Peter Hodgson invited me to co-teach with him Professor Farley's old survey course "God in the Western Tradition." For some reason one of the alterations I suggested to his syllabus was to add Book One of the *Summa Contra Gentiles*. Some reading of Aquinas had been imposed on me in graduate school, and I had assigned a few passages in a previous course, but these had passed right over my head. But in preparing to teach Aquinas seriously, and in front of a colleague whom I knew to be both acute and unsympathetic to the scholastic tradition, I really began paying attention. The more closely I read and the more thoroughly I pondered, the more galvanized I became by the power, coherence, and subtlety of Aquinas' conception of God and world. I realized I could no longer ignore him; further study seemed called for, though when and how I did not know.

The unexpected opportunity presented itself in autumn of 2004, when PhD students requested a seminar on John Milbank. A large and complex essay on Aquinas by the latter appeared on the syllabus; so intrigued and yet puzzled was I by Milbank's wonderfully creative yet not quite convincing take on Aquinas that I decided after the seminar had ended to work systematically through all 150 or so of the passages cited by Milbank. The public result was my book *Aquinas and Radical Orthodoxy*; the private (and personally more important) result was my increase in understanding of Aquinas, and my growing sense that here was a general conceptual framework for my theological thinking that was sophisticated, highly adaptable in face of modern scientific and intellectual challenges, and fitted by design to supportively interpret the ancient creedal consensus of the Church. Yet another collegial invitation cemented this turn in my thinking, when Patout Burns offered to let me co-teach his Aquinas seminar in the autumn of 2006. The example of his masterly exposition of the medieval doctor, and my study of Bernard Lonergan upon his urging, were the final incentives: from that point on, and to this day, I have chosen to think of myself as some kind of Thomist, though determined to belong to no school and to remain open to additional inspiration from multiple directions.

The last stage of the journey toward this book developed from my decision to include a discussion of Catherine Pickstock in *Aquinas and Radical Orthodoxy*. Although I came to disagree with her interpretation of Aquinas, I remain in her debt for her strong and creative reading of the role of the divine ideas. After the book was finished in 2011, a few questions on this issue remained unsettled for me; what I initially regarded as a technical side-issue in time issued in surprisingly large vistas. From my reading of David Burrell I was alerted in 2013 to the percipient essays of James F. Ross; these became the catalyst for my attempt at a fresh account of ideas in Aquinas.[21] He initially pointed me as well to the broader philosophical relevance of the debate on the ideas; the more I ranged within the history of philosophy, the more the

---

[21] It was also around this time that Sean Hayden, then a PhD student in Vanderbilt's Graduate Department of Religion, made me aware of the highly significant studies in the philosophy of subjectivity made by the "Heidelberg School" (Dieter Henrich, Manfred Frank). In various ways this strand of thought has contributed much to my thinking, merely hinted at by brief references in Chapter 10. I remain deeply grateful to Professor Hayden for turning my attention in this fruitful direction.

issues involved kept popping up in all sorts of unexpected places. Thus the genesis of Part Three of this book.

As the example of Pickstock shows, engagement with a probing thinker can be a great gift, in spite of (or even because of) sharp disagreement. Here I must conclude this record of relevant influences by singling out three theologians to whom I am greatly indebted but who appear in this book only as objects of critique. Eberhard Jüngel remains for me an exemplar theologian: elegant, cultured, and compassionate, he shows us all how to rethink the doctrinal heritage from the ground up, on the grandest scale and in intricate conversation with the modern world and with the depths of philosophical tradition. I had the good fortune to have Kathryn Tanner as a teacher, as well as drawing upon her writings. To me as to many others she remains an inspiration for her systematic breadth, her clarity and conceptual prowess, and her superb marriage of openness to a changing culture with faithfulness to the gospel of Jesus Christ. Finally, John Milbank, in spite of the rancor he has often aroused, has been a gift to theology. Through his sweeping originality and encompassing vision, his fearless urge to do theoretical battle on almost any disciplinary field, and his sensitivity to where the theologian stands in current world history, Milbank has catalyzed our field in more ways than we realize. He has not yet received his due, but someday he will. In the chapters below, my vigorous disagreements with these three are clearly foregrounded, but these quarrels should not be taken as either my complete or as my final word. Even if Jüngel, Tanner, or Milbank never read these lines, at least young theologians might take occasion from my expression of gratitude to benefit from the wealth of insight to be found in their work. I, at any rate, intend to keep learning from all three.

IV.

Aquinas, envisioning the Holy of Holies as a schematic of the creator's impingement upon the world, cross-references the cherubim upholding God's empty throne (the mercy seat) with the cry of the seraphim in Isaiah's vision (*STh* I/II q. 102 a. 4 ad 6). A nice juxtaposition, but more, an essential expression of creative monotheism: it is just the overwhelming proximity of the infinite, the saturation of every point of created space with the *doxa tou theou*, that defeats our representations. That is why the Jews' adytum housed no icon. John Chapman, former abbot of Downside Abbey, marvelously described contemplative prayer thus: "The intellect faces a blank and the will follows it."[22] In part, this book is attempting to expound what is meant by God as "blank." The limitless ground and goal of every limited thing ("nothing in particular— which is God of course"), the creator presents the mind not so much with an object for apprehension as a sheer scarp extending up forever. But as the second half of Chapman's

---

[22] Sebastian Moore, "Some Principles for an Adequate Theism," *Downside Review* 95 (1977): 201. In this essay Moore, himself a monk of Downside, draws out in a lovely way the theistic implications of contemplative practice. It is my hope that the forays made in the chapters below will be judged faithful to his principles.

aphorism suggests, the climb is the thing. The continually renewed connection made in these essays between God's immensity and the ascending impulse that propels our intelligent-voluntary acts suggests that words like "infinite" and "incommensurable," necessary though they are, can tend to make of God merely an obstacle or an absence. A less inadequate description of the God theoretically imagined in these pages would be "sublime." *Sublimis* means not just high up but also borne aloft, elevated; unlike "infinity," it has a verbal form: *sublimare*. Human subjectivity, embodied and willing mind, cannot grasp God, but it aspires still; it points to God, aims at God, and (when divinely aided and drawn) can even rise to God, its one completely satisfying end. To think this divine sublimity can be more than a conceptual indulgence; as continually informing the will's pursuit of freedom to its eternal source, it becomes the mind's own liturgy.[23]

That is a way for Pascal to forgive Descartes.

---

[23] Kierkegaard remains the greatest philosophical guide to this path. Readers would not go far wrong if they traced many of the leading thoughts of this book to a forbidden hankering to yoke together Kierkegaard with Aquinas. If the resulting marriage of modern Protestant and quintessential Catholic appears incongruous, I answer that in my own experience the great figures of nineteenth- and twentieth-century Protestant theology are among the most important dialogue partners for Catholic theology in this century. In particular, learning how to read Kierkegaard's anthropology and Dietrich Bonhoeffer's ecclesiology as truly Catholic achievements continues to enrich my own thinking. Though neither would have been happy about it, I number those two among my favorite Catholic authors.

Part One

Cultus Mentis: Accommodating the Endless Object

1

Can Pascal Forgive Descartes?
God's Ambiguous Infinity

I cannot forgive Descartes. In all his philosophy, he would have been quite willing to dispense with God. But he had to make Him give a fillip to set the world in motion; beyond this, he has no further need for God.

Pascal
Pensées

I have never written about the infinite except to submit myself to it, and not to determine what it is or is not.

Descartes
Letter to Mersenne

"God is not a name but a concept." Thus writes Kierkegaard, speaking through the persona of Johannes Climacus.[1] Presumably he means, at least in part, that God is not a thing, an ostensible referent toward which one can gesture and to which a name can consequently be applied. Instead, the use of the word "God" involves not direct reference but an effort of thought, a conceptual synthesis of ideas and experiences. There are many such concepts inhabiting our speech (one usually does not say, "That's Truth, right over there next to the window"); they require a certain amount of learning and practice of those who would use them properly. The striking, in fact the crucial, thing about the concept "God" is that the list of situations or contexts that guide its use is potentially without limit. There is no idea or experience to which God is not in some way relevant, at least if we grasp what we mean by the concept. As Charles Wood has

---

[1] Søren Kierkegaard, *Philosophical Fragments / Johannes Climacus*, ed. and trans. Howard V. Hong and Edna H. Hong, vol. 7 of *Kierkegaard's Writings* (Princeton: Princeton University Press, 1985), 41; *Søren Kierkegaards Skrifter*, ed. Niels Jørgen Cappelørn et al. (Copenhagen: Gad, 1997–), 4: 246. Henceforth volume and page number of the Danish collected works will appear in brackets following the English page citation.

pointed out, "An understanding of 'God' relates to and affects one's understanding of everything else, one's own self in particular."[2]

The concept "God" is (potentially) infinitely relevant because God is (actually) infinitely relevant. Ironically, this unlimited divine relatedness is why Kierkegaard, speaking through yet another persona (Anti-Climacus), can also say that God "has no concept."[3] That is, God knows or relates to all particulars directly without needing the mediation of a cognitive abstract, a universal. As infinitely relevant God needs no concept. But *we* do, if we are to speak of or think about God at all. Are not the special problems associated with our use of the concept "God" a direct reflection of the fact that God relates with such unfathomable immediacy (and hence "has no concept")? In fact, it could be argued that these problems are such that we cannot even limit ourselves to *a* concept of God. To think God is not to arrive at an adequate single concept, the quintessence of divinity; it is to master a shifting ensemble of concepts that implicate and check each other in various ways. This pattern of concepts must be constantly renegotiated, drawing on and responding to particular historical contexts of thought, speech, and action.

The dynamics of this process, and the criteria by which it can be judged, are dependent on the goal toward which a particular "thinking" of God aims, and the communities or traditions to which it is responsible. Thus, even where the definition of a concept is agreed upon, its "freight," its meaning and implications for reflection on God, can be judged in sharply divergent ways. A most instructive example of this is provided by the differing readings offered by two contemporary thinkers of one concept (infinity) as used in reference to God by one great philosopher (Descartes). Of course, much has been written of late about the "Cartesian subject" and the salutary results for theology and philosophy that occur when it is abandoned.[4] But what of the Cartesian idea of God? I turn to the "infinite" Cartesian deity as read through the eyes of the German Lutheran theologian Eberhard Jüngel and the French Roman Catholic philosopher Jean-Luc Marion.

I. God in the Epistemological Revolution: Two Readings

The juxtaposition of two quotations with intriguing similarities will provide a point of entry into this discussion. The first, from Jüngel, comes from his great work, *Gott als Geheimnis der Welt*, written in 1977:

---

[2] Charles M. Wood, *The Formation of Christian Understanding* (Philadelphia: The Westminster Press, 1981), 25.
[3] Søren Kierkegaard, *The Sickness unto Death*, ed. and trans. Howard V. Hong and Edna H. Hong (Princeton: Princeton University Press, 1980), 121 [11: 232–3].
[4] Unfortunately, as with much of the currently fashionable theological posturing with respect to the key figures of "modernity," this too often smacks more of compulsive repetition than of actual insight into the thinker in question. For a witty if tortuous attempt to retrieve the real "Cartesian subject" from current misunderstandings, see Slavoj Žižek, *The Ticklish Subject* (London: Verso, 1999).

Thereby, however, the being of God necessarily falls asunder. For on the one hand God, in accordance with his essence—that is, as that which is absolutely superior to me—cannot be thought of as limited to the presence of the ego. Even for Descartes, it belongs to the essence of God to be more than merely present with me. On the other hand, God's existence can only be asserted when he is present within the horizon of my existence. Because for "Descartes being-ness means: being represented through and for the subject," which "I" am. Thus the following aporia emerges:

a) The existence of God is secured through me when the essence of God is represented by me.
b) In terms of his *essence* God is of course the almighty creator who exists necessarily through himself and through whom I exist (and also through whom I am *what* I am).
c) In terms of his *existence*, however, God is through me, inasmuch as even *his* existence can be understood only as a being-represented through and for the subject, which "I" am.[5]

The second quotation comes from Marion's book, published in 1981, *Sur la théologie blanche de Descartes*:

Descartes makes no final settlement in favor either of ontic precedence or of the primacy of thought; the result is that the one and the other are put into practice alternatively, indeed conjointly, via two competing cases. As always, this paradox is nowhere more obvious than in the [case of God as] *causa sui*: God appears as an infinite essence, so much so that it is completely summed up in an *exuperans potestas* [overwhelming power]. Thus God appears as the absolute creator of beings—the ontic foundation of the *res cogitans* [human being as thinking substance] as well as of other beings. But at this very same point in the theory, God, in order to exist, or rather in order that his existence might become intelligible to the *cogitatio* [human thought], must satisfy a rational demand of the finite ego (*causa sive ratio cur existat* [a cause or reason why he exists]). The ego becomes the epistemological foundation of the *cogitatio* of God as well as of other beings. Thus the foundation is divided in two, between *cogitatio* and creation, a finite and created rationality and an incomprehensible and infinite power.[6]

---

[5] Eberhard Jüngel, *Gott als Geheimnis der Welt: zur Begründung der Theologie des Gekreuzigten im Streit zwischen Theismus und Atheismus*, 6th ed. (Tübingen: Mohr Siebeck, 1992), 165. Translation by Darrell L. Guder under the title *God as the Mystery of the World* (Grand Rapids: Eerdmans, 1983), 125. Citation of page numbers in the original will henceforth be followed in parenthesis by citation of page numbers in the translation, although the latter is to be used with caution. All translations of quotations are mine unless otherwise noted. For Jüngel's relation to Descartes, see also Paul DeHart, *Beyond the Necessary God: Trinitarian Faith and Philosophy in the Thought of Eberhard Jüngel* (Atlanta: Scholars Press, 1999), 43–68.
[6] Jean-Luc Marion, *Sur la théologie blanche de Descartes: analogie, création des vérités éternelles et fondement*, 2nd ed. (Paris: Quadrige/PUF, 1991), 451.

Both Jüngel and Marion see a curious tension in the way Descartes tries to conceive of God, the human mind, and the interrelation of the two. Their accounts are not identical but they evidently overlap in an intriguing way. To see more clearly the similarities and differences, I will deal with each in a bit more detail. This will unavoidably involve considerable haste and oversimplification in summarizing two very complex readings of Descartes, but it is necessary to lay the groundwork for what follows.

To begin with Jüngel, the "aporia" he describes (not, strictly speaking, a contradiction but a baffling difficulty blocking a consistent course of thought) must be understood against the background of a traditional presupposition about conceiving God. God is metaphysically unique as one whose essence is logically inseparable from existence (somewhat crudely stated, *what* God is, God's identity, and *that* God is, God's mode of actuality or "esse," to use Thomist language, mutually imply and define each other). In this unique case, to exist as God is God's identity; existence is not a contingent fact separable in principle from essence, as it is with creatures. This insistence had been a commonplace of philosophical and theological thinking about God long before Descartes, and he accepted it without question. If God is to be conceived, it must be as one in whom essence and existence are thought together.[7]

But Descartes's discussion of God, itself traditional in so many ways, is part of a larger argument, one of revolutionary import for the self-conception of human reason. It is well known that Descartes located the foundation for cognition and rationality in the human "ego" or self, which "clearly and distinctly" apprehends its own presence as well as its own defining activity, thinking.[8] Heidegger, whom Jüngel closely follows in this discussion, argued that one result of this new foundation of thought is that the existence of things outside the self is strictly a function of their perception by the self, their "being present" to thought. This is neither a logical inference nor a stipulative definition, along the lines of Berkeley's "To be is to be perceived." Rather, Heidegger claims that the meaning of any assertion of existence is now implicitly determined as a mode of being present ("re-presented") with the cognizing self making the assertion; to say "X exists" henceforth means or implies that X is within the horizon of the self's presence to itself.[9]

In the passage cited, Jüngel is pointing out the difficulty of maintaining the traditional assertion of the identity of God's essence and existence, once the import of this new understanding of existence is absorbed. Divine essence and divine existence can no longer be brought into a single movement of thought, so to speak; the mind

---

[7] Jüngel, *Gott als Geheimnis*, 139–41 (106–7). See, e.g., René Descartes, *Principles of Philosophy* I.14 (PW I, 197–8 = AT VIIIA, 10) and *Meditations on First Philosophy*, Meditation V (PW II, 46 = AT VII, 66). All citations of Descartes are from John Cottingham, Robert Stoothoff, Dugald Murdoch, and Anthony Kenny, trans., *The Philosophical Writings of Descartes* (Cambridge: Cambridge University Press, 1984–91), abbreviated PW with volume number and page. This is followed by the corresponding reference to Charles Adam and Paul Tannery, eds. *Œuvres de Descartes* (revised edition, Paris: Vrin / C.N.R.S., 1964–76), abbreviated AT with volume number and page.

[8] Descartes, *Meditations* VI (PW II, 54 = AT VII, 78) and Second Set of Replies (PW II, 103–5 = AT VII, 144–6).

[9] Martin Heidegger, *Nietzsche, Volume IV: Nihilism*, ed. David Krell, trans. Frank Capuzzi (San Francisco: Harper & Row, 1982), 114–17.

assigns them to separate locations. God's essence is defined as absolutely superior and transcendent to human reason, indeed as the creator of that reason. But if there is to be knowledge of God's existence, if that existence is to be meaningfully asserted, then the divine essence must be somehow re-presented, it must be given in some idea to that human reason and thus constructed by the human subject as an object, similar to any other existent. This is because in this new Cartesian epistemological scheme, "to exist" becomes virtually identical with "to be present in the form of some attribute which affects the knowing human subject."[10]

Now Descartes is certainly aware that God cannot be present in the manner of ordinary objects. To be sure, God and created things (minds and material objects) have this in common: both are characterized by a degree of ontic independence, that is, they are substances. But God's independence is absolute, that of created substances only relative, since they depend on God holding them in being.[11] Another way of putting this is to say that God is infinite substance. Thus, the word "substance" is not used in the same sense of God and created things; we can know substances, and hence God, but the qualification "infinite" signals that the concept "substance" is not used univocally of the divine. Descartes in this way tries to salvage God for his own epistemology, bringing the divine into the representational scheme while at the same time allowing enough ambiguity in this unique case to conceal the fault line that Jüngel claims to uncover.

The fault line is still present despite this concealment; I will indicate later what happens, according to Jüngel, when this fault line began to widen. But initially the nature of the "aporia" described in the quote with which we began must be grasped as carefully as possible. God's essence is defined by Descartes (following venerable traditions) in such a way as to problematize its relation to the new role of the human subject in constituting knowledge. Existence now means objectifiable presence within the human cognitive horizon.[12] But how can the absolutely transcendent creator appear within this horizon? Descartes's denial of the univocity of substance suggests that God's appearance in this horizon is possible but problematic, a quasi-availability qualified by infinite unavailability. To know God as God involves a claim about God's essence and a claim about God's existence that do not exactly negate each other but that are resistant to harmonization, threatening to move off in separate directions. This puts a question mark on the traditional metaphysical claim of identity of essence

---

[10] Descartes makes this latter point explicitly in *Principles*, I. 52 (PW I, 210 = AT VIIIA, 25):

> We cannot initially become aware of a substance merely through its being an existing thing, since this alone does not of itself have any effect on us. We can, however, easily come to know a substance by one of its attributes. ... Thus, if we perceive the presence of some attribute, we can infer that there must also be present an existing thing or substance to which it may be attributed.

Jüngel cites this passage in part in *Gott als Geheimnis*, 166 (125).

[11] Descartes, *Principles* I. 51 (PW I, 210 = AT VIIIA, 24); *To Clerselier*, 23 April 1649 (PW III, 377–8 = AT V, 355–6).

[12] That is, the possibility or impossibility of something's existence coincides precisely with the possibility or impossibility of its being clearly and distinctly perceived by a human subject. Cf. Descartes, *Meditations* VI (PW II, 50 = AT VII, 71).

and existence. In short, Descartes's traditionalist theism sits awkwardly with his revolutionary epistemology.

Turning to the Marion passage a similar theme is discernible, although placed in a different interpretive context. Marion is making a general statement about a constitutive ambiguity in the Cartesian metaphysical system; uncovering this ambiguity is the task of the entire book on the "white theology" and continues a course of investigation begun in his earlier book on Descartes's "gray ontology."[13] In the specific paragraph quoted, Marion points to an example of Cartesian discourse about God that furnishes a particularly revealing instance of this ambiguity: the claim that God is self-caused (*causa sui*).

Marion's argument is that a "double onto-theo-logy" characterizes Descartes's metaphysics; this gives it its ambiguous character. As with Jüngel, Heidegger provides many of the conceptual tools which Marion uses to analyze Descartes.[14] In this case, Heidegger makes the claim that the entire metaphysical tradition of the West (which in his understanding arises with the ancient Greeks, culminates in Hegel, and meets its dissolution at the hands of Nietzsche) must be labeled onto-theo-logical, because every metaphysical treatment of the "being" that grounds the structures of reality has implicitly traded on two different senses of the word "being." On the one hand, being represents the general and undifferentiated power of being shared by all things which are. In the "school metaphysics" of the later seventeenth and eighteenth centuries, this "being-*qua*-being" was eventually codified as the special concern of ontology.

Heidegger argues, however, that there is another sense of the word "being" embedded in every metaphysical scheme. Alongside being in general, such schemes have made use of the notion of a "highest being," a particular (not abstract) entity that stands at the pinnacle of the hierarchy of beings and through its power grounds the being of all other beings. If being-*qua*-being is the abstract power of being shared by entities, then the highest being is the entity that enables this participation. (Of course, this dual structure gives rise to many confusions and ambiguities, such as the issue of which sense of being is truly foundational, but to point out these difficulties is precisely Heidegger's intention.) If ontology denotes the study of being-in-general, then theology indicates that part of metaphysics devoted to analysis of the highest being.

Metaphysical systems have variously if consistently deployed both an ontology and a theology; but Heidegger believes they have only been able to obtain a certain level of apparent consistency by trading in hidden ways on this distinction, oscillating between the meanings of being in order to account for different aspects of the "groundedness" of beings. Unable to decide where the foundation truly lies, metaphysics has needed to

---

[13] Marion, *Sur la théologie blanche*, 5–7. Cf. Jean-Luc Marion, *Sur l'ontologie grise de Descartes: Savoir aristotélicien et science cartésienne dan les Regulae* (Paris: Vrin, 1975).

[14] For what follows, see especially Martin Heidegger, *Identität und Differenz* (Pfullingen: Neske, 1957), 50–9. For further discussion, see also Jean-Luc Marion, *Sur la prisme métaphysique de Descartes* (Paris: PUF, 1986), 92–3. English translation of the latter by Jeffrey L. Kosky under the title *On Descartes' Metaphysical Prism* (Chicago: University of Chicago Press, 1999), 86–7. Citations of this work will be to the original, with the corresponding pages of the English translation following in brackets.

keep in play both interpretations of being; hence, Heidegger's claim is that onto-theology is the hidden scaffolding of all Western metaphysics.[15]

One of Marion's purposes in his magisterial studies of Descartes is to probe the adequacy of Heidegger's conception of metaphysics as onto-theo-logy.[16] Can the Cartesian metaphysical project be characterized as onto-theo-logical? His answer is only a qualified yes. For in fact, the metaphysical thought of Descartes reveals two distinct onto-theo-logies, that is, one ontology and its corresponding theology are operating in tandem with a parallel ontology and theology. This unique state of affairs arose due to the radically innovative nature of the Cartesian epistemology. In his study of the gray ontology, Marion argues that the epistemological principles first sketched out by Descartes in his *Rules for the Direction of the Mind* (c. 1628) actually, if unconsciously, reorganize the discourse of being-*qua*-being in such a thoroughgoing way as to provide the hidden sketch of a general ontology. When Descartes establishes the procedures governing the knowledge and certainty of any and all existents, he is tracing an ontology in gray, so to speak.

The ontology is gray because it is shadowy; it is operative yet unacknowledged. This is not to say that Descartes does not also have an explicit ontology, a conception of being-*qua*-being. He believes it to be a fundamental principle of reason that anything that exists must have a reason or cause (*causa sive ratio*) why it is, and why it is what it is. On this reading, the principle of the being of all beings is their participation in a causal order grounded in God's creative power.[17] But Marion's point is that Descartes's radical epistemology casts an ontological shadow, as it were: a rival set of ontological principles emerges in which the being of beings is not understood primarily in terms of their being caused but rather in terms of their being conceived or thought by a knowing self.[18]

On Heidegger's reading of metaphysics, a fully fledged scheme must combine an ontology with a theology, an account of the highest principle or being that grounds the being of beings. One might suspect, then, that if Descartes's thought is truly metaphysical, the indeterminacy of being-*qua*-being signaled by the presence of the gray ontology might lead to ambiguities in fixing the identity of the "highest being" that rules the realm of being. It is Marion's thesis in *Sur la théologie blanche* that this is indeed the case. The indecision characterizing Cartesian ontology (i.e., between the putative ontology of being-as-caused and the "gray" ontology of being-as-thought lurking behind his epistemology) is carried over into Descartes's attempt to locate an ultimate principle determinative of beings.[19]

Thus, the search in Descartes for a highest being, a determinative ground, a theology (or, more abstractly, a theiology, concerning that which is granted "divinity" or divine status) is stamped by the dual character of his ontology. "The foundation, and thus the the*i*ology, remains burdened by the ambivalence which already characterizes the

---

[15] Marion, *Sur la prisme*, 93 [86].
[16] Ibid., 7–8 [6–7].
[17] Descartes, *Replies to Objections* I (PW II, 78 = AT VII, 108–9). Cf. *Replies* II (PW II, 116, 119 = AT VII, 165, 169).
[18] Marion, *Sur l'ontologie grise*, 186.
[19] Marion, *Sur la théologie blanche*, 450–2.

gray ontology."[20] For insofar as the being of beings is understood as a being-caused, Descartes deploys a conception of God as the highest causal power, indeed as the cause of her own being as well as of every other (*causa sui*).[21] But within the epistemological realm where knowledge of existents is concerned, it is the ego, the knowing self that bears away the prize of divinity. For the being of beings as known is grounded in that which knows them, which represents them.

The result is a theology that cannot finally specify where the true ground of being lies: is it in God or the ego? In calling Descartes's theology "white" (i.e., blank), Marion is emphasizing this anonymity; like a blank document with the king's signature, where the actual bearer of the missive (and hence of the royal authority) is not specified, the bearer of the title of highest principle is indeterminate, indeed the subject of a kind of competition between divine causality and human thought. And this indeterminacy of the highest being simply mirrors the original indeterminacy of being-*qua*-being. "The theology becomes white because the ontology remains gray."[22]

To speak of a double onto-theo-logy is one thing, but is it truly necessary to see them as "competing cases" as the initial quotation states? Can they not be brought into harmony? Why not simply say that the onto-theo-logy ruled by the thinking ego is subordinated to or embedded within the more encompassing onto-theo-logy ruled by God's causality? After all, Descartes assumes that God is the creator of the human ego in the first place. This should settle the precedence question once and for all. But this is to miss Marion's point: in Descartes such a straightforward reduction proves impossible; the "doubling" of the onto-theo-logies is basic, it cannot be resolved by reducing one to the other. This is the "paradox" he is emphasizing in his discussion of God as self-caused. For the way in which Descartes tries to specify divine superiority leaves unsettled the question of whether God really is superior to human reason.

The naming of God as self-cause is the prime exhibit of this "paradox" because it involves the claim that God transcends human rational consideration even as it subordinates God by grounding this claim in a principle of reason! As the cause of the being both of himself and of every other being, God can only be conceived as an infinite power; such a being, Descartes insists, can be apprehended in a certain way by human reason but never comprehended. But this claim is undermined by the way in which Descartes derives *causa sui* as a divine name in the first place. It is a basic demand of human reason, he says, that anything that *is* must have a reason or cause *why* it is.[23] If God exists (in the only intelligible sense of existence that Descartes's scheme will allow), then God must have a cause, and of course the only conceivable cause of the infinite power is that power itself.[24]

---

[20] Ibid., 451.

[21] Descartes shows great care in explaining the precise meaning of this formulation, cautioning the reader that it is "not too inappropriate" to understand God as self-caused but that a notion of efficient causality is not appropriate. See, e.g., *Replies* I (PW II, 79–80 = AT VII, 109–11). Cf. *Replies* IV (PW II, 164–5 = AT VII, 235), God is similar only "in a sense" to an efficient cause of himself; *To ****, March 1642, II (PW III, 213 = AT V, 546), a notion of formal causality is preferable.

[22] Marion, *Sur la théologie blanche*, 451.

[23] Descartes, *Replies* I (PW II, 78 = AT VII, 108).

[24] Marion, *Sur la prisme*, 282 [267]. Marion discusses (270–6 [256–61]) the extraordinary philosophical difficulties Descartes lands himself in by employing the notion of a self-cause, especially as such a

Thus, Descartes seeks to have it both ways. God hovers uneasily at the limit of reason, secure neither in her transcendence of it nor in his immanence to it. Indeed Descartes must have it both ways. It is crucial to his entire scheme that God be an object of human knowledge. The human subject must know with utter certainty that God *is*, even if the essence of God remains incomprehensible. But then Descartes is, in effect, conceding some kind of subordination of God as object to the epistemological demands of the self-grounding human knower. God grounds this knower by creation even as this knower grounds God, so to speak, by "cogitation."

Enough has been said at this point to begin to see a clear convergence between the interpretations of Jüngel and Marion. Both discern at the heart of Descartes's metaphysics a disjunction, signaling a hidden struggle for precedence between a God who is infinite and absolute, ruling the realm of beings, and a human knowing subject who subordinates every claim to being and existence to its immanent cognitive procedures. Both lay particular stress on the strong metaphysical claims for God's transcendence insisted on by Descartes. Both emphasize as well the new and radical epistemological context within which Descartes attempts to situate his discourse on the divine. Somehow, he cannot quite bring the human mind and the almighty creator into a settled and proper alignment, in spite of the fact that he evidently desires to do so and no doubt thinks that he has succeeded.

It would seem that these two interpreters are offering a common diagnosis, even if their angles of approach and terminology differ. Perhaps the best way to relate the claims made in the passages cited is to see Marion as providing a much more encompassing context, based on exhaustive research in the works of Descartes, for an insight that Jüngel had already arrived at in the course of a more general theological study. It is interesting that both authors use different ideas by the same thinker, Heidegger, to arrive at such similar conclusions. Jüngel appeals to the Heideggerian discussion of "re-presentation" as the grounding of beings through subjectivity. Marion looks instead to his hypothesis about metaphysics as "onto-theo-logy."

Both authors seem to discern the same instability hidden in the Cartesian edifice: God and the knowing self cannot find stable positions relative to one another within a single, comprehensive metaphysical scheme. But when the further question is raised of the significance of this instability for thinking about God, the differences begin to emerge between Jüngel and Marion. These differences will be seen to pivot around their distinct interpretations of the rhetoric of infinity in Descartes's theism. But first the passages cited above must be placed within the larger discussions of each author, discussions in which Descartes is given a role to play within the narrative of the historical course of Western philosophy. Although within the narrow focus of the discussion so far Jüngel and Marion seem to be discussing the same figure, he becomes two different characters when reintroduced into the two different stories they tell.

---

notion had been explicitly rejected as incoherent by his scholastic predecessors (Anselm, Aquinas, Duns Scotus, and, more ambiguously, Suarez).

II. The Philosophical Legacy of the Cartesian God: Two Narratives

We begin, once again, with Jüngel. The role in his account of the notions of essence and existence and their identity in God has already been mentioned. The rise and dominance of these ideas form the narrative background to his perspective on Descartes's significance. The roots in the philosophical and theological tradition of this insistence on identity of essence and existence are far too complex to be entered into here. Suffice it to say that it was a claim that could be made on the basis of many interrelated considerations, including the demand for the utter simplicity of divine being (it thus cannot be a compound of essence and existence) as well as the claim that God's existence is necessary (and hence part of his very essence, not an adjunct to it). Jüngel, while not unaware of this variety, construes this and most of the other traditional metaphysical claims about divinity (necessity, simplicity, omnipresence, omniscience, etc.), as essentially variants on a common theme. All serve to guarantee God's absolute superiority by distancing God from the finite, the worldly, the human.

God's characteristics are always determined in relation to prior philosophical judgments concerning relative value and excellence among beings. What is deemed of value must be found eminently in God, while what is despised must be expunged from the divine being. The different approaches to the unity of essence and existence in God can without difficulty be seen as reflecting this tendency. Simplicity, for example, derives ultimately from the role of God as the unifying source and ground of a multiplex and fragmentary world; to take another example, the affirmation of the necessary and ubiquitous presence of God, and hence the linking of existence to the divine essence itself, is in deliberate contrast to the flux and decay associated with temporality.[25] Either way, there can be no separation of essence and existence in God as metaphysically defined because God's absolute superiority to the world and its human inhabitants must be maintained.

This fundamental stress on the superiority of God (including the particular ways of affirming the identity of essence and existence in God that derive from it) decisively informs Jüngel's assessment of the Cartesian difficulty discussed in the first section. The standard epistemological expression of divine superiority had long been the human inconceivability of God's essence. Descartes accepted this bit of tradition, too, as part of the inherited conceptual apparatus of theism. But, as has already been suggested, when Descartes tried to incorporate these time-honored claims (by now codified in the late scholastic philosophy in which he was steeped) into his radical new epistemology, he introduced a structural instability in his theistic conceptuality. In so doing, he adumbrated a "disintegration" of divine being that was only to be revealed in the later denouement of metaphysical theism. This narrative is, in fact, one of the central themes of Jüngel's book.

---

[25] For the former point: Jüngel, *Gott als Geheimnis*, 139, 142 (105–6, 108). For the latter: ibid., 136 (103).

According to this story, later thinkers tried with increasing futility to bring into harmony the traditionally conceived absolute divine essence and the radically reconceived human cognitive capacity. As Heidegger argued, the Cartesian revolution made judgments of existence a function of presence to the human knower.[26] The unintended result was the "temporalization" of existence; "to be" in any meaningful sense was to be a spatiotemporal object in some kind of cognitive relation to the structures of human rationality, a development that triumphed with the ascendancy of Kant.[27]

In the wake of Kant, philosophical discourse on the divine seemed to drift inexorably toward one of two different but equally self-refuting alternatives. It could salvage an absolute divine essence, but only by making it strictly unthinkable as an existent. Or else it could accept the horizon of human capacities as ultimate, embrace the flux of worldly existence, and deny completely a transcendent absolute. Either way, metaphysical theism as any kind of useful adjunct to theology was shipwrecked. The final inheritors of the theistic legacy of Descartes (Fichte, Feuerbach, Nietzsche) could only allow the traditional conception of the identity of divine essence and existence to wither away, and with it the philosophical conception of God that had become standard in Christian theology. This was quite contrary to Descartes's intentions, of course, but according to Jüngel it was a conclusion rigorously derived from the premise of his thought.[28]

Like Jüngel, Marion also tells a story, a story involving both Descartes's relation to preceding traditions of thought as well as the legacy he bequeathed to later thinkers. But the plot and characters are rather different, thereby throwing a light on the difficulty of Cartesian theism that contrasts with Jüngel's reading in interesting ways. Marion situates Descartes in a larger struggle among sixteenth- and seventeenth-century thinkers over the abilities of human rationality to comprehend the nature and mind of God. This dispute pitted more mystically inclined thinkers (Benoît de Canfeld, Pierre de Bérulle, François de Sales) who stressed the utter mystery and incomprehensibility of God against a growing group of thinkers associated with the new scientific worldview (Kepler, Galileo, Marin Mersenne). The latter group saw the logical and mathematical laws governing natural processes to be direct insights into the creative divine mind itself; the human mind only perceives more dimly what the divine mind perceives with perfect clarity. But the infallible necessity of these "eternal truths" is the same for both.[29]

---

[26] It [i.e. the principle of *cogito ergo sum*] says that I am as the one representing, that not only is *my* Being essentially determined through such representing, but that my representing, as definitive *repraesentatio*, decides about the being present of everything that is represented; that is to say, about the presence of what is meant in it; that is, about its Being as a being (Heidegger, *Nietzsche*, 114).

[27] Jüngel, *Gott als Geheimnis*, 173–4 (131).

[28] Ibid., 200–3 (150–2).

[29] Jean-Luc Marion, "The Idea of God," in *The Cambridge History of Seventeenth-Century Philosophy*, vol. 1, ed. Daniel Garber and Michael Ayers (Cambridge: Cambridge University Press, 1997), 268–72.

Descartes completely rejects this position as an infringement of divine transcendence. In a letter to Mersenne he exclaims, "Indeed to say that these truths are independent of God is to talk of him as if he were Jupiter or Saturn and to subject him to the Styx and the Fates."[30] In response he makes it a basic premise of his thinking that God is the creator of the "eternal truths" that human reason perceives. The principles of logic and mathematics are just as contingent from God's point of view as any other aspect of created reality. Marion explores the implications of this position in a variety of ways, but the important point in the present context is that this claim places crucial limitations on the way in which God's attributes can be spoken of. In *Sur la prisme metaphysique de Descartes* (the culminating volume of that series of studies which looked first at Descartes's "gray ontology" and then his "white theology"), Marion devotes a chapter to the incoherences forced on the Cartesian discourse of God by the demands of his epistemological method on the one hand, and the claim that God creates the eternal truths of reason on the other.

After a close analysis of the various formulae in the *Meditations* that Descartes uses to define God's being and argue for God's existence, Marion uncovers three philosophical "names" of God, basic determinants of divine being. Although they are employed more or less interchangeably by Descartes, Marion argues that they serve different purposes in his philosophical system and, in fact, do not cohere with each other. Consider that an immediate consequence of the claim that the truths of reason are contingent divine creations is the radicalization of divine transcendence. All reflection on the nature and attributes of God based on logical inference or extrapolation from worldly reflection now faces a drastic limitation. This should imply not only that God's being is, strictly speaking, incomprehensible but also that discourse about the divine should not be subject to the basic logical and epistemological procedures constituting Descartes's new "method" of knowledge itself. The problem as Marion sees it is that two of the three "names" of God that perform vital functions in Descartes's philosophy seem to infringe on the kind of divine transcendence he is putatively committed to.[31]

The three concepts or "names" that structure Descartes's theism are God as infinite, God as the most perfect being, and God as self-cause (*causa sui*). With respect to the second of these, Marion argues that it deploys a set of perfections that turn out on closer inspection to be extrapolated characteristics of created entities; the latter are themselves comprehended and manipulated by the human reason that "clearly and distinctly" perceives them. Descartes is attempting to construct a clear concept of God in order to rescue the reality of the created order that had been put in question by the hyperbolic doubt of his method, but this construction takes place using those very resources of method and clearly perceived realities that are hypothetically in doubt.[32] In a similar way, the third "name," self-cause, falls foul of Descartes's own strictures for reasons that have already been discussed. In invoking God as the self-caused cause of all things, Descartes has brought God once again into the realm dominated by rational

---

[30] Descartes, *To Mersenne*, April 15, 1630 (PW III, 23 = AT I, 145).
[31] Marion, *Sur la prisme*, 257–92 [244–76].
[32] Ibid., 277–8 [263–4].

inference and what Leibniz christened the "principle of sufficient reason." God appears to answer the summons of a basic principle of rational thought, in spite of the fact that as the one who creates eternal truth itself God should be in no way subject to such considerations.[33]

Of the three "names," only infinity truly meets the demand for radical divine transcendence set up by Descartes's position on the creation of eternal truth.[34] The question of God as infinite will be revisited in more depth, but here it will suffice to summarize the course of theism in the post-Cartesian philosophical situation as Marion sees it. Descartes is finally unable to bring his thoughts about God into a coherent structural relationship; the three different ideas jostle against one another but are never connected or hierarchically arranged in a stable way. In his contribution to the *Cambridge History of Seventeenth-Century Philosophy*, Marion shows how ideas about God in that century can be organized according to their preference for one or the other of the Cartesian ideas about God. Some thinkers mirrored Descartes's own indecision, but the greatest figures (Malebranche, Spinoza, Leibniz, etc.) tried to give precedence either to the idea of the highest perfection or to the idea of God as self-cause. It is highly significant, though, that the third "name," the idea of God as infinite, did not seem to find a prominent echo in the philosophical situation immediately following Descartes.[35]

For Descartes the naming of God as infinite marks the fact that God radically transcends the resources of human thought and language. It represents a retrieval of a central strand of the classic theistic tradition, relying in its specific formulations upon Duns Scotus and some more recent mystical thinkers. But the intellectual climate was growing increasingly hostile to appeals to a mystical, radically transcendent infinity. In fact, Marion speaks of a "growing empire of metaphysical rationality" that demanded comprehensible concepts and univocal language even when dealing with the divine essence.[36]

In the very incoherence of his "naming" of God, Descartes represents for Marion a question mark put against all earlier and later attempts to define the being or essence of God in strictly philosophical terms, that is, apart from theology. A moment's reflection on this point will reveal a subtle difference of emphasis that informs the different "narratives" of Jüngel and Marion. In the story Jüngel tells, Descartes appears primarily as a traditionalist when it comes to the metaphysical picture of God. The various titles for God that he uses are lifted unproblematically from the standard discourse of absolute divine superiority. Indeed it is this very traditionalism, this faithfulness to a course of thought permeating both philosophy and theology for centuries, that makes Descartes the crucial figure he is for Jüngel. At once perfectly representative of metaphysical theism and yet also the initiator of that upheaval in the human cognitive self-image that stamps later thought as "modern," his God is the proleptic announcement of its own philosophical death. But for Jüngel this usefully clears the ground for a fresh

---

[33] Ibid., 283–4 [269].
[34] Ibid., 287 [271–2]. See also the summary chart on p. 285 [270].
[35] Marion, "The Idea of God," 291–2.
[36] Ibid., 293.

encounter of theology with philosophy because the standard metaphysical portrait of God is thereby revealed in its terrible fragility, indeed in its utter unsuitability for use by a theology that proclaims the identity of God with a tortured and dying human being.[37]

In contrast to this, Marion questions whether the Cartesian discourse of God can be reduced finally to metaphysics at all. Marion is aware, like Jüngel, of the traditional metaphysical provenance of the divine "names" that Descartes makes use of. But the way these concepts are employed by Descartes, the irreducibly pluriform character they force on his theistic language, becomes paradoxically the very marker of his radical originality. By demanding all three names and at the same time denying their coherence, Descartes bears witness to two imperatives that uneasily confronted each other in his day: the simultaneous demands that God be rationally fully intelligible and yet transcendent to human reason. In this way, Cartesian theism "attests to the fact that God cannot adequately be conceived within the limited discourse of metaphysics"; this makes it "*the* radical position on the question of God at the beginning of modern thought."[38]

The convergence between Jüngel and Marion on Descartes discussed earlier thus seems to give way to a divergence. The basic "aporia" of Cartesian theism, described so similarly by the two authors, does not by itself settle the question of Descartes's relation to the metaphysical tradition. For Jüngel, he is a spokesman for the grand tradition of the God of metaphysics. Ironically, Descartes's very invocation of that God is in the service of establishing a revolution in the self-conception of human reason, which will eventually issue in the death of the metaphysical God, a death that Jüngel believes should help theology to see the dubiousness of making "absolute superiority" the basic determinant of divine being. But for Marion, what Descartes says about God marks a turning point in philosophical theism; far from passively absorbing this tradition, he brings it into a new constellation of thought, which simultaneously invokes the past and calls it radically into question.

The divergence in these two interpretations of Descartes turns on the question of divine infinity. For both thinkers it is Descartes's utterance of an old word ("God is infinite!") in a radically new situation that marks his unique importance. For Jüngel, the infinity of God in Descartes perfectly suits its function within metaphysics. For Marion, that infinity demonstrates how the concept of God is not reducible to its function as capstone of a metaphysical system. In fact, his "incoherent" concept of God

---

[37] Jüngel, *Gott als Geheimnis*, 167 (126). In light of the complexity of Jüngel's stance toward Descartes, it is somewhat misleading for Fergus Kerr (on p. 8 of his *Theology after Wittgenstein* [Oxford: Blackwell, 1986]) to characterize Jüngel's perspective bluntly as "anti-Cartesian" on the grounds that he showed how the "turn to consciousness" initiated by Descartes "nearly ruined" theology. Jüngel's basic point in the passage cited by Kerr is rather more subtle. In fact, he warns that an immediate rejection of the self-grounding of thought initiated by Descartes (in order to "save" the traditional God of theology) would be a "short-circuited" theological conclusion. To be sure, theology must rethink the premises of modernity, but the basic lesson Jüngel draws from Descartes is the inadequacy of the pre-modern theistic tradition he inherited. His response to the Cartesian epistemological revolution, while by no means uncritical, is quite nuanced and deserves more attention than it has received.

[38] Marion, "The Idea of God", 278.

served to open up, even explode, metaphysics from within.³⁹ How can the identical concept indicate for one the culmination of metaphysical theism and for the other its (implicit) rejection? The ambiguity of divine infinity must be brought to light.

III. The Infinite God: Reinscribing Metaphysics or Marking Its Limit?

It is telling that one will not find in Jüngel's discussion of Descartes any specific attention devoted to the description of God as "infinite"; he takes up this term in passing as simply one more expression of the metaphysical way of defining the divine essence. Even these glancing references, however, suffice to show the connotations this word has for Jüngel. The "metaphysical concept of God" shared by "the entire Western tradition" is that of the "perfect and infinite being, tolerating absolutely no limitation."⁴⁰ His discussions of Hegel and Nietzsche suggest a certain sympathy for their critiques of the traditional infinite as a fixed opposition to the finite, and to the human in particular.⁴¹ Shaped by this strain of thought, Jüngel tends to construe Descartes's usage in light of the "bad infinite," that infinite which is, as Nietzsche says, "hostile to humanity" (*menschenfeindlich*). He suggests that the driving force in conceiving the infinite (at least in the pre-modern metaphysical tradition inherited by Descartes) was the negative association of finitude with the deficient and transitory.⁴²

Jüngel thus treats infinity as an adjunct to the concept of absolute metaphysical superiority and evaluates Descartes's use of the term accordingly.⁴³ It is all the more striking, therefore, that Marion, in the course of a much more extensive examination of Descartes, perceives in his invocation of infinity the key to his transcendence of the metaphysical framework of thought. When Descartes labels something infinite,

---

[39] Cf. Marion, *Sur la théologie blanche*, 443, where he claims that incorporating the "incomprehensible idea" of the infinite within metaphysics forestalled the linguistic and conceptual closure of a univocal concept of God, thus "opening up" metaphysics to transcendence.

[40] Jüngel, *Gott als Geheimnis*, 186 (140).

[41] Ibid., 195–6 (147), cf. 96–9 (72–5).

[42] Ibid., 275–6 (203): "The idea of God taken over from the old metaphysics does not tolerate the finitude of thought."

[43] There is a parallel to this in the way Jüngel reads Anselm's definition of God. In the only citation by Marion of Jüngel's work of which I am aware, the former criticizes Jüngel (among other thinkers) for too hastily interpreting Anselm's celebrated "that than which nothing greater can be thought" as equivalent to a "most perfect being" (*ens perfectissimum*), a phrase that does not appear in Anselm. The distinction is important to Marion because he wishes to insist that Anselm's determination suggests an "open" juxtaposition of qualities intensified to their maximum, not a rigorously or methodically (i.e., metaphysically) deduced and definable category of perfection. It is possible that in this case, as with that of the infinite, Marion has remained more sensitive to nuances in the conceptual usage that Jüngel elides in his "grand narrative" of the metaphysical tradition. The citation in question is at Marion, *Sur la prisme*, 268 [254]. Marion has developed his "non-metaphysical" interpretation of Anselm further in "Is the Ontological Argument Ontological? The Argument According to Anselm and Its Metaphysical Interpretation According to Kant," *Journal of the History of Philosophy* 30, no. 2 (1992): 201–18. A different version of the latter appears as Chapter Seven of Jean-Luc Marion, *Cartesian Questions: Method and Metaphysics* (Chicago: University of Chicago Press, 1999), 139–60.

he signals that it is finally "indeterminable by concept."[44] It cannot be conceptually comprehended. Indeed that which is infinite is known and represented precisely as incomprehensible.[45] Marion argues that naming God as infinite follows strictly from the "inaugural rupture" that marks Cartesian thought from its beginning: the claim first made in the *Rules* that God creates the eternal truths. As infinite God is not brought into the circle of finite representations and causes, and, moreover, is "unreachable through the method [and] incomprehensible to objective science."[46]

Properly understood, the naming of God as infinite by Descartes deftly shifts the concept of the divine being outside the proper sphere of metaphysics, strictly defined. Marion has labored to show how precisely Cartesian metaphysics conforms to the Heideggerian definition of metaphysics as "onto-theo-logy." As was seen, there are in fact two distinct onto-theo-logies operative in Descartes. Of the three divine names in Descartes, two are closely connected to the two onto-theo-logies: the "highest perfection" functions to mark the divinity in the cogitative onto-theo-logy, while "self-caused" characterizes God in the causal onto-theo-logy. But Marion argues that the third figure of the divine, God as infinite, has no constitutive role to play in either of these components of Descartes's metaphysical scheme; accordingly, it "does not depend on the Cartesian constitution of metaphysics" at all.[47]

For this reason, Marion can claim that the infinite should be considered less a metaphysical concept of God than an echo of the tradition of the "divine names."[48] The infinity of God marks in Descartes a key differentiation between the creator and created substances.[49] Among the Cartesian designations of the divine, infinity has a certain primacy, at once informing the more properly metaphysical concepts and transcending them.[50] Etymological appearances notwithstanding, infinity for Descartes is not a purely negative determination; it does not indicate the merely "indefinite," nor is it reducible to an expression of merely human cognitive limits with no positive content.[51]

Both Jüngel and Marion agree in effect that the use of the idea of infinity by Descartes allows him to "protect" the divine, as it were, from the pretensions of philosophy to comprehend the divine essence. But as Jüngel sees it, the end of this maneuver is merely to hide the rift Descartes had opened up between God's essence and existence. Infinity becomes an expression of epistemological "false modesty" concerning God's infinitely superior essence; it allows Descartes to obscure the incommensurability of

---

[44] Jean-Luc Marion, *God without Being: Hors-Texte*, trans. Thomas A. Carlson (Chicago: University of Chicago Press, 1991), 23.
[45] Marion, *Sur la prisme*, 262–3 [250]. Cf. Descartes, *Meditations* III (PW II, 32 = AT VII, 46).
[46] Marion, "The Idea of God," 276.
[47] Marion, *Sur la prisme*, 288 [273].
[48] Ibid., 291 [275]. The reference to the "divine names" is meant to recall those trends within the traditions of dogmatic theology, especially following Pseudo-Dionysius, which situated utterances about God within a discourse of revelation and the *analogia fidei*, a procedure that was increasingly excluded from early modern philosophical discussions about God due to the decline of the doctrine of analogy and the rise of a putatively self-grounded, rational conceptuality of the divine.
[49] Ibid., 238 [226]. Cf. Descartes, *Meditations* III (PW II, 31 = AT VII, 45).
[50] Ibid., 287 [272]. See also p. 240 [228].
[51] Ibid., 306 [290]. For Descartes's definition of the difference between the infinite and the indefinite, see *Principles of Philosophy* I. 27 (PW I, 202 = AT VIIIA, 15).

that essence with the finite human reason asserting its existence.[52] It "covers over" the aporia at the heart of Cartesian theism, the basic indecision with respect to the relation of the transcendence of God to the cognitive mastery of the ego. The concept of God's being is caught in this struggle and disintegrated in the process.

However, for Marion, the infinity of God serves to remove God from the site of this struggle, insuring that God's being cannot be reduced to its role in competing onto-theo-logical schemes. Ultimately Marion values the infinite in Descartes as the guarantor of a divine transcendence that cannot finally be defined metaphysically. But Jüngel can see in the infinite only another instance of just such a metaphysically defined transcendence. Their disagreement (if that is not too crude a word to use) cannot be adjudicated on the basis of definitions of "infinity" itself. They evidently agree on the basic meaning and function of infinity (denying all limitation of God and hence removing God's essence from the finitizing mise-en-scène of the human intellect). But whereas Jüngel sees this as perfectly replicating the basic dubiousness (from a theological standpoint) of metaphysical theism, Marion celebrates it as a potential "opening" of metaphysical reason toward theology. Any attempt to trace further the roots of these different readings of the infinite quickly leads into the larger question of the relations between philosophy and theology.

IV. Conclusion: Submitting to the Infinite

How does thought honor the divine? How does it properly "submit" to the infinite? The introduction to this chapter spoke of the different contexts, traditions, and goals that determine the success or failure of thought and speech about God. What is at work in the divergent readings of Descartes we have been exploring is a clash of intellectual "styles" associated with the different orientations of Christian doctrinal theology and philosophy. The historical traffic in concepts between these two traditions is so complicated and intimate that a hard distinction is unwarranted, but this much can be suggested. Jüngel the philosophically invested theologian is committed to a mode of reflection on the divine in which one tries to start with concentrated attention to the saving, grounding event presupposed by the community of faith; only then and on that basis does one work "outward," shaping broader generalizations about God and world. Marion the theologically invested philosopher tries to follow the internal logic of philosophical reflection to that point where its limits or aporias indicate the threshold of a possible divine revelation (the actuality of which, however, remains beyond strictly philosophical assertion).[53]

---

[52] Jüngel, *Gott als Geheimnis*, 165 (125).
[53] Cf. Jean-Luc Marion, "Metaphysics and Phenomenology: A Relief for Theology," *Critical Inquiry* 20 (Summer 1994): 590: "Between phenomenology and theology, the border passes between revelation as possibility and revelation as historicity." It should be pointed out that this interpretation of the differences between Jüngel and Marion is by no means exhaustive. Another fruitful avenue for exploring their differences might involve a comparison of Protestant and Roman Catholic theological appropriations of philosophy. Not to fall into easy caricatures, can one see here Marion's

Jüngel's suspicion of the Cartesian infinite lies in his conviction that Christian theology can fashion adequate concepts of God only when it allows its thinking to begin with and be guided at every point by the "givenness" of God's being in the event of Jesus Christ.[54] But such an approach cannot be sustained if defined with excessive rigor; even in service of this project, theology must necessarily and constantly resort to "experimenting with the rhetoric of its uncommitted environment." It will rely particularly on conceptual borrowings from philosophy, bending them to its own purposes perhaps but without evacuating them of the precision of meaning that makes them useful in the first place.[55] Jüngel's approach springs from a genuine concern. History illustrates the risks of an insufficiently critical handling of philosophical borrowings; theology has continually imported usefully rigorous conceptions of the divine at the cost of burdening itself with dangerously abstract notions of divine transcendence and superiority.

The Cartesian infinite is thus limited to the role assigned it by Jüngel's Barthian theology of revelation. It becomes one more indication that the philosophical God as classically conceived, the "highest being" that dutifully undertakes its important metaphysical functions, cannot perform its crucial theological role: living and dying humanly. As Jüngel memorably says, the cross could only collapse under the weight of this God.[56] Against that fetishization of philosophical concepts within theology that historically eventuated in a putatively "rational" *deus unus* eclipsing and finally supplanting a "revealed" *deus trinus*, he argues that thought submits to the infinite *theologically* when it reconceives the infinite within the stance of faith in the crucified. The result is no longer the alien infinite of overwhelming power but the love without limit historically uttered in the word made flesh.

But can theology envision another role, a positive one, for the divine infinity? Can there be a theological submission to the infinite that, rather than expunging it, incorporates it as a philosophical validation of divine transcendence, as thought's *philosophical* submission to transcendence? Marion shows the way. It was Descartes who spoke of a proper disposition of thought toward the divine infinite (as opposed to the merely "indefinite") as a submission or even a "surrender."[57] Just as one can never

---

"Catholic" willingness to call the philosophical tradition to the aid of theology versus Jüngel's more dialectically suspicious, "Lutheran" relating of the two?

[54] Thus, Jüngel faithfully upholds Barth's dictum that, at least where God is concerned, the Christian theologian must begin from the *actuality* of the divine among us (i.e., in revelation) and only then move to define the corresponding *possibility* in the divine being. Nor should it be forgotten that the phrase "event of Jesus Christ" in Jüngel's usage is a shorthand expression, which also includes the pneumatological and ecclesial dimensions. What is really at stake in the phrase is Jesus Christ present through God's Spirit in the faithful community. In other words, as with Barth, the strong "Christological concentration" should not obscure the basically trinitarian assumptions of Jüngel's thought.

[55] Rowan Williams, *On Christian Theology* (Oxford: Blackwell, 2000), xiv.

[56] Jüngel, *Gott als Geheimnis*, 163 (123).

[57] Descartes, *To Mersenne*, January 28, 1641 (PW III, 172 = AT III, 293); *Replies* I (PW II, 81–2 = AT VII, 114). The former is the source of the epigraph at the beginning of this chapter. The use of the image of the ocean in the latter citation (and the similar example of viewing a mountain, *To [Mersenne]*, May 27, 1630 [PW III, 25 = AT I, 152]) almost suggests a kind of "overload" of the cognitive apparatus. This use of natural images as symbolic of properly cognitive judgments is reminiscent of Kant's famous discussion of the sublime in the *Critique of Judgement* (Book II, § 23). For a fascinating theological development of this idea of "overload" as the basis for a phenomenological

"see" the ocean (i.e., as a whole) but can indeed hardly miss the water at close hand, so the finite mind does not even try to "take in" the divine essence in its integral infinity but rather submits to an ever-deepening inspection or contemplation of the individual divine perfections clearly and distinctly perceived. The result can be a kind of cognitive joy, a "natural" love of God.[58] He is, however, careful to deny any salvific merit to this love in itself; in fact the same divine infinity that is the object of this rational eros is also invoked as reason's limit, eluding its drive to comprehension. Infinity, as it were, "reveals" to philosophical reason that there is more to God than reason or philosophy can grasp, thus securing doctrines "such as the mystery of the Incarnation or of the Trinity" from rational dismissal.[59] Marion's more "charitable" attitude toward the Cartesian infinite might be seen to develop imaginatively this line of thinking.

What makes Descartes the great thinker he is for Marion is that he acknowledges the failure of rational comprehension of the divine even as he refuses simply to abandon the drive to comprehend (in the manner of that "orthodox" Pyrrhonism which embraced skepticism and reveled in the confusions of reason in order to show the necessity of revelation). For the failure of philosophy to adequately define the divine essence can only be shown philosophically by the very attempt to do so. Only by thinking metaphysics to its limit could Descartes show (in philosophical terms) what it would mean for the divine to transcend that limit. Thus, the infinite can signify not only the hubris of reason but its humility as well. Naming the divine as infinite is an attempt to find the conceptual resources within philosophy to gesture toward that which eludes its grasp. This endeavor to conceive God within philosophy as the "outside" of philosophy does not curb the drive to comprehend, which is the élan of reason; it speaks of God as that which meets reason at the limit of its comprehension.

Of course, philosophy can always refuse what transcends its cognitive horizon, seeing only the empty or the meaningless where a Christian philosopher like Marion expects the elusive freedom of the divine. In other words, the ambiguity of the infinite persists. Marion's "charitable" philosophical reading is at the outset implicitly informed by a theological interest. Against a reading like Jüngel's he sees that the transcendence implied by the Cartesian infinite need not be the negation of the immanence of incarnation but rather its ground of possibility. But no more than Descartes himself can he decide this using purely philosophical resources. In the end, he and Jüngel are united in their belief that the ambiguity of the infinite can only be resolved when it attests itself, when thought learns that the infinite is not a concept but a name.

---

understanding of revelatory events, see Jean-Luc Marion, "The Saturated Phenomenon," *Philosophy Today* 40 (1996): 103–24.

[58] Descartes, *To Chanut*, February 1, 1647 (PW III, 309–10 = AT IV, 607–09).
[59] Descartes, *Principles* I. 24–5 (PW I, 201 = AT VIIIA, 14).

2

Absolute Dependence or Infinite Desire: Subjective Alignment with God in Schleiermacher and Kierkegaard

In the youthful Søren Kierkegaard's unfinished satirical play, *The Battle of the Old and the New Soap-Cellars*, the philosopher Mr. von Jumping-Jack finds his grand monologue summarizing the course of modern philosophical development cut short by the presider for violating the allotted time limits. Just as the beadles come to drag him from the podium, he evades them long enough to blurt out his conclusion: "Since I see that force will be used, I cannot do the piece on Schleiermacher, but it was Hegel who speculatively drew together the previous systems, and therefore with him knowledge has reached its proper dogmatic peak."[1] These lines unintentionally predict the further course of Kierkegaard's own engagement with the two thinkers mentioned. We know that while still a university student he studied Schleiermacher's dogmatics carefully with Hans Lassen Martensen, but the overwhelming cultural and academic influence of Hegel in Denmark, and Kierkegaard's growing sense that Hegelian idealism represented all that was most dubious and dangerous about his own age, relegated his treatment of Schleiermacher to a few scattered references in the journals and the published works.[2] This relative lack of attention, in turn, has proven prophetic of later scholarship as well, where close comparisons between Schleiermacher and Kierkegaard, surely the two greatest anti-Idealist theologians of the first half of the nineteenth century, have been surprisingly sparse.

Whatever other reasons we may adduce for such scarcity of discussion, the very difficulty of performing this particular comparative operation probably plays some role. In what terms are we to frame such a comparison? How can we bring these two sprawling worlds of thought into a common conceptual field? Their very different styles of literary presentation, the divergent challenges they sought to respond to in their maneuvers at the boundary between dogmatics and philosophy, and above all the originality, complexity, and subtlety of the distinct conceptual apparatuses they

---

[1] Søren Kierkegaard, *Early Polemical Writings*, ed. and trans. Julia Watkin (Princeton: Princeton University Press, 1990), 118–19 [17: 292].
[2] For his study of Schleiermacher, see Alastair Hannay, *Kierkegaard: A Biography* (Cambridge: Cambridge University Press, 2001), 50–1.

developed to facilitate these maneuvers, all these have been at work, amply justifying suspicion of any simple and straightforward comparative formulation. Nor can we readily appeal to either one of the figures themselves for a substantive treatment of the other; obviously not to Schleiermacher, who died when Kierkegaard was still a student, but neither, it would seem, to Kierkegaard, whose own slender comments on Schleiermacher are frequently cryptic and present no unambiguous assessment of his contribution to theology. Nonetheless, perhaps there is a clue in Kierkegaard's very ambivalence.

Let us present this ambivalence at its sharpest. Early in *The Concept of Anxiety* (1844), Vigilius Haufniensis speaks of Schleiermacher's "immortal service" to the science of dogmatics, one scarcely understood by contemporary theology and in fact "left behind long ago when men chose Hegel."[3] Compare with this the sharp tone of a journal entry from a few years later (1850), where Kierkegaard complains that by conceiving religiousness in "esthetic-metaphysical" rather than in "ethical" terms "Schleiermacher may be said to have falsified Christianity."[4] What sort of "immortal contribution" to Christian theology, it might well be asked, can be made by a falsifier of Christianity?

Before appealing too quickly to the explanation that Kierkegaard's views on Schleiermacher underwent some sort of profound alteration in the period between these citations, and instead of indulging the tempting reflex of strongly dissociating Kierkegaard's own views from any assertion by one of the pseudonyms, perhaps we might explore the ways in which both statements can be taken simultaneously as genuine Kierkegaardian responses to Schleiermacher's thought. A brief examination of what is meant by praising Schleiermacher's "immortal service" will unexpectedly point us toward the nature of Kierkegaard's negative judgment on him, and in turn the bulk of this chapter will use this negative judgment (without necessarily agreeing with its diagnosis) as the clue to the true nature of the divergence between these two authors, a divergence that has proven very hard to formulate in terms which are not biased toward one or the other of the two.

One reading of Vigilius's encomium to Schleiermacher's "immortal contribution" has been that it refers to Kierkegaard's indebtedness to some of Schleiermacher's ideas about original sin (which is, after all, the topic of *The Concept of Anxiety*).[5] But the context suggests, I think, that Kierkegaard in fact has something else in mind, something that goes much more to the heart of the dogmatic enterprise. To put it briefly, what Kierkegaard praised Schleiermacher for was the latter's practice of a "pure" dogmatics in opposition to a "speculative dogmatics." According to Vigilius, when dogmatics is treated properly or "purely" it does not try to "explain" its basic presuppositions, or rather it explains them by presupposing them. As examples he

---

[3] Søren Kierkegaard, *The Concept of Anxiety*, ed. Reidar Thomte (Princeton: Princeton University Press, 1980), 20 [4: 327].

[4] Søren Kierkegaard, *Søren Kierkegaard's Journals and Papers*, ed. and trans. Howard V. Hong and Edna H. Hong (Bloomington: Indiana University Press, 1967–78), vol. 4, entry 3853 [23: 58]. Further citations to this English edition will be abbreviated *JP*, followed by volume and entry number. Following the practice established above, citation of the Danish collected works, by volume and page, will then follow in square brackets.

[5] This is the suggestion of Reidar Thomte: Kierkegaard, *Concept of Anxiety*, 228 n.47.

mentions the dogmas of original sin and of Holy Scripture.⁶ Dogmatics must always begin with the actual; it presupposes a set of "historical" circumstances as the horizon within which it must work, a set of purely "factual" coordinates which include both the sinful incapacity of human beings to achieve the ideality of ethics and the positive scriptural proclamations of incarnation and atonement.

Dogmatics can and does, of course, bring matters such as the dogma of sin or the authority of scripture under intelligent and critical scrutiny, but it must do so in a way proper to its own nature, its "heterogeneous originality." It can, for example, bring these various presuppositions into an ordered relationship, it can probe their logical interconnections, and it can reinterpret them in light of the tasks of proclamation in the current cultural situation. By providing a consistent and rigorous understanding of how Christian dogmas must be unfolded and applied for the contemporary upbuilding of faith, dogmatics is thereby "explaining" the dogmas and their authority precisely by presupposing them. But dogmatics goes astray when it attempts to subject these fundamental actualities upon which it is based to the kind of "explanation" practiced by speculative philosophy. That would mean bringing them into that dialectical development of concepts by which philosophy attempted to penetrate the contingent play of actuality and uncover the necessary logic of its development. In this way the meaning of Christianity, of sin and faith and atonement, would be rendered an episode within the immanent and necessary career of absolute spirit, a development that, although temporally worked out among finite subjects in the sphere of history and human choice, is in fact reducible by human reason to a set of conceptual transformations and mediations.

Kierkegaard's hostility to this entire idealist conception of history is well known: the famously dense "interlude" in the *Philosophical Fragments* merely discusses in detail what Vigilius briefly asserts near the beginning of his book, that "contingency ... is an essential part of the actual [and] cannot be admitted within the realm of logic."⁷ What is not so often recognized is that he could regard Schleiermacher as a predecessor in this attack on a speculative approach to dogmatics. For Schleiermacher, too, rigorously delimits the dogmatic field to the always presupposed Christian consciousness of sin and redemption, a consciousness that itself involves the achieved historical proclamation of the gospel and the historical proliferation of communities nurturing the human response to that proclamation. The dogmatic task involves the clarification and conceptual articulation of the specific contents of redeemed consciousness (i.e., faith) for the purposes of upbuilding communication; it in no way involves a speculative metaphysics of the absolute being, or a speculative philosophy of religion in which the basic concepts of Christianity in their historical facticity are subsumed within the larger project of reason's self-articulation.⁸ In short, for Schleiermacher as

---

⁶ Ibid., 19–20 [4: 327].
⁷ Ibid., 10 [4: 318]. Cf. Kierkegaard, *Philosophical Fragments*, 72–88 [4: 272–86].
⁸ Friedrich Schleiermacher, *Der christliche Glaube. Nach den Grundsätzen der evangelischen Kirche im Zusammenhange dargestellt. Zweite Auflage (1830/31)*, ed. Rolf Schäfer, vol. 13 [in 2 books] of *Kritische Gesamtausgabe, Erste Abteilung: Schriften und Entwürfe*, ed. Hans-Joachim Birkner et al. (Berlin: Walter de Gruyter, 2003), 13.1: 19–59; 127–50. English: Friedrich Schleiermacher, *The Christian Faith*, trans. H. R. Mackintosh and J. S. Stewart (Edinburgh: T&T Clark, 1928), 5–31; 76–93. (Citations of the English will henceforth appear in parentheses following the German page reference.)

for Kierkegaard, a speculative dogmatics is a contradiction in terms, as dogmatics cannot bring its basic foundations into its own field of vision in such a way as to render them transparent to reason, as stages in a comprehensive self-unfolding logic of actuality.

But it must be immediately pointed out that, in spite of this harmony, Schleiermacher and Kierkegaard have quite distinct reasons for this resistance to theological speculation. Kierkegaard's negative comments on Schleiermacher can be understood in light of these different grounds. For Schleiermacher, dogmatics is ordered to the redeemed God-consciousness whose self-identical essence is immediate consciousness of one's self as absolutely dependent on a grounding power beyond the self, which is named as God.[9] In other words, the criteria of meaningfulness and validity to which dogmatics submits the doctrinal material proliferating within the Christian community turn crucially on the ability of that material to express that foundational moment of the self, which strictly speaking precedes the self's cognitive and volitional acts. There can be no speculative dogmatics because the use of concepts in dogmatic expressions is limited to articulation of those precognitive states of immediate self-consciousness or "feeling" that Schleiermacher calls pious; this is to be sharply contrasted with the metaphysical use of concepts as the ordering of cognitive experience in its widest scope.

Kierkegaard, while fully approving of Schleiermacher's strictures against handling the dogmatic material from the standpoint of philosophical reason, does so on different grounds altogether. For him, reason is in no position to reduce the symbols and demands of the gospel to the conceptual order because the situated, existing individual self that employs that reason is confronted with the "paradoxes" of sin and atonement. Why paradoxes? Sin (the fact that freedom in history has through its own act become unfree and lost its transparency to the power that grounds it), as well as atonement (the fact that this situation has been countered by the presence of God in history as an individual human being), are matters that simply cannot be comprehensively grasped and reduced to an immanent conceptual ordering by the finite reason embedded within an existentially situated individual.[10] Only fundamental commitment of the self to the act of God in Christ and the ever-renewed resolve to live before God on the basis of repentance and forgiveness, only faith, properly determines the standpoint of the dogmatician; and this stance of faith, as Kierkegaard insists again and again, simply cannot be harmoniously subsumed within the stance of a sovereign, speculative reason.[11] But, to state the heart of the matter in concentrated form, he must also therefore severely criticize Schleiermacher for a conception of the self that discounts the absolute centrality for its relation to God of individual subjective choice and striving in favor of a stabilized awareness of its having been posited within the total created order.

Adequately determining the nature of Kierkegaard's approval of Schleiermacher has at once pointed us to the deepest grounds of his disapproval. But then do the two turn

---

[9] Ibid., 13.1: 32–40 (12–18).
[10] Kierkegaard, *Philosophical Fragments*, 15–7, 47 (sin), 51–4, 61–2, 65–6, 193–4, 222 (atonement) [4: 222–6, 251–2, 255–6, 263–4, 266–8; no *Skrifter* reference for last two English citations].
[11] Kierkegaard, *Concept of Anxiety*, 10–21 [4: 318–29].

out to be mounting a *common* front against speculative dogmatics for reasons that, ironically, spring from essentially *divergent* orientations? To suggest this is the burden of the remainder of the chapter, in which we must probe more carefully what separates them. For their contrasting anti-speculative portraits of faith or religiousness suggest that differing theories of the human self before God underlie the divergence between the two. My thesis, in other words, is simply that the best way to approach the ultimate differences separating these two Christian thinkers is to examine their respective theological anthropologies, unpacking so to speak the all too brief formulation offered above. First, I will attempt a broad construal of their different understandings of the nature of the self and of God's role in its constitution, and then I will briefly delineate what might be the most striking dogmatic result of these differing anthropological conceptions. For there is, I will suggest, a close connection between the fundamentally differing notions of the self before God that Schleiermacher and Kierkegaard develop, and the tellingly divergent Christologies that they set forth.

Space limitations obviously preventing any exhaustive treatment, I will begin by examining their two distinctive positions on theological anthropology from three angles that seem particularly suggestive for comparative purposes. For both thinkers, I will first determine which human faculty provides the locus for the characteristic unity and identity of the self; second, I will suggest how the constitutive relation of the self to God is understood; and third, I will try to sketch the way the self is situated within the broader creation and God's providential purposes there.

As a first approximation, it can be proposed that Schleiermacher grounds self-identity primarily in terms of awareness or consciousness, and Kierkegaard does so primarily in terms of choice and action or will. In Schleiermacher's anthropological scheme, the human person's awareness of being an individual is primarily defined neither in terms of acting nor of knowing but in terms of feeling. Of course, the self's interactive traffic with the world in action and cognition is ongoing and essential, but these would resolve into an incoherent series of atomic or punctual moments were there not an immediate precognitive awareness of centered consciousness. Feeling (*Gefühl*) is obviously a weighty, even quasi-metaphysical, concept; it cannot be understood in terms of our current, highly attenuated notion of "feelings" or "emotions." Feeling, in fact, is what it *means* to be a self, this self, my self, and all that the individual experiences, knows, does, and suffers vis-à-vis the surrounding world is woven collectively into the lived texture of the immediate consciousness of selfhood, which in turn informs, interconnects, and colors all those separate volitional and cognitive acts, thereby making them *my* acts.[12]

Kierkegaard's contrasting vision of selfhood places much greater emphasis on the central role of choice, deliberation, and action. It might be said that, contrary to Schleiermacher, freedom here is visualized not so much as a projection of the self outward into the world, and the individual's action is not simply expressing an already-achieved and ever-present self-awareness. Instead, the choices made by the self are seen as a kind of never-ending choosing of the self itself, of my unique

---

[12] Schleiermacher, *Der christliche Glaube*, 13.1: 22–32 (6–12).

selfhood in this time and place and under these circumstances. In a striking way, the unity and identity of the self are not prior to the exertion of will but posterior to it and dependent upon it. Freedom is an aggressive appropriation of an unending series of choices, demanding vigilant resistance to any reliance on putative compulsion to act (by inward disposition or outward circumstance) as an evasion of the true task of selfhood. Similarly, Kierkegaard does not stress the way in which shifting engagements with the larger world-forces beyond the self are constantly feeding into the self and being processed as part of its self-identity in feeling. Rather, the ceaseless pressure to choose courses of action in the world, when acknowledged and willingly embraced, leads to the inward intensification of the sense of individual selfhood over against all that is not self.[13]

Emphasizing these differences exclusively can easily lead to caricature, and it would be as wrong to portray the Schleiermacherian self as dissipating into passivity and undifferentiatedness as it would be to see the individual in Kierkegaard enclosed in a sheer solipsistic voluntarism. So we speak here not of a simple anthropological opposition between Schleiermacher and Kierkegaard but of a real and significant contrast in emphasis. Put aphoristically, the Kierkegaardian self is always "running to stand still" (like the Red Queen in *Alice through the Looking Glass*); the human being is not so much a self that wills but a restless will to be a self. For Kierkegaard, freedom, not feeling, is what it means to be a self.

The basic distinction comes out even more clearly when Kierkegaard says that the essence of selfhood is not immediate consciousness but "consciousness raised to the second power,"[14] by which he means that awareness of what is other than the self must be ceaselessly mediated by the free act of inwardly disposing the self toward all that is given, appropriating it only from the unique locus of the particular individual and thereby heightening "inwardness." The consummation of this process in Christian faith is a new, recovered immediacy, not prior to and grounding freedom but issuing from freedom.

Both thinkers understand that the self's relation to God's creative power plays a constitutive role in its structure; in light of the differing understandings of selfhood just seen, telling differences of emphasis will not surprisingly manifest themselves on this point as well. Here we might juxtapose two citations. In *The Christian Faith*, Schleiermacher refers to "the immediate self-consciousness of absolute dependence" as "the only way in which, in general, one's own being and the infinite Being of God can be one in self-consciousness."[15] Compare with that the pronouncement of Johannes Climacus in *Concluding Unscientific Postscript* that "an infinite negative resolution"

---

[13] The synthetic account above is not to be found fully expressed in any particular passage of Kierkegaard's writings, but some of his most complete schematic discussions of selfhood can be found in Kierkegaard, *Concluding Unscientific Postscript to "Philosophical Fragments,"* 2 vols., ed. Howard Hong and Edna Hong (Princeton: Princeton University Press, 1992), 129–250, 301–48, 387–430 [7: 121–228, 274–319, 352–91]. Cf. Kierkegaard, *Sickness unto Death*, 13–74 [11: 127–88], and Kierkegaard, *Concept of Anxiety*, 1–162 [4: 309–461].

[14] Søren Kierkegaard, *Fear and Trembling / Repetition*, ed. and trans. Howard Hong and Edna Hong (Princeton: Princeton University Press, 1983), 324 [15: 87].

[15] Schleiermacher, *Der christliche Glaube*, 13.1: 201 (131).

is "the individuality's infinite form of God's being within him."[16] While not strictly parallel in intent, the two utterances neatly suggest the decisive point at issue.

If, for Schleiermacher, feeling is what it means to be a self, then that special form of feeling, that immediate awareness of being a self absolutely dependent upon a founding power, is what it means to be "before God." Indeed, he famously claims that the original and essential meaning of the term "God" must simply be a reference to the source or "whence" of that founding gesture. The self always bears within its immediate self-awareness its distinction from what is not the self, what is "other," but this resolves itself into two forms. The "world" is the total field of reciprocal interactions conceived as a unified whole; it is all that which is both capable of influencing the self and yet is susceptible to the self's counteracting actions. But the consciousness of absolute dependence distinguishes itself from self-awareness and world-awareness as indicating that power which embraces and upholds both world and self; it is the source by which the self finds itself "placed," always already oriented toward a world and empowered to act. It is also the source sustaining that ordered field of interactions which constitutes the world.[17] Thus, as Schleiermacher sees it, for the self to be before God means for the self to apprehend its own positedness, from which can never be separated its co-positedness along with and as part of a created cosmos.

When Kierkegaard, on the other hand, speaks of the self's "infinite negative resolution," he is defining its togetherness with God not in terms of a deep awareness of a state of affairs but in terms of an ongoing, willed self-orientation. The word "resolution" marks the self's relation to God as fundamentally an "ethical" matter in Kierkegaard's sense of that word, that is, as a matter of the existing, choosing, striving individual. The ethically oriented subject is engaged in continually and rigorously struggling to actualize the universal truth of the human in the always shifting circumstances of finite temporal existence. Only in this cultivation of inwardness, this deepening of its particular subjectivity, does God become meaningful and real to the self, because "the expression for the utmost exertion of subjectivity is the infinitely passionate interest in its eternal happiness."[18] In other words, God is present indirectly or negatively as this "absolute interest" of the acting and existing self in its eternal end or well-being. Hence Kierkegaard's famous claim that "freedom ... is the wonderful lamp. When a person rubs it with ethical passion, God comes into existence for him."[19]

The self resolves with concentrated pathos to be itself and only in so doing finds itself before God. Kierkegaard qualifies this resolve as "negative" and "infinite." It is negative because this determination of the self involves a break with the immediacy of everything given. This is partly because God, though omnipresent in creation, is nowhere present directly; "only in the inwardness of self-activity" does the self "become aware and capable of seeing God."[20] But this turning away from the finite world is no contemplative retreat from the temporal or finite, no stoic nonattachment.

---

[16] Kierkegaard, *Concluding Unscientific Postscript*, 35 [7: 41].
[17] Schleiermacher, *Der christliche Glaube*, 13.1: 32–40 (12–18).
[18] Kierkegaard, *Concluding Unscientific Postscript*, 53 [7: 57].
[19] Ibid., 138 [7: 129].
[20] Ibid., 243 [7: 221].

It is a painful and wrenching affair because the existing self is always deeply committed to acting in its particular situation, even as it must reject any reliance on that situation turning out in accord with its intentions. Thus, "in his acting the finite elements are once and for all reduced to what must be surrendered in relation to the eternal happiness."[21] This resolution is also infinite. This means it is never finally achieved; the resolve to be passionately interested in being oneself in the world (and hence in the presence of God) is unfinished because the infinite element of the human self takes the temporal form of being "continually in the process of becoming."[22] This means that freedom itself can only be actualized anew in each new situation; the free self can only exist by continually "repeating" itself.[23]

To put it schematically, Schleiermacher envisions the self as always already oriented to free action toward the world by a relation to God that is simply given in and with selfhood, while for Kierkegaard, the self must strive to exist freely in the world in order to dispose or orient itself toward a God-relation that is never given. Following Hans Frei, we can suggest that Schleiermacher's understanding of the relation of the self to God is a kind of non-metaphysical critical realism. It is a realism because it affirms a content given to the self, thus refusing to simply identify God with the self's apprehension of it. It is non-metaphysical because it denies that self and God confront one another as subject and object. And it is critical (in Kant's sense) because "every attribute or quality [of God as the "whence" of dependence] is qualified by its being a content of [human] consciousness."[24] But Kierkegaard downplays the immediate givenness and stability suggested by this notion of the God-relationship in favor of its intensive subjectivity and instability. God is related to the person not as a given or datum but as the object of an unending desire. The infinite and eternal God encounters the subject only as the latter freely immerses itself more and more deeply into the finite and transitory through self-committing acts in the world. And this God encounters the subject precisely as this particular subject's most intense and passionate self-interest: "God himself is this—*how* one involves himself with Him."[25]

The third point of comparison between the Kierkegaardian and the Schleiermacherian vision of the self involves placing the individual in a landscape, as it were. God is creator of the world, not just of the individual human subject; where is the self located within the larger scheme of world development, understood as providentially maintained by God? The question is difficult, and here we must confine ourselves to some too-brief suggestions. One way of approaching this problem is to recall the old division between general and special providence, where the former represents God's governance as mediated by the total causal nexus of the world (operating by natural laws) and the latter represents God's particular care for chosen individuals or groups through a more

---

[21] Ibid., 391 [7: 356].
[22] Ibid., 86 [7: 85].
[23] This "self-repetition" implies the willed continuity of my selfhood, but the "repetition" involved cannot be reduced to merely perpetuating the self that temporally preceded this moment; it is the eternal idea of my individual agency that is replicated in time. See Chapter Three that follows.
[24] Hans Frei, "Niebuhr's Theological Background," in *Faith and Ethics*, ed. Paul Ramsey (New York: Harper & Row, 1957), 37–8.
[25] *JP* 2, 1405 [23: 215].

direct involvement in the world. The point of invoking this (dubious) distinction is to suggest that part of what distinguishes Schleiermacher and Kierkegaard on the notion of the human self is the very different ways they see that self as a particular individual in its relation to the general or universal order or structure of the created world.

Schleiermacher clearly understands himself to be retrieving properly Reformed notions of providence and election when he refuses to make a hard distinction between general and special providence: "We stray from the right path the moment when we assume for some individual thing a special divine causality in any way separate from connection with the whole."[26] His point is that we must attribute the entire, interconnected web of creation to a single, undifferentiated act of divine creative power; there is no individual thing that can be extracted from the total network of relations. Individuals cannot be played off against the general classes of which they are expressions, as if they were any more properly the subject of divine creation than the nested wholes of which they are a part. He is not at all claiming that the particular must therefore be denied reality or subsumed into the general without remainder; in fact, he wants to say that the entire development of the natural cosmos is providentially guided to issue in the perfected community of human individuals. That is, special providence drives or guides general providence, not vice versa, but the crucial point remains that an absolute harmony reigns between the whole and its parts, the general and the particular.

Kierkegaard's very different temperament on this point is well known, though it is much more decisively shaped by opposition to Hegel rather than to Schleiermacher. It is not just that Kierkegaard's vision of divine providence is much more oriented to the particular individual, a "personalist" rather than a "cosmic" vision of divine guidance, we might say. But beyond this, for Kierkegaard, the field of individual human existence is an intersection of clashing forces or regimes, of temporal and eternal, of general and particular. Especially, where for Schleiermacher the particular self is called to the harmonious expression of its location within the generic whole, for Kierkegaard the individual is a site of contradiction: "'Self' signifies precisely the contradiction of positing the universal as the particular." Put even more strongly: "The point about the particular is precisely its negative relation to the universal and its repellent relation to it."[27] As far as Kierkegaard's view of providence is concerned, he can even concede that the entire course of general history (natural or human) might appear an awesomely wasteful or meaningless battleground of impersonal forces, in which as such no divine purpose can be discerned but which nonetheless provides the arena within which God can guide or draw individual human selves into their most intensive development toward perfection.[28] This throws into even sharper relief the "negativity" of faithful resolve discussed earlier; utter devotion to God, far from issuing in a profound accord with a larger developmental or evolutionary trajectory of the cosmos, results instead in the deepest heterogeneity between the particular individual and the world at large. In light of this conflict, faith cannot appear as the health of the natural self but only as

---

[26] Schleiermacher, *Der christliche Glaube*, 13.2: 496–7 (725).
[27] Kierkegaard, *Concept of Anxiety*, 78 [4: 381].
[28] *JP* 2, 1450 [26: 340–1].

a wound whose mark is suffering: "One who in truth has become involved with God is instantaneously recognizable by his limp."[29]

I would reiterate that in spite of the manifest divergence in sensibility between these two thinkers at this point, it would be misleading to speak of anthropological schemes that are diametrically opposed. There are in fact numerous intriguing similarities between these two conceptions of the self which I have no time to explore. If I have emphasized their differences, it is because I believe that these differences are fundamental to the way Schleiermacher and Kierkegaard retrieve and interpret the Christian dogmatic tradition. Their anthropological sensibilities represent a somewhat submerged tension, a fault line so to speak, but one that issues in doctrines of sin and Christology that clash in sharper and more evident ways. Although I have no time to explore their doctrines of sin, they clearly represent the important link between their respective anthropologies and Christologies. Given their differing orientations toward the nature of the self and its relation to God, quite different understandings of human alienation from God are inevitable; these, in turn, logically demand different accounts of the overcoming of that alienation in Jesus Christ. Nonetheless, the links between anthropology and Christology may not be immediately apparent.

Surely the Christologies of Schleiermacher and Kierkegaard are most tellingly distinguished by their strikingly different understandings of the way God and Christ are related, what the New Testament refers to when it says "God was in Christ." We might formulate this difference by referring to Schleiermacher's Christology of the "Second Adam" and Kierkegaard's Christology of the "God-Man." For Schleiermacher, Jesus Christ is the self-diffusive presence in history of perfected creaturehood; for Kierkegaard, Jesus Christ is the paradoxical presence in history of the creator. For both thinkers, Christ represents the final and inexhaustible possibility for every human self in any circumstance to be in proper relation with God. But for Schleiermacher this calls for a perfect creature emerging from the developing world, a new creation advancing the old creation from within, while for Kierkegaard it demands nothing less than the transgressive advent of the eternal creator in time. Conceiving the self in terms of absolute dependence on the one hand, and in terms of infinite resolve on the other, provides a clue to the significance and function of these Christological alternatives.

For Schleiermacher, the basic predicament of sin is the utter inability of unredeemed persons to allow their God-consciousness to control and permeate their temporal experience in the world. The salvific ideal is to free the consciousness of absolute dependence from its crippled and distorted marginality in the ongoing experience of self and world, and to bring the continuous and joyous awareness of being grounded in the infinite, active power of a wise and loving God into a new and dynamic resonance with each moment of knowledge and action. Christ effects this not just by being the absolute exemplar of just such a total God-relation but also by bringing into being within history that self-proliferating community which communicates the power of this triumphant consciousness of creaturehood.

---

[29] *JP* 2, 1405 [23: 215].

Such is the work of Christ. For his person, the classic question is not whether he is divine but in what sense we should understand his divine status. How must God have been in Christ, according to Schleiermacher, in order for him to have effected salvation in this way? Schleiermacher insists that the only way God, understood as pure, omnipresent creative power, could be said to be "in" a particular creature would be if that creature could in its dependence "receive" the totality of God's founding creative act in all its depth and richness, thus (we might say) "mirroring" or "expressing" the creator. The world as a whole, of course, is precisely this expression of the creator; but can an individual part of the world perform this function? Yes, given a creature that could apprehend the structure of the entire cosmos by means of an active consciousness and then submit this reception to a kind of aesthetic processing in order to issue in living thought and activity that creatively express what is received. In other words, God could be present "in" the world only in the form of a perfect apprehension and reconfiguration of the world-creature itself in the form of a conscious, rational, and active life. Human being represents the only possibility of God's being "in" the world, and Jesus Christ represents the actualization of that human possibility.[30]

For Schleiermacher, the relation of the self to God involves an awareness of the reception of God's creative power, an awareness that must merge with and decisively condition the totality of knowledge and action. For Kierkegaard, it rather means the maximum intensification of subjectivity itself as an unending process of freely choosing the self, which involves the paradox of embracing a maximum exposure to the unstable flux of temporal process as the only means of absolute orientation to its eternal (transtemporal) *telos*. Much of his corpus represents an analysis of the various substructures of selfhood as they determine the succession of fundamental choices the self faces at each point of its intensification; these choices present it with greater and greater enhancements of freedom but only as paired with alternatives of deeper and more subtle evasions of selfhood, each a different cul-de-sac of despair. To oversimplify, for Kierkegaard, sin indicates the freely willed flight of freedom from itself. This represents the rejection of its divine call, its eternal end as a temporal creature, to grow by means of temporality into its eternal selfhood as God's free counterpart in love. Such rejection takes the form of submerging freedom into immediate enjoyment of its world, or into objective contemplation of it, or into titanic defiance of it; but in each case the self freely entangles itself in the world and hides from its harsh but essential exposure to time rather than exercising true choice and thus solidifying its identity. The paradox of time and eternity here is utterly central to Kierkegaard's entire way of thinking. The self realizes its *eternal* end in God only through the enhancement of its proper involvement in the instability and contingency of *temporality* through deliberate choices.

As with Schleiermacher, the work of Christ, and consequently the way his person (his divinity) is conceived, bears evident marks of this portrait of the nature and failures of selfhood. But in this case, the Christological result points in quite another direction. Indeed, Kierkegaard is explicitly aware of the refusal of Schleiermacher's path involved here. In an 1850 journal entry he complains that Schleiermacher is "unable to pick up

---

[30] Schleiermacher, *Der christliche Glaube*, 13.2: 54–6 (386–8).

very much from dogmatics" because "he treats religiousness in the sphere of being", whereas for Kierkegaard "every Christian qualification is characterized by the ethical oriented to striving" and becoming.[31] By "dogmatics" it is clear from other instances of his usage that Kierkegaard has especially in mind the Christian doctrines of sin, incarnation, and atonement, in all of which the "possibility of offense" is constitutive. Indeed, it is Schleiermacher's vision of the self before God that must, as Kierkegaard judges the matter, render him incapable of grasping the centrality to faith of the pathos of the striving self and of the Christian paradoxes with which the intellect necessarily but happily collides. The startling claim that Schleiermacher cannot "pick up very much from dogmatics" must be interpreted from Kierkegaard's own retrieval of the doctrinal tradition, of which his Christology is an illuminating case in point.

To summarize just as quickly and crudely as I did with Schleiermacher, Jesus Christ for Kierkegaard brings that difficult synthesis of temporal and eternal that defines the self to a point of unimaginable concentration: the total coincidence of a specific, past human subject (thus irreducible to objective assimilation both as an historical entity and as a person) with the eternal salvation or end of the human believer. The absurdity of such a conjunction, its mysterious opacity that resists any satisfactory conceptual synthesis, is merely the intellectual aspect of the more fundamental "offense" of the Christ, who confronts the self with the final, sharpest crisis of accepting its vocation to freedom. The man Jesus as savior must be God in time because, as we saw, God is present with and in the self's infinite concern to be itself; as in all cases, so chiefly with Christ, faith is the *creatrix divinitatis* in the believer (following Luther).

The results of the different Christological paths of our two thinkers are too extensive to enumerate here. Suffice it to say that for Schleiermacher, the mystery or miracle of the Christ is the appearance in history of sinless creaturehood, but this appearance is of a piece with the broader mystery of the emergence of creative novelty in the course of world-development. For Kierkegaard, on the other hand, the Christological mystery follows the classical lines of Chalcedonian orthodoxy, where the creator himself steps onto the world-stage as a human being. Seen from another angle, this means that Schleiermacher's merging of general and special providence into a single, immanent development is here challenged by Kierkegaard's claim that "creation is really fulfilled only when God has included himself in it."[32]

The conclusions of this all too hasty and preliminary examination may be stated this way. At the heart of the dogmatic distinction between Schleiermacher's Christology of the "Second Adam" and Kierkegaard's of the "God-Man" lie fundamentally distinct anthropological options. Rather than a Schleiermacherian anthropology of absolute dependence, where the individual's identity is rooted in self-consciousness and harmoniously expresses the larger general orders of creation, Kierkegaard offers an anthropology of infinite resolve, where identity is defined as the issue of an unending striving and the individual is called not to express the universal so much as paradoxically subsume it.

---

[31] *JP* 4, 3852 [23: 58].
[32] *JP* 2, 1391 [22: 177].

This has throughout been a structural comparison; the genesis of these different sensibilities has been left to one side, but we might close by considering the following comment of Charles Larmore comparing the sublime and the beautiful: "The sublime expresses the transcendence of freedom, the ability to move beyond all that experience has made of us. Beauty, by contrast, is an ideal of unity, in which our noblest humanity feels at home in the world of experience."[33] That Schleiermacher is deeply inspired by a romantic, aesthetic vision of harmonious unity, and typically strives to overcome the Kantian dichotomy of freedom and nature, is just as certain as that Kierkegaard the personalist aggressively reasserts such dualisms in the name of human transcendence. In both cases as well there is a productive conjunction of these philosophical tendencies with their respective theological traditions. Would it be too far from the mark to suggest that in Schleiermacher's thought a radicalized version of Calvin's doctrine of election is the vehicle for a worldview defined by the ideal of the beautiful? And that with Kierkegaard we have an equally radicalized version of Luther's teaching about faith that conceives reality under the sign of the sublime? As a first approximation, at any rate, such a general formulation might be worthy of consideration.

---

[33] Charles Larmore, "Hölderlin and Novalis," in *The Cambridge Companion to German Idealism*, ed. Karl Ameriks (Cambridge: Cambridge University Press 2000), 144.

3

"The Passage from Mind to Heart Is So Long ..." Kierkegaard's Repetition and the Ontology of Agency

In what seems almost a throwaway line, Constantin Constantius, the pseudonymous narrator of Søren Kierkegaard's enigmatic book *Repetition*, remarks, "*Repetition* is a crucial expression for what 'recollection' was to the Greeks. Just as they taught that all knowing is a recollecting, modern philosophy will teach that all life is a repetition. The only modern philosopher who had an intimation of this is Leibniz."[1] Constantius, however, quite fails to elaborate on what might seem an important philosophical filiation; indeed, Kierkegaard himself, when we range beyond this particular book, is scarcely more helpful. Scattered, invariably brief references to Leibniz in his other publications and a set of jottings from his journals shed no obvious light on Constantius's claim. The result has been that commentators for the most part either ignore the statement or offer tentative readings that do not really dispel its obscurity.[2]

It might be replied that solving this minor puzzle is far less important than discerning the conceptual shape of 'repetition' (the notion) itself and disentangling it from the

---

[1] Søren Kierkegaard, *Fear and Trembling/Repetition*, vol. 6 of *Kierkegaard's Writings*, ed. Howard Hong and Edna Hong (Princeton: Princeton University Press, 1983), 131 [4: 9].

[2] A representative selection from the large literature on 'repetition' of passages that at least broach the issue of Constantius's appraisal of Leibniz might include: John D. Caputo, "Kierkegaard, Heidegger, and the Foundering of Metaphysics," in *International Kierkegaard Commentary: Fear and Trembling and Repetition*, ed. Robert L. Perkins (Macon, GA: Mercer University Press, 1993), 223; Niels Nymann Eriksen, *Kierkegaard's Category of Repetition: A Reconstruction* (Berlin: Walter de Gruyter, 2000), 119; Ronald Grimsley, "Kierkegaard and Leibniz," *Journal of the History of Ideas* 26 (1965): 391-2; Håvard Løkke and Arild Waaler, "Gottfried Wilhelm Leibniz: Traces of Kierkegaard's Reading of the *Theodicy*," in *Kierkegaard and the Renaissance and Modern Traditions, Tome I: Philosophy*, ed. Jon Stewart (Farnham: Ashgate, 2009), 71; Johannes Sløk, "Die griechische Philosophie als Bezugsrahmen für Constantin Constantius und Johannes de Silentio," in *Materialien zur Philosophie Søren Kierkegaards*, ed. Michael Theunissen and Wilfried Greve (Frankfurt: Suhrkamp, 1979), 285-6. These sources provide brief conjectures that vary greatly both from each other and from the approach taken here, though the speculations of Eriksen and of Løkke and Waaler come closest. Two other sources on 'repetition', richly informative though they are, simply avoid the Leibniz issue altogether. See Edward F. Mooney, "*Repetition*: Getting the World Back," in *The Cambridge Companion to Kierkegaard*, ed. Alastair Hannay and Gordon D. Marino (Cambridge: Cambridge University Press, 1998), 282-307; and Louis Reimer, "Die Wiederholung als Problem der Erlösung bei Kierkegaard," in *Materialien*, 302-46.

deliberate obfuscations, boasted of by Constantius, of *Repetition* (the book).[3] For even though 'repetition' as a technical concept appears only a handful of times outside of the work of that title, it seems that Kierkegaard regarded what that word named as in itself central to the entire theological anthropology that he so painstakingly built up through the entire pseudonymous authorship. So we learn that 'repetition' is basic to any understanding of what freedom is, that it is central to grasping personhood and spirit, that in fact 'repetition' names both the fundamental task and the eternal fate of the human being (Constantius).[4] Other pseudonymous voices can be heard claiming that 'repetition' is a "transcendent" category corresponding to "the passion of the absurd" (Vigilius Haufniensis), or that it indicates the "new immediacy," that it safeguards the proper understanding of "hiddenness," "faith," and the "religious paradigm" (Johannes Climacus).[5]

Placing 'repetition' at the center of such a web of fundamental Kierkegaardian concepts indeed suggests what Constantius's witty persona tries to camouflage: "the word ... means everything."[6] Unfortunately, inflation leads to devaluation: 'repetition' might turn into a category so all-encompassing that it becomes shorthand for Kierkegaard's entire analysis of subjectivity, at which point any useful specificity it might have had is lost. In particular, attention would thereby be diverted from a fairly straightforward question which has tended to receive only the haziest answers: why are all these things 'repetition', that is, *what is it that is being repeated*? Until such a basic question is successfully answered, doesn't it seem in order to defer attention to the rather peripheral issue of Leibniz's supposed intimation of 'repetition'?

The first task of the present chapter will be to demonstrate that this sensible appraisal of hermeneutic priorities is mistaken. Comprehending the fleeting reference to Leibniz must not be delayed until the overall problem of 'repetition' is solved; rather, our overall grasp of 'repetition' will depend precisely on catching the meaning behind that curiously offhand remark. What is thereby revealed will then, later in the chapter, make it possible to indicate how the concept of 'repetition' encodes an incipient metaphysics, whereby Kierkegaard's anthropology of the acting, existing subject can be seen to unfold and make sense within the framework of an account of being itself which he only obscurely delineated.

The first section will show how Leibniz provided Kierkegaard with some basic categories for defining the tension between ancient and modern notions of selfhood. The second section will show how this tension issues in the crucial juxtaposition of 'recollection' and 'repetition'; in so doing, it will reveal how solving the riddle of the latter turns on grasping just what is repeated in 'repetition', namely, God's eternal "idea" of the individual temporal agent. A hitherto little-noticed discussion in Leibniz's *Theodicy* turns out to be the key both to his intimation of repetition and to this reading of the concept as a whole. A shorter third section will comment on how the failure

---

[3] In the following, the word "repetition" as the title of Kierkegaard's book will be capitalized and italicized (*Repetition*), but as a technical usage of Kierkegaard's more broadly it will not be capitalized but set in single quotation marks ('repetition').
[4] Kierkegaard, *Repetition*, 305, 308, etc. [15: 66–7, 70].
[5] Kierkegaard, *Concept of Anxiety*, 17–8 [4: 324]; *Postscript*, 262–3 [7: 238–9].
[6] Kierkegaard, *Concept of Anxiety*, 18 [4: 324].

to attain 'repetition' characterizes not only the ancient Greeks but also Kierkegaard's immediate predecessors and contemporaries in romanticism and idealism. The last major section before the brief conclusion will build on all the foregoing in order to sketch the ontological assumptions built into 'repetition'. The basic argument of the chapter, then, is twofold: only when we have solved the smaller riddle of Leibniz's presentiment of 'repetition' will we come to weigh properly the import for Kierkegaard of this specific term and to decipher its literal application (i.e., what is "repeated"); and only after unraveling that bigger riddle, the riddle of 'repetition' itself, will we be able, at the end of the chapter, to discover in that master image the conceptual building-blocks of Kierkegaard's implicit ontology of agency.

I. The Christian Vision of the Self Confronts the Ancient Greek Deficit of 'Spirit'

One of the most important clues to understanding the mystery of Leibniz's intimation is in plain sight, in Constantius's choice of words. If the quote is read with care, it will be obvious that Leibniz is not simply being credited with a presentiment of 'repetition' in general but rather with a quite specific aspect of the idea, determined in two ways. First, Leibniz has been the modern philosopher who at least implicitly grasped that 'repetition' was a modern notion, indeed a notion that marks the difference between ancient (i.e., Greek or pagan) views of life and those that succeeded them in the West (i.e., not just postclassical, but especially Christian). Second, he somehow glimpsed that this historical or cultural opposition was mirrored by a conceptual or structural one, such that 'repetition' can be defined exactly by its opposition to 'recollection', the master concept of the Greek worldview according to Kierkegaard.

It will be argued in this section that his reading of Leibniz helped stimulate Kierkegaard's own formulation of the general opposition between Greek and modern (i.e., Christian) notions of selfhood. Three quotes from Leibniz's *Theodicy*, in each case highlighted by Kierkegaard in his notebooks, will reveal the basic pattern of the opposition.

1. Leibniz: "The ancients attributed the cause of evil to matter, which they believed uncreate and independent of God: but we, who derive all being from God, where shall we find the source of evil? The answer is, that it must be sought in the ideal nature of the creature, in so far as this nature is contained in the eternal verities which are in the understanding of God."[7]

In other words, the Christian doctrine of creation *ex nihilo* marks a degree of divine transcendence of the cosmic order that the Greeks did not envision. It is difficult

---

[7] Gottfried Wilhelm Leibniz, *Theodicy: Essays on the Goodness of God, the Freedom of Man and the Origin of Evil*, ed. Austin Farrer, trans. E. M. Huggard (1951; reprint, La Salle, IL: Open Court, 1985), 135. Elsewhere he speaks of "the philosophy of Christians, which recognizes better than that of the ancients the dependence of things upon the first Author" (ibid., 57).

to overstate how foundational this general notion of divine transcendence is for Kierkegaard's entire way of thinking, but the idea itself he could have drawn from any number of sources. What especially intrigued him about Leibniz's use of it, as shown by his journal reference to this passage, was the conclusion that "the ground of evil is not to be found in matter, but in creation's ideal nature."[8] Whatever it is that challenges and limits the flourishing of creatures, especially free and rational ones, its origin is first and ultimately to be located in the intentions of the creator, that is in the world as "ideal," as foreseen in God's mind prior to its actualization. The important point at this stage is how this "modern" understanding of the creator's transcendence enables a more radical approach by Kierkegaard to the issue of the spontaneity of selfhood.

Prior to the elaboration of the idea of creation, the ancient notion of divinity's relation to the world was typically that of a shaper or artificer, or alternately an infused spirit animating the cosmos; either way, the divine act is limited by the refractoriness of the material substrate that God works upon or inhabits. The result is that in the drama between God and human beings, a third, quasi-independent actor intervenes. Both human suffering and human wickedness thereby find a mitigating explanation, and the fundamental goodness of God and of human beings can be rationally salvaged with some ease. But Kierkegaard will have none of it. On the one hand, matter as independent interferes with a strong notion of providence, the idea that God's oversight of events plays out on even the minutest level, the day-to-day conundrums of individual existence. On the other hand, and more importantly for Kierkegaard's theological anthropology, the ancient idea of matter is linked with the meaninglessness of worldly necessity, the opaque bulk of circumstance that ultimately controls the fortunes of individuals. This is of course the notion of fate, and Kierkegaard in many places expresses his conviction that a modern-Christian understanding of selfhood must utterly reject any hint that the ultimate destiny of an individual person might reside in accidental worldly circumstances beyond their control.

Appropriating the Leibnizian themes of the transcendence of God and the denial of fate prompts Kierkegaard to a remorseless ratcheting-up of every individual's self-responsibility. This insight escaped the Greeks but modern thought must take hold of it as truly its own. As revealed by an analysis of the difference between ancient and modern tragedy, only the agent conceived from the modern point of view is truly responsible for his or her guilt, truly *acts* (without a vitiating mixture of passivity). The ancient tragic hero, by contrast, is only partially free, both because there is always an admixture of the fateful in his or her downfall and because (to use Hegelian language) the hero's subjectivity never attains a silhouette distinct from the social collectives which ground it and give its acts meaning. "The ancient world did not have subjectivity reflected in itself. Even if the individual moved freely, he nevertheless rested in substantial determinants, in the state, the family, in fate."[9]

---

[8] Søren Kierkegaard, *Notebooks 1–15*, ed. Niels Jørgen Cappelørn et al., vol. 3 of *Kierkegaard's Journals and Notebooks*, ed. Bruce H. Kirmmse and Brian Söderquist (Princeton: Princeton University Press, 2010), 389 [19: 391]. Note that Kierkegaard refers to the Leibniz text by section number, in this case §20.

[9] Søren Kierkegaard, *Either/Or, Part One*, vol. 3 of *Kierkegaard's Writings*, ed. and trans. Howard V. Hong and Edna H. Hong (Princeton: Princeton University Press, 1987), 143 [2: 143].

Again and again Kierkegaard returns to this failure of the ancient worldview to fathom the true radicality of personhood. "The Greeks did not in the profoundest sense grasp the concept of spirit"; "with the Greeks freedom is not posited as freedom."[10] This is shown most tellingly for him in the Greek attitude to morality. The inexorable demand laid upon every human being to realize the human ideal that for Kierkegaard defined the authentic notion of the ethical was guilelessly evaded by the Greeks through their intellectual dalliance with fate. Thus, Aristotle ("with amiable Greek naiveté") revealingly concedes "that virtue alone does not make a man happy and content, but he must have health, friends, and earthly goods and be happy in his family."[11] In this way the good life, instead of maintaining its exalted "ideality" as the defining goal of all human striving ("the task for every man"), turns out to depend as much upon good luck as upon earnest effort.[12] Hence, "Greek ethics ... was not ethics in the proper sense but retained an esthetic factor."[13] So the sheer freedom and total responsibility of the human individual becomes a first marker of the Christian advance over paganism.

2. Leibniz: "Whatever perception [one's understanding] may have of the good, the effort to act in accordance with the judgment, which in my opinion forms the essence of the will, is distinct from it. Thus, since there is need of time to raise this effort to its climax, it may be suspended, and even changed, by a new perception or inclination which passes athwart it, which diverts the mind from it, and which even causes it sometimes to make a contrary judgment. Hence it comes that our soul has so many means of resisting the truth which it knows, and that the passage from mind to heart is so long."[14]

Kierkegaard in his journals calls attention to this passage in noting the question to which it is an answer: "What is the relationship between the will and the concluding act of the understanding[?] Does it [the will] necessarily follow the understanding's concluding thought[?]"[15] Two aspects in particular of Leibniz's account turn out to resonate strongly with Kierkegaard's understanding of the greater insight into selfhood that should characterize the advance from paganism. The first is the notion of the "long" passage from knowing to doing, a temporal elongation within which an obscure conflict plays out. For Kierkegaard, the relative naiveté with which the Greeks spoke of performing the good or failing to do so, already noted under the first number, finds its source not only in the role they conceded to the accidental "external" impact of destiny but also in the relatively unconflicted "internal" continuity they assumed in a given individual between knowing and doing. In other words, given accurate insight and favorable outer circumstances, the Greek mind tended to regard the performance of right actions as straightforward: "all ancient ethics was based

---

[10] Kierkegaard, *Concept of Anxiety*, 87 [4: 391]; *Repetition*, 297.
[11] Kierkegaard, *Concept of Anxiety*, 17 [4: 324].
[12] On the "task for every man," see Kierkegaard, *Concept of Anxiety*, 18 [4: 325].
[13] Ibid., 16 [4: 324].
[14] Leibniz, *Theodicy*, 314.
[15] Kierkegaard, *Notebooks 1–15*, 391 [19: 393].

on the presupposition that virtue can be realized."[16] The failure of virtue in a given individual comes down either to ignorance or unfavorable circumstances, or some combination of both.

In other words, the Greeks realized that the choice of the good is often thwarted, but located the source of that blockage in the essentially extraneous. Kierkegaard, in a move that deepens the theme of the spontaneous or self-responsible subject, in effect internalizes the obstacle, thereby complexifying agency itself by emphasizing the gap between vision and act. The Socratic definition of sin as ignorance "lacks a dialectical determinant appropriate to the transition from having understood something to doing it."[17] This Greek automatism ignores what Kierkegaard in his journals insists is the "pathos-filled transition," which, for an existing person, must mark the passage from thought or ideality to action or reality.

The second implication of the distance which Leibniz opens up between the knowing self and the acting self follows directly from the first. The new solidity that is given to the notion of the will in its distinctness from that of the understanding permits a new and grimmer genealogy of moral fault. Socrates had to define sin as ignorance because he lacked the category of willed "defiance." Indeed, that one could, knowing the greater good, deliberately allow the lesser to occlude it in one's actual choices: this was something the pagan mentality found difficult to countenance. "The intellectuality of the Greeks was too happy, too naïve, too esthetic, too ironic, too witty—too sinful—to grasp that anyone could knowingly not do the good, or knowingly, knowing what is right, do wrong."[18] The gap or articulation between understanding and doing, and the consequent enhancement of will: this marks a second theme drawn from the *Theodicy* and used by Kierkegaard to juxtapose the Greek and Christian ideas of the self.

Characteristically, Kierkegaard is not afraid to draw radical consequences from this point. "In the life of the spirit there is no standing still [*Stilstand*] (really no state [*Tilstand*], either; everything is actuation)."[19] In other words, the self, which the previous section has shown to be "turned over to itself" in its freedom, is at no moment not faced with the choice of what it will do, and hence (unavoidably) of what sort of self it will be. Spirit, because freedom is essential to it, is never simply "at rest" in a particular state but is continually active in shaping itself in accord with its concrete decisions. Each such decision becomes, in its turn, a further deposit shifting the interior landscape in which the succeeding decision will have to be made. This is a consequence of the radical status granted to "spontaneity" in Kierkegaard's anthropology: fate has become interiorized, as it were, indeed voluntarized.

3. Leibniz: "[The damned] will rather choose to be, and to be that which they are, than not to be at all. They will love their state, unhappy as it will be, even as angry

---

[16] Kierkegaard, *Concept of Anxiety*, 19 [4: 326].
[17] Kierkegaard, *Sickness unto Death*, 93 [11: 205].
[18] Kierkegaard, *Sickness unto Death*, 90 [11: 203].
[19] Ibid., 94 [11: 206].

people, lovers, the ambitious, the envious take pleasure in the very things that only augment their misery ... They will not be able to refrain from desiring perpetually things whose enjoyment will be denied them."[20]

Leibniz is facing a question: Why does Christianity affirm eternal condemnation for merely temporal and finite human sins? His answer is that the punishment is perpetual because the damned sin perpetually; having freely embarked during their lives upon a course that increasingly alienates them from their own meaning and felicity, they willingly maintain the impetus of that perverse willing in a kind of self-reinforcing cycle.

As is well known, poetic renderings of the damned personality occupied Kierkegaard's reflections from an early period. This gloomy fascination was more than a morbid eccentricity, however; the real possibility that the individual subject's essential project of free self-choosing could eternally miscarry was an important element in his developing theory of human selfhood. In light of this overall concern, Kierkegaard flags the Leibniz quote in his journals: "This passage deserves a second reading."[21] And well it might have, as it comprises a striking anticipation of what he will later thematize as "despair."

The notion of perpetually choosing against one's own happiness as a model for understanding damnation implies that the dynamic of human willing, where one is constantly in the process of choosing to be oneself in one way or another, finds no natural or purely immanent limit. Kierkegaard obviously assumes that the dissolution of the human body at death cannot decisively alter the inexorable working-out of choices accumulated in earthly life. Hence, the trajectory of self-mastery never really terminates, even if "free choice" has long since degenerated into the convulsive self-affirmation of a human ruin. This horrible possibility stands as another boundary marker for Kierkegaard between the Christian and pagan worlds. The latter will answer the eschatological questions otherwise than the Christian. For Greek thought, how and when does self-choice end? In only one way: with the soul's return to its homeland at death.

Although the Greeks indulged in mythological pictures of post-mortem justice, where especially wicked figures suffered fitting torments, these stories could not, for Kierkegaard, serve the same function for them as the doctrine of eternal judgment does for Christians. The latter concerns the relationship between finite existence in time and the transtemporal realm of utter reality, that is, the Eternal, the Divine, God. The issue is the ultimate and timeless significance vis-à-vis the ground of reality itself of each human being's temporal career. At this point the Greek mentality, in its consummate philosophical form, must balk at Christian eschatology; it could conceive neither such a direct connection between the temporal and the eternal, nor could it suspect that the upshot of temporal choice might somehow lead to the forfeiting of that blessedness that must surely result from death's release of the soul into its birthright: the regime of ideal or divine truth. It appears that for Kierkegaard

---

[20] Leibniz, *Theodicy*, 292–3. This is actually a citation by Leibniz of a review summarizing one of the arguments of Archbishop William King's 1702 work on the origin of evil.
[21] Kierkegaard, *Notebooks 1–15*, 391 [19: 393].

the true Greek analogue to the modern-Christian eschatology, with its tension between two exclusive eternities, is to be found not, surprisingly, in their poetic depictions of Elysium and Tartarus but rather in the quiet enthusiasm of Socrates on his deathbed.

Kierkegaard employs several expressions for what must be seen, from the Christian standpoint, as the Greek mind's failure of nerve. For example, he speaks of the "commensurateness" of temporal choice with an eternal outcome that Christianity recognizes but paganism never did.[22] But another way he articulates this eschatological opposition of Greek and Christian is especially important for what follows. Recalling the New Testament judgment that the pagan is "without God in the world," he insists that "the pagan did not have his self directly before God."[23] This has nothing to do with theoretical atheism but rather concerns the criterion used to judge the significance of the moral successes or lapses of the existing self. Of course, for the pagan there are failures of obligation to the gods, but these ultimately are in the same order as failures of piety toward one's parents, or toward the state. None of these can claim a final, transcendent significance with regard to the ontological status of a human soul; they, indeed all moral failings, are judged according to a purely human standard. "The pagan and the natural man have the merely human self as their criterion."[24]

Thus, the absolute significance of human actions implied in the doctrine of eternal punishment, their direct impingement upon the very ground of cosmic order, and hence the fact that they are matters of actual divine concern: this is lost on the pagan with his "superficial Pelagian conception" of sin.[25] That is, the pagan simply cannot imagine that the ideality of human persons, their link to the timeless divine realm as their authentic homeland, could somehow hinge upon the relative trivia of earthly decisions. Only the Christian *exists* "before God," grasping what Kierkegaard calls the sheer "reality" (*Realitet*), the transcendent weight, of the existing individual precisely as existing (not as a "soul" detachable, in the last resort, from its temporal history). By contrast, "a pagan, the natural man, is very willing to admit that sin exists, but this 'before God' that actually makes sin into sin, this is too much for him… [I]t makes too much of being human."[26] This third and last Kierkegaardian variation on a theme of Leibniz, the burden of eternity pressing upon our finite decisions, is continuous with the two previous in disclosing a transcendent significance within the human individual and its free decisions. With the general picture now in place of the modern notion of "spirit" and its corresponding absence prior to Christianity, we are finally ready to broach the particular issue of Kierkegaard's 'repetition' with its defining opposition to 'recollection', the very opposition Constantius uses to define Leibniz's "intimation."

---

[22] Kierkegaard, *Postscript*, 270–1 [7: 245].
[23] Kierkegaard, *Sickness unto Death*, 81 [11: 194].
[24] Ibid.
[25] Ibid., 81 [11: 195].
[26] Ibid., 87 [11: 200–1].

II. What Is Repeated? Leibniz's "Lazy Sophism" Solves the Riddles of 'Repetition'

During one of Kierkegaard's discussions of the essential opposition between Greek and Christian views of human existence, he tucks away in a footnote a curious comment upon the famous inner divine voice or *daimon* by which Socrates claimed to be guided. "Socrates' genius, as is well known, was only dissuasive, and this is how the humorist, too [i.e., the one, like the pagan philosopher, possessed of the highest "immanent" human wisdom but falling short of Christian truth], must understand his relationship with God." Within the Christian truth, however, "it is the reverse; there the spirit [the inner divine guidance] is inciting."[27] Upon this apparently slight distinction hangs the entire issue. For the Greek, the relation between the call of the divine and any particular concrete decision in this life is a negative one; that the divine voice wards one away from this or that act dramatizes the fact that the soul's conjunction with the divine order is closely aligned with suspension of action in face of particular situational demands, by restraint from rather than by commitment to the business of embodied freedom. Correspondingly, the Holy Spirit is precisely a call to individual existence here and now, to enter utterly into the minutiae of the self's day-to-day options.

The choice between pagan and Christian worldviews is finally a choice about the relationship between the individual's temporal existence in freedom and his or her eternal destiny before God. Does our connection with God, the source bestowing upon each self such time-transcendent significance as it may have, in some sense *await* the working out in time of our dilemmas of choice, or rather is it an *already given* inheritance always present, hovering behind the petty dramas of temporal life? Does God wait, so to speak, in front of the existing individual, or behind? In a way, everything which Kierkegaard has said about the Greek view of life can be summed up by this latter option, in which (to repeat a phrase from above) the human being "has his eternity assured *behind*." Kierkegaard has a name for this way of relating existence and eternity, temporal freedom and ideal telos: he calls it 'recollection'. "When eternity's essential decisiveness is to be reached backward in recollection, then quite consistently the highest spiritual relationship with God is that the god [as in Socrates's case] dissuades, restrains, because existence in time can never become commensurate with an eternal decision."[28]

To understand fully Kierkegaard's 'repetition' it is essential to grasp it in its opposition to this Greek ideal of 'recollection'. The nature of the Greek-Christian polarity has begun to come into focus through the pattern of oppositions set up in the previous section. Clearly, it has everything to do with the opposed assessments of the value, in light of eternity, of individual existence in time which characterize, respectively, the Greek (or "pagan," or "natural," or "immanent," or "speculative," or "ancient") understanding, and the Christian one. The antithesis is succinctly expressed by juxtaposed temporal orientations of the agent: one either faces forward, pursuing

---

[27] Kierkegaard, *Postscript*, 271 [7: 245].
[28] Kierkegaard, *Postscript*, 271 [7: 245].

the time-transcendent significance of one's selfhood (one's "eternal truth") only in and through the successive free decisions which make up this life, as in some sense constituted by those decisions; or else one looks back, wary of full immersion in the sideshows of worldly existence lest they distract one from one's inherited and always-already-possessed kinship with the ideal realm. The opposition, at least in broad outline and with all oversimplifications duly acknowledged, should by now be evident enough. But now the question must be asked: why is that worldview which denies 'recollection' and which characterizes (or rather, should characterize) modernity called 'repetition'? The search for an answer will now move in a surprising direction, by way of a curious passage in Leibniz which, it will be suggested, is the key to that "intimation" praised by Constantin Constantius.

Leibniz:

> Men have been perplexed in well-nigh every age by a sophism which the ancients call the "Lazy Reason," because it tended toward doing nothing ... For, they said, if the future is necessary, that which must happen will happen, whatever I may do. Now the future (so they said) is necessary ... because the Divinity foresees everything, and even preestablishes it by the control of all things in the universe ... for there is a truth in the future event which is predetermined by the causes, and God pre-establishes it in establishing the causes.[29]

This might seem at first to be raising the issue of fate again, but something far more important is going on in Leibniz's discussion of this odd "sophism," something which draws not just Kierkegaard's close attention, but his enthusiasm: "It is excellent what Leibniz says about 'the lazy reason' [*den dovne Fornuft*]."[30] But what is so excellent about it? Kierkegaard does not say, but what will now be proposed is that Leibniz's remarks on this bit of sophistry are what Kierkegaard had in mind when he made Constantin Constantius speak of an "intimation" of 'repetition'. The crucial point lies in the way Leibniz, in dissolving the fallacy, describes the relation between the free agent and the all-creating God. To see this relation in its significance requires a last bit of background.

Leibniz repeatedly emphasizes that the created order in its entire spatial and temporal range is the result of the creative causality, both intelligent and willed, of God. This means that all that comes about is, in some sense, intended by God, and thus "seen" by God "prior" to its actualization in the course of events. (The "priority" here is not literally temporal, since God's transcendence is understood by Leibniz along the "classic" lines established in late antiquity and the middle ages by the great Jewish, Muslim, and Christian theoreticians of creation from nothing: the divine reality is not distended within any arrangement of duration or temporal succession; only created

---

[29] Leibniz, *Theodicy*, 54.
[30] Søren Kierkegaard, *Journals EE-KK*, ed. Niels Jørgen Cappelørn et al., vol. 2 of *Kierkegaard's Journals and Notebooks*, ed. Bruce H. Kirmmse and K. Brian Söderquist (Princeton: Princeton University Press, 2008), 140 [18: 150]. I have altered the English translation from "idle reason" (with no definite article), which obscures the fact that "reason" here refers not to the human rational faculty but rather to a rationale or demonstration (in this case a sophistical one).

reality is dispersed into past, present, future, whereas each created moment is equally "present" to the divine gaze constituting it.) This means that the events making up the created order each happen "twice," so to speak; in one way, in the timeless and ideal realm of the creator's intention, in another way, as temporally unfolding within the zone of finite actualization which is the created universe.

The choices and acts of free human agents are just as much events within this universe as anything else, and therefore find their ultimate cause in the divine will to create them. The "lazy sophism" seizes on this point, of course: God has seen all "beforehand," indeed has arranged the converging causal chains to bring about precisely what happens at every moment. Freedom, therefore, is purely illusory; my choosing this as opposed to that course of action, in fact my decision to do something rather than nothing, all are equally futile since the future is preordained. As the song says: what will be, will be. Leibniz, however, insists that this is a *non sequitur*, whether taken as a theoretical refutation of freedom, or as a practical counsel against responsible action. Kierkegaard notes one of the relevant passages where Leibniz explains: "the effect being certain, the cause that shall produce it is certain also; and if the effect comes about it will be by virtue of a proportionate cause. Thus your laziness perchance will bring it about that you will obtain naught of what you desire."[31] Earlier in his book Leibniz had similarly laid bare the "fault of the sophism": "It is untrue that the event happens whatever one may do: it will happen because one does what leads thereto; and if the event is written beforehand, the cause that will make it happen is written also."[32] In short, the "lazy reason's" claim that all choices are vain because the causal trajectories of the future have "already" been established by the creator is itself vain, because one can never rule out that one's own acts, as a free agent in the world, are themselves necessary links in the chain, visible to God but quite hidden from us, leading to that future. Hence, the counsel should be: choose wisely and act, because only your free acts can grant you the dignity of a willed causal participation in the divine constitution of any desired outcome.

Thus, Leibniz argues that the lazy sophism is specious on the practical level; but it is also theoretically flawed, because it draws the creative divine cause of things into the created order, as if it were simply an additional component to the temporally prior causes conditioning an event. This is to forget the transcendence of the creative act, which is not itself one among created causes but rather their ground of possibility. In any worldly event, including the choice and action of a free agent, God's causality and worldly causality always coincide but are never yoked together alongside each other; God's causality is uniquely the simultaneous ground of all worldly causal interactions and precisely for that reason cannot be numbered among them. As Leibniz says, "The actions of the will are determined in two ways, by the foreknowledge or providence of God, and also by the dispositions of the particular immediate cause, which lie in the inclinations of the soul."[33] But that God sees those dispositions and actions from all eternity, and enables them, does not make them any less contingent or free within the

---

[31] Leibniz, *Theodicy*, 153.
[32] Ibid., 57.
[33] Ibid., 344.

created causal network: "the decree to give existence to this action no more changes its nature [i.e. makes it compelled rather than free] than does one's mere consciousness thereof."[34] In other words, one's seeing something happen means, *ex hypothesi*, it necessarily is happening, even if nothing prior necessitated it; likewise, even God's creative "vision," which makes my free act possible, does not shift its inner-worldly modality. It isn't just free in spite of being "foreseen" by God; it is free exactly because God has "foreseen" it as free.

The well-known puzzles which such discussions generate for us (since the relation of a transcendent God to a temporal world can be rendered rational but not imaginable) do not need to be rehearsed, and anyway Kierkegaard's real interest does not seem to lie in Leibniz's philosophical argument (though he presumably acquiesces in it). What really came to grip him, it will now be proposed, is the sort of image of God's relation to my free activity that arises from Leibniz's language and that Kierkegaard found highly suggestive for his own philosophy of the self.

Consider the relation between temporal existence and the realm of eternal or ideal truth that is implied by the worldview that 'repetition' opposes, namely, 'recollection'. The accounts of the "Greek" mind above have consistently fostered the assumption that the ideal and the actual, the eternal and temporal, the world of truth and the world of appearance or becoming, are polarized in a relatively undialectical fashion. For 'recollection', a human individual's degree of participation in the domain of authentic reality and truth is equivalent to that individual's abstraction from the field of temporal change in which human life or existence ordinarily goes forward. It is not as though the ideal and the real planes bear no relation to one another; the former for the pagans was, in its sublimity, deficiently reflected in the lower order. One thinks here of Plato's famous definition of time as a "moving image" of eternity. But the "motion" here represents precisely the distorting medium of the reflection; change and becoming are, in themselves, mostly meaningless noise. Participation in the truth, for things and persons, happens as unmoving ideas or forms are glimpsed in their persistence through the temporal flow. The path of wisdom for human beings is to develop their intellectual grasp of the unchanging, positioning themselves for a maximal share in the ideal world through a discipline of detachment from the living struggle of the everyday.

The Leibniz passages that drew Kierkegaard's eye, however, pointed toward a radically opposed stance for existing individuals who sought their own eternal significance. On the alternative model of 'repetition', the eternal truth to be sought by human beings is not something always already presupposed, self-contained on a plane prior to and separate from the "shadowplay" of existing agency; it is precisely the affirmation, the truth of that very agency, its ideal reality as eternally grounded in the divine mind whose creative act is nothing other than the positing of the creature as agent along with all of its individual acts. Note how Leibniz repeatedly phrases it: "If the event is written *beforehand*, the cause that will make it happen is written also." "[A]ll these connexions of the actions of the creature and of all creatures were represented in the divine understanding … *before* he decreed to give them existence." "[T]hese good

---

[34] Ibid.

or bad actions today were *already* before God when he formed the resolution to order things." "When God does leave it to a man [to work out his own destruction], it [i.e. his activity] has belonged to him since *before* his existence." "[*A*]*nterior* to existence ... [the human soul] was determined from all eternity in its state of mere possibility to act freely, as it does, when it attains to existence."[35]

In each instance, the same two notes are sounded together: that of the existing creature as causal agent, and that of the anterior, eternal presence of just that agency in the divine mind (and not the presence, say, of an abstract idea or detached "soul"). To assume that this ideal "beforehand" somehow obviates the temporal causal act is precisely the fallacy of the "lazy sophism." The truth of the matter for Kierkegaard is that only as human beings enter fully into their embodied course of freely willed existence do they appropriate and affirm their own time-transcendent meaning. The eternal "beforehand" does not evacuate creaturely freedom but rather charges it with unlimited meaning. That God freely creates the freely acting agent is just what makes that created agent real, and it is also what makes its created act to be of transcendent significance in itself. Hence 'repetition': instead of retreating from the flow of material life, withdrawing to effect a backward connection with an ideal realm finished and indifferent to one's existential dramas, one's only hope of mapping oneself onto the pattern of eternal truth lies in an unreserved involvement with one's own ongoing existence. The road to the eternal does not lie behind the individual agent, but ahead. My transcendent truth does not float above my history, always available to my "recollecting" intelligence; it can only be pursued through it, volitionally.

What is repeated, then? It is my own ideal truth, my identity in and before the creator. And why must it be repeated, instead of recollected? Because the transcendent significance of my life, my "eternity," will turn out to be exactly and exclusively identical with the self I have constructed through the acts I have chosen. Because the God who creates me *ex nihilo* thereby constitutes me precisely as this particular free causal operator of these particular acts, my ideality (in the eternal truth of God's mind) is precisely my actuality (my role as an existing, acting self), and my conjunction with eternity lies only in my temporally executing the existence that already timelessly defines me, that is, in my "repeating" it.

Note too that on this model 'repetition' involves not only fulfilling my eternal identity in time, but also knowingly doing so, which means acting with some consciousness that my acts have an eternal significance. Just as the possibility of 'recollection' turns on the awareness that the self has a status that transcends its temporal career, so too the possibility of 'repetition' involves a similar awareness. In each case, the tasks of existence "stand between" the self here and now and its eternity, but in different senses; for 'recollection', they threaten to become impediments or luring byways to be evaded, while for 'repetition' they form the unique road to be followed, although in such a way that the "I" in its abiding significance is not lost, dissipated amid the various finite outcomes that are pursued as means to that infinite significance. The Leibnizian themes discussed in the previous section converge upon this conclusion. The radicality

---

[35] Ibid., 57, 149, 152, 195, 321. Italics added.

of self-construction, the perilous gap between contemplated truth and willed act, the awful risk of perpetually choosing misery rather than God: all fall into place as elements of Kierkegaard's philosophical/theological anthropology of 'repetition'. Also significant is the way Leibniz makes the metaphysical point fundamental for a psychological issue; Kierkegaard's appropriation of the motif of 'repetition' will consist in prolonging and amplifying this move.[36]

The opposition to the Greek understanding of the meaning of human existence stands out in this context with peculiar sharpness, as displayed by some of Kierkegaard's unpublished notes on *Repetition*: "With the Greeks freedom is not posited as freedom… [For them] only in recollection did [freedom] possess eternal life. The modern view, however, must be to express freedom forwards, and herein lies repetition."[37] 'Repetition' is thus freedom's task; that is, the individual must choose to act in such a way that her or his status as a free cause is continually affirmed and not dissolved as a meaningless connecting point within the necessary pattern of causal chains. "The moment it is apparent that the individual can lose himself in events, fate, lose himself in such a way … that freedom is taken up completely in life's fractions without leaving a remainder [i.e. is "evaporated" in events], then the issue becomes manifest … to freedom's concerned passion."[38] For "the Greek mentality" freedom encompassed its eternal significance "by moving backward into it"; but "the modern view … must seek freedom forward… [F]reedom must press forward, not retreat."[39] Only assuming the risk of acting will realize and solidify the individual in its status as agent.

The understanding of 'repetition' that has been won here by querying the Leibnizian intimation gains in plausibility by the way it illuminates certain other difficult notions in Kierkegaard, such as those of temporal enhancement, of the moment, and of pantheism. This section will end by looking at each of these in turn, since they all have ramifications for the ontological reflections of the final section.

1. The advance in worldviews or "stages," from the esthetic and metaphysical through the ethical and into the religious, is measured by "the degree that time is accentuated."[40] Change, movement, and temporality are those aspects of material existence that even the greatest Greek mind could not properly evaluate: "It is Socratic to disparage all actuality and to direct man to a recollection."[41] Socrates' supreme achievement was his passionately existing into the idea of self-knowledge, an unending pursuit against the backdrop of his own penetrating ignorance of himself. To center his pathos on

---

[36] The different conjectures of the earlier cited passages of Eriksen and Løkke/Waaler concerning the link between Leibniz and 'repetition' each have hold of one side of the issue. While Eriksen turns to monadology to speak of the way God predetermines monadic acts without infringing in the slightest on their spontaneity as self-expressions, Løkke and Waller think the answer lies not in the doctrine of monads but rather in the way that intelligent agency involves the actualization of what is ideally envisioned prior to action. As can now be seen, both accounts are partial but correct and indeed complement each other.

[37] Kierkegaard, *Repetition*, 297.
[38] Ibid., 315 [15: 80].
[39] Ibid., 317 [15: 81].
[40] Kierkegaard, *Postscript*, 299 [7: 272].
[41] Søren Kierkegaard, *The Concept of Irony with Continual Reference to Socrates*, vol. 2 of *Kierkegaard's Writings*, ed. and trans. Howard V. Hong and Edna H. Hong (Princeton: Princeton University Press, 1989), 60 [1: 120].

his own selfhood is what marks him as the first ethicist ("the founder of ethics"), but this "movement of infinity," as pagan, still remains within the bounds of the humanly attainable.[42] It is a species of what Kierkegaard in *Fear and Trembling* calls "infinite resignation," and resignation means the grasping of one's self in a realization of its transcendent worth, but only by breaking the ties that bind one's desire to the world of finitude. It is "to renounce the whole temporal realm in order to gain eternity."[43]

While the essence of pagan 'recollection' is that nothing truly crucial happens in time *qua* temporal, characteristic of 'repetition' is the extreme pressure brought to bear on a person's spatio-temporal transactions as such: in Constantin Constantius' words, "Repetition—that is actuality and the earnestness of existence."[44] But it must not be thought that the modern-Christian stress on the temporal simply mirrors the Greek stress on the eternal, as if the truth lay in merely imposing a reverse one-sidedness, embracing the temporal and dismissing the eternal. In 'repetition', it is the very involvement of eternity in the temporal that bestows such importance on the latter, while 'recollection' virtually demands the sacrifice of time in order to salvage the eternal. 'Repetition' in fact constitutes the free, existing self as that site where the temporal and the eternal are drawn into the closest proximity despite their opposed valences for human understanding. This is at the heart of what Kierkegaard means by "paradox."

Already Socrates recognized the difficulty involved in relating eternal truth to an existing person but resolved it through the movement of 'recollection'; such a resolution does not disrupt the immanence of the understanding. The advance that 'repetition' makes beyond Greek wisdom lies in its closing off this intellectual doorway out of existence, instead imposing on decisions within existence the freight of the eternal. "The paradox emerges when the eternal truth and existing are placed together, but each time existing is accentuated, the paradox becomes clearer and clearer."[45] The intensity of the paradox increases as both elements are "accentuated" in their opposition to each other, culminating for Kierkegaard in the revealed Christian dyad: on one side, temporal existence become sheer enmity to God (original sin), confronted on the other side by the divine truth entering into a conjunction with historical flux that repels reason and demands faith (incarnation as "the God in time"). What is important for now, however, is that 'repetition' at any level is defined by the paradoxical yoking of time and eternity to each other within the very structure of individual personhood.

Temporal or existential accentuation through direct contact with the eternal, to the point of paradox: this, as proposed earlier, is one of the Kierkegaardian ideas which comes into view more prominently in light of our account of 'repetition'. Two more ideas that follow closely upon that paradox are likewise thrown into sharper relief: the moment, and pantheism.

2. Kierkegaard's discussion of the "the moment" is too evocative and involved to be entered into fully; all that is necessary here is to see how 'repetition' as expounded

---

[42] On Socrates as founder of ethics, see Kierkegaard, *Sickness unto Death*, 89 [11: 202].
[43] Kierkegaard, *Fear and Trembling*, 69, 49 [4: 161–2, 143].
[44] Kierkegaard, *Repetition*, 133 [4: 11].
[45] Kierkegaard, *Postscript*, 208 [7: 191].

above reconfigures the temporality of subjectivity. "This category [i.e. the moment] is of utmost importance in maintaining the distinction between Christianity and pagan philosophy."[46] Why? Because "only with Christianity does eternity become essential," that is a basic component in the constitution of the existing self, defining its "temporality."

To be sure, the Greek thinker was deeply aware of his own eternity, but not in such a way that eternity entered concretely into the process of existence itself. Recall how Kierkegaard defines the task of "permeat[ing] one's existence with consciousness," that is, existing in the full and authentic sense: "simultaneously to be eternal, far beyond [existence], as it were, and nevertheless present in it and nevertheless in a process of becoming."[47] It was always a sign of the seriousness of Greek philosophy for Kierkegaard, in contrast to the frivolousness that he saw among modern "assistant professors," that in Greece "a thinker was also an ardent existent person impassioned by his thinking."[48] But even this philosophical *pathos* labored under the crippling limitation of all pagan thought. Because "all thinking is eternal," the passionate commitment to thought demanded a radical break with existence. It was the acknowledgement that all thinkers are existent beings that made the commitment to thinking eternal truth a passion for the Greek mind; it made the "beyond existence" into a kind of death in life, whether by "dying in the Pythagorean sense" (i.e., bodily asceticism) or by "being dead in the Socratic sense" (i.e., the infinite resignation of irony). Either way, the Greek "was aware that he was a thinking being, but he was also aware that it was existence as medium that perpetually placed him in a process of becoming."[49]

The intractability of "the moment" (the atomic temporal unit) for the Greeks was based on their attempt to define it in purely time-immanent terms; defined abstractly as neither past nor future, but as their site of meeting (where future shifts into past), the Greek moment signaled the elusiveness of the present, its status as a restlessly moving mathematical point, always vanishing and without content.[50] This is to conceive time and eternity "abstractly," that is, in confrontation or juxtaposition: "By the moment, then, [Plato] understood that abstraction from the eternal that, if it is to be the present, is a parody of it."[51] The Christian conception, in contrast, gives transcendent content to the moment, gives it "presence," by defining it as "that ambiguity in which time and eternity touch each other," or as "time in the fateful conflict when it is touched by eternity."[52]

Kierkegaard clearly signals that with this latter notion we are once again in the sphere of "repetition, by which eternity is entered forwards" (while "for the Greeks, the eternal lies behind as the past that can only be entered backwards").[53] This forward bearing of existence means that in post-Greek personhood the (so to speak)

---

[46] Kierkegaard, *Concept of Anxiety*, 84 [4: 385].
[47] Kierkegaard, *Postscript*, 308 [7: 280].
[48] Ibid.
[49] Ibid., 309 [7: 281].
[50] Kierkegaard, *Concept of Anxiety*, 87 [4: 389–90].
[51] Ibid., 86 [4: 390].
[52] Ibid., 89, 87 [4: 392, 390–1].
[53] Ibid., 90 [4: 393].

placeholder within time for eternity is the future; the moment's eternal ingredient takes psychological shape as a future-orientation. The apocalyptic image employed by St. Paul, where the world ends "in the blink of an eye," perfectly captures the commensurability between the temporal decision in the "now" and its eschatological ballast, the ultimate judgment that will declare its eternal validity (or eternal shortfall). In sum, the Greek and Christian conceptions of "the moment" oppose one another: the former has the abstract juxtaposition of time and eternity within human existence, the latter their concrete (if paradoxical) synthesis. The eternal creative presence of my existence "behind" me, once it enters decisively into the structure of my living choices (as 'repetition' demands), reappears, as it were, "ahead" of me, as my eternal future. The eternal is not fully present within my temporal existence, of course, but takes the concrete form of eschatological hope and fear (myself as either conjoined with, or alienated from, my timeless truth in God). Here "where everything is in a process of becoming ... only so much of the eternal is present that it can have a constraining effect in the passionate decision [and] the *eternal* relates itself as the *future* to the *person in a process of becoming*."[54]

The deadly gravity infused into the business of existence by the constitutive proximity to it of the eternal obviously marks crucial progress beyond the Greek anthropology. Kierkegaard's verdict here is implacable: baffled by "the synthesis of the temporal and the eternal" in the individual's living "moment," the Greeks "lacked the category of spirit."[55] So benighted, pagan irony can make a jest of this life, "ris[ing] above the world's opposition and foolishness with a smile"; it lacks "Christianity's true, earnest, eternally concerned conception of the truth."[56] But, given the tight conjunction in Kierkegaard between conceptions of selfhood and conceptions of God, it is hardly surprising that he will transform this infirmity of Greek anthropology straightaway into a theological lapse. This pivot is especially visible in his discussion of suicide: not being "conscious before God as spirit," thus failing to recognize spirit as "the ethical-religious category," the pagan failed to realize the self as essentially constituted by its "God-relationship."[57] Without "the spirit's definition of a self", the Greek could finally sanction "self-murder" as "no one else's business," rather than seeing it for what it is: "escaping from existence ... mutinying against God."[58]

This reiterates the basic lesson of 'repetition': my own existence here and now is my eternally, divinely assigned post; I may not abandon it.[59] Suicide goes beyond a breach

---

[54] Kierkegaard, *Postscript*, 307 [7: 279–80].
[55] Kierkegaard, *Concept of Anxiety*, 88–9 [4: 392].
[56] Søren Kierkegaard, *Works of Love*, vol. 16 of *Kierkegaard's Writings*, ed. and trans. Howard V. Hong and Edna H. Hong (Princeton: Princeton University Press, 1995), 197 [9: 196].
[57] Kierkegaard, *Sickness unto Death*, 46, 45 [11: 161].
[58] Ibid., 46 [11: 161].
[59] Alert readers will note that the moral propriety of suicide was condemned along just these lines by Socrates himself, utilizing the identical analogy of deserting one's post (*Phaedo* 61c-62c). How can this be accounted for in terms of the opposition between Greek and Christian views on this matter that Kierkegaard is stressing? One might invoke Socrates's status as a borderline figure, the founder of ethics who occasionally peers beyond his own Greek limitations; however, Socrates in the above passage suggests that his refusal of suicide is nothing innovative but rather reflects earlier Greek ethical discussions. It might, therefore, be more useful to use this little anomaly to illustrate what should have become obvious over the course of the present discussion: Kierkegaard's rendering of

of duty to the universal ethical norm; it is a crime against that "private relationship to the divine" that the pagan never suspected.[60] This brings us to Kierkegaard's curious remarks about the "pantheism" of the Greeks.

3. "The pantheist is eternally reassured backward; the moment that is the moment of existence in time, the seventy years, is something vanishing." In other words, 'recollection', where "all existence-decisions become only shadow play compared with what is eternally decided from behind," is made equivalent to pantheism.[61] Why?

That God is to be encountered everywhere is an axiom of both pagan and Christian piety, but with a critical difference. Looking out on the beauty and immensity of the natural order, the pagan is immediately struck by the presence of the majestic power of its divine ground. But this "worship," where "God is related directly to the human being, as the remarkably striking to the amazed," is what Christianity names idolatry.[62] The opposed position ('repetition', in effect) is one where God is indeed to be found in every worldly circumstance, but only as the hidden providence that arranges every moment as a possible encounter with my eternal creative ground through the medium of decision. Any direct relation to God, any presence of God in creation as such, immediately available for apprehension, is cut off for the Christian. God's omnipresence is precisely God's invisibility. The encounter with God in the world is always indirect, that is, as mediated by a person's interiority, in the struggle of free decision. "Nature, the totality of creation, is God's work, and yet God is not there, but within the individual human being there is a possibility (he is spirit according to this possibility) that in inwardness is awakened to a God-relationship, and then it is possible to see God everywhere."[63] To contemplate the divine as everywhere directly at hand, unmediated by a free, personal act, is pantheism, and pantheism is another name for recollection.[64]

III. Interlude: Kierkegaard Unfair to Schlegel?

"Kierkegaard unfair to Schlegel"

Donald Barthelme

The essence of 'repetition' is the intimate involvement of an eternal divine intention with the self-consciously forward orientation of a freely self-constructing self as it advances into each irremediably obscure future moment. The very image of "repeating" encodes the paradox of a transcendent creator of free agents: in utterly contingent choices here

---

the opposition between the pagan and Christian mentalities is highly simplified and schematic, blurring or ignoring many nuances and overlaps in the historical development of ideas. This need not call into question the basic force and insight of his account, but it is as well to acknowledge it.

[60] Kierkegaard, *Fear and Trembling*, 60 [4: 153].
[61] Kierkegaard, *Postscript*, 226 [7: 207].
[62] Ibid., 245 [7: 223].
[63] Ibid., 246 [7: 224].
[64] This necessity that the non-idolatrous God-relation must be indirectly mediated via freedom is otherwise expressed by Kierkegaard's equation of pantheism with any account of sin that obscures its positively willed character. Kierkegaard, *Sickness unto Death*, 96 [11: 209].

and now, one is reaffirming the eternal pattern of one's true self. The modern-Christian discovery of authentic existence, of genuine "subjectivity" or "spirit" in Kierkegaard's terms, is marked by the demand for a conscious existing within this paradoxical juxtaposition of time and eternity. "The difficulty is to exist in them [i.e., between the contrasting poles of existence and eternity], not abstractly to think oneself out of them and abstractly to think about, for example, an eternal divine becoming and other such things that appear when one removes the difficulty."[65] At this point, just before the turn to ontological considerations in the section to follow, it might be in order to indicate, all too briefly, how the "Greek" mind is not the only foil against which Kierkegaard defines 'repetition'; though we have not yet noted it, Kierkegaard detects the fatal attempt to relax the tension of existence not just in the ancients but in his own idealist and romantic contemporaries. They are, as it were, moderns who refuse to be modern.

One example of the kind of speculative *détente* he wishes to resist is explicitly instanced in the quote. The language of a "divine becoming" immediately calls to mind Schelling with his "theogonic process."[66] It is not necessary, however, to limit the idea to any particular thinker. What Kierkegaard seems to have in mind is the way in which speculative philosophy in his period (in both its romantic and idealist modalities) tends to understand the absolute itself as somehow undergoing the same kind of temporal adventure as existing human persons. But by subjecting God to a process of actualization, no matter how exalted and idealized, the divine ground of being is robbed of its vital time-transcendent status. One result is that the self's definitive encounter with its divine truth can now come to be seen (with Hegel) as the playing out of a rationally discernible logic, rather than the paradoxical abyss only traversed in faith. Besides this diluted theism there are, however, "other such things" that take the paradoxical sting out of 'repetition's' time / eternity synthesis. Even the radical temporalization of the human (instead of the divine) in the name of embracing individual existence is an evasive maneuver; it vitiates just what it claims to protect.

"Hegelian philosophy culminates in the thesis that the outer is the inner and the inner is the outer ... But this principle is essentially an esthetic-metaphysical principle, and in this way Hegelian philosophy ... finishes in a fraudulent manner by combining everything (also the ethical and the religious) in the esthetic-metaphysical."[67] For Hegel, interiority characterizes the abstract and undeveloped; in the human individual, as in everything else, the process of actualization signifies the development and flowering of any merely internal principle, its completed external expression. As one appropriates the multiple and contingent forms of one's own appearing, one casts off all accidental and extraneous factuality and comes fully to be oneself in a final and complete coincidence of internal idea and external appearance. The real is what is fully self-expressed in the public order of causal interaction or history. Indeed, for a human person this taking up of the inner into the outer is a maturation beyond the cherished quirk of individuality. Self-expression means entering fully into the larger movement

---

[65] Kierkegaard, *Postscript*, 354 [7: 323].
[66] Cf. Kierkegaard, *Philosophical Fragments*, 10 [4: 218].
[67] Kierkegaard, *Postscript*, 296 [7: 270].

of historical spirit in its social and cultural expressions, and the abandoning of all that is merely contingent in oneself, the private idiosyncrasies of "my soul."

So, for Hegel, the coincidence of inner and outer really amounts to an expression of the superiority of the latter: "the outer (externalization) is higher than the inner."[68] Any such conclusion is repudiated by Kierkegaard's entire theory of selfhood as 'repetition', where each person's authentic existence demands the mediation of all external relations by an interiority intensified in response to the most personal demand of the eternal. Already the imperatives of ethics imply that "the outer as the material for action is a matter of indifference, because the purpose is what is ethically accentuated," that is, the shape and internal disposition of the agent. Once religion enters the picture, this indifference of inner to outer is heightened to a relation of sheer contrast. The situation becomes one defined by "suffering," where "the inner infinity of interiority" must be continually reclaimed through painful renunciation of any happiness in the external order.[69] Only in the Christian paradox of faith is there an authentic kind of reconciliation of inner and outer, for faith means "to exist in such a way that my contrast to existence constantly expresses itself as the most beautiful and secure harmony with it."[70] This is 'repetition' in the fullest sense, but Hegel's model fails even to attain the authenticity of the prior religious movement of "inner infinity." For Kierkegaard, Hegel's form of 'recollection' is a merely speculative assurance that lacks the ethical passion of its Greek predecessor; the philosopher as an existing individual is not affirmed, but dissolved.

And what of German romanticism? It might seem that the existence-strategy of the romantics, with its heightening of ironic detachment and exaltation of creative individuality, would find in Kierkegaard a sympathetic response. But again, as with Hegel, what mimics a kind of return to the Greeks (in this case to the master of irony, Socrates) is in fact a betrayal of their best insights. Here the ethical dimension of existence is sacrificed to the esthetic, rather than to the metaphysical, as with Hegel; but the upshot is the same, from Kierkegaard's point of view. When he attacks the worldview expressed in Friedrich Schlegel's novel *Lucinde*, he is not motivated by prudish disgust at its notorious (by contemporary standards) obscenity but rather taxes it for a misplaced and poisonous nostalgia. The romantics yearn to recapture the Greeks' naïve and guilt-free attitude to embodied life, but the "secret of all Greek culture" is that "when beauty must reign, a synthesis results, from which spirit is excluded."[71] The Christian discovery of spirit has forever disrupted the immediate union of mind and body. The fated historical location of the romantics in the wake of Christianity's polarization (in the name of the conscious self-mastery of ethics) of "flesh and spirit" renders impossible the reconstruction of any untroubled unity of the two. Instead, in all such attempts it turns out that one eye is always slanted contemptuously toward regnant ethical demands. The result is that the romantic's imitation of carefree

---

[68] Kierkegaard, *Fear and Trembling*, 69 [4: 161].
[69] Kierkegaard, *Postscript*, 296–7 [7: 270].
[70] Kierkegaard, *Fear and Trembling*, 50 [4: 144].
[71] Kierkegaard, *Concept of Anxiety*, 65 [4: 369]. This point is related to the conclusion of Chapter 2 and to the development of a concept of the "sublimity" of the divine that is the concern of this entire volume.

bliss is actually "extremely refined, because it not only wishes to enjoy naively but in its enjoyment also wants to be conscious of the destruction of the given morality."[72]

Thanks to this "smirk at the morality under which others, so it thinks, are sighing" every poetic attempt to return to humanity's childhood finds its putative innocence already curdled. Worse, because romanticism cannot reunite flesh and spirit, its opposition to their Christian sundering merely takes the form of an embrace of flesh at the expense of spirit: "its difference from Greek culture is that in its enjoyment of the flesh it also enjoys the negation of the spirit." Thus, Schlegel's novel is "an attempt to suspend all ethics" in the name of "living poetically." But Kierkegaard counters that "true inward infinity comes only through resignation, and only this inner infinity is truly infinite, and truly poetic."[73] What romanticism offers is only the "free play of ironic arbitrariness," a sham infinity that diffuses the "infinite interest in existing" that is ethics into an estheticized existence of refined enjoyment.[74]

Kierkegaard takes K. W. F. Solger's sympathetic theoretical appropriation of romantic ideas and turns it against the romantics. In the attempt to free the self from all finite constraints (including ethical ones), romantic irony thinks "to find in art and poetry the higher actuality that emerges through the negation of finite actuality." But because that higher actuality "can only be perceived in the infinite approximation of intimation," every poetic work in turn becomes an approximation that itself must be treated with ironic distance.[75] The higher actuality never is, but is only continually becoming, hence full self-commitment to existence is endlessly deferred. In jettisoning the divine demand upon the self, romanticism loses the eternal component within 'repetition', leaving only the shapeless flow of esthetic sensuousness.

Note that romanticism and Hegel, from different starting points (and in spite of the latter's often severe critique of romantic irony), end up with the same result from a Kierkegaardian perspective. The self-constructive project for Kierkegaard is always the attempt of the temporal individual to come into alignment with an eternal, divine imperative normative for selfhood (what he calls the ethical as "the Deity's eternal stamp").[76] External circumstances confronting the self continually enter into its ongoing self-definition, but only as the parameters of each ethical choice. This process makes freedom an exacting struggle ("suffering"), where the external must be converted from a meaningless, refractory clutter through inwardly appropriating one's self in and through it. In quite different ways, Hegel and Schlegel abandon this "inner infinity" of selfhood in the name of a "beautiful" synthesis of inner and outer, the self identified with and released into the endless movement of externality. The result for Kierkegaard is a calamitous abandonment of that interiority which anchors the self amidst its ongoing transformations. Once the ethical passion that infused the discovery of Socratic irony is rejected in order to define the human subject's horizon in world-metaphysical or individual-esthetical terms, then even the serious jest of

---

[72] Kierkegaard, *Concept of Irony*, 289 [1: 323].
[73] Ibid., 289 [1: 323–4].
[74] Ibid., 289 [1: 323], cf. Kierkegaard, *Postscript*, 315 [7: 287].
[75] Kierkegaard, *Concept of Irony*, 319 [1: 349].
[76] Kierkegaard, *Postscript*, 152–3 [7: 142].

the Greek *contemptus mundi* ("resignation") degenerates into the false wisdom of an absolutized irony, where all, God, self, and world, seem to Kierkegaard to be lost in undifferentiated flux.

IV. Being and Agency: 'Repetition' and Kierkegaard's Ontology of *Interesse*

Following Constantius' reference back to Leibniz, we have thought to construe 'repetition' primarily in light of the latter's "excellent" riposte to the "lazy sophism." The resulting picture is one in which the individual human being moves through each moment of life aware that every temporal decision adds one more essential contour to the perpetual figure of her individual truth in God's eye. Since it is precisely that particular agent as self-created in her acts that is always already inscribed in God's idea, the desired embrace of her own eternal truth is not to be consummated through abstraction from the existence-tasks that infest each moment of embodied life, but only by consciously plunging into them as so many temporal sites of eternal encounter. The agent's eternal truth is nothing other than the truth of her own actualization; her eternity lies ahead, on the other side of its temporal 'repetition'.[77]

Otherwise put, though the eternal order can be abstractly grasped in thought, as an existing person one's authentic, living connection to it must be circuited through the will and its acts; hence the importance both of the connection of understanding and will, and also of the joint between them, the point of articulation (freedom) whose range is the array of action possibilities grasped in intelligence but whose fulfillment is the enacted decision. As self-mastery becomes more conscious, the risks involved increase. Only grasping free action before God in its eternal resonance maintains the conditions for freedom in the future; however, even defaulting on this challenge of free existence, the self cannot cease choosing but is progressively channeled by disordered and self-deceiving choices into narrower and narrower straits. Thus, Kierkegaard can speak of 'repetition' as a repetition of one's self, as the "taking back" of one's self from the particularity of its acts. But this clawing back of the self from its web of self-undertaken

---

[77] From the standpoint now achieved a light can be turned back upon some of Constantius's unhelpfully oracular pronouncements concerning 'repetition'. *God willed a 'repetition' in creating* by volitionally enacting something timelessly foreknown. *'Repetition' is a transcendence* in that it disallows the resolution within the immanent sphere of individual consciousness of the contradictions of personal existence, demanding instead the continual resort to a transcendent anticipation. This *raises consciousness to the second power*, i.e., it involves a recursive awareness of selfhood as itself a task for freedom that encompasses all particular self-aware acts: a consciousness of consciousness. It is the *password* that conducts one into the sphere of existence as ethical demand and that also allows safe-passage beyond this sphere into the "absurdity" of faith, once the impossibility (in light of sin) of ethically repeating the eternal forces a deeper dependence on the transcendent, a reception not just of every act from God but of selfhood itself. This in turn shows the requisite conception of selfhood as the dynamic point of intersection between time and eternity to be *the necessary condition of Christian dogmatics*; the gospel does not abandon the temporal-eternal confrontation that defines the free self but rather hones it to the point of intensified paradox. Kierkegaard, *Repetition*, 133, 186, 229, 149 [4: 10–11, 57, 94, 25–6].

commitments is possible precisely because of its faith that each act repeats an integral identity anchored in the timeless vision of the creator.

The final turn in this chapter is now to suggest how the faint lineaments of an ontological scheme can be discerned as the presupposed metaphysical context for the preceding, basically anthropological reflections. We have discussed how 'repetition' defines the human self as caught in, or rather constituted by, a field of tension between time and eternity. As Constantius asserts, this both explains the ancient oscillation between the Eleatics (all is and nothing comes to be) and Heraclitus (all becomes and nothing is), and unmasks it as a fruitless standoff between equally one-sided perspectives.[78] The shorthand here employed for the pre-Socratic positions marks a furtive emergence of the terminology of *being*, tactically absented from the discussion up to this point. Adding Constantius's further claim that 'repetition' is "the *Interesse* of metaphysics" allows the ontological problematic to shoulder its way fully into view.[79] Were Kierkegaard's thought to be mined as a resource, not just for an "existential" psychology, nor even a phenomenology of *Dasein*, but for an ontology of agency, then the concept of 'repetition' developed in the previous sections might well provide the indispensable orienting point. Here, with the discussion nearing its end, all that can be done is quickly to assemble a handful of elements that suggest that such a reading does no violence to Kierkegaard but in truth excavates some of his deepest concerns.

The first element is Kierkegaard's differentiation between the concepts of existence and being, with the former seen as a kind of dilution of or deficient participation in the fullness of the latter. In discussing "the moment," Kierkegaard suggests that the Greek abstraction of time from eternity results in the inherent emptiness and volatility of the temporal "now." Because the moment so conceived was thereby construed as the appearance of nonbeing under temporal determination, nonbeing itself was equated by the Greeks with the fugitive, the marginal, the vanishing point. In contrast, "the Christian view takes the position that non-being is present everywhere as the nothing from which things were created."[80] In the sphere of temporal becoming, nonbeing is pervasive; it cannot be trivialized as the nonexistent, because existence itself is definable as constituted by the conjunction of being and nonbeing (i.e., actuality dispersed into the multiplicity and mutual delimitation of finitude). The task of existence is therefore "to do away with [non-being] in order to bring forth being"; since nonbeing is "the temporal forgotten by the eternal," the expansion of being within existence is by implication the union of the eternal and temporal in the moment, for only the connection with the eternal keeps existence from being defined by its nonbeing. With this the faint outlines of an ontological scheme begin to take shape. For the pagan thinker, what is, exists; what is not, does not exist. But for the Christian, what is, absolutely speaking, *ipso facto* does not exist, since existence is the space demarcated by the differentiation being / nonbeing.

A second Kierkegaardian element in this nascent ontological structure is the peculiar kind of existing which characterizes human personhood. Thought knows

---

[78] Kierkegaard, *Postscript*, 307 [7: 279]; *Repetition*, 148 [4: 25].
[79] Kierkegaard, *Repetition*, 149 [4: 25–6].
[80] Kierkegaard, *Concept of Anxiety*, 83 [4: 385].

its ideal object as both universal and timeless, but also as abstract ("the good, the beautiful, the ideas").[81] Over against the abstract being of the ideal are the plethora of concrete existents; most of these have no apprehension of the idea, that is, they do not think: a rose, say, or (more prosaically) a potato. Their concrete mode of existence is defined precisely by the absence of any grasp of the ideal via thought. The concreteness of human existence by contrast is characterized by that participation in the timeless idea which is called thought.[82] In sum, the realm of concrete, individual existents lies in between, lacking the perfection of the eternal being of the ideas but more perfect than what has no being at all. Within that in-between realm, the human existent as thinking is more perfect than what has no relation to the idea, making the human person the between-being (*Mellemvaesen*) par excellence.[83]

This points right away to a third component of the Kierkegaardian ontological construct. Human being is, of course, not the thought-being of the ideal, yet it must somehow participate that ideal. With this one becomes aware of the unique character of human existence as a problem confronting the existing individual. As a concrete existent the human being as thinker is cut off from any immediate abstract unity of thinking and object-thought: "Existence separates the ideal identity of thought and being; I must exist in order to be able to think, and I must be able to think (for example, the good) in order to exist in it."[84] The ideal and abstract unity of thought and being is not actuality but only possibility; it is the concrete and temporal character of individual human existence, its actuality, which disrupts any such "hypothetical" unity. Thus, human existence, as that which always intrudes between any abstract unity of thought and being, is called by Kierkegaard an "*inter-esse*."[85]

This peculiar ontological status makes human existence a problem, a task defined by the goal of concretely uniting thought and being such that one doesn't just think an idea, one "exists in it." Kierkegaard's specification of the form of this task has already been cited: "to permeate one's existence with consciousness, simultaneously to be eternal, far beyond it [i.e., existence], as it were, and nevertheless present in it and nevertheless in a process of becoming."[86] Note the implications of this trilemma. For an existing individual, truly thinking an idea becomes a matter of "existing in it," permeating one's existence with consciousness of the idea; this in turn means that authentic thinking becomes saturated with the concrete circumstances of the individual's ongoing struggle to exist in freedom. As the Greek thinkers knew so well, it becomes a matter of will, of decision, a self-discipline infused with pathos. It can now be seen how the gap between thinking and being created by the actuality of human existence maps rather closely onto the gap between understanding and will. But here a parting of the ways opens up. The passionate Greek thinker construed his existence-task to be that of dying to everyday, temporal embodiment with its endless small- or large-scale problems and attempted solutions in order that he might grasp and be grasped by the timeless idea.

---

[81] Kierkegaard, *Postscript*, 329 [7: 300].
[82] Ibid., 330–1 [7: 301–2].
[83] Ibid., 329 [7: 301].
[84] Ibid., 330 [7: 301].
[85] Ibid., 314 [7: 286].
[86] Ibid., 308 [7: 280].

He immersed himself in existence, but only in order to turn away from it toward an already completed ideal realm. The Greek aim was 'recollection'.

The elements so far enumerated might fit together in the following way. What keeps existence turned toward being and away from the emptiness that infects it is always some connection to the eternal; for the specifically human existent, this connection with the eternal must come via some participation in the ideal realm through thought. Without this, human existence devolves into directionless, chaotic activity: it becomes "noise."[87] But for Kierkegaard, living in the modern-Christian epoch means that the Greek way of practically solving the problem of existence can and must be surpassed. Now the fourth and final element comes into play. If existence is not finally to be evaded in thought (as in 'recollection'), one must in some sense become oneself the being one thinks. Otherwise put, one's very own freely undertaken maneuver through the forking paths opening up at each moment must itself become the idea one passionately thinks, again and again. In Kierkegaard's terms, the metaphysical problematic of human existence, inter-esse, is only resolved on the level of conscious subjectivity, as interest, that is the infinite interest in one's own existing spoken of above. Beginning as an ontological concept, interest has now fully crystallized into an ethic of subjectivity, but without leaving its ontological signification behind.

The Greeks could not have arrived at this resolution because they lacked the category of spirit. They did not grasp the radicality of finite spirit as freedom: the ideal self must be constructed in action, and thus each moment is filled with eternal significance. They also missed the other side of this: God as infinite, creative spirit grounds the human agent precisely in her most minute and trivial circumstances, and thus anchors finite existence in the ideal realm. These are the ingredients of what Kierkegaard named 'repetition', inchoately assembled long before by Leibniz. 'Repetition' itself is the fourth and final element that would have to be incorporated by any attempt at a truly Kierkegaardian ontology of agency. That this quintessentially modern category has yet to be discovered by the moderns can only be due to modernity's own feebleness, its incapacity to assimilate the grand implications of its own Christian heritage.[88] Kierkegaard sees in contemporary Hegelianism yet another iteration of this tragic history; how else to characterize the way Hegel's brilliant insight, namely, that the passage from antiquity to modernity involves exchanging the ultimacy of the categories of substance for those of subject, had come to be frittered away in a half-return to Greek intellectualism?

How, finally, will an ontology of agency that turns on the category of 'repetition' bring together these elements (existence as participated being, humanity as middle-being, the problem of human existence as the task of infinite interest in itself) into a discourse of being? An early turn of phrase from Kierkegaard's dissertation makes a critical first step: "the true actuality becomes what it is [*den sande Virkelighed vorder hvad den er*]."[89] A remarkable set of variations on this cryptic principle echoes through later writings, clarifying its meaning. Jumping ahead three years, Johannes Climacus

---

[87] Kierkegaard, *Repetition*, 149 [4: 25].
[88] On the modern failure to discover 'repetition', see ibid., 148 [4: 25].
[89] Kierkegaard, *Concept of Irony*, 319 [1: 349].

characterizes the scenario of Socratic 'recollection' as one in which "the individual has existed, before he came to exist [*har Individet vaeret til før det blev til*]."[90] Reminiscent of the first phrase but, it turns out, opposed to it. This is shown by an earlier appearance of an almost identical formulation from Kierkegaard's notes on Leibniz, who is chided for thinking he can defend the universal validity of the particular Christian truth by comparing it to the timeless rules of harmony that exist prior to, and quite apart from, their actually being discovered and enacted by musicians. Kierkegaard's jottings protest that this "enervates the essence of [Christianity], for the historical is precisely its essential aspect, whereas in the case of other ideas, it [the historical] is the contingent."[91] That is, for Christianity, the eternal truth for existing human beings must itself become historical; its contingent occurrence (as the Christ) is essential to its very truth. Thus, it is quite the opposite of an abstract idea like "harmony," whose truth is indeed independent of any particular historical actualization. It can be said of any such idea that contingent actualization is accidental to its truth-status, and therefore (anticipating Climacus's phrase above almost word-for-word) "it existed before it came to exist [*at den har vaeret til førend den blev til*]."[92]

This verbal mimicry uncovers the meaning of Climacus's indictment of 'recollection'. To say that an individual "existed before he came to exist" amounts to the proposition that his eternal truth is indifferent to and untouched by the contingencies of his temporal becoming; what is truly meaningful about him subsists, logically prior to the accidents of actualized existence. Kierkegaard's 'repetition', of course, is what he brings forward to oppose, in the name of Christianity, this seductive pagan invitation to human beings to live the life of the ideas. The juxtaposition is made in no uncertain terms by Constantin Constantius: "When the Greeks said that all knowing is recollecting, they said that all existence, which exists, has existed [*hele Tilvaerelsen, som er til, har vaeret til*]; when one says that life is a repetition, one says: existence, which has existed, is now coming to exist [*Tilvaerelsen, som har vaeret til, bliver nu til*]."[93] The first phrase unmistakably lines up verbally with the Climacus quote and the Leibniz notation: 'recollection' means that an individual's temporal existence with its choices can add nothing fundamentally novel to her ideality, her essential truth existing in every way prior to her existence now. The opposition of 'repetition' to this is registered with the subtlest shift in wording: what is eternally abiding about the individual is nothing other than what is happening here and now. One must 'repeat' one's transcendent truth by existing in time, because that truth is in the creator's mind and exactly mirrors, from its 'prior' position, that unfolding action which the creator grounds.

The "true actuality" which Kierkegaard spoke of in his dissertation is there equated with "faith" in the gracious creator God: "when [faith] has struggled, it has won the victory over the world; and yet it had won the victory over the world before it struggled."[94] The notion of 'repetition' as developed in conversation with Leibniz is the

---

[90] Kierkegaard, *Philosophical Fragments*, 96 (translation altered) [4: 294].
[91] Kierkegaard, *Notebooks 1–15*, 390 [19: 392].
[92] Ibid. (translation altered).
[93] Kierkegaard, *Repetition*, 149 [4: 25].
[94] Kierkegaard, *Concept of Irony*, 319 [1: 349].

ontological elaboration of this paradox. For the Greek, what exists now does so because it has already existed eternally: it feebly mimics the preexistent. For 'repetition's' faith in a creator *ex nihilo*, because all preexistence is nothing but God's knowledge of what will be enacted in time, what exists eternally does so because it is now becoming. In short, the human subject's eternal truth is not an alternative to its becoming, but is the creator's intention ever to be repeated in becoming.

The following pronouncement could just about provide a schematic for the ontological framework within which agency as envisioned here begins to make sense: "God does not think, he creates; God does not exist, he is eternally [*er evig*]. A human thinks and exists, and existence separates thinking and being."[95] The first three elements just discussed each find their place. First, existence merely participates the fullness of eternal divine being; second, human existence in thought participates eternity, but abstractly, such that thinking and being cannot be united in thought itself; third, this awkward straddling of the gap between thinking and being (inter-esse) is the actuality which forms the task of human existence, to act in order to enact the unity of thinking and being which eludes thought in abstraction (i.e., to "exist in the idea"). If these three elements present the problem of human existence, 'repetition', the fourth element, marks the turn toward its solution. The only possibility of my freely acting so as to create a self which traverses the gap of abstraction lies ultimately in a God who "creates," that is, whose idea is the concrete unity of thought and being which my acts can repeat.

V. Do It Again: Rescuing the Kierkegaardian Agent

If the three elements that have just been described as defining the Kierkegaardian problematic of existence are strikingly reminiscent of Heidegger's analysis of *Dasein*, that is surely no accident. In his own bringing together of being and agency, Heidegger proved himself a close student of the Dane; his phenomenological elaboration of the latter's scheme is (in many ways) the richest and (certainly) the most influential attempt to adapt a Kierkegaardian ontology of agency for the peculiar configuration of modernity incubating in Weimar Germany (and perhaps not yet behind us). But Kierkegaard's own scheme was drastically truncated in the process, when Heidegger decided he had to refuse the fourth element, 'repetition' itself, as an anthropological possibility because it was premised upon a time-transcendent all-creating intelligence. With God removed from the ontological horizon, only "being and time" come to define human existence, such that the latter is forced into a shotgun marriage with temporality.

Though carefully developing Kierkegaard's ontological legacy, Heidegger was notoriously reticent concerning his deep debt to him. The other Weimar figure who arguably could best lay claim to appropriating the Dane's theorization of agency was, by contrast, one of that earlier generation's most accomplished scholars and promoters

---

[95] Kierkegaard, *Postscript*, 332 (translation altered) [7: 303].

of Kierkegaard: the brilliant Göttingen theologian Emanuel Hirsch. This pioneering translator of Kierkegaard's Danish prose into German pulled off on the level of ideas a more questionable translation of Kierkegaard's ethic of authentic subjectivity into the German political context, reading his theory of agency through Carl Schmitt's decisionism and Karl Holl's neo-Lutheran absolutization of conscience. In the hands of such an eager participant in seething Weimar nationalism the obscure and fearful predicament of existence in Kierkegaard underwent a terrible clarification, reemerging as a nakedly willed embrace of the historical "moment" of Germany's imminent rebirth, a moment grasped by "conscience" as divine providence and hence triumphantly absolutized.

The disastrous allegiances of Heidegger and Hirsch are well known: for both, Germany's great "moment" arrived in 1933. What does it say that the two thinkers most engaged between the wars in taking up the Kierkegaardian ontology of agency could come so enthusiastically to welcome the Nazi pseudo-revolution? Whatever the answer (and it will not be a simple one), a new retrieval of that ontology must do its part to extricate Kierkegaard's theory of selfhood from these sinister associations by essaying an alternative merger of theism and "existentialism," one that can lay a more trustworthy claim to continue his project. But though such a retrieval must draw back from the peculiarly dark abyss into which Heidegger and Hirsch looked, it will nevertheless have to acknowledge the unavoidable chasm which, Kierkegaard knew, must always mark the encounter of human and divine freedom.

In trying to solve the puzzle of Leibniz's anticipation of 'repetition', the preceding exploration has here and there surfaced a clutch of notions the odd familiarity of which no doubt lies in their remarkable proximity to traditional Christian doctrines (creator, providence, immortal soul, faith, heaven and hell). This should not surprise, for, even apart from any reference to justification or Christology, Climacus's proud admission is relevant here: look behind Kierkegaard's dazzling parodies of speculative language and "what always emerges is old-fashioned orthodoxy in its rightful severity."[96]

Examined from a slightly different angle, the concluding analysis of *Interesse* suggests that this stealthy traditionalism is not just theological but philosophical as well, recalling the grand scholastic themes of created being as participation, of human moral life as an accumulation of habituated virtuous or vicious dispositions, and of creatures as temporal "repetitions" of eternally known archetypes. Leibniz's own incorporations of scholastic thought into the *Theodicy* no doubt played a mediating role here. If Heidegger's imperious dissociation of the discourses of divinity and of being can no longer claim the status of a philosophical or theological axiom, the further elaboration of Kierkegaard's ontology of agency positively invites a reexamination of his largely hidden and indirect scholastic influences. And if his selective reaching back behind idealism, behind even early modernity towards the resources of a pre-modern conceptuality of creator and creation is pursued, might not the thought of Thomas Aquinas provide an especially encompassing metaphysical scheme, one conceptually intricate and flexible enough to incorporate and extend the implicit ontology within

---

[96] Ibid., 275 [7: 249].

Kierkegaard's account of existence? Then, too, can Kierkegaard's phenomenologically rich psychology, so much more sensitive to the living texture and dynamics of concrete self-consciousness, supplement in its turn Aquinas' more schematic accounts of soul and virtue? This is only a wager, to be sure, but it has been entertained before now. The distinguished Italian philosopher Cornelio Fabro long ago began some astute forays in this direction; the present chapter can be read as a small tribute to the fertility of his ideas.[97]

An appeal to the "closed" medieval world of Aquinas on agency might seem inadequate to the dilemmas of the contemporary self, notoriously decentered within a post-Copernican, infinite universe. But the discovery of merely spatial infinity is existentially ambiguous. Pascal's anxiety is famous: "The eternal silence of these infinite spaces frightens me."[98] Hardly remembered is the nearly contemporary reaction of Leibniz:

> The ancients had puny ideas on the works of God ... for want of knowing modern discoveries... [I]t must be acknowledged that there is an infinite number of globes, as great as and greater than ours, which have as much right as it to hold rational inhabitants ... [T]his immense space encircling all this region may in any case be filled with happiness and glory.[99]

More decisive for considerations of pre-modern relevance is another limitless abyss that Pascal confronted, the "infinite distance between mind and charity" opened up by the "eyes of the heart" that alone can perceive it.[100] This other infinity of Pascal, at least, was not at all hidden from Aquinas: because "sin is infinite" as "the turning away from the immutable good, which [itself] is infinite," so too the infusion of charity opens out into "the eternal good of a share in the Godhead," which in any given individual is "greater than the good of nature in the whole universe."[101] The truly "infinite space" within which this immeasurable good can be installed is located within each human individual's freedom, the bottomless expanse between the transcendent self-possibility implicit in intellect and its hazardous, piecemeal actualization (cognitively

---

[97] Cornelio Fabro, *Participation et Causalité selon S. Thomas d'Aquin* (Louvain: Publications universitaires de Louvain, 1961), 29:

> Such an infinity which, in God, expresses being and, in the creature, expresses non-being explains what Kierkegaard called the infinite qualitative difference between God and the creature. This difference is fully expressed in the Thomist distinction of *essentia* and *esse*, [itself] expressed by means of the notion of a participation which involves the total dependence of the creature with regard to God, thanks to the emergence of the *esse* upon which creation is founded.

Cf. also 634–7 and Cornelio Fabro, "Kierkegaards Kritik am Idealismus: Die metaphysische Begründung der Wahlfreiheit," in *Der Mensch vor dem Anspruch der Wahrheit und der Freiheit: Festgabe, Johannes B. Lotz S.J. z. 70. Geburtstag am 2. August 1973 gewidmet*, ed. Josef de Vries and Walter Brugger (Frankfurt a. M.: Knecht, 1973), 151–80.

[98] Blaise Pascal, *Pensées*, trans. W.F. Trotter (1932; reprint, London: J. M. Dent & Sons, 1956), 61.
[99] Leibniz, *Theodicy*, 134–5.
[100] Pascal, *Pensées*, 234.
[101] *Sth* I/II q. 87 a. 4, q. 113 a. 9.

unanticipated in its concreteness) through the will to exist from God alone. The point of 'repetition' as Kierkegaard came to see it was that between each thought and its willed enactment, an interval must be traversed that is interminable, in a way, because true freedom interposes an ever-repeated detour via timelessness: between each moment and the next an infinite distance must be crossed, the never-finished errand of petitioning the divine eternity that alone can span the distance between myself and myself.[102] In this way, there is a passage from mind to heart that is longer even than that from intellect to will. So much longer.

---

[102] Cf. on this point Chapter 2 of this book.

4

$f(S)\frac{I}{S}$: The Instance of Pattern in Kathryn Tanner's Theology

Isskustvo kak priem (Art as Device)

Viktor Shklovsky
Theory of Prose

Kathryn Tanner's reflections on the Trinity have a self-effacing character. She operates within a rhetorical register that prizes quiet and careful exploration of her chosen themes rather than grandiose claims or noisy polemics. Although closely attuned to a variety of contemporary problems, she maintains throughout her doctrinally oriented work a resolute and deeply appreciative conversation with formative pre-modern figures. This combination of stylistic restraint and fealty to classic traditions, one mark of her unique presence on the current scene, tends to lull the reader, concealing the more innovative and even subversive elements of her Trinitarian thinking.[1] Notably, in the doctrinally focused constructive work (to be found in *Jesus, Humanity and the Trinity* and *Christ the Key*) that will be the concern of this brief chapter, her developing positions on theological anthropology and grace are shaped by a certain motif extracted from the standard pre-modern discussions of the Trinity. That is, Tanner makes use in a highly original way of the notion that the Trinity is to be understood as a pattern of differentiated but mutually interlocking relationships; this idea of constitution through a relational pattern is consciously drawn upon as a structuring element at several crucial points of her nascent systematic theology.

We will attempt in the short reflections that follow to pay homage to this creative aspect of Tanner's work, not just by trying to locate and describe it, but also by taking it seriously enough to raise some questions about it from a more Catholic and Thomist direction. The first section will identify the basic motif at work, showing how the

---

[1] It is perhaps more apt to speak tentatively of her "Trinitarian thinking" rather than of her theology of the Trinity because, as she modestly reminds us, she has not yet attempted a full theological treatment of this subject. Kathryn Tanner, *Jesus, Humanity and the Trinity: A Brief Systematic Theology* (Minneapolis: Fortress Press, 2001), xviii–xix.

Trinitarian pattern of constitution through mutual other-relation is connected with Tanner's reflections on creation and Christology. The three following sections will turn to the way in which this pattern works itself out in different aspects of her soteriology; in each case, the way her position is structured by this pattern will be shown to have rather startling consequences from a more traditional point of view. The final section will indicate some potentially disquieting features of the resulting soteriological picture, tempered by a sense of appreciation for the uniqueness and promise of her overall achievement.

I. Mutual Other-Relation as a Replicating Pattern

The structural role played by the dominant relational pattern in Tanner's thinking is most clearly on display in the "brief systematic theology," which laid out the basics of her vision. It might seem surprising at first to speak of a reigning Trinitarian motif in her work since she has repeatedly drawn attention to the centrality of Christology for her entire approach. The dissonance is only apparent. The incarnation of God in Jesus Christ is indeed pivotal for her, and one can only admire the architectonic imaginativeness with which she ingeniously applies and unfolds a range of illuminating consequences for the standard theological topics, consistently beginning from and returning to this close attention to Christ. But when seen in context, just this incarnational emphasis on the union of divine and human in Christ not only links her theological appraisal of Jesus to her broader position on God's relation to the created order but also refers both incarnation and creation to the Trinity itself as founding instance.

Since the publication of her first book, Tanner's work has rightly been associated with an acute sensitivity to the conceptually unique causal complexity involved whenever divine activity is brought into relation with creaturely event.[2] Her often-invoked "non-competitive" account of the matter refers to her strictures (perfectly justified and quite traditional, to Thomist eyes) against any lapses that allow divine causality to stray into a parallel alignment alongside created causality, as if they were simply different instances of a common class of agency. Less discussed has been the Christological application of this principle. She regards the general picture of God's providential agency within the world as providing a vital context for any understanding of what happens in the special case of the particular incarnational appropriation of the humanity of Jesus, happily joining the company of other theologians like Athanasius, D. M. Baillie, Robert Sokolowski, and Karl Rahner.[3]

The incarnation is best understood as the unique and total creative impact of the divine reality upon the constitution of Jesus's humanity. At this one site within the created order, the product of the divine activity is one with, a kind of direct transcription of, that activity itself. She puts it well: "Here the effect of divine agency is not external to divinity."[4] For this reason Jesus can be the subject of actions that are describable,

---

[2] Kathryn Tanner, *God and Creation in Christian Theology: Tyranny or Empowerment?* (Oxford: Basil Blackwell, 1988).
[3] Tanner, *Jesus*, 5.
[4] Ibid., 21.

literally, as acts at once of a human being, and of God. Lest this unprecedented alliance with the particular selfhood of Jesus itself prove a mere spectacle without inherent relation to others, Tanner immediately develops the implications for humanity as such of this divine conjunction. Although the details are not worked out fully, she insists that in God's union with the human Jesus, human nature itself is already gifted; the very meaning of humanity has been constituted anew, and to the degree that other individuals take up in their attitudes and acts the human path opened by that one man, they "already" come to share (though imperfectly) in his total intimacy with the creator.[5]

How is this intimacy to be understood? It is here that the Christian discourse of the Trinity begins to play a central role for Tanner. The event whereby Jesus's humanity undergoes the total shaping force of divinity must be understood through the terminology of relations, a vocabulary evolved in the early Christian centuries to describe the interplay of three moments within the one God. His human career is a perfect reception and reflection of that divine sourcing called the Father, initiated and energized at every point by that dynamic impulsion called the Spirit, and hence becomes the created presence of that eternal image of the Father called the Son. So the divinity of the humanity of Jesus Christ is solely a function of its entering into the relational pattern that defines the being of God. Although this entry, because it necessarily unfolds within human temporality, can be described as a process coinciding with the human history of Jesus, Tanner strongly reminds readers that this is in no way a cooperative effort between God and human. Jesus's humanity, simply as such, is always primarily the recipient of this unfathomable grace.[6] And what holds for him holds even more emphatically for humans who participate in the grace he incarnates. That grace must always be fundamentally "alien" to the rest of us; it arrives too late, having to compete with our own already sinfully constructed subjectivity rather than constituting the subject from the beginning as in the case of Jesus. This, too, is inevitably a process; Tanner sees it in our case extending itself beyond the temporal enclosure of the present created order. Availing herself of Gregory of Nyssa's conception (itself developed from Phil. 3:13), she envisions an endless approximation toward perfect reception of divinity on our part, a stretching and straining toward the goal (*epektasis*).[7] But though our fate may be different than Christ's, in his case as in ours the basic description of salvation or union with God is always for Tanner the entering of the human into the network of Trinitarian relations.[8]

Christ is "the key" for Tanner because in him, in his life and death and resurrection, the paradigm of God's saving intent becomes visible. But that intent itself can only be understood according to a Trinitarian logic. Indeed, the way in which she works out her entire theological project in terms of a single trajectory of divine initiative is one of its most deeply impressive aspects. Memorably: "God is doing [in the incarnation] what God is always doing, attempting to give all that God is to what is not God."[9] In

---

[5] Ibid., 51.
[6] Ibid., 50.
[7] Ibid., 43.
[8] Ibid., 47.
[9] Ibid., 15.

Christ there appears to the eye of faith the perfect self-bestowal of God upon creature; this gift then empowers all the derivative receptions of God's gracious presence that shape the lives of other human beings, while it in turn is itself a natural extension of the divine life in itself, which consists in the perfect communion of God's own giving to herself in the Trinity.[10] Thus, the eternal pattern of divine self-giving enlarges itself through a single, majestic movement, penetrating into and transforming the created cosmos. This is the agency, the authority, what German names *die Instanz* of the pattern, both in the world and in her theology.

II. The Algebra of Redemption

Though not many could match Tanner's skill in weaving together the themes outlined above, taken individually they do not represent innovations. They stand for the most part in the best tradition of pre-modern theology and speculation, both patristic and medieval (as her own numerous citations attest). But when she comes to apply this grand scheme in more particular ways to the understanding of human salvation, the result is in several cases far more surprising from a traditional standpoint. We will start in this section with the case of theological anthropology, before turning in the next section to theological ethics, then in Section IV to eschatology. A set of what might be called soteriological instincts or conscious biases plays a strong role in all three cases and suggests a dominance of the Trinitarian pattern in a different register than that uncovered in the discussion just completed.

I would argue that in the case of theological anthropology, the best place to begin exploring Tanner's unique conclusions is with the classic Protestant suspicion of Catholic notions of created grace. Tanner at several points announces her adherence to the Protestant orientation on this matter. The concern is clear: she sees as an ever-present danger the temptation for Christians to assume "possession" of the divine gifts, as if they could be detached in some way from the continual and necessary presence of their divine giver.[11] To avoid what the tradition following Luther perceives to be an overriding danger, a drastic solution is proposed. Unlike other human acts, which must arise and take their character from the particular powers of human agency, the acts that mark redeemed human living are themselves properly divine and always remain so. They cannot be traced back to a divine transformation of the immanent capacities of the human agent, in the manner of the supernatural bestowal spoken of in the Catholic tradition. Tanner prefers to abandon the idea that part of the gift of grace itself lies in such an augmentation of human knowledge and willing as could make reception and exercise of the gift an act authentically attributable to the human being as such; the threat of becoming entangled in the dangerous rhetoric of "merit"

---

[10] Ibid., 35–6.
[11] Ibid., 91. See also Kathryn Tanner, *Christ the Key* (Cambridge: Cambridge University Press, 2010), 98.

is judged too great. This is what she means when she insists that there are no "created versions" of divine powers.[12]

Human reception of the gracious presence of God in union with Christ is not, according to Tanner, mediated by a supernatural but fully human "habitus." In the Catholic tradition one speaks of faith and charity as theological "virtues" precisely because they represent the elevation and disposition of already naturally given human capacities for knowing and willing. Although this elevation itself is not merited or effected in any way by the human being, once initiated by God it allows a new range and efficaciousness to human action, one that is in discernable relation to what are recognized to be human excellences in cognition, affection, and self-direction. In other words, for the theological tradition that Tanner wants to distance herself from, the theological virtues that orient us to friendship and communion with God do not contradict but rather augment and extend that human goodness, the traces of which remain even in the unredeemed in spite of sin, bearing witness to the peculiar gifts of human nature itself. And because human beings are made for communion with God, these peculiar gifts are dim reflections of the wisdom and love of the divine being itself. Indeed, at just this point Tanner takes a more radical step. Not satisfied with denying that faith and love are created analogues to divine powers, she denies that faith and love have any inherently superior qualities in themselves, as human dispositions, in comparison with other human qualities. In other words, it seems that the propriety of faith and love as human counterparts to the reception of divine grace has nothing to do with any relative superiority they display simply as human dispositions, in "natural" terms. Only their purely "passive" or "open" quality toward the divine marks them out; any pretensions they may have in strictly human terms are illusory.[13] But if faith and love defined in a Christian way thus inhabit a quite distinct moral universe, one scarcely recognizable from within the horizon defined by our innate human capacities, then they are really not virtues except in a purely equivocal sense.

The upshot of Tanner's approach here can be put this way: what might be called the "psychological" character of faith and love, their particular range, modes and interconnections within the overall organization of the human subject, become matters of relative indifference to her investigation. Indeed, her account of the human self is oddly truncated when it comes to discussing human capacities generally. This comes out particularly clearly when she speaks of the results of the fall: human operations are totally corrupted, though the human nature remains completely intact.[14] Only an anthropology that detached nature and act to an extraordinary degree could countenance what looks like a paradox. For on a more traditional reading, human acts arise from human powers, and the array of human powers with their inbuilt orientations and limitations is itself a function of the particular nature of the human being. Tanner clearly wants to suppress attention to "potencies" as inherent structures that mediate

---

[12] Tanner, *Jesus*, 50, 91. Tanner, *Christ the Key*, 82–3. The creative extension here of Luther's scheme of forensic justification is evident; the relation of grace and sin in the believer can only be dialectical (*simul justus et peccator*), ensuring that the process of sanctification is strictly isolated from the moment of justification.

[13] Tanner, *Christ the Key*, 17, 93–5.

[14] Ibid., 67.

between a shared general nature and the particular activities of the individual, for only in this way can she sustain such a stark separation of nature and operation. Since they are not tied to human nature via human potencies, human operations are conceived in more abstract, functional terms.[15] Once again a Protestant worry seems to be at work, since in another context she warns that the orientation of the human person to God (i.e., that which determines God as the proper end of any given human existence) should not be understood in terms of "internally self-generated" inclinations; it is as if the gratuity of grace would somehow be compromised if it had to link up with or work in terms of a set of already given capacities.[16]

Tanner's striking refusal to grant a theological role to an analysis of human subjective components is signaled, finally, by her deep ambivalence in face of the rhetoric of "human nature." For the counterpart of what might seem a positive insistence on the post-lapsarian integrity of our nature is a resolute tendency to downgrade the traditional pretensions of that nature. This can be seen in several ways. She implies that there must be some connection between the peculiarities of human nature and the fact that God in becoming incarnate assumed a human being, but just in those passages where a reader might look for some clue as to the "aptness" of human nature for this dignity one looks in vain.[17] Granted only human nature, as fallen, required this saving condescension; but does that mean one could equally well conceive the divine assumption of, say, an oak or a lobster? Indeed, when expounding on human nature as such, Tanner prefers to stress its limitation, its finitude, its lack of fitness to express the divine word. Our nature seems, at times, quite closely connected to what is wrong with us. Her unwillingness to discuss a positive role for natural human endowments within the salvific economy, and its link to a particular reading of the incarnation, is nowhere better displayed than in her description of the social existence of the redeemed as an "unnatural community," comparable in its juxtaposition of the "naturally disparate" to the union of divine and human in Jesus![18]

That these ways of speaking are deliberate cannot be doubted. The classically Protestant sensibility at work here is clear, as when, going against the grain of Aquinas' notion of grace as perfecting nature, Tanner prefers a reading in which grace corrects nature without really building upon it.[19] We have also indicated the role of her understanding of the incarnation. But in the final analysis it is possible to see here a deeper motif at work. On a certain reading of the ancient tradition, the Trinitarian persons in their mutual distinction are exhaustively describable from the pattern of relations in which they originate or are originated by each other. We saw in the previous section that the humanity of Christ is distinguished by its subsumption within this relational pattern; human redemption, consequently, can equally be rendered as our being defined by these relations. All this is fairly standard, but at Tanner's hands it receives a more creative and radical reading. In the Trinity, in Jesus Christ, and in

---

[15] Ibid., 108.
[16] Ibid., 125.
[17] For the implied connection, see Tanner, *Jesus*, 111. For the missing note of "aptness," see, e.g., ibid., 48–9.
[18] Tanner, *Christ the Key*, 242.
[19] Ibid., 61–2.

redeemed humanity the same mechanism is at work: the constitution of persons, in something like their totality, through mutual relation. That being the case, the relational pattern itself takes on a kind of ontological priority, while the actual related units become derivative; little attention need be directed to their individual contribution to or agency within those relationships, or indeed to the internal structures or capacities that enable such a role. This move is naturally allied to another "strong" reading of the tradition by Tanner, where she takes up the "stretching" image used by Gregory of Nyssa and boldly reimagines it to include not just a stretching forward but also a stretching wider, such that the increasing capacity to receive God on the part of the human is the direct result of the increased "flow" of divine self-giving.[20] Hence, there is no need to analyze the graced augmentations of particular human powers, since as such the latter are irrelevant. The divine giving is all.

If it is asked what role is played in the ongoing redemptive process by human intelligence and freedom in their created integrity, Tanner finds little to say other than to read both in terms of radical receptivity. Both the ancient understanding of intellect as the capacity to formally "become" anything knowable, and the notion of human freedom as a detachment from pre-programmed patterns of behavior, become simply two more ways for Tanner to stress human beings as somehow radically malleable. Hence the relative lack of interest in human nature, which is by definition the realm of the relatively "fixed." The end result is that the specifically anthropological side of Tanner's soteriology has a uniquely "algebraic" feel, with the human being playing the role of an "x" whose redeemed status is predominantly rendered as its being "slotted" into the triune relational network. In algebra, the variable in itself is nothing; its value is only defined by the operational relations specified for it. In the same way, in Tanner's account the human individual remains rather empty, in fact intentionally so; all initiative is granted to the Trinitarian relationships that, in conjunction with Christ, determine that individual anew, and to all appearances in a manner radically tangential to any discernibly given structure (nature, proper potencies, virtues) of the "human" as such. The new human only "appears" at the prompting or request (the instance) of the Trinitarian pattern. As we will now see, some such picture underlies the ethical and eschatological dimensions of her soteriology as well.

III. From the Social Trinity to a Trinitarian Economics

The same priority of relationships over things related plays itself out in a different way in Tanner's forays into theological ethics. We will have to be brief here, as this aspect of her position is less forthrightly developed than in her anthropology; it emerges as a by-product of her urgent critique of what has come to be called social Trinitarianism. By the latter is meant that theological tradition in which the doctrine of the Trinity, and especially those general characteristics that are held to be abstracted from the relations that constitute the Trinity, are proffered as a divinely authorized model for

---

[20] Tanner, *Jesus*, 43.

human social relations. Such characteristics as mutual conditioning of identity, utter receptiveness or openness to others, radical equality, individual dispossession in favor of communal sharing of goods, and so on are made programmatic for a Christian critique and reformulation of societal arrangements; the ecclesial community in an idealized mode is sometimes held to represent in imperfect and local form this perfected realm of human relations that will hold universally in the eschatological Kingdom.

Tanner has, of course, become known as one of the most articulate critics of this entire way of thinking. She has argued repeatedly both that this approach either misunderstands or ignores key elements of the classical Trinitarian teaching, and that it is unable to provide any kind of effective social prescription because the analogy between finite and fallen human beings and the divine "persons" is so terribly remote. The recommendations for the common life and flourishing of humanity that are derived from this scheme, she argues, end up too vague and platitudinous to have much political purchase.[21] The details of her powerful critique (with which I am in complete sympathy) are unimportant here. Though it derives partly from her mastery of the implications of classical Trinitarian theory, at least equally important is her sense that social Trinitarianism fails to issue in a set of strong and detailed ethical commitments that can challenge current social malformations from the standpoint of an alternative communal vision. It is yet another of Tanner's strengths as a theologian that she is acutely aware of the connection between the understanding of doctrines and the shape of actual Christian living, just as she is wary of the manner in which that connection is sometimes (as in social Trinitarianism) rendered in ways that are too direct, unnuanced, and simplistic. In other words, her critique of the social Trinity is in the interest not of purifying Christian doctrine of its political or ethical implications but rather of rendering those implications more effective.

So the structure of human action should reflect our relation to God, but instead of a direct "modelling" of human relations on Trinitarian ones, Tanner insists that the human analogue must be located with reference to the general pattern of divine self-giving, which takes on different forms in God's being, in Christ's being, and in the being of the redeemed.[22] Social Trinitarianism tries to short-circuit this necessary attention to the different levels of instantiation of the divine giving relations, ignoring the appropriate mode of application to the fallen human condition.[23] However, in pushing for this new method of linking the redemptive relation to God with theological ethics, she arguably remains, in a curious way, under the hidden sway of the social Trinitarianism she opposes. In seeking to recover the social relevance of Trinitarian doctrine without joining the "social Trinitarians," she nonetheless keeps one foot in the latter camp, because in outlining her vision of ethical transformation she directs her attention almost exclusively to the level of social or communal relations rather than persons.

---

[21] Ibid., 77–83; Tanner, *Christ the Key*, 233–43.
[22] For the relation of human action to the God-relation, see Tanner, *Jesus*, 79.
[23] Ibid., 81–2.

The result is an intriguing and original set of theological "principles of sociability or relationality."[24] But what is relatively absent from her considerations at this point is much of an account of what redemptive transformation looks like on the level of the individual, as opposed to the level of the group. Her approach here stands, presumably deliberately, at the opposite extreme from the individualism that has lamentably dominated so many traditionalist understandings of salvation. Tanner can hardly be faulted for making clear in this way that every Christian account of redemption must be articulable in political terms. Even so, this overriding emphasis on the communal dimension of sanctification follows naturally from the characteristic bias of her redemptive vision, which has already been noted in her anthropology. In her description of the way the new life of grace changes us, the priority rests exclusively with the pattern of relationships; communal renewal is not a function of new gracious endowments on the level of particular persons, but rather persons are assumed to be reshaped in and through the renewed force of community.

This focus on the systemic character of redemption mirrors the way she tends to talk about sin; the stress on human entanglement in a "body" of exploitive and corrosive structures is surely correct, and corresponds to what is meant classically by "original sin." But there is hardly any discussion of its traditional counterpart, "actual sin," the sin that is the willing, daily contribution, in a million large or small ways, of individuals (in fact, of all of us) to the system of death. Thus, our own souls deform themselves. But though Tanner knows that our sinful persons "are constituted" as sinful, she chooses to leave the agency here undifferentiated, because the question of our own individual complicity in our corruption seems a marginal concern.[25]

How can we describe this tendency? If we imagine the ethical problematic as always involving a spectrum of agency that ranges from the individual on one side to the group on the other, then "politics" might be the mediating term between the extremes, since it seeks to draw together and integrate the choice of and struggle for just social arrangements with the virtues demanded of the individuals who must "operate" those negotiations and arrangements. Toward one end of the spectrum, where the individual is the exclusive focus, we speak more of "morality" and of "virtue"; toward the other side, where prime agency rests with the "block" behavior of groups and the concentration, dispersal, and circuits of material and symbolic capital, we might speak of "economy." When Tanner speaks of "a debt economy in conflict with God's own economy of grace" she reveals the leitmotif of her entire ethics of redemption.[26] The new humans are not turned and transformed from within; they are summoned into being by "relations of production" of which Marx knew nothing, an economy of grace that replicates the triune self-giving: the instance of pattern.

---

[24] Ibid., 83–95.
[25] For sinful constitution, see ibid., 57.
[26] Ibid., 88.

IV. Enjoyment without Desire

One final example of Tanner's highly innovative appropriation of traditional dogma is provided by her eschatology. In general her reflections in this area are well argued and profound. Her recommendation is that the new conditions of creaturely existence marking the advent of God's reign are not to be thought of as a crude interruption of the temporal course of the natural order, a miraculous suspension of the world's physical decay in order that a new, better time series can be tacked on, as it were, picking up where the old one left off. Cosmic senescence is no more a threat to eschatology than that of individual human beings; in either case, it is the entire temporal career of humans and their common world that will be taken up and transfigured. The mere passage of worldly time in itself brings the Kingdom not a bit closer; each moment of the life of creation is equally close to the new creation because each moment will be redeemed.[27] Tanner's detailed reflections on this point are highly suggestive. However, there is one aspect of this eschatology that is sharply stamped by the idiosyncratic anthropology that we have tried to identify, and that extrapolates it into eternity. Putting some classic eschatological questions might render this more visible. How should we envision the elevated state of communion with God that is the human face of the new creation? In particular, in what way can that communion be understood as the perfection or consummation of human being as such?

In the Western tradition, a fairly sharp distinction has been drawn between the status of redeemed humans in this life (*in via*) and their state in heaven (*in patria*). The difference between the light of grace they experience now and the light of glory that awaits is such that it demands an entirely distinct category of anthropological description: the beatific vision. The first hint of Tanner's unique approach in this area is her reluctance to employ such a category. We recall that a dominant structural element in her theology is the suggestion that God's triune being, the incarnation in Jesus, and the entry of grace into the human sphere are all to be construed as linked moments of a single arc; in each case it is a matter of the one intention of God to bestow the divine being, with Jesus's reception of God approximating as closely as possible the perfect self-giving of Father to Son, and that of the redeemed approximating in even less perfect ways that of Jesus. One result is that Tanner construes human redemption as a sort of deficient version of the hypostatic union; as discussed above, our human nature, by sharing in the humanity of Jesus, assumes the same structural position with regard to the triune relations that constitutes Jesus's own personhood. One unexpected result of this understanding of redemption is that it allows both our existence in grace now as well as our eschatological attainment of communion with God to be described in exactly the same terms. Our existence in the new creation will be a heightened participation in the triune relational pattern, closer to that of Jesus himself; "glory" is just more "grace," more intense but structurally identical.

In a way this follows from the moves already indicated. Tanner, as we have argued, regularly directs attention away from the anthropological dimension of redemption,

[27] Ibid., 97–124.

that is, the way in which grace meets up with and alters already given structures of human personhood. This is true even in the case of Jesus: just as humanity in general has no "aptness" for being the vehicle of incarnation, so Jesus himself is pure receptivity, an empty vessel shaped totally by the bestowal of the eternal Word. Because this union of God and humanity is "unnatural," in Tanner's view the language of grace as a "supernatural" gift enhancing our natural powers is not strong enough. Grace is always something "alien" to the redeemed.[28] The seriousness with which she intends this claim is shown by the way she cuts the Gordian knot of the long-standing dispute over how best to affirm the intrinsic human fittingness of grace while safeguarding its sheer gratuity. She canvasses the various positions in this argument only to conclude that it is insoluble on the traditional terms; the only way to escape the dilemma is to deny that human beings have a natural desire for union with God.[29]

More precisely, her bold move at this point is to claim that any desire we have for God is not "internally self-generated" but is itself a product of the proximate offer of the Holy Spirit that constitutes humanity from its origin.[30] The Barthian overtones of this decision are obvious, but to be noted here is the way all this affects Tanner's picture of human fulfillment in the eschaton. The very notion of a desire that is not somehow rooted in human appetition as human has something paradoxical about it. More than this, as something like a "new" desire created *ex nihilo*, it seems to lack a specifiable relation to the natural range of human affections. "Humans, it is true, are determined to God ... But that is just *not* to be determined in any particular direction as other things are, since God is the absolute good and not a limited one."[31] The more traditional approach on this issue is to see an inherent connection and orientation between our desires for finite goods and our desire for God; our affective orientation to the divine is by ordering our many finite acts of will in such a way that they do not obstruct but rather serve the infinite quest as so many partial incarnations of it. But Tanner's language here is more disjunctive; our determination to God must be conceived as alternative to limited determinations to our fellow creatures.

As already noted, Tanner creatively reconfigures human intellect and will as our very lack of firm definition, our constitutive openness to the "alien," our ability to be "stretched" without limit in order to take in God's self-gift. To secure the radicality of grace as she understands it, Tanner is willing to pay a high price: if it means abandoning the attempt to discern how the myriad finite acts of grasping truth and loving things that form the texture of human life are all, in spite of their confusion and corruption, stubbornly aligned toward the one goal that is God like filings in a magnetic field, then so be it. The divine gift meets in us no already existing desire, but, she argues, none is necessary: it is not attractive to us because of the sort of desiring creatures we are, but rather "in and of itself," as "superior" and "source of our own good."[32] The holiness that makes us fit to dwell with God is not the completion of our natural, frustrated

---

[28] Ibid., 51; Tanner, *Christ the Key*, 12.
[29] Tanner, *Christ the Key*, 106–39.
[30] Ibid., 125.
[31] Ibid., 49.
[32] Ibid., 127.

tendency. It is, she insists, foreign to us, even when we are translated beyond the current created realm. It is never "within" us, it "adheres" to us "externally."[33] Since Christ's righteousness is ours in the sense that it stands in place of ours, salvation at his hands is better described as our cooptation than our completion.[34]

It is surely more in accord with the Western tradition to see, with a thinker like Maurice Blondel, all the dispersed acts and partial yearnings that make us who we are as so many expressions of a foundational desire for God that defines the space of the human within the natural cosmos, just as all our fragmentary intellectual achievements of finite truth inherently grasp creatures as genuine signs of the creator. In this sense a final loving vision of God "face to face" is not just incomprehensible gift (though it is that too) but is just as much the fitting reward of humanity's persistent faithfulness to its own truest desire. But for Tanner our intellect and will are precisely our lack of definition, and our final enjoyment of God can be called a consummation of our very humanity only in the most oblique way. True to her intuition that grace finds no proper point of insertion within our given nature, Tanner's descriptions of our final reconciliation with God render it more as a structural arrangement, a perfected juxtaposition "cleanly separating" God's giving from the immanent workings of its human receptor.[35] God's offer of communion meets in us no merely human desire for it; it rather creates a desire that, in its way, is therefore just as little "ours" as the gift itself is. Our final enjoyment of God is the triumphant outworking of an inexorable pattern of divine giving, not a fullness whose shape matches that of the mysterious lack at the heart of human freedom; it is not there because we want it, it is instead wanted because it is there.

V. *L'automatisme de répétition* and the Effacement of Interiority

Following the path of Tanner's theory of salvation through three different theological spheres (anthropology, ethics, eschatology) has brought us to the same result. The individual human person as present in her doctrinal theology presents a strangely "hollowed out" appearance. There is a resolute lack of interest in what we might call "interiority": the deep structures and dynamics of selfhood in their own right, logically distinct from (even if always imbricated with) the "economy" of bodied and cultural transactions. The role played in the story of redemption by the internal topography of the subject is ignored in what seems a systematic, not an incidental, way. Instead, in her various descriptions of the salvific process the initiative is almost always taken by relational patterns, grounded ultimately in schemata drawn from Christological and Trinitarian dogma. Can any clues as to the possible reasons for this be drawn from characteristics of her work more broadly?

---

[33] Ibid., 90, 65.
[34] Tanner, *Christ the Key*, 97.
[35] Ibid., 96.

A number of possibilities tentatively suggest themselves. Theologically, there is the characteristic Barthian allergy to granting systematic status in the theology of divine acts to any anthropological "point of connection." In regard to non-theological resources, the sensitivity to cultural anthropology that has formed the Yale theological tradition also probably plays a role, perhaps enhancing suspicions against any appeal to supposedly universal subjective structures unmediated by particular communal linguistic formations. Ethically, it is possible to wonder whether there is a wariness, drawn from feminist and queer theory, of the rhetoric of the "normal" and "natural," which often operates oppressively to police polymorphous humanity. Methodologically, finally, one could point to a tendency defining Tanner's work since her dissertation (and especially connected with George Lindbeck), namely that of tackling theological problems primarily by trying to discern quasi-grammatical "rules" embedded within faithful Christian discourse. Hence, some issues like the nature of divine acts in the created order, or the role of human beings in the redemptive process, present conundrums that are not susceptible of solution through translation into speculative or introspective languages but which the theologian should formally situate within the space defined by protocol assertions deeply encoded within the affirmations of Christian tradition.

But more important than the hunt for sources is the evaluative question: how should we respond to this tendency? Any answer tentatively offered in closing this all too short chapter will be taken, not as a final verdict on the issue, but as a sort of query put to Tanner's project (which is still very much underway); it can only register qualms coming from a particular theological standpoint, in fact the one being developed in this book. In other words, it should be seen not so much as an attempt at refutation as a perplexity or dissatisfaction springing from a theological sensibility admittedly different than Tanner's own. The hesitations to be summarized here will hopefully be read against the background of my warmly confessed admiration for her work overall. That work is highly unusual and quite invaluable for theology today due to its unique combination of gifts. Who are the theologians currently writing who bring together such logically clear-headed argumentation, such commanding grasp of the depth and possibilities of traditional Christian thought, and such a delicate but transformative incorporation of contemporary insights springing from ethics, economics, and politics (considerations of gender and sexuality as well, though the latter are present in Tanner more often as a hidden pressure than as a topics in their own right)? If her work is here engaged critically I hope thereby to honor my old teacher, by attempting the sort of hard thinking she so marvelously modelled for me and tried to instill in me. In the end, the difficulty uncovered and named in this chapter is only one aspect of her work; it remains to be seen how that work will further unfold. But for now, it seems necessary at least to try and signal the difficulties that appear from the standpoint of thinking the Christian creator God and her subjective accommodation by the human person.[36]

---

[36] Apart from the theme discussed here, it might also be suggested that the way Tanner exegetically roots Trinitarian thought in a reading of the gospel narratives, salutary though it is, seems to underplay the role of the monotheistic problem. The fact that the inchoate Trinitarianism of the New Testament is never allowed to problematize the faith shared with Israel in the one, omnipotent creator God of Israel is given insufficient attention.

Some of these difficulties spring from arguments or assumptions specific to only one or another of the theological topics touched on above. On the anthropological side, Tanner attempts to render human intellection and volition in negative terms, as a kind of omnideterminability marking human nature as uniquely lacking essential inner-worldly definition for its cognitive modes and affective drives. Besides representing a more abrupt break with traditional notions than she acknowledges, the claim appears dubious on its face, fashionable philosophies of radical human malleability notwithstanding. Closely related to this is her disallowing any normative status to human being in purely creaturely terms; neither being human nor being redeemed have a properly natural dimension on her understanding. Eschewing a theory of the supernatural, this denatured anthropology leaves the human as such shuttling between "unnatural" states and ungraspable outside the sphere of revelation. For all the oppressive possibilities that lie within attempts to determine the normatively human, the refusal to discern the natural contours of human belonging can have its troubling side as well. With regard to her structural and communal bias in ethics, it can be argued that reflection on the full range of human goodness cannot succeed where the focus on ideal interpersonal and collective relations occludes attention to the virtuous habituating of inherent capacities needed for individuals to actualize such relations. As for eschatology, Tanner's unwillingness to connect our consummation in God solidly to a dynamic subjective orientation inherent to the creature as such results in a strangely attenuated theology of human desire, prohibiting a more robust development of the affective and sensual psychology of spiritual life.

In all these cases, the impoverished stock of concepts with which Tanner attempts to analyze human nature leaves her theological account of individual personhood distressingly shapeless. But this is a subsidiary set of concerns. They are preliminary contributors to what seems the larger issue, namely, the way in which Tanner's theological turn away from personal "interiority," demonstrable in the various ways just outlined, leads to an inability to specify in a convincing way just how grace, or holiness, or God, are really and truly "in" me, transformatively ingredient to my very selfhood. How will her scheme finally stave off the accusation that God's saving arrangement is ultimately just arbitrary in human terms? From a Catholic perspective, it must appear that her Protestant fear of even the slightest claim to "ownership" of Christ's merit, intensified by fidelity to Barth, results in a sort of "scorched earth" policy to the created, properly human dimension of grace. Is this necessary? It has not been sufficiently shown by her that any reference to salvation as truly befitting and perfecting the human as such harbors a covert and illicit claim on the divine favor. Besides, it seems a desperate measure that, in spite of her best efforts, threatens her scheme with a massive extrinsicism and formalism of grace, the very thing she is seeking to avoid.

On the note of formalism, let us return to the Yale heritage of a "regulative" approach to doctrine. Referring to her master image of the mysteries of faith as a series of events of God's self-bestowal, repeated in different modalities but always occurring along a single line of divine intention grounded in God's triune eternity, Tanner offers a brilliant and revealing commentary on her own method of elucidating doctrine:

Situated within this theological structure of many different parallel or analogous relations of gift-giving unity, human life ... gains a greater intelligibility, as each aspect becomes a kind of commentary on the others. Intelligibility here is like that of myth according to Claude Lévi-Strauss, where conundrums are naturalized, rather than resolved, by repeating them across a variety of domains. Or it is like the intelligibility provided by a Freudian recounting of the compulsive repetition of traumatic events in a person's life .... meaning is enhanced as a similar structure variously permutated becomes visible.[37]

So then, repetition rather than resolution? In some situations perhaps, but where the intelligibility of the faith is concerned surely more hard hermeneutical work is going to be required to squeeze some human *meaning* from the incarnational and Trinitarian formulae. The attempt to illuminate our condition can only get so far with purely structural juxtapositions. "Colorless green ideas sleep furiously." Noam Chomsky's famous sentence provided an unforgettable reminder that flawless syntactical arrangements can still coincide with semantic gibberish.[38] Tanner's bet that Trinitarian theory and the nature of human redemption in Christ can and should cast a reciprocal light on one another is a good one. But its full payoff will prove elusive without a much richer theology of selfhood than she has developed so far; the danger is that fuller accounts of the Trinity and of redemption will be hampered by an approach that is too formalistic and insufficiently humanistic.

Classically, of course, it was the concept of the human being as *imago Dei* that helped to mediate between the austerities of Trinitarian grammar and the richness of human self-experience. But the entire approach outlined in the sections above signals a shift in the use of "image" talk: the second person of the Trinity as eternal image of the Father ends up, via the paradigmatic role of the hypostatic union, usurping human nature's positive imaging role as accessible in the rest of us. Only our inherent plasticity is left, a kind of negative image identical with our ability to be stamped by the primary image that is Christ.[39] This way of theorizing the image does indeed "turn attention initially away from the human altogether."[40] The concern is that adequate theologizing of the human image never recovers from this "initial" neglect. The resulting danger is of a severe formalism in depicting the human dimension of redemption.

A tiny aside Tanner tucks away in a footnote on the Trinity might offer a little parable on this humane deficit. Searching for analogies to the eternal generation of the Son, she offers a model of utterance used by Nyssa and Damascene.[41] But the imagery is purely concerned with the physical mechanics of vocalization: the Spirit is the "breath" that "sustains and empowers the Word" as it leaves the Father's mouth. In a note, Tanner quietly affirms that this failure to attend to the classic Trinitarian model of mental process, where the Son as Word is the intelligible emanation, the perfect "concept"

---

[37] Tanner, *Jesus*, 38.
[38] Noam Chomsky, *Syntactic Structures* (The Hague: Mouton, 1957), 15.
[39] Tanner, *Christ the Key*, 4.
[40] Ibid., 1.
[41] Ibid., 177–8.

or "judgment" issuing from God's self-knowledge, is no accident: "This analogy of an exterior word stands in contrast to an Augustinian focus on an interior word." We could hardly have failed to take the hint, for it can be no surprise at this point that Tanner would resist an analogy that thematizes human psychology.

But the deeper worry here is that such decisions signal a characteristic void in her theology. The function of the Augustinian analogy was never to map human psychodynamics directly onto the divine being, a fact of which Aquinas was well aware even if many later thinkers have not so noticed. Its vital role is to invite prayer into the intelligibility of the Trinitarian mystery, pivoting on the splendid natural privileges we exercise daily, even though sinfully, in living our humanity. Our intellective grasp and our desiring volition are genuine natural perfections and truly present in God their prime instance though in a way opening out our notions of them toward their infinite depth. Only granting this positive sense to the human image allows the further precious increment of light upon the divine mystery that the psychological analogy provides: the eternal utterance of the Word is no mechanism but the production of an unlimited meaning. The Son doesn't just "come from" or "exit" the Father but *expresses* her: God is her own symbol, her own icon. From the analogy of our mind the eternally uttered Word takes on properly living, organic, even intelligent and creative associations, beyond the mere mechanics of audible production; it is art beyond device.

The restriction of Trinitarian analogy to subhuman models is of a piece with the larger issue, namely, applying the Trinitarian relational pattern to the understanding of redemption in a way that remains "external" to redeemed subjectivity. The rather "algorithmic" feel of such an application could tempt the adventurous to discover in the mathematical symbolism of our title a sort of formal grammar of the Trinity: (*f*)ather, (S)on, (s)pirit, perhaps? Tantalizing as that might be (and in the spirit of Tanner's own coding[42]), that is neither the origin of the formula nor its point of relevance. Tanner's evasion of a mental analogy for the Word is referenced here only as an indirect reflection in her God-talk of the formalist risk involved in her reduction of human interiority to pattern, a reduction that has more serious consequences in its enfeeblement of theology's attempt to speculatively imagine union with God as a truly *human* good. The title of this chapter has merely taken a cue from Tanner's own reference to Lévi-Strauss and Sigmund Freud, following the inevitable associational trajectory of structuralism and psychoanalysis to playfully evoke a bit of Lacanian psychological mathematics. Tanner's initial stroke of insight was structurally to align the theological loci of "Jesus, humanity and the Trinity" by making them replications of a single motif: divine self-donation to the other. The risk is that this fertile decision will become simply the reverse side of an anti-humanist evacuation of selfhood as such.

According to the Lacanian formula, the delusory integrity of the human subject is a function of signifying processes more or less opaque to it, whereby the unconscious (*le Inconscient*) endlessly works to master the signified meaning forever "barred" from direct access.[43] Here, too, subject is reduced to pattern, slipping along the unending

---

[42] Ibid., 195.
[43] Jacques Lacan, "L'instance de la lettre dans l'inconscient ou la raison depuis Freud," in *Écrits* (Paris: Editions du Seuil, 1966), 493–528. The formula is found at p. 515.

chain of signifiers. The Christian can welcome the insight that we are constitutively "unfinished" but will do well to stipulate that this lack represents the unlimitedness of a concrete desire for the infinite it images, not the deceptive quest to cover over an unfillable void of meaning. Can Tanner's theology, as so far developed, readily support this affirmation of the positive dignity of humanity as divine image? The relatively vacated humanity that appears at the heart of her systematic account lacks the sort of ontological solidity that would make it something other than a mere by-product of putatively more fundamental impersonal transactions.

Repetition in itself is never resolution; it could be simply pathology. Neither the cyclic reassembling of mythemes nor the forced iteration of psychic gestures signifies anything in itself but a problem. If such patterns give way to light, it is only as they are hooked back into the deeper region of undeformed personhood from which they have been temporarily expelled. Their significance is derivative of larger reservoirs of human meaning; only when reintegrated thence, through the irreplaceably human labor of interpretation, do the mechanics of blind reproduction cease. It is this "deeper region" of selfhood that appears insufficiently explored (at least to this point) by Tanner; her rendering of soteriology as a formal reproduction of her Trinitarian and Christological relational schemes looks sterile if intended as a substitute. Here the "instance" of the pattern, understood as its summoning persons into being as a result of its logical and ontological priority (the mirror image of the posteriority and poverty of individual selves in Tanner's scheme), passes into Lacan's notion of a compulsory repetition, the relentless insistence (*l'instance*) of a pattern that tyrannizes over the subject. For all its undeniable wealth of insight, barely sketched in our discussion, Tanner's Trinitarian soteriology threatens to leave a disturbing blank space just where theological attention directs us to the intricacies of human selfhood. Her automatism, which claims to be a substitute for that resolution, seems more a symptom. Of what? I am compelled to repeat: Kathryn Tanner's reflections on the Trinity have a self-effacing character.

Part Two

Dogma and the Infinite God: Trinity, Christology, Grace

On the Contrary: Thomistic Second Thoughts on Eberhard Jüngel

Es gibt allerdings Unaussprechliches. Dies zeigt sich ...

Ludwig Wittgenstein
Tractatus Logico-Philosophicus

Les théologies moderne de la Parole sont nées de cette réduction: Dieu est le moyen de sa révélation.

Christian Duquoc
"La théologie naturelle"

Upon reflection, I find myself opposed to myself. That is to say, to an earlier version of myself. For some time I have been more and more drawn to the precision and elasticity of the Christian metaphysical theism of Thomas Aquinas and its characteristic readings of the ancient ecclesial traditions (on negative theology, sacramental ecclesiology, God as *ipsum esse*, and creation *ex nihilo*). But my current conviction that his vision offers the most promising orienting point for constructing a reasonably defensible and encompassing articulation of the Christian gospel has brought with it an uncomfortable corollary: I have fallen quite out of sympathy with at least some of the convictions of the author of my first book.[1] This shift would be trivial in itself, merely autobiographical; what makes it embarrassing is that it also necessitates a public demurral from some of the most basic affirmations of Eberhard Jüngel, one of the truly formidable theological intellects of our time, whose writings were critical to my own education and remain objects of my special esteem. How do I properly honor Jüngel in spite of the bafflement that has gradually and unintentionally emerged in me in face of his brilliantly conceived central project? Unable to shake off the awareness

---

[1] Paul DeHart, *Beyond the Necessary God: Trinitarian Faith and Philosophy in the Thought of Eberhard Jüngel* (Atlanta:, 1999). David Burrell's curt response to that work (see his short notice in *Theological Studies* 62 (2001): 207), a skeptical shrug in face of a certain style of theological thinking and argumentation characterizing both the book and its hero, now strikes me as strangely prophetic of my future trajectory.

that my own contributions can only be dwarfed by the stature of his achievement, I will nonetheless remain his student even here by trying to follow his example, for Jüngel has consistently reserved the dignity of explicit detailed contradiction for those opponents he deems most worthy of respect, calmly laying out the precise points at issue with all due care. One such honored opponent of Jüngel's has in fact been Thomas Aquinas himself, and what follows is accordingly one sort of rejoinder from a position inspired by the latter.

The constructive scheme laid out in Jüngel's great work *God as the Mystery of the World* at its heart demands the explicit rejection of two theses embraced by Aquinas: on the one hand, Jüngel's book develops an account of language and revelation intended to counter any claim that "the Deity, therefore, is ineffable and incomprehensible"; on the other hand, it culminates in a cruciform interpretation of the triune divine being that, in his words, "has destroyed the axiom of absoluteness, the axiom of apathy, and the axiom of immutability."[2] *Au contraire*, says the Thomist. No more can be done here than to register some almost telegraphically brief defensive objections, raising questions about his revisionary rejections of these classical formulations pursuant to more detailed discussions in the future. The first section will deal with his critique of Aquinas on analogy and negative theology, while the third section will concern itself with his theistic (or anti-theistic!) reconstruction of the divine triunity. The second section, shorter and more tentative, will serve as a hinge between the main sections, hinting at some probable submerged Christological and ecclesiological assumptions that respectively inform both Jüngel's stances on revelation and Trinity as well as the outlined alternatives proffered in the spirit of Aquinas. The final section will conclude with some broader historical reflections upon this clash of theological conceptions and its implications. What follows covers much ground in haste and would need extended development before it could lay claim to the title of an argument with Jüngel; it merely reflects a set of concerns and hesitations prompted by a stance, some contours of which are quite unsystematically noted, more sympathetic to the ancient tradition than his own.

I. Language against Language

References to Aquinas can be found scattered throughout Jüngel's writings; sometimes approving, sometimes not, they confirm the status of Aquinas in Jüngel's mind as one of those crucial moments within the Western tradition (an "*epochale Umbruch*") that serve as abiding points of reference for his own thinking.[3] The seriousness with which Jüngel enters into his critical dialogue with tradition is one of his more appealing qualities, but although Aquinas is frequently noticed, substantive engagement is scarce apart from the treatment of ineffability and analogy within the chapter on divine "speakability" in *God as the Mystery of the World*. This discussion forms the centerpiece

---

[2] Jüngel, *Gott als Geheimnis*, 316 (232); 511 (373).
[3] Eberhard Jüngel, *Wertlose Wahrheit: Zur Identität und Relevanz des christlichen Glaubens. Theologische Erörterungen III* (Tübingen: Mohr Siebeck, 1990), 135 (quoting Rahner).

of a larger argument that indicts the entire tradition of negative theology for the crime of suppressing the linguistic mode of God's presence in the saving proclamation of the gospel. As Jüngel narrates it, Aquinas, maintaining the tradition of Pseudo-Dionysius, offers a doctrine of analogous naming of God's attributes that must finally undermine the believer's confidence in God's nature and identity. For Jüngel, in the Christ event God has entered the world of the human, the speaking animal, by graciously annexing its fundamental capacity, language itself. But Aquinas speaks for those who, refusing this most intimate conjunction of divine self-utterance and human proclamation, insist instead on a God finally incompatible with speech. How can this fail to result, generally, in a divine hostility to language perhaps tipping over into an enmity (decried by Nietzsche) to the human as such? More particularly, under the conditions of modernity, the faceless and silenced God of negative theology must confront the human search for meaning with an "unbearably sinister riddle," eventually dissolving any significance of God for a humanity come of age.[4]

In response, it should be said that Jüngel's description of analogy in Aquinas' own writings displays for the most part his usual sensitivity but strikes two or three false notes as well. These in turn skew the evaluative conclusions he draws from the discussion, for the careful reader of Aquinas will have difficulty recognizing the dire results Jüngel insists upon as in any way necessitated by the foregoing account itself. Two sorts of consideration need to be raised in order to understand what is questionable in Jüngel's diagnosis. The first is that Jüngel seems to be working with an unwarrantedly flattened notion of cognition, one that fails to recognize the modes and limits of Aquinas' measured agnosticism. Second, Jüngel can only delineate the modern consequences of analogic naming in such grim terms because he sees it against the background of his own contestable understanding of what divine revelation should entail.

One approach to the first point can be made by simply pointing to a strange feature of Jüngel's discussion of analogy: after an admirable summation of Aquinas on the matter (marred mainly by a misbegotten attempt to uncover a secret dependence upon the analogy of proportionality), he begins his critique of analogy by turning, not to Aquinas' version, but to that of Immanuel Kant.[5] Indeed, Jüngel can even promote Kant to a sort of spokesman for the negative theological tradition.[6] But this will not do, for as Jüngel himself rightly concludes, the whole thrust of Kant's position on analogy is utterly to seal God off from any cognitive access by playing off our possible grasp of a divine relation to the world against the sheer unknowability of God, the "x" at one term of that relation.[7] Thus, God's "love" for Kant amounts to no more than the assertion of an infinitely superior, and hence unknown, causal efficacy. But this flat-footed result is only compelling once one accepts the relevant Kantian definitions of cognition and of

---

[4] Jüngel, *Gott als Geheimnis*, 378 (277).
[5] Jüngel, *Gott als Geheimnis*, 358–63 (263–6). The wrongheadedness of this attempt at assimilating Kant to Aquinas has already been pointed out by John Milbank in *The Word Made Strange: Theology, Language, Culture* (Oxford: Blackwell, 1997), 7–16. Although the details of his account of Aquinas are quite problematic, Milbank's overall point is well taken. For Jüngel's claim about proportionality, see *Gott als Geheimnis*, 375–6 (276).
[6] Jüngel, *Gott als Geheimnis*, 380–1 (279).
[7] Ibid., 361–2 (265).

belief, which Aquinas certainly does not. Jüngel's discussion of analogy shows no sign of being aware of these distinctions.

Unlike for Kant, "knowledge" in Aquinas is itself an analogical term. The fact that humans can have no knowledge of God's essence in this life means that they can neither grasp nor name "what" God is as they can name finite material objects by discerning their causes and defining their quiddities vis-à-vis other finite things. But humans can cognitively and truthfully assert the reality of an infinite ground of all things; they can know the authentic presence of goodness, wisdom, and love within that ground in a grade of perfection which transcends all earthly experiences; and finally, through the revelation in Christ, they can come, through growth in relationship, to know the eternal co-inherence of Word and Spirit within the divine identity. Of course, God remains sheerly mysterious to the categorizing and defining intellect, but the fragmentary glimpses of this mystery are such as to invite the believer further and further in, drawn by the affective touch of faithful desire coaxing her out always beyond, but never against, what she can know within the zone illuminated by reason. The role of analogy is crucial here because it informs our willing with the knowledge that the direction of its reach is indeed along an unlimited extension rooted in, though expanding beyond, the goodness and love we concretely experience in this world.

This "agnosticism" of Aquinas operates in a dialectical fashion, whereby the repeated denial of the modal adequacy of our own affirmations of divine wisdom and benevolence in no way simply negates the authentic content of those affirmations but rather draws us willingly to grow up into that content beyond our cognitive limits. Jüngel, however, insists on seeing here a zero-sum game where negation simply trumps and frustrates every affirmation, such that God as revealed is even "more" unknown.[8] He evidently does not believe Aquinas' assurances that revelation decidedly increases our assimilation of saving truth. This is completely in line with his conjoined reading of Pseudo-Dionysius, where Jüngel fails to note the epistemic dynamism involved in the fact that for Dionysius even our negations of the divine names are themselves endlessly negated in our living engagement with the mystery itself. Instead, the picture Jüngel offers of negative theology is that of a machine that perfectly immobilizes itself. Empty negativity always has the last word.

Because he does not sufficiently appreciate in this whole tradition the living interplay in faith between a cognitive affirmation and negation that are themselves embedded in a larger existential progression involving will and feeling, Jüngel regards with apparent surprise Aquinas' incorporation of transcendent perfections in his discourse of God's attributes, as if this involved a "reversal" based solely on scriptural necessity that is at odds with the way of negation.[9] But Aquinas' notion of faith involves a more flexible and multivalent understanding of what can constitute knowing than Jüngel's account, apparently keyed to a Kantian definition of cognition, can countenance. Jüngel's conclusion, then, on the entire negative theological tradition is that it ends up in a sterile opposition between God's existence, a naturally available but nugatory thesis, and God's essence, admitted as utterly superior but empty of all

---

[8] Ibid., 330 (243).
[9] Ibid., 332 (244).

cognitive content.[10] Whatever role such a debased scholastic inheritance may have played in mediating the hidden atheism of early modern thought, it cannot pass for a satisfactory reading of Aquinas.

But an insufficiently nuanced appreciation of the role of knowledge in negative theology is not the only factor at work in Jüngel's sharp disapproval of Aquinas' position. The second element is a presupposed notion of what a saving revelation of God is or should be. Reading Paul in such a way that justifying faith means our being assured of the personal "acknowledgement" of our person by the divine person, Jüngel construes God's revelation primarily in terms of an act of self-identification.[11] Only in Jesus Christ, in other words, are human beings first confronted with "who" God really is. A similar understanding pervades his interpretation of Paul's discourse of the cross, where Jüngel, guided by a particular reading of the Johannine utterance that "God is love," makes the inference that for Paul the event of the crucifixion is the defining disclosure of the divine identity, and that identity in turn is equivalent to the divine essence.

This moves quickly into a host of detailed exegetical matters that cannot be resolved here, but it can at least be signaled that this reading of the New Testament data is eminently debatable. On the one hand, the God revealed in Jesus the Son was not a previously unknown God but was none other than the creator, the God of Abraham, Isaac, and Jacob, of the law and the prophets and the covenant people. Paul knew "who" God was before the Damascus road experience. For this reason, is it really correct to see in Paul's theology of the cross the answer to the question "Who is God?"? Should we not reverse Jüngel's judgment and admit that it is more proper to say that Paul confessed God's presence in Christ crucified on the basis of his prior confession of Israel's creator God, rather than vice versa?[12] That God has spoken definitively and climactically in Christ presupposes the confession of Israel, it does not retroactively ground it. On the other hand, what are the warrants for understanding the crucifixion of the word made flesh as God's self-definition, as Jüngel is wont to do? At any rate, the famous Johannine equivalence of *theos* and *agape* is hardly, taken in context, to be understood as a definition of the divine essence, nor does it demand the sort of exclusive connection with Paul's "word of the cross" that Jüngel gives it.

Given the different roles played by "essence" in their respective schemes, Jüngel and Aquinas are talking at cross purposes. The point is that Aquinas' strictures against our knowledge of God's essence call forth such vigorous opposition from Jüngel because he already relies upon an understanding of God's revelation in Christ precisely as the articulation in language of the divine essence itself. As Jüngel reads the New Testament, the good news is not so much the announcement of God's ultimate saving gesture in Jesus as rather in some way itself identical with that saving gesture, as God's informing humanity "Here is who I am!," thereby grounding anew their own identities. This is a powerful interpretation, but neither a necessary nor an unproblematic one, especially when literalized and made the master model for what revelation must mean.

---

[10] Ibid., 320–1 (235).
[11] Ibid., 314–15 (231).
[12] Ibid., 296 (218).

In sum, a Thomist will be inclined to see the discussion of Aquinas in *God as the Mystery of the World* as tendentious: the doctrine of analogy expounded by Aquinas is both misunderstood on its own terms and wrongly construed as an "unbearable" concealment of God when juxtaposed against the assumption of revelation as God's essential self-disclosure. If analogy in the tradition of negative theology is nothing more than the self-negating deployment of language against itself, without remainder, then the silencing of revelation as Jüngel conceives it is indeed the only result. All language is condemned to inauthenticity, and God is defined as the negative opposite of the linguistic animal until modern atheism justifiably ushers this God off the stage. But first, even if all language is finally inadequate to the divine being, it by no means follows that silence about God is the only authentic way to be faithful. Language is used against language, not to neutralize language entirely, but to show by the very shape of its inadequacy its genuine residual possibility as an element within worshipful existence. It is just in this way, second, that the upshot of analogical naming in the manner of Aquinas could never be, as Jüngel accuses, the mutual exclusion of the divine and human natures.[13] Just the opposite: human nature could never be defined in opposition to God precisely because the protocols of analogical speech concerning ultimate mystery prevent God and any created nature inhabiting a common logical space, within which such exclusion is alone possible.

Finally, as to revelation, perhaps God in the gospel has not so much defined himself into our speech as he has initiated a worldly event of real divine presence around and through which, as a series of embodied experiences, a persistent communal sign of final mystery can take historical shape. If so, then language must undergo a therapy in which all its genuine advances as the articulation of our thinking of God are repeatedly brought up against the constitutive limits of thought itself. The hopeful result is not a barren muteness but the incorporation of language into a totality of experience now freed to grow beyond itself. That is why the words of the 1215 Lateran Council so often and ominously quoted by Jüngel find their better interpreter in Przywara, in spite of the former's criticism.[14] That every affirmed similitude of God and creature must trigger an awareness of even greater dissimilitude signals not a peculiar impoverishment of language but a peculiar richness of possible experience. In revelation, the eternal utterance, because unutterable in human words, personally arrives. "There is, to be sure, what cannot be said. It *shows* itself ...."[15]

II. Body against Body

Just a word or two more about this arrival, this showing, is in order to illuminate the rather different conception of revelation Jüngel seems to work with, the pressures it is responding to, and some insights it possibly occludes. The Christian doctrine of

---

[13] Ibid., 382–3 (280).
[14] Ibid., 388–9 (285).
[15] Ludwig Wittgenstein, *Tractatus Logico-Philosophicus,* trans. D. F. Pears and B. F. McGuiness (London: Routledge & Kegan Paul, 1961), 73 [6.522]. The translation here is my own.

revelation must balance different tendencies. On the one hand, there is the majesty of what takes place: the divine itself, resident within the house of creation; on the other hand, there is the feebleness and unworthiness of the human hands that must somehow receive this immense gift. The Christian tradition has been united in proclaiming the necessity of the gracious descent of the divine Spirit itself to mobilize and direct the receptive human capacities, in order that revelation, the genuine transferral of divine utterance into human hearing, succeed at all. But there are different ways of conceiving how this happens. Jüngel's own account of the matter is fascinating but raises some questions from a Thomist perspective.

He renders his scheme briskly in *God's Being Is in Becoming* (1965).[16] Indeed, *God as the Mystery of the World*, though written later (1977), can in some ways be regarded as an immense historical and philosophical prologue to that earlier book, situating its Trinitarian argument within an account of the story of God's lingering cultural death over the course of modern intellectual development. In fact, it might be suggested that the particular theological construal of revelation that Jüngel presents in the early work makes most sense when it is seen as also attempting to provide the answer to a question put by the unfolding of modernity as narrated in the later book. According to that narrative, the affirmation of human objectification, the cognitive control exerted by the knowing subject upon every datum that purports to obtain human meaning, can be understood both as the indispensable founding charter of the modern world as well as the most disastrous efflorescence of humanity's perennial perverted self-assertion. Granting this view of things, Jüngel supports an understanding of revelation in which the saving disclosure of the divine presence is cast as the perfect riposte to human objectification: a perfected knowledge event in which God utterly controls, at every stage, her appearance within the horizon of human cognition. Never objectified by us, God instead must ever anew objectivize himself and thus remain the inviolable subject of his givenness.

But what sort of "givenness" is this? There are grounds for suspicion that the incarnation of the Word has here become so hedged about with caveats, so "protected" from any entry into the causal interchanges of historical human agency (lest it become a "predicate of history"), that anything like a human presence of God has become volatilized and evanescent. One is tempted at this point to recall Hegel's acute observations on the logic of Protestantism as recounted by Jüngel himself. Because Reformation faith "avoids, for the sake of God's infinity, the finite perception of God in the institutions of finitude," the Protestant believer "desires the grief of not being able to *have* God" for if the subject "*had* God, then the infinite would be dissolved into objectivity."[17] It is at least arguable that the picture of the revelatory event that Jüngel recounts in *God's Being Is in Becoming*, where the saving truth of God in Christ takes objective form in human consciousness ultimately not via the subjective and

---

[16] Eberhard Jüngel, *Gottes Sein ist im Werden: Verantwortliche Rede vom Sein Gottes bei Karl Barth—Eine Paraphrase*, 4th ed. (Tübingen: Mohr Siebeck, 1986). English translation by John Webster under the title *God's Being Is in Becoming: The Trinitarian Being of God in the Theology of Karl Barth—A Paraphrase* (Edinburgh: T&T Clark, 2001).
[17] Jüngel, *Gott als Geheimnis*, 95–6 (72).

intersubjective agency of human cognition itself but only by means of a kind of repeated "vertical" invasion of divine agency (the Holy Spirit), is still subject to the pathos described by Hegel.

Much more would have to be said here to substantiate such suspicions, but the issue is raised at this point in order to indicate two kinds of consequence for Jüngel's theology. If revelation is the inexorably triumphant sort of event imagined in this account, and any truly humanly constructed objectivity is denied to it, then, first, any extension of the event of revelation on the plane of historical causation becomes problematic. In particular, what becomes of the entire traditional understanding of the "whole Christ," where the very bodily presence of Godhead is, through the gift of the Spirit, continued in the material availability of the Word in the Eucharist and in the living bodily society of believers that historically both perpetuates and is perpetuated by that fleshly memory? It would seem that an "actualist" account like Jüngel's runs the danger of resulting in an "occasionalist" repetition of revelation where events of disclosure tend to harmonize with certain human actions but no real interlock of creaturely and creative agency occurs.

Second, if God cannot truly give herself in Christ in such as a way as to be received on genuinely human terms, what becomes of the claim, so central to Jüngel, that in revelation God truly identifies himself, truly gives herself to be known? The answer, as will be seen in the next section, lies in his particular understanding of the doctrine of the Trinity. For it looks like revelation for him is less fittingly imagined (along more patristic and Thomist lines) as a self-communicating divine agency taking authentically creaturely shape as an organic event within the world's temporal order than it is a self-enclosed pattern of giving and receiving that mirrors an eternally prior event of divine self-constitution; it hovers, so to speak, in the intermittent consciousness of elect recipients yet remains somehow spooky, never quite attaining worldly status. Even if one-sided, this exaggerated characterization hopefully brings out an alternative construal of revelation that places the accents somewhat differently. The worry is that an account like Jüngel's is missing the fleshly heft of revelation, the divine utterance as the living human body of Jesus, a historical force with its own impetus, aggregating the community of Eucharistic prayer that carries it forward. The body of the whole Christ pressing against the body of the world: this is a different sort of vision of achieved revelation than a punctuated series of perfectly controlled receptions of divine self-objectification. To be sure, this is not the whole of Jüngel's doctrine of revelation, but it is uncomfortably central.

III. God against God

Jüngel's concern to protect the act of divine self-disclosure from exposure to the historical, objectifying processes of human knowledge, as well as his insistence that what takes place in revelation is the self-identification in language of the divine essence, not only present certain problems in themselves but also play a crucial role in a series of interpretive decisions he makes concerning God's triunity. The resulting affirmations are troublesome not just for those working from a Thomist perspective but for any theologian broadly committed to the ancient and medieval heritage of

Christian thought. The matter is highly complex, but three distinct moves in Jüngel's argumentation can be tentatively identified.

(A) In an important paper Ralf Stolina has shown the peculiarly modern circumstances under which arose the opposition between a so-called immanent and an economic Trinity, an opposition that, *pace* Jüngel, does not correspond to the ancient distinction of *theologia* and *oikonomia*.[18] The paired concepts only secured a continuing role in theological discussion as a result of the controversies in the wake of Friedrich Schleiermacher over the eternal status, apart from creation, of the personal distinctions of Father, Son, and Spirit. As the terminology stabilized, so too did the relatively new way of thinking about the relationship between Trinity and revelation associated with it. This thinking attempted to answer the question, become urgent in a context both modern and Protestant, about the epistemic ground of our assurance of God's eternal triune distinction in light of the acknowledged absence of an explicit scriptural teaching (or natural disclosure to reason). The answer runs like this. The New Testament tells a story in which God is disclosed through the interplay of three agents accorded divine status (Jesus, the Spirit inspiring believers in him, and the one Jesus called Father), and we may name this interplay the "revealed" or economic Trinity. If this narrative is supposed to constitute the definitive revelation of God, indeed the self-disclosure of the absolute truth of divinity, then its threefold character cannot be an arbitrary instrument but must itself reflect perfectly God's eternal life. Hence, if revelation is truly God's self-revelation, there must be in the eternal being of God a corresponding triunity that must serve as the ground of possibility for both the self-revelatory character of the revealed one and the freedom of the act itself.

That the above account will strike many theological readers today as natural and obvious, indeed perennial, is a testimony to how deeply its assumptions have pervaded theology since the mid-nineteenth century, particularly the key presupposition that the doctrine of the Trinity must be fashioned as the solution to a certain kind of epistemological problem. At any rate, simplifying a bit one can say that, by way of contrast, the original emergence of the classical doctrine of the Trinity fixed at the great councils was driven by the necessity of reconciling the exclusive claim to divine status of Israel's God, creator of heaven and earth, with the salvifically ultimate status of the living Jesus and the communal sharing of his body. The economy here is not triune in itself but is the twofold sending into the world by the Creator of the Son and Spirit. The sendings or "missions" are identical with created complexes of events, one personal and the other collective, but the divine modalities they present to faith are eternal and integral to the divine identity. The central Trinitarian problematic therefore becomes the discernment of how the *created* divine "sendings" are radically grounded in their divine source (Jesus's "father") precisely as real participations of timeless or *uncreated* "proceedings" grounded in the eternal Father, the source of their shared divine essence.

Whatever the difficulties involved in laying out the Trinitarian problem in this traditional way, it has definite advantages from a more classical or Thomist perspective. For one thing, it places front and center as a basic datum of all Trinitarian thinking

---

[18] Ralf Stolina, "'Ökonomische' und 'immanente' Trinität? Zur Problematik einer trinitätstheologischen Denkfigur," *Zeitschrift für Theologie und Kirche* 105 (2008): 170–216. On Jüngel, see p. 171.

the foundational commitment to God as creator *ex nihilo* of all that is not God, with the resulting conditioning of all our God concepts (dialectically elaborated in classical fashion by Aquinas' conclusions concerning the divine essence). In particular, this installs strict conceptual safeguards within any discourse that combines creature and creator, time and the time-transcendent (i.e., the eternal), a great need given the tendency of Trinitarian constructions to veer off into mythology or divine "psychology." Another advantage of the more classical approach is that it does not attempt to construct a "created Trinity" by differentiating God's causal agency in the world into three distinct centers. It is presumably because he supports something like the latter that Jüngel denounces the axiom that "the works of the Trinity outside God are undivided," suggesting that it leads to the separation of trinity and economy and eventuates in practical monotheism.[19] It can be said in reply that even though vis-à-vis the created order as such the triune God's causal agency is always and only directed to the unified act of founding and maintaining the total world-event, the effect of this one act within the created order can be and is the constitution of two centers of *creaturely* agency that reflect, indeed coincide perfectly with, the eternal roles of particular intra-divine persons. In other words, the Son and Spirit are "sent" into creation ("missions") not as distinct divine efficient causes but as quasi-formal causes assuming patterns of created agency in self-presenting ways (though different ways in Jesus and in the Church, respectively). Finally, this way of arguing avoids the entire epistemic resort to an inference back (*Rückschluss*) from a supposedly available "economic Trinity" to a logically prior "immanent" ground of possibility that replicates it. Such a way of thinking is not only deeply woven into Jüngel's argument, but as Stolina shows, has entered widely into current theological discussion. Unfortunately, it generates two Trinities, resulting in endless discussions as to how to reunite them; perhaps the intractability of the question is a sign that it has been hopelessly framed. For Aquinas as for all before him, the issue cannot arise: there are not two Trinities.

(B) With superb insight, Herbert McCabe suggested the image of "projection" as fruitful for conceiving the missions, especially the incarnation.[20] That is, the pattern of eternal relation of origin and reception/reflection between Father and Son is thrown onto the created and sinful human world as onto a screen. The timeless relation of Son to Father, now reconfigured as that of Jesus to God, takes a particular worldly and human shape, even to the point where the Son's total receiving and expression of the given divinity of the Paternal source inevitably plays out on the screen of sinful human history as a path of obedience descending into alienation and execution. The essential point of this is to maintain the genuine entry of the divine Word into the world without assuming that this involves any alteration or development on God's part. In incarnation, that is, the world is creatively maneuvered into the field of intra-divine personal relations; the point of intersection is marked by the temporal unfolding of those very relations, the presence of the creaturely counterparts bearing the identity of the divine persons (Son and Spirit). This avoids fairytale theologies of

---

[19] Eberhard Jüngel, *Entsprechungen: Gott – Wahrheit – Mensch. Theologische Erörterungen* (Munich: Christian Kaiser, 1980), 268.
[20] Herbert McCabe, *God Matters* (London: Geoffrey Chapman, 1987), 48–9.

the eternal interplay of Father and Son that ultimately amount only to more subtle conceptualizations of the scene conjured by Milton in *Paradise Lost*, where there is imagined a kind of celestial board meeting of the three persons before all creation, where the Father commissions the Son to be incarnate and the Son heroically agrees. In particular, the obedience and suffering that define the existence of Jesus are the created analogous expression, the worldly "projection" of the eternal relation of Father and Son, and should not be thought of as literal transcriptions of intra-divine realities.

It is remarkable, however, that Jüngel has a tendency to speak in ways suggestive of just this kind of pretemporal scenario. This is partly due to his understanding of the divine freedom in self-revealing, partly due to his questionable elevation of the crucifixion itself as the defining disclosive moment of the divine essence, rendered (in a conspicuously non-analogical way) in terms of a human psychology of love. The result is that the "projection" is, in effect, allowed to "rebound" into the divine being, so to speak. The humiliation and death of Jesus here come to be retrojected into the divinity as eternal moments, connected with a choice or "election" of the Son to become identified with fallen humanity. The questions that must arise at this point are legion; I will limit myself to two. First, does this not open the door in Jüngel's discussion of God to a problematically enthusiastic interpolation of the speculative discourse of negation? Thus, we hear, on the one hand, that the "nothing" from which God creates is a kind of internalized death-moment eternally being overcome, so that the divine being "ek-sists" into nothingness in what looks like a blown-up version of the being-toward-death of *Dasein*.[21] In addition, we are told in several places that God must say "no" to herself in order to create "space" for creation, a recrudescence of cabbalistic mythology that rests on an unaccountably competitive view of divine and created being.[22]

Second, is it not astonishing how within a theological position so suspicious of natural theology because of its putative "anthropocentric" extrapolation of God from distorted human self-understanding that the saving communion of God and humanity effected in Jesus must be read back into an eternally prior position as a primal partnership (covenant) chosen, to be sure, by God but nonetheless defining his very identity? These are profound issues, but it is initially hard to see how this does not amount to a kind of backdoor enthronement of humanity as the meaning of reality as such, a move that is in no way rendered innocuous by insisting that it is freely "elected" by God. Nor is the intoxicating whiff of this backhanded human exaltation really dispelled by initially confining it to the humanity of Jesus. All of this, it can be suggested, is allowed in by the basic assumption that God must somehow pre-eternally "get into position" to be incarnate and crucified, meaning that the Trinitarian persons must as it were define themselves vis-à-vis one another in specific ways determined by the elected covenant with the fallen creature.[23] On the more Thomist "projective" understanding suggested above, the Son does not need to choose or do anything to "prepare" to be incarnate;

---

[21] Eberhard Jüngel, *Unterwegs zur Sache: Theologische Bemerkungen* (Munich: Christian Kaiser, 1972), 220–1; *Gott als Geheimnis*, 303–4 (223–4).
[22] Jüngel, *Unterwegs*, 120; *Wertlose Wahrheit*, 8.
[23] Equally obscure is the related implication that God's elective decision somehow determines or even concretizes God's being, as in Jüngel, *Gott als Geheimnis*, 44–50 (35–9). How could the infinite fullness of being be abstract?

Jesus (living and dying) just is what the Son looks like when the Son is a human creature in a world distorted by sin. Aquinas is taxed in some theological circles with being "metaphysical" and insufficiently "biblical." Here, though, he not only comes off looking remarkably sober in comparison with this remarkable "retrojective" tendency of Jüngel's, but he also need fear no embarrassment at the hands of the exegetes. He might be forgiven for asking: Does a theological reading of the New Testament witness in any way necessitate this extravaganza?

(C) Once the Trinity is deployed to block any human objectifying initiative in revelation, with the events constituting God's disclosure seen as withdrawn from creaturely determination by an exercise of perfect divine control, the path is opened to seeing those events as "really" taking place within the divine being itself. Jüngel marches determinedly down this path. After all, in accord with the logic of the "*Rückschluss*," if God really communicates herself in revelation then what prevents its very historical character, its status as event, from also being read back into God? If God is to be the subject of his being known in a truly radical way, how better to ensure this than to conceive her as subject of his being *tout court*? This in turn nicely converges with the "retrojection" of Good Friday into the divine identity as one of its constitutive moments. Jüngel's master concept for integrating these moves is, as already suggested, love (again illustrating the determination to read John as providing a definition of the divine essence). But love here is explicated (in unproblematized reliance on human relationships) in a highly characteristic and dialectical way, as intensity of self-relation only via an even greater intensity of other-relation or selflessness, or as the unity of death and life for the sake of life. So God is an event, and God is the event of love, demanding the incorporation of a fundamental moment of self-abandonment. As eternally elected, God's presence in the life and death of Jesus is itself somehow the actual occurrence of her divinity itself. Jüngel's ultimate move, then, is to recover the primal and absolute status of divinity, which might seem to be threatened by the inclusion within God's identity of this identification with the creature, by stressing the radical "decision" character of all this. God's love, in which his covenant with humanity even unto death in some way determines her being, is nonetheless sovereignly free, because God's being is always already an event of divine choosing.

So the divine self-identification that takes place in revelation is, for Jüngel, grounded in an understanding of divine being as itself an act of eternal self-definition. The triune divine existence is ever and anew the event of deciding about the divine being. This is an exhilarating display of speculative imagination, but from the alternative perspective that is here assumed it is cause for considerable bewilderment. Two issues need to be highlighted. First, what understanding of freedom is at work here, and how coherently can it be maintained? For instance, what sense can be made of radical freedom as self-defining being, which seems to fall into logical conundrums similar to those of the concept of self-causality? The power of will is exercised as anteriorly situated within the existent whose capacity it is; no amount of stressing the will's "radicality" in the divine case would seem to allow it to get back behind itself, as it were. God cannot choose to be God "in some way" without already being God in some more fundamental way. But even more strangely, it seems that divine freedom is here being defined solely in terms of choice or decision. There is nothing inevitable about this. Willing, on Aquinas' understanding, is primordially dynamic impetus toward the good understood, a good desired as sought when absent but desired equally in fulfillment, as determined possession. Choice or decision is a derivative moment of willing that only comes into play in face of multiple paths toward a desired end, and God's being itself, as always already the ultimate concentration of all perfection, cannot provide God with a field for decision. Only the endless alternative orders of creation bring election into play.

The second issue concerns what happens to the divine triunity when it is understood as an eternal love-event defined on Jüngel's dialectical terms. In trying to think the relations between the three divine modes of being as a logic of self-definition or auto-election, Jüngel sees the moment of suffering obedience or self-sacrifice instanced in Jesus's crucifixion as the expression, indeed the execution, of an intra-Trinitarian interplay between the Father and the Son of positing (self-relation) and negation (selflessness), both of which are preserved while their opposition is overcome in the event of divine unity (the Holy Spirit). Jüngel can even speak of the way in which the Son, as the necessarily moment of opposition or negation, hereby serves to "mediate" the divine being to itself.[24] A Thomist will have to question the need, indeed the wisdom, of the venture undertaken by Jüngel here. It is no longer just a matter of Trinity against Trinity (economic versus immanent) but has become a kind of crisis within the divine being: God against God. What can be said to this? At this point Aquinas and Jüngel seem to exhibit a clash of fundamental visions of the divine, each so encompassing that detailed adjudication (based, say, on direct scriptural appeal) is hardly possible. For Aquinas, God is not on a journey but is the point of arrival of all journeys. For Aquinas, God's being is not self-mediated, because that which is the end of all ends can never be a means, even to itself. To use language from the opening quote from Christian Duquoc, Jüngel's splendidly consistent but drastic exercise in a theology of the word has God's being itself made to play the role of medium of revelation by construing it as an eternal self-mediation. From the more traditional perspective, this can only be called what Duquoc calls it: a reduction of the divine being.[25]

IV. Conclusion: The School of Peterson and the Protest of Kierkegaard

Rückschluss, retrojection, *réduction*. The puzzle presented to Thomist eyes by Jüngel's Trinitarian experiment, indeed by his entire theology of revelation, has only been sketched above. Much of what has been said stands in need of further elaboration and explanation, to say nothing of actual argumentation. Such arguments, in fact, are already underway, albeit directed more to Jüngel's prime predecessor.[26] Many readers

---

[24] Ibid., 521–3 (380–1).
[25] Christian Duquoc, "La théologie naturelle. Son enjeu dans le débat ouvert par la Réforme," *Lumiere et Vie* 32 (1983): 80.
[26] See the interesting discussions in Bruce L. McCormack and Thomas Joseph White OP, eds., *Thomas Aquinas and Karl Barth: An Unofficial Catholic-Protestant Dialogue* (Grand Rapids, MI: Eerdmans, 2013).

will have wondered how I could get this far without even mentioning Karl Barth and, of course, Barth is the huge figure behind Jüngel, inspiring so much of the latter's overall approach as here outlined, even if not all its development in detail. Much that has been said in this chapter in response to Jüngel could be applied to Barth as well. It was Barth, it could be argued, who first commandeered the doctrine of the Trinity and yoked it to a unique and radical departure in reconceiving revelation (a reconception so consciously anti-modern as to be perversely defined by modernity). In this Barth nonetheless, though somewhat in spite of himself, perpetuated elements of the long tradition of German Protestantism (including the *de rigueur* opposition to the twin bogies, "mysticism" and "metaphysics"). But what of the even older tradition: the ancient creeds, the great Fathers and scholastics, that Barth also did so much, in his way, to reinstall as contemporary dialogue partners in Protestant theology? His achievement here is laudable and marks Jüngel as well. And yet the burden of the discussion above has been to emphasize how that ancient consensus is nonetheless undermined in crucial ways by the Barthian project (and Jüngel's sometimes scathing criticism of ancient and medieval theological decisions intimate that this was not unintentional). The question is currently being asked, and rightly so, as to just how traditional Barth's trinitarianism, say, really is, in spite of his respect for ancient formulae. Is it even Nicene?[27] Without attempting a definitive answer, the nature of the opposition between a more classically oriented approach like that of Aquinas and this more recent development can be captured, maybe, by playfully inverting the title of an essay by Jüngel treating Barth's beginnings.

Jüngel spoke of the critical influences upon Barth's development of both the "school" of Kierkegaard and the "protest" (*Einspruch*) of Erik Peterson.[28] My reversal is certainly not meant to imply that Barth attended the wrong school in learning from Kierkegaard (though one may question his connected judgment that the wise theologian will also grow up and move on from the Dane). But perhaps a spell in the school of Peterson would have been salutary as well, for it was Peterson who strove to rescue dialectical theology from an excessively "idealistic" view of revelation by rooting theological practice in a heartily non-docetic realism of God's presence in history. The theologian is properly defined as one incorporated into that body of the Word that continues, through its ecclesial and dogmatic extension in the present, to press up against the body of every worldly institution.[29] A flirtation with idealism, I have suggested, characterizes Barth's position on revelation (as recounted by Jüngel) even in its mature expression, and slants his reconstruction of the doctrine of the Trinity in distinctive ways.

As for Kierkegaard, Barth learned much from his stark opposition between faith and offense, his refusal of any access to God's reconciling presence, whether in history

---

[27] It is a great service of Bruce McCormack's "strong" position on Trinity and election in Barth that it has engendered a wide-ranging discussion in which these issues are being aired. Some examples are collected in Michael T. Dempsey, ed., *Trinity and Election in Contemporary Theology* (Grand Rapids: Eerdmans, 2011).

[28] Eberhard Jüngel, "Von der Dialektik zur Analogie: Die Schule Kierkegaards und der Einspruch Petersons," in *Barth-Studien* (Gütersloh: Gerd Mohn, 1982), 127–79.

[29] Erik Peterson, "What is Theology?" in *Theological Tractates*, trans. Michael J. Hollerich (Stanford: Stanford University Press, 2011), 1–14.

or feeling or knowledge, unmediated by creaturely self-divestment in faith. God is revealed to us only in our decision for God. But Barth's suspicion ultimately was that Kierkegaard's theological anthropology led to a "philosophical" analysis of faith as a purely human possibility. Jüngel rightly questioned this particular suspicion, but then in turn complained that the Kierkegaardian "paradox" of the God in time must mean that God in becoming human "contradicts himself."[30] This is doubtful in two ways. First, it misinterprets the paradox of the incarnation as involving a logical contradiction when it points instead to an aporia of the existentially situated human intellect. (Something similar occurs when Jüngel opposes Kierkegaard to Aquinas on the continued possibility of the past; this forgets that the lingering possibility of the actualized is not, for Kierkegaard, a metaphysical demotion of actuality but a quality of purely human historicity)[31].

Second, Jüngel's reading of paradox literalizes Kierkegaard's essentially poetic account of the God "becoming" human. Everything turns on how one properly reads Kierkegaard's line about God's "eternal essence" being "conjugated into the dialectical determinations of becoming."[32] While Jüngel quotes this in support of his own position, it seems rather that he has reversed the direction of the movement, transferring the determinations of becoming into the eternal essence in a way Kierkegaard would never have approved. What Jüngel does not seem to hear is the "protest" or "veto" (*Einspruch*) registered by Kierkegaard that limits theological concept formation in the name of God's eternity, the utter transcendence of temporality. While Jüngel, following Barth, tries to play down the time-eternity opposition and its paradoxical opacity that conditions every attempt to penetrate the unity of God and humanity in thought (a repeated injunction of Jüngel's), it is arguable that Kierkegaard's entire scheme pivots on it. Where Jüngel sees a stark opposition between a soteriological (concrete) and a metaphysical (abstract) distinction of God and world, Kierkegaard's paradoxical understanding of the eternal moment in temporal human existence is a resolute attempt to distinguish and unite creator and creature through a metaphysics of freedom toward God.[33]

Kierkegaard, in other words, might well be closer to a "traditional" figure like Aquinas than either Barth or Jüngel suspects. On the larger issue of the Barthian stance toward tradition, it hardly requires a reactionary outlook to greet with some skepticism Jüngel's reading of theological history, in which the supposedly fundamental truth that God's eternal identity is uniquely defined by the crucifixion has in effect been suppressed or misunderstood by virtually every theologian in history save for Luther, Hegel, and Barth.[34] Indeed, this supposedly Pauline truth (but is it?) was scarcely recognized in most of the New Testament! That Jüngel in defining God as the unity of identity and nonidentity, or as the eternal overcoming of an eternal negativity, has drunk deeply from Schelling and Hegel would be obvious even apart from his repeated praise especially of

---

[30] Jüngel, *Wertlose Wahrheit*, 87–9.
[31] Jüngel, *Gott als Geheimnis*, 292 (215).
[32] Ibid., 305–6 (225).
[33] I argue these claims about Kierkegaard and eternity in more detail in Chapter 3.
[34] Jüngel, *Gott als Geheimnis*, 50–1 (39–40).

the latter.[35] But is it so clear that this is an advance over the "Greek" instincts infusing the Fathers and Scholastics? As for Luther, Jüngel's fealty is expressed in almost every one of his writings. But here, beyond the obvious question of whether Luther quite warrants the overwhelming stature in theology that the Germanic Protestant tradition has tended to grant him, there is the more subtle matter of Luther's own alliances with the Catholic tradition broadly speaking, highlighted by Jüngel's contrastively selective retrieval of him. Even a Thomist can plead for a reading more appreciative than Jüngel's of Luther's affirmation of the hiddenness of the divine essence in abiding tension with, and not resolved by, election and revelation.[36] And while Luther's fierce opposition to the "theologians of glory" can perhaps be turned into a blanket opposition to natural theology along Barth's lines, there is also his equally determined defense of the fleshly availability of God in the Eucharist, a note of true divine "givenness" that followers of Barth should reckon with more sympathetically: less Heidelberg, more Marburg!

Before offering a concluding reflection, it is urgent at this point to reaffirm that none of the critical concerns raised in this chapter around revelation and the divine essence and triunity mean that we have somehow dispensed with Jüngel or his constructive masterpiece (which, to echo his own assessment of Przywara's *Analogia entis*, likewise a book he wished to resist, "cannot be admired enough").[37] In fact, there is so much to praise even in his wider oeuvre, the sermons, the many rich and beautifully crafted essays, and of course that little masterpiece of exposition *God's Being Is in Becoming*, which even as it seemingly ventriloquizes Barth slyly arranges to undercut Barthian repudiations of the Bultmannian legacy by revealing their secret kinship. Even the sympathizer with Aquinas will continue to find more than enough to learn from and savor. Wonderful moments abound, such as his trenchant remarks on theological "relevance," his fascinating suggestions on eschatology, his powerful synthetic reflections on the historical Jesus, and many more.[38] Especially remarkable are the pleas, at once eloquent and exasperated, against the tired invocation of Pascal's "god of the philosophers" complaint and in favor of a theology that intimately joins faith to the rigors of thought, in the closest critical conversation with philosophy's history and concepts.[39] *D'accord*, says the Thomist. And even more than the content of his writings, what is irreplaceable is the space they have afforded in theology for such a cultured and deeply humane voice.

But the questions remain. In attempting to think through the consequences of creation *ex nihilo* along the lines under development in this book, one ends up forced to question Jüngel's reliance upon a Barthian doctrine of revelation; the latter will come to appear a dubious translation of Luther's extreme position on justification by faith into epistemological terms, prompted by an exaggerated allergy to human objectivizing. In its place we should explore a more radical "giving over" of the

---

[35] For the first definition, see Jüngel, *Gottes Sein*, 36 n. 98, quoting Barth. For the second, see Jüngel, *Gott als Geheimnis*, 302–3 (222–3).
[36] Jüngel, *Gott als Geheimnis*, 267–9 (197–8).
[37] Ibid., 357–8 n. 1 (262 n. 1).
[38] Ibid., 2–3 (4–5), 292 (215); Eberhard Jüngel, "The Dogmatic Significance of the Question of the Historical Jesus," in *Theological Essays II*, ed. J. B. Webster (Edinburgh: T&T Clark, 1995), 82–119.
[39] Jüngel, *Gott als Geheimnis*, 61–2 (48); Jüngel, *Gottes Sein*, 128–9.

Word's knowledge into the bodily jostle of history, where the divine self-utterance is really borne by the church in all its sinful misery and hypocrisy, its truth protected from failure ("infallible") not so much by a unique epistemic mechanism as by the continual cunning of providence. On the Trinity, too, one must wonder at the irony of a development whereby the Barthian theological approach that initially provided the greatest impetus for the Protestant recovery of the Nicene doctrine has at Jüngel's hands somehow come close to a deconstruction of the patristic Trinitarian heritage in the name of the Reformation, not unlike the one called for by Schleiermacher.[40] Aquinas shares with the ancient Trinitarian thinkers the conviction that God even as triune is more happily conceived as the unimaginably simple and sheerly actual than as an event defining itself through its own self-alienation. "*Nemo contra deum nisi deus ipse*" was the tagline for much of Jüngel's more daring speculation to the contrary.[41] During the writing of my book on Jüngel, I was taken with this radically decisionist view that rendered the divine being a freely elected achievement, a triumph over a necessarily internalized principle of negativity. Doesn't this mean that the living God is the one who, more than we, truly undergoes death, perfectly and eternally?[42] It was one theologian who (rhetorically) asked that question then; it is the same yet another who thinks he should now answer, "No." In his stirring conclusion to *The Problem of Pain*, in lines that beautifully encapsulate Aquinas' vision of deity, C.S. Lewis says it: the God "who could never have been otherwise" can only be the God who "has no opposite."[43] To the source of all necessity (and hence of all freedom) no countervailing principle is possible, not even an internalized one. In other words, and in reply to Jüngel (and to the final line of my book on him), I would venture to say, *Nullum contrarium dei, ne ipse quidem*.

---

[40] Jüngel, *Gott als Geheimnis*, 507–8 (371).
[41] See especially ibid., 498–9 (363–4), and Eberhard Jüngel, *Ganz Werden: Theologische Erörterungen V* (Tübingen: Mohr Siebeck, 2003), 231–52.
[42] DeHart, *Beyond the Necessary God*, 177.
[43] C. S. Lewis, *The Problem of Pain* (New York: Macmillan, 1943), 142.

6

John Milbank's Divine Comedy: Not Funny Enough

There is something funny, there is something crazy about myth for it shares with the comic and the insane the quality of obsessiveness. Nothing, in principle, is allowed to elude its grasp ... But this obsessiveness, this claim to universality is relativized by the situation ... Myth ... [like] other forms of human speech such as the joke or riddle ... gains its power, knowledge and value from the play between ... We may have to become initiated by the other whom we study and undergo the ordeal of incongruity. For we have often missed what is humane in the other by the very seriousness of our quest.

J. Z. Smith
Map is Not Territory

As St. John shrank from baptizing Christ, but it was required of him so that human action and divine action should coexist, so reason and nature remain immanent in grace. Let no one, then, suppress them.

Maurice Blondel
Letter on Apologetics

In one episode of his shrewd narrative meditation on the afterlife (called *The Great Divorce* in protest against Blake's *Marriage of Heaven and Hell*), C. S. Lewis stages a posthumous confrontation between two souls who had been artists in life. The blessed one tries to entice the damned one to abandon his alienation from divine Reality, appealing to that vital relation to Beauty that originally motivated their creative work on earth. (To pursue Beauty truly, it is suggested, is, effectively even if unknowingly, to aim oneself toward God.) But the attempt fails; the lost artist has ultimately staked his soul on the triumph of his personal vision of beauty rather than upon Beauty itself.

"My friend," said the Spirit [the beatified artist], "Don't you know?" "Know what?" "That you and I are already completely forgotten on the Earth?" "Eh? What's that?" exclaimed the Ghost [the lost artist], disengaging its arm, "Do you mean those damned Neo-Regionalists have won after all?" "Lord love you, yes!" said the Spirit, once more shaking and shining with laughter ... "We're dead out of fashion." "I must be off at once," said the Ghost. "Let me go! ... I must write an article. There must be a manifesto. We must start a periodical. We must have publicity. Let me go. This is beyond a joke!"[1]

The scene is as comic as it is painful. And, Lewis reminds us, the theologian no less than the artist is faced with the same fateful tradeoff: "There have been men before now who got so interested in proving the existence of God that they came to care nothing for God Himself."[2]

Is there a methodological analogue to this fatal existential incongruity? Prior to and foundational for the expression of God in an individual's life is the communal witness of God's people, the church. As the church seeks, in ever new ways fitted to its circumstances, to display to the world through its collective life the God disclosed to it and present in it, theology seeks the intellectual articulation of this communally referenced God and her relation to the human present. Among the basic criteria for this articulation will be the cultural terms within which this articulation will prove most comprehensible and effective. But here a new version of Lewis's problem also comes into play. Prior to its selection of specific ideas or language for its proclamation and reflection, theology is informed by deep assumptions and expectations in regard to the very nature of its cultural engagement with the world. What does it expect from the post-Christian society of the present, for example, and how can it employ its cultural resources to work out a faithfulness that can be "legible"? What constitutes effectiveness or "success" if the goal is not just cultural diffusion or intellectual persuasion but a letting become visible of God through the life of a public community? Ultimately, what is the political and cultural "stance" of theology vis-à-vis the "world" that will allow the harmonious display of the particular God to which it claims to witness; and what stances risk falling into "performative contradiction" with this display, no matter what their accompanying cultural or intellectual promise?

In methodological terms, the question might takes this form: what relations hold between the conceptual articulations of Christian teaching about God and salvation, and the strategy and rhetoric informing the discursive productions presenting those articulations? In service to Christian witness, or ecclesial transparency to God before the world's gaze, theology will seek to harmonize the manner of address with the content. Theological communication will prove at once most faithful and most effective when there is discernible resonance, rather than discord, between the account it provides of God's way with the world and the "stance" toward the world rhetorically assumed within it, between substance and style. ("Style" here would signify not just expressive technique but the entire range of assumptions about the nature and goal of a communication that is implicit within it.) In short, the stylistic question is as much about faithfulness as it is about effectiveness. The present chapter makes no claim to present rigorous reflections on this issue generally. It only seeks to suggest one way of connecting certain truths about the Christian God with an account of the church's

---

[1] C. S. Lewis, *The Great Divorce* (New York: Macmillan, 1946), 81–2.
[2] Ibid., 68.

engagement with the human cultural world, an account that performatively supports or exhibits those truths rather than undermining them.

John Milbank, one of a handful of the most creative and powerful minds in Western Christian theology at the turn of the twenty-first century, has produced an extremely impressive body of work. These writings are particularly useful for the present discussion because they represent a conscious attempt to supply his quite original theological vision with a fitting set of assumptions about the kind of cultural engagement this vision demands.[3] According to Graham Ward's keen analysis, this mode of engagement can broadly be described as an "allegorization" of secular discourses, that is, an unveiling "of their [disavowed] dependence upon metaphysical and theological assumptions." Like Dante's great poem, Milbank's *Theology and Social Theory* "embraces secular discourse … within a theological metanarrative," leading Ward to characterize Milbank's work as a contemporary *Divina Commedia*.[4] With all due respect for this achievement, Milbank's understanding of theology's mode of cultural engagement will serve the present chapter as a foil for what I take to be a more satisfying way of solving the problem. Nothing like a critique of Milbank's important project is provided, or attempted; indeed, a theological or metaphysical scheme as detailed and encompassing as his is not subject to refutation as such, short of the presentation of an alternative scheme of at least comparable scope and coherence. The focus here will instead be on indicating, merely in outline, an alternative approach to Milbank's: a different reading of the import of certain central Christian claims, coupled with a style of cultural engagement that befits them.

The alternative laid out here repeatedly takes its orientation from the writings of Rowan Williams, another vitally important contemporary voice in Christian theology.

---

[3] Although Milbank's texts (along with those productions allied with or taking off from his project, earlier united under the banner of "radical orthodoxy") have received widespread and intense discussion, much of the vigorous polemic surrounding them so far fails, it seems to me, to appreciate the scope and depth of his theological accomplishment. There are many possible reasons for this failure. One is the intimidating abstraction and complexity of his writing, along with the formidable range and depth of the arguments, both of which encourage among readers piecemeal rejoinders, wary distance, or defensive dismissal. When his work is not simply ignored, the critical literature suggests it is easier to render peremptory (often stereotyped) judgments from afar than to critically engage it in detail. Another factor lies in the (real or perceived) nature of the brash political vision now associated with his work, aggravated by his public interventions on touchy social questions. But more relevant to this chapter is a third possible reason: the rhetorically constructed "voice" that speaks in his texts, and the intellectually aggressive subject-position it implicitly enunciates, can be off-putting. The resulting irritation evident among many readers may well be, at least partly, intended by Milbank, but it has hindered his serious reception. For all these reasons, much future work remains in assessing his overall significance and debating the many specific arguments he has provided, presumably when the time arrives for calmer judgments. As for the position developed in the present volume as a whole, it shares Milbank's deep yet creative commitment to Catholic orthodoxy; his critical engagement with ancient, medieval, and modern culture; and his drive toward an encompassing speculative scheme; but many of its basic assumptions are obviously different. These differing assumptions lead in the present chapter to a demurral from some of his most characteristic (and "radical") positions. Such specific disagreements do not alter my overall assessment: the routine hostility or, increasingly, indifference Milbank's work has widely met with represents a lost opportunity for contemporary theology.

[4] Graham Ward, "John Milbank's Divina Commedia," *New Blackfriars* 73 (1992): 311.

Both Milbank and Williams begin from the basic claim of classic Christianity: God, the unique and absolute creator of all things, has graciously designed, through his incarnation in Jesus, to bestow on human beings not just healing for the wounds of their willed alienation but (astonishingly) a share in her very deity that enables a personal communion with him utterly beyond anything available to the created cosmos as such. God gives herself, then, to us; but in created terms what, exactly, is given? God is given as Christ and the Spirit; but how, exactly, does that work? In their respective approaches to these questions, Milbank and Williams begin from a similar place but end up laying the emphases quite differently, and implicit within that difference, I wish to suggest, lies the key to their distinct assumptions about the necessary shape of Christian witness in our time.

So then, the different models of this latter problem (the relation of Christian claims to the cultural "stance" of theology) are rooted in different theological construals of God's self-gift or of grace. This difference will be specified by comparing certain claims of Milbank and Williams, with Williams's incipient approach being elaborated and considerably extended along my own lines. The divergence at issue might be imaged by the following question: In graciously giving himself to the creature, does God have to "come to" the creature *within* the "worldly" world (Williams), or rather has she always already, as it were, given himself to the creature *through and as* the world as "divinized" (Milbank)? This is the eschatological conundrum proposed by the piano scene from the Marx Brothers film *Animal Crackers* (1930), where, well into Chico's stately, interminable rendition of "I'm Daffy Over You" the following exchange takes place:

CHICO: I can't think of the finish.
GROUCHO: That's strange, and I can't think of anything else.

As human we are all oriented to God as our perfect end, our finality; but does this mean that the divine self-gift is "somehow" already given, its effects reaching back to constitute the creature as its receiver, and, on the plane of human culture, already anticipating the true meaning within every human expression? Something like this is Milbank's position, as will be argued. For him, the divine self-gift is so overwhelming in its transcendence that it has already, from the beginning as it were, qualified and permeated every created immanent horizon. In its various moments, the giving of this gift is marked by an ultimate identity between the receiver and what is given; God's gift does not "encounter" a recipient with an integral identity but rather pre-constitutes its identity as that of the receiver of just this gift.

Or do things stand differently? Is there another way to understand the relation between the created world and God's gift of herself to it? An alternative picture would have God's self-gift arriving as "something more" within an already-given world; its arrival would be, as it were, unanticipated by the world (though befitting it). As a human end, even after its initial advent, it would remain so incommensurable a consummation of human nature as to require divine disclosure for it to be thought. The ultimate goal of the chapter will be, by first sketching out an alternative to Milbank's account of grace along just such lines, to eventually suggest an alternative to his strategic positioning of theology within human culture. This two-stage approach reflects the assumption with which we began: a coherent theological position involves a harmonic relation between the way Christian claims about God and salvation are understood, and the way theology imagines and theorizes the church's, and its own, cultural transactions with the world.[5]

The chapter is divided into six sections. Milbank's cultural strategy accords with certain speculative interpretations of the doctrines of God, creation, and grace; hence, the outline of a systematically distinct position will first need to set up alternative interpretations of those doctrines, before going on to suggest how an alternative mode of cultural interaction can be envisioned arising from them. As already indicated, certain ideas of Williams will provide initial direction for our alternative. Section I ("Two Paths from Balthasar") will compare claims of Williams and Milbank arising from an early period that seem crucial for their future theological paths; against the background of several areas of agreement I will trace the evidence of a divergence concerning the cultural stance of theology, largely rooted in Williams's developing Christology. The mature fruits of this incipient divergence will be discussed in the next four sections, even as the doctrinal focus shifts; that is, attention will be directed to the doctrines of creation and grace as at least equally important as Christology for understanding both Milbank's position and the proposed alternative. The Thomist inspiration of the conceptual framework used to develop Williams's alternative to Milbank will also become clear in these sections. Specifically, Section II ("Mere Being") will be concerned with the doctrine of creation, and Section III ("Mere Nature") with the doctrine of grace. With the dogmatic bases thus laid, Section IV ("Mere Culture") will at last be able to turn to the question of the nature of Christian claims within the world of human meaning, returning to Williams to show how he already strongly signaled a different answer to this question than Milbank, before going on to argue that Williams's understanding accords well with the doctrinal interpretations outlined (under Aquinas' inspiration) in the previous two sections. The claim, to anticipate the overall argument, will be that in Milbank's fundamentally "anticipatory" scheme, God's self-gift is ontologized and naturalized in such a way that its transcendence can be strategized or deployed in the church's cultural transactions. By contrast, in the more "historical" alternative, God's self-gift arrives in such a way that "mere" being and "mere" nature are preserved in their integrity; an interrogative or mythic "tactics" becomes the fitting ecclesial stance, as opposed to Milbank's metanarrative "strategy." Section V will probe the ludic or comic dimensions of Christian witness brought to light by this stance, while Section VI will sum up the argument of the chapter as a whole.

---

[5] The position developed here in response to Milbank, beyond pursuing suggestions of Rowan Williams, relies extensively upon Thomas Aquinas. In so doing it reads Aquinas in a way that is rejected by Milbank, trading upon the strong distinctions between nature and grace, and between the natural and the supernatural, which Milbank has worked so vigorously to overturn. I have presented Milbank's interpretations of Aquinas and responded to them in some detail. Paul DeHart, *Aquinas and Radical Orthodoxy: A Critical Inquiry* (New York: Routledge, 2012).

I. Two Paths from Balthasar

Von Balthasar's highly implausible claim [is] that the success of Christianity has wiped out all other forms of religion and metaphysics ... This is a pretty wild story.

Fergus Kerr

In order to understand the development of the differing approaches of Williams and Milbank, it is important to begin with certain shared commitments that appear in their writings from an early period.[6] Two are significant in this context, the first being their shared admiration for Hans Urs von Balthasar, and in particular the large-scale theological interpretation and critique of Western metaphysics found in the fourth and fifth volumes of *The Glory of the Lord*.[7] Balthasar's concluding reflections appear to have been especially suggestive for both writers, and Williams's rendition of its crucial themes in his 1986 paper "Balthasar and Rahner" strikingly foreshadows the ontological shape of Milbank's still developing project. On one side there is the broad acceptance of Heidegger's critique of Western metaphysics, tempered by a sharp verdict on his ontology as "nihilistic and tragic," rendering being ultimately as "an organic, impersonal and alien process of fate or necessity." The Christian alternative proposed by Balthasar will involve a "fundamental Platonism," where Being grasped as "formal limitlessness" cannot possibly "be the source of beings, of concrete forms"; instead, they are sourced in the triune divine Being as "particular creative intentions, dependent upon the eternal Logos who is the divine ground of the possibility of all otherness, all differentiation."[8] The result is a unified interrelation of beings "in which beauty is intelligible," and a subjective orientation in which "the fundamental cognitive moment is the apprehension of participation" in God.[9]

Williams, strongly sympathetic to Balthasar's critique of Rahner throughout the paper, concludes with two significant descriptions of the Christological assumptions

---

[6] Although at several points throughout this chapter I highlight what seem to be tensions and conflicts between the published ideas of the two authors, I neither presuppose nor imply anything regarding the personal relations of acquaintance, influence, or disagreement between Milbank and Williams themselves, a topic on which I am uninformed, and which is anyway superfluous for the exposition. (The two authors have referenced each other numerous times, almost always appreciatively. It might also be noted that Milbank studied with Williams when the latter taught at Westcott House in Cambridge, around 1978–80.) The discussion is based solely on their publications, and the convergence or divergence of their ideas as perceptible on that basis. The concern here is with claims and arguments, not personalities.

[7] Hans Urs von Balthasar, *The Glory of the Lord: A Theological Aesthetics*, ed. Joseph Fessio, S.J. and John Riches, vol. 4: *The Realm of Metaphysics in Antiquity* (Edinburgh: T&T Clark, 1989), and vol. 5: *The Realm of Metaphysics in the Modern Age* (Edinburgh: T&T Clark, 1991). Williams was deeply engaged with this material in the late 1980s, as he was part of the team translating these volumes into English.

[8] Milbank would single out the coda to the metaphysics volumes as the place where Balthasar "brilliantly contended" for the position Williams identifies here, that of absolute being as the unity of infinity and determination. John Milbank, "Can a Gift Be Given? Prolegomena to a Future Trinitarian Metaphysic," *Modern Theology* 11 (1995): 153–4.

[9] Rowan Williams, "Balthasar and Rahner," in *The Analogy of Beauty*, ed. John Riches (Edinburgh: T&T Clark, 1986), 21–2.

driving Balthasar's reflections. "Whether there is ... a metaphysics of the Cross [i.e. an ontological vision that would situate the conflict of divine goodness and human tragedy without "philosophical evasion"], is precisely the issue to which Balthasar's monumental *oeuvre* addresses itself." Then shortly after: "Balthasar's Christ remains a question to all human answers."[10] A metaphysics of the Cross and Christ as universal interrogation: two powerful images for the systematic theological role of Christology. Further essays of Williams would begin energetically exploring Christology in the next few years, but Milbank, too was not idle; the late 1980s was the period of gestation for his own "monumental" contribution *Theology and Social Theory* (1991). But as each sought to exploit Balthasar's weighty insights, their paths began to show a serious divergence.

The roots of this divergence can be traced not only to differing appropriations of Balthasar but also to differing developments of the other commitment shared between Williams and Milbank. One of the most characteristic positions maintained early on by Williams was an insistence that the Christian story, and the older story of Israel from within which it arose, can only be understood if the notion of divine "revelation" is seen in the closest connection with, indeed in some sense as derivative of, the notion of a "people of God." The fundamental meaning of Christian existence is not to be found in texts or doctrines, nor directly "read off" objective events; rather, all these are given only within the social-interpretive labors constituting the community in which God has chosen to disclose his "name." Whatever is meant by revelation or salvation is finally located in the struggles of a human collective to image or represent, in its institutions and rites, its shared meanings and social patterns of belonging, who "God" is.[11] This special sociocultural orientation marks Milbank's work just as deeply as that of Williams, and it provides a vital element in his unique elaboration on the Balthasarian ontological quest. Surprisingly, the key to the divergence in the positions of Williams and Milbank lies in the different ways each brings together the two things they have in common: the debt to Balthasar and the communal understanding of revelation.

The roots of Milbank's approach, which can only be sketched here, can already be seen in a very early essay (1982) on "Christological Poetics."[12] As the human (hence cultural) event identical with the eternal self-representation of God, Jesus Christ is the divine fulfillment of all human creative intent, that is, of that work of *poiesis* by which human existence is constituted as a labor of creative interpretation. In his life-act he realizes the fullness of human meaning as charity. Moreover, the interpretive response of his followers over time amounts in its own right to an ongoing actualization of his fulfillment of human meaning, thus sharing in it. Notable here is the participative dimension, whereby William's emphasis on the community itself as the disclosure of God is turned by Milbank into a claim that the church extends and realizes Jesus's divinity as the act of consummating human meaning. Within a few years Milbank

---

[10] Ibid., 34.
[11] See, e.g., Rowan Williams, "The Finality of Christ," in *On Christian Theology* (Oxford: Blackwell, 2000), 98–9.
[12] John Milbank, "A Christological Poetics," in *The Word Made Strange* (Oxford: Blackwell, 1997), 123–44.

had elaborated this vision more fully, suggesting that the church's communal cultural practice of continuing Christ's consummation of human meaning implies and requires the explicit deployment of an ontological scheme. "The *logic* of Christianity involves the claim that the 'interruption' of history by Christ and his bride, the Church, is the most fundamental of events, interpreting all other events."[13] The history of Jesus as God incarnate must inform, and can only be effectively present through, a community whose practice is marked by absolute difference from every other, incipiently nihilistic communal practice. This historical community with its ethical structure stands as a (fragmentary but real and continually realized) achievement of the fullness of human belonging together, from which fullness it is in a position to deconstruct and correct every other social and cultural arrangement. This unique status, in turn, is licensed by an ontology that articulates the "framework of reference implicit" within the communal history, tracing the ecclesial singularity to the donation (in Jesus) to that community of the knowledge and presence of the unique creator God.[14]

In this way, Milbank was pursuing his own version of that "metaphysics" of the Christ-event that, according to Williams, was the goal of Balthasar's huge output; and he was situating the pursuit within that self- and world-interpreting communal practice that Williams argued was integral to God's self-disclosure. But a surprise awaits, for during the same period in which Milbank was developing this ontology of Christ, Williams was rethinking the very desirability of that kind of project. The catalyst seems to have been some brief comments found in an essay by Cornelius Ernst.[15]

Citing modern belief's unavoidable awareness of the historical relativity of the different theological schemes developed over time, Ernst called for a radical interpretation of "the *meaning* of this historical succession of theologies" that would not presuppose any one of their viewpoints, but would situate itself within the horizon of "*the* theological problem of the meaning of God and man for one another."[16] It might be thought that the disclosure of God in Jesus Christ should give the theologian confidence in tackling this question, but Ernst warns against underestimating the difficulty; it is in explaining this difficulty that he provides the brief, almost cryptic distinction that would become seminal for Williams's own Christological reflections during this period. Are Christians, even as possessing the gift of Christ, now in a position to answer the question of creation, incarnation and salvation, of "the meaning of God and man for one another"? Yes and no.

> The substantive ("ontic") answer to this question we already have in Jesus Christ, and can have no other. It is the ("ontological") meaning of this substantive meaning we must continually search for without expecting any final answer ... [The articulation of this ontological meaning] could only exist as a total human

---

[13] John Milbank, *Theology and Social Theory: Beyond Secular Reason* (Oxford: Blackwell, 1990), 388.
[14] Ibid., 381.
[15] Ernst had been a Dominican teaching at Blackfriars, Oxford, from the mid-1960s until his retirement in 1975. A couple of years after his death in 1977 there appeared a volume of his essays, including the one that caught Williams's attention: Cornelius Ernst OP, *Multiple Echo: Explorations in Theology*, ed. Fergus Kerr OP and Timothy Radcliffe OP (London: Darton, Longman & Todd, 1979).
[16] Ibid., 85.

culture, the progressive discovery of a single human identity in Christ as the historical process of the diverse but related processes of self-discovery going on in the distinct cultures all over the globe.[17]

Three elements of this remarkably compact statement make themselves felt in Williams's reflections: the distinction between conceiving Christ as humanity's "ultimate" meaning in substantive versus ontological terms; the claim that the latter (ontological) conception in its universality could only be articulated as ingredient within a universal communal culture; and the realization that such a culture is not yet here, but is being built within history, and that Christians as such, with their gift of Christ, have been given an integral role to play alongside all other humans in building such a culture.

No less than Milbank, Williams affirms that in Christ and his Spirit, God truly "gives" himself into the world, particularly the social world of human meaning-making. As divinely perfected human, Jesus clearly has universal human significance; but in what way is this universality, this finality, accessible to Christians short of the eschaton? Having it in one sense, are they not still seeking it in another? Pondering this problem suggested by Ernst's distinction apparently prompted Williams to a serious rethinking of the entire enterprise of constructing an ontology of Christ as consummating or subordinating all human meaning, the attempt, as he also put it, to articulate a "cosmic Christ."[18] He had earlier characterized the Christological engine of Balthasar's project both as a search for a "metaphysics of the Cross" and as the promotion of Christ as "a question to all human answers." Now it seems that these Christological modalities are in conflict with one another. Or at least that a proposed "ontology" that shows how Christ "already" incorporates all human meaning is dangerously premature for a pilgrim church; it wrongly anticipates a universality that has not yet arrived, even granting the arrival of the Christ. No, in Christ the church rather possesses the universal "interrogation" to be put to all communities of meaning, including its own (a particular concern of Williams), in cooperative pursuit of a self-critical, non-self-possessed and non-tribal human culture.[19] Above all, such an interrogative process would be part of a history: it would take time, it would be filled with unanticipated turns, and it would involve inevitable failures, but every encounter would become an opportunity for the church to learn anew about its own "final" truth from the world beyond it.

Thus, from similar starting points, Milbank and Williams had by around 1990 arrived at what look like divergent assessments of the "stance" of Christian culture

---

[17] Ibid.
[18] The central document of this rethinking is the above referenced "Finality of Christ" from 1990; Milbank's *Theology and Social Theory* appeared the same year.
[19] Williams, "Finality of Christ," 94, 96, 102–3. This is not at all a rejection of Balthasar tout court. In fact, other motifs identified in Balthasar by Williams might also have played a role in suggesting or reinforcing William's position. The emphasis on drama, for example, or the notion of contemplativity and non-mastery, particularly if the latter becomes an ideal not only in the Christian stance toward the natural world but also the world of human meaning. See Williams, "Balthasar and Rahner," 23–4 (on "contemplative receptivity") and 26–7, 32–3 (on drama).

and of theology vis-à-vis the world.[20] A more detailed exploration of the nature of this tension must wait till the fourth section. The next two sections will be devoted to developing the doctrinal positions that underlie or connect with these different assessments. As seen, for Williams Christology was apparently the doctrinal consideration playing the key differentiating role. In Sections II and III, however, attention will shift to doctrines more central for the "stance" promoted by Milbank. Theology must become what he calls a "metadiscourse," that is, it can and must seek discursive mastery over all non-theological discourses; it must especially reject the "false humility" that seeks accommodations to "secular" reason or that countenances any truly *fundamental* challenge from non-theological disciplines or philosophical arguments. Why is this stance required? The answer might surprise: "Once theology surrenders its claim to be a metadiscourse, it cannot any longer articulate the word of the creator God."[21] To understand this lapidary formula, it will be necessary to investigate in the second and third sections some of Milbank's speculative interpretations of God, creation and grace. Only then can it be suggested in Section IV how these doctrinal commitments contribute to his insistence on theology as metadiscourse.

Of course, the true goal of these sections is not to analyze Milbank's thought; it is to suggest an approach to creation and grace that differs from his, an alternative reading of these doctrines that can then fund an alternative account of theology's cultural stance. As citations will show, the account of what witness to the world is like eventually developed (in the fourth section) will elaborate upon, while remaining fundamentally in sympathy with, Williams's reflections in this area. Sections II and III, in contrast, will abandon discussion of Williams temporarily in order to ally with Aquinas against Milbank's doctrinal speculations. Even so, those two sections can be seen as proceeding along a path Williams already pointed out, even if only suggestively. A passage in "The Finality of Christ" lays out the very themes that will be central in the doctrinal exploration of creation and grace. Invoking the powerful reflections of the French theologian Jacques Pohier, Williams cites a series of claims that begin with Christology but end up with the creator God that Christ reveals: "The resurrection of Jesus Christ and the Pentecost of his Spirit do not mean that Jesus Christ is henceforward

---

[20] There are other tensions not discussed here. A fascinating example concerns Williams's warning against (presumably poststructuralist) philosophical epistemologies that amount to "linguistic idealism" ("Balthasar and Rahner," 24). Milbank, for his part, has not hidden his sympathies for this strand of "postmodern" French speculation. See John Milbank, "'Postmodern Critical Augustinianism': A Short *Summa* in Forty-Two Responses to Unasked Questions," *Modern Theology* 7 (1991): 225–37 at 225. His retort to Williams's concern is that theological realism is actually the enemy of philosophical realism (i.e., it will inevitably appear as "idealism" from the latter's perspective). See Milbank, *Theology and Social Theory*, 5–6, and "Intensities," *Modern Theology* 15 (1999): 487. But for Williams, part of the stress on a "contemplative" approach to reality (following Balthasar) is the demand to recognize the opposition, the intractability of reality as given, checking and overflowing our linguistic constructions of it. This is perhaps a kind of fealty on Williams's part to the theologically informed epistemic realism of Donald MacKinnon's thought (Williams's partial critique of the latter notwithstanding). See Rowan Williams, "Trinity and Ontology," in *On Christian Theology*, 148–66. Milbank remains with the rejection of "givenness" in favor of the poetic, interpretive shaping of the real (there are only interpretations).

[21] Milbank, *Theology and Social Theory*, 1.

the answer to everything ... They indicate that God bears witness that the question [N.B.] raised by Jesus Christ is the one by which God manifests himself ... Jesus Christ does not manifest himself as being the totality of meaning ... [Thus Christians] do not have omnipotence of meaning ...." So God is indeed unsurpassably given, disclosed, to Christians. But who is this God? Williams's summary of what Pohier is saying can serve this chapter almost as an epigraphic retort to Milbank's "metadiscourse" of the creator: Christ reveals "a God who is authentically creator of a world because this God [echoing a phrase of Pohier] does not wish to be everything.... Jesus 'uniquely' reveals the God whose nature is not to make the claim of unique revelation as total and authoritative meaning."[22]

These lines adumbrate the relation between God's mode of creating and saving the world on the one hand (topic of the next two sections), and the cultural pretensions of theology on the other (the concern of the fourth section). Indeed, Williams's choice of interlocutors obliquely suggests the prime theological resource for this exploration. Both Ernst and Pohier were Dominicans, each in his own way deeply inspired by the theologian of their order, Thomas Aquinas. Similar inspiration will be sought here; themes of Aquinas will be drawn on again and again to construct models of creation and of grace alternative to those of Milbank, so that in the end a model of Christian cultural engagement in tension with his, but in harmony with Williams, will suggest itself. Of course, Milbank, too, draws on Aquinas in his own way. He stands with Aquinas in affirming that, in Jesus Christ, the creator God gives himself to the creation in such a way that it is elevated to a direct participation of the Triune relations constituting the divine being. This self-gift requires a bestowal upon creation that transcends its natural capacities, that is, the "supernatural"; and it results in the creation's transparency to the triune essence, as the intra-divine processions take up residence within it. But how best to understand this self-gift and the resultant transparency is the key question for Sections II and III; what it does and does not license the church to claim over against the world can then be assessed in Section IV.

Precisely how this discussion will develop defies brief summary, but the created image of God (*imago Dei*) as analyzed by Aquinas can serve as a connecting leitmotif, the three forms of the image corresponding to the three sections. As just indicated, the argument with Milbank concerns how grace perfects created nature, enabling the indwelling of uncreated Being within the creature. For Aquinas, the transparency of creation to the triune relations, their participated representation in the world, is inextricably linked with created intellect and created will, the mark of angels and (central to our concern) of human beings.[23] Since these two capacities involve a twofold intending of being in its universality, the cognitive intention of Truth linked with the desiring intention of Goodness, I will in what follows sometimes use "intentionality" as a shorthand expression for what Aquinas usually calls the rational or intellectual creature or the human being. Indeed, the ultimate end or goal served by the existence of intentional being within creation, the reason for its creation as a

---

[22] Williams, "Finality of Christ," 104–5.
[23] The questions of angelic intentionality, and of angelic beatitude, are not at issue here. The potentially complicating discussions in Aquinas will be bracketed.

kind, is to "image" God specifically.[24] For Aquinas, the focal analogy for grasping the triunity of God lies in intentional production and relation: it is most closely likened to a unity of God as intentional activity (Father), God as object of his cognitive intention of himself (Son), and God as object of his affective or desiring intention of himself (Spirit). Consequently, the created representation of the Trinity will replicate these intentions; the human being as "*imago Dei*" will understand or intellectually see God *qua* God, and will love God *qua* God. But why are there three forms or stages of the created image of God? Because this image of God in the human being exists in three, progressively more perfect modes: first, simply as the possession of intellect and will, that is, as the (unactualized) capacity for these intentions that amounts to "a natural aptitude for understanding and loving God"; second, as actualizing this intentional capacity, actually knowing and loving God, albeit imperfectly, through the gift of grace in this life; third, as achieving this knowledge and love perfectly, after death "in glory."[25]

With this threefold distinction in mind, it is possible to restate in different terms the structure and the broad thesis of the three sections to follow; these form the heart of the chapter's argument toward a proposal concerning theology's cultural stance, while the fifth section draws the "droll" implications of that stance. Section II in effect explores the first mode of the image, the creature as "*capax dei*." It takes issue with Milbank over his tendency to merge grace with a general ontology, to distribute the capacity or possibility to be transparent to the triune God or to represent the divine self-gift throughout created being as such; by contrast, it will insist upon Aquinas' strict localization within human, intentional being of the capacity to receive divinizing grace. Section III, in turn, is keyed to Aquinas' second mode of imaging God, looking at the actual bestowal of supernatural grace and its relation to nature. Here Milbank pursues a model of grace as intrinsic and, indeed, essential (i.e., definitive for the very nature of the human); the response will play up those elements of Aquinas' account that picture the bestowal of saving grace as less intrinsic than adventitious, less essential than accidental (using these terms in their Aristotelian sense). In both these sections it will be argued that for Aquinas the worldly advent of God involves a gap or "play" between, on the one hand, a defined created zone of structural or essential ambiguity vis-à-vis the divine gift, and, on the other hand, its localized mediation into transparency to that gift (i.e., the resolution of the ambiguity) by way of cosmic process or history: totality, temporality, and contingency. The different models of creation and grace (Milbank's and the proposed alternative) developed in these second and third sections will issue, in turn, into two quite distinct programs of Christian cultural intervention (the subject of Section IV). Here Aquinas' third, perfected mode of human imaging of God will come into its own, but only by its deferral. The crucial realization that the full triune presence within the creature is not yet an embodied possibility within the current order of creation, not even within the community of Christ's body, will provide the rationale for an alternative to Milbank's picture of the total mastery of Christian discourse.

---

[24] Aquinas differentiates human intentionality as "image" from the broader "similitude" that all creatures bear to God. *STh* I q. 93 aa. 1 and 2.

[25] *STh* I q. 93 a. 4.

II. Mere Being

Candidly speaking, and I do want to keep strictly to the point, by the way, but I feel I simply must explain that Fate, so to speak, treats me absolutely without mercy, just like a storm treats a small ship, as it were. I mean to say, supposing I'm wrong, for instance, then why should I wake up this morning and suddenly see a simply colossal spider sitting on my chest? like this ... [Makes a gesture with both hands.] Or supposing I pick up a jug to have a drink of kvass, there's sure to be something frightful inside it, such as a cockroach. [Pause.] Have you read Buckle?

Anton Chekhov
The Cherry Orchard

One of Milbank's better known positions is that for Christian belief there can be no merely rational discourse of being-as-such; any such "immanent" attempt to speak of being must bring fatal distortions in its train, since created being can be adequately articulated only from its relation to the Triune creator. As he forcefully puts it, "Christian theology ... utterly appropriates to itself the ontological task."[26] A theological ontology will be one where "the 'beingness' of finite being is always referred to transcendent *esse*," the divine act of being; this is opposed to an "immanent ontology, where one does not have to explain the essences of this world ultimately in terms of the lure of the ineffable," that is, their constitutive desire for union with God.[27] In other words, there must be no aspect or "space" within created being that is not fundamentally *defined* by its origin from and drive for return to God. Hence, only the doctrine of Triune creation gives a theologically relevant account of being; faith can neither be informed by, nor even allow the cogency of, the claims of a merely philosophical ontology.

What results from this theological appropriation? Milbank has given scattered hints that suffice to indicate at least the outline of a properly theological ontology.[28] With Balthasar he often casts his discussion of creation in terms of Heidegger's distinction of Being and beings, drawing upon the former's ontology of creation in which beings participate, not in an immanent act of being (i.e., "*ens commune*" as sheer indeterminate existence, negating essential differentiation), but in the "subsistent being" of God, in which "plenitude of actuality" amounts to the coincidence of existence with "infinitely determined essence." Milbank interprets this relation of existence and essence as in fact a Trinitarian distinction, with the Father as the endless *giving* of existence, forever arriving not at a mere fulfillment of potency that would "close" the divine being but rather receiving himself as the likewise endless *determination* of his "other," the Son. Crucially, for Milbank this eternal triune relation of total actuality (existence) and determinate content (essence) is continued in the act of creation, such that "creatures ... only *are* as sharing in God's arrival"; in creation God continues to be the infinite giving

---

[26] Milbank, "Can a Gift Be Given," 131–2. This is arguably one of the areas in which Balthasar has been a decisive influence upon Milbank, even if the latter develops in his own way the former's insistence upon a theological appropriation of metaphysics.

[27] John Milbank, *The Suspended Middle: Henri de Lubac and the Debate concerning the Supernatural* (Grand Rapids, MI: William B. Eerdmans, 2005), 29–30.

[28] For the account given in this paragraph, see Milbank, "Can a Gift be Given," 153–4.

of existence *as* the infinite giving of determinacy. Beings as such, in their givenness by being *qua* being, are constituted by and exhibit this fecundity of the Trinity.

A number of metaphysical emphases found in Milbank can be closely connected with this account of created being as Triune participation. On the one hand, the creature's very identity as recipient of the gift of being is itself given, hence the creature's existence is *radically* donated and, as it were, not truly its own; on the other, this ceaseless giving is construed as an endless play of determinacy. One result of this speculative scheme is the inherent nothingness of the creature in itself: "The Creature only is, as manifesting the divine glory, as acknowledging its own nullity and reflected brilliance."[29] That is, the total existence of creatures must be construed as nothing but their "general ontological drawing back towards God": "Beings only *exist* as longing in their own mode for God." Milbank's claim is not that all beings *have* such a call but rather that they are *nothing but* that call, it essentially defines their being; the zero sum logic here is intentional, for he equates their *existence* as desire for God with their being "nothing of themselves."[30]

A second result, closely linked to the first, is the systemic metaphysical demotion of the subsistent, identifiable thing; the totality of the creature's givenness is understood in such a way that its distinctive shape and agency as recipient is overwhelmed, the ceaseless flow of creative determinations meanwhile eliding all stable identities. Creation means "suspicio[n] of … fixed 'essences,'" envisioning "a reality without substance, composed only of relational differences and ceaseless alterations."[31] Third and finally, any distinction between the mutually limiting components of created reality and their ordering as parts of the whole, any notion of inherent structure, comes close to dissolution. This is because the goodness radically bestowed upon creation by an infinite God escapes the logic "of scarcity, of limited being." The goodness of the whole is the goodness of every locus and moment, and it is our feeble imagination that would assign it in greater quantity to "the whole," or to an "end" eventually arrived at, for at any point God can bring about a good greater than the whole.[32]

As is the case with Milbank's theology more generally, on occasion Aquinas is read in ways that provide some support for these particular claims; but at other moments Milbank indicates that he might be going beyond Aquinas, and freely draws on other resources from the tradition. In response, a contrasting ontological picture will now be outlined that relies more broadly on Aquinas, and takes issue with some of Milbank's

---

[29] Milbank, "Can a Gift be Given," 135. Cf. Milbank, *Suspended Middle*, 52.

[30] Milbank, *Suspended Middle*, 26–8. Aquinas' language here need not be construed in the way Milbank does. Yes, Aquinas knows that the creature "taken in itself" is nothing (*STh* I/II q. 109 a. 2 ad 2: *in se considerata est nihil*), but he also knows that "being created is not part of the *ratio* or definition of created being, i.e. participated being" (*STh* I q. 44 a. 1 ad 1), else the very notion of being as such would denote creatureliness, and uncreated *ens* would be impossible. The language of "nothing in itself" is further clarified by *De veritate* q. 8 a. 7 ad 12: "nothing" does not describe the essence of the creature, rather the point is that creatures would not exist in any way or at any moment apart from God's agency. In other words, the term "nothing" tells us nothing about what any creature, as such, is.

[31] Milbank, "Postmodern Critical Augustinianism," 267. Cf. Milbank, "Can a Gift Be Given," 137: In a "theological ontology" relations will be at least on the same level as substances, and in fact "one might want to dispense with, or downgrade," the latter.

[32] John Milbank, "Enclaves, or Where is the Church?" *New Blackfriars* 73 (1992): 349–50.

more contestable or selective readings of him. It will not necessarily be utterly opposed to Milbank's at every point, but it is bound to display serious divergences from it. The emphases will be placed differently, with consequent differences in the inferences drawn. There are two features of Aquinas' thinking that will here be highlighted in pursuing a different path toward theological ontology. The first is the role of organic order, or of parts adapted to the whole, in Aquinas' understanding of the created universe; the second is the role of temporal change and development, whether naturally regularized, contingent, or rooted in free created agency.

For Aquinas, God's creative act in the full sense is not exhausted in the constitution of a multitude of things, the participation of limited beings in the unlimited act of being. A full account must include the two features just mentioned. Oversimplifying somewhat, for the purposes of this chapter we will refer to the former feature of creation as that of world order, while the latter feature we will call providence.[33] God's creative bestowal upon the world fundamentally involves both structural ordering but also a temporal course of interaction, an unfolding history of agency, for the creatures so ordered. Now, according to the account of Milbank just given, it would seem that divine grace is granted to the world on the most universal, ontological level. His scheme resists identifying any sphere within the created realm that is not touched by, or in fact constituted by, the gracious ordering to supernatural communion with God. On such an account, being simply as such is always already graced, and it is pointless, indeed dangerous, to allude to the differentiated structure or the history of creatures to specify the working of grace, since this might suggest a "zone" of nature over against one of grace. Such a dualism he strives to overcome. Hence, a doctrine of grace virtually becomes identical with a doctrine of creation, taking the latter in the narrow (ontological) sense of the divine grounding of finite entities, or of the relation of (divine) Being to beings. But Aquinas' fuller account of creation complicates the picture. For there are aspects of any created order on Aquinas' understanding that do not fall explicitly within the horizon of ontology as the first or most universal science, the science of being as such. And, as will be seen, the more differentiated picture of the created order that results will provide just the kind of "zoning" of grace that Milbank rejects.

For Aquinas, the completion or perfection of a created thing does not lie only in the bestowal of existence on its essence, that is, in the actuality of this thing as this kind of thing, in this identifiable form. As he explains, only God is good essentially, just by being an identifiable "this." Every creature for its completion, its full goodness, require three things beyond identity or essence: it must have actuality (it must receive or participate existence, i.e., it must be created), but then also it must exercise the

---

[33] This narrow definition of providence is a departure from Aquinas' own usage, since he can include both of these two features, i.e., (a) the necessary constitution of a world consisting of various kinds of creatures fitted to one another in various ways, and (b) the governing of their developing causal relations over the course of time, under the one rubric of providence. This must be kept in mind when reading Aquinas, but it will serve to clarify the discussions of this chapter if the term "providence" (as is commonly the case in the use of this term) is especially linked with God's guidance of the world's history, including all the activities and interactions, necessitated or contingent, of the entities within it.

actions or operations proper to its identity, and finally it must attain the goal proper to its identity. For only God is actual simply as essence (what God *is* is to-be); only in God is this act of existence completely identical with operation (in creatures potencies must be actualized beyond mere existence); and only in God is the act of existence itself the attainment of end (since God consists in being the highest end and attaining himself as the highest end, both at once).[34] This means that the ultimate metaphysical debility that defines all creatures as such, namely, that they are not God, puts them in need of more than their appropriate act of essential being. They also require both defined, telic relations with other creatures and operational agency. This inevitably determines the two aforementioned characteristics of our world.

First, there must be a multiplicity of created beings, arranged within an overarching order.[35] God's rich immensity could only be finitely represented by a world of many things, of many different kinds, situated within fitting arrangements of mutual orientation both vertical (hierarchy of beings determined by the range and excellence of their perfections) and horizontal (the causal functioning of beings for each other as means and/or as ends). The complex beauty of such an organic arrangement is absolutely necessary; creation as a mere collection of finite beings would fail in an essential way to reflect the divine goodness, when compared with a total world order in which all the beings are "fitted" to each other. Indeed, for Aquinas, given the representative function of creation, the world as a whole is the highest created good *qua* created; all individual creatures, even humans and angels, take their relative places as subordinated to the world, parts to whole. (Aquinas would agree with Milbank that all creatures must pay the tribute of their nullity to God, but for him they do so via their inter-creaturely relations, that is, as mediated by the world order. This is obscured by Milbank's devaluation of the holism of creation as a prior, encompassing good in its own right.)

Second, in order that a further echo might be found within the created order of the dignity of infinite agency grounding it, the positioning of beings one to another is not static, like a crystal lattice, but is a dynamism. Each being is a limited agent, acting on others, and is in turn the object of actions of others upon it. As Aquinas explains, "[God] governs things inferior by superior, not on account of any defect in His power, but by reason of the abundance of his goodness; so that the dignity of causality is imparted even to creatures."[36] The world order is not a framework for inert units but connects these agents and their interactions into a mechanism of change. Not being God, created things, even the mightiest, are limited not just in the range and power of their acts; apart from immaterial realities (angels), all created things are also limited by their inherent potentiality, which means their agency is spatially and temporally circumscribed (i.e., they are embodied or material). Nothing is continually displaying all of the operations definitive of its specific excellence; most material realities must first be generated by other realities, and even then their operations are sporadic, put in motion according to a complex set of internal and external factors.[37] So the world of

---

[34] *STh* I q. 6 a. 3.
[35] *STh* I q. 47 aa. 1 and 2.
[36] *STh* I q. 22 a. 3.
[37] On the inability of creatures to display all operations, see *STh* I q. 54 a. 1.

created agents is a world of potencies continually being reduced to act, and that means a world of process, a temporal world.

Thus, the world is only possible for Aquinas as an interplay of elements in tension. Again bracketing angels as immaterial, nothing can attain fulfillment, nothing can truly be what it is supposed to be, save as in some sort of ordered, interactive relationship with other created things, since its good cannot subsist simply in itself, as its own existence. And further (again bracketing immaterial angels), this involvement with other things necessary for the attainment of its good takes the form of action, or what Aquinas calls motion. Hence, Aquinas says that beyond the good of subsistent creatures there is the higher good of their ordering to each other; and he says that God's governance of the world (which is the created actualization of the eternal plan of providence), besides preserving things in their subsistence, moves all things to their respective goods (i.e., all *mutatio* of things by God or by each other falls under providence).[38] Though creation is a single, simple act of God, considered as effect it is complexly structured, and the constitution of participating beings, what falls under the view of metaphysics, is only part of it. To account fully for beings in their total arrangement, physics, the science of material things in motion, is required; hence, even a "theological ontology" strictly speaking would give only an inventory and a schematic, an architecture; it would not provide a functional model. The creature demands a world, and a world takes time.

Put another way, the creative act presents an irreducible duality to our analysis: God is both first act (an object of metaphysics) and first mover (an object of physics). The excellent discussion at *STh* I q. 105 a. 5 clarifies the ways God acts in every created agent according to the three causal principles of action. God is active in every creature (1) according to final causality since God, the good of whom every lower good is a participation, is the final cause of every created act; (2) according to efficient causality since God as first mover moves all things to their operation "as it were applying their forms and powers to operation" (see below on "universal instrumentality"); and (3) according to formal causality since God does not just "apply" the forms but also supplies to all agents, and preserves in them, these very forms through which they operate, participations of the infinite divine formality. This same pattern is replicated in the discussion of grace at *STh* I/II q. 109 a. 1. God as first act provides the gracious habitual form; God as first mover moves to supernatural operations via that form but also disposes to the reception of that form; and all this is in service to God as supernatural finality, that is, deiformity.

We now turn from these general Thomist reflections to their specific point of application: the image of God. The creaturely display of God's triune essence, it was said above, is the specific capacity of a certain kind of entities, namely, those capable of universal intentionality (intellect and will). But human beings, though intention-capable, are still beings; they exist only as mediated by the structure of dynamic order just outlined. They are only one class of members of this order, confined to a relatively small "possibility space" over against, and positioned by, the universe of other beings incapable of intentionality; moreover, individual human instances only take place briefly

---

[38] For the first point, *STh* I q. 22 a. 1. For the second, *STh* I q. 103 a. 4.

in terms of cosmic time, flickers of intentional activity that exist only when generated by other such flickers, as a result of partly contingent factors. So the very possibility of a created image of God, of exhibiting the divine triunity, must "happen" as a series of events within a dynamic order made up of temporal intercausality, partly necessary, partly accidental, partly free. The contrast in emphasis with Milbank's "theological ontology" is striking; as was seen, the latter suppresses as much as possible identifiable things, their "ownership" of their proper being and agency, and their subordination within a world order. All this can be dispensed with because, for Milbank (as was seen above), it is the very universal fact of participant being as such, the relation of Being to beings, present throughout creation, that displays or replicates the internal procession within the divine essence: the perfect givenness of infinite being as infinite essence.

If the giving of created being as such thus universalizes the presentation of triune being, how does Milbank (who clearly seeks harmony with Aquinas) account for the latter's limitation of the very capacity for such a presentation to intentionality (for only beings with intellect and will are "*capax dei*")? Here Milbank argues that created intentionality or human "spirit," as in fact the apex and (as microcosm) the summation and intentional reflection of all created being, in effect shares with the entire cosmos its own orientation to the triune being. Thus, his universalization of the triune image stands because of this "trumping [!] of *esse* by *intelligere*, being by spirit."[39] Although this position admittedly develops more "radical" themes of Henri de Lubac and his reading of Pico della Mirandola, Milbank seeks support from Aquinas. Human being mediates the universal desire for God and stands proxy for God as the created object of that desire, since as Aquinas argues at *ScG* III 111–2, intellectual existence is the divinely intended end or *telos* of all created being.[40]

Whatever the inherent power of these speculative suggestions, it can briefly be suggested, without entering into a detailed exegesis, how the attempted reading of Aquinas is too strained to undermine our alternative: an insistence on a spatiotemporal limitation of the potential triune exhibition solely to human intentionality. First, Milbank's "microcosmic" reading of humanity is superfluous, because for Aquinas the cosmic desire of each being for God is in fact mediated by their location within the total created order itself and not by humanity.[41] Second, Milbank's reading of his textual authority encounters problems, for *ScG* III 112 nos. 5 and 8 show that the telic role of humanity for other creatures is itself a result of their common subordination to the world order, not a replacement for it. Indeed, no. 9 shows that the ordering of all other creatures to human beings as, in a way, their end (since non-intentional being exists for the sake of intentional), is not an ordering of individual beings to each human being but rather the ordering of all nonhuman species to the human species as a whole. In other words, the role of humanity simply exemplifies hierarchic world order itself. There is no warrant, then, for reading the privileged capacity of humanity for the Trinity back into the universal givenness of being.

---

[39] Milbank, *Suspended Middle*, 52.
[40] Ibid., 98–9.
[41] This claim will be explained in the next paragraph.

The contrast developed here can be summarized in this way. On one side, Milbank's ontology baptizes poststructuralist flux; the infinite gift of existence is always surpassing and disrupting essences, not by destroying them but by always generating more determinations of them. On the other side is Aquinas' picture preferred here, where created existence is always determined or "fitted" to essence; this stress on the appropriation or "ownership" of existence by essence befits Aquinas' emphasis on God's genuine gift to creatures of identity and especially agency, which unfolds a world of meaningful (and irreversible) temporality. In his account of creation, Milbank seems as wary of granting a central role to the world or the whole as he is of granting it to the thing or substance. Indeed, for him spirit or intellect mediates the world's relation to God. For Aquinas, the opposite holds: in the created order, the world as a whole mediates the relation of spirit, indeed of all individual creatures as its parts, to God. The good of the cosmos is twofold: the ordering of things to each other (their belonging to a world) and the ordering of this ordered whole to God. The latter order does not replace or "trump" the former; rather the former is for the sake of the latter.[42] All things are ordered to God as the ultimate "external" end, as source and goal of all things; but this is through their prior ordering to one another: everything is ordered to God via its worldly coordination with everything else. The rational creature, even granted its unique possibility of imaging God through its intentionality, is in no way made an exception to this worldliness through this more direct connection: "Of all creatures the rational creature is chiefly ordained for the good of the universe."[43]

The role of the adverb "chiefly" in this quotation, taken out of context, is ambiguous. This role should be specified, lest it invite a misreading of the position just summarized, and developed throughout the chapter. Aquinas' main point in context is that rational creatures, as incorruptible, are among the essential ("structural," as it were) components of the universe; their number is therefore precisely ordained by the creator for the good of the universe. The point of "chiefly" (*principalius*, "more principally") here is that the rational creature is even more fundamental to the overall created order than the other structural or "eternal" parts Aquinas mentions (celestial spheres, stars, elements, natural species). On the other hand, "chiefly" should in no way be read here as if implying some kind of alternative between the rational creature's ordering to the world versus its ordering to God, as if Aquinas were saying, "The rational creature is chiefly ordained for the good of the universe ... rather than for God." On such a reading, which forms no part of the argument of this chapter, the ordinance of the rational creature would be "first" to the world order, "then" to God.

In fact, the approach taken in this section and the next should imply the rejection of any such "competitive" view of world-ordinance and God-ordinance. The human creature's ordinance to God is indeed via (by way of or by means of) ordinance to the world, but only with the proviso that the ordinance to the world is for the sake of the ordinance to God. This I take to be the import of the image of an army that Aquinas often uses (e.g. *STh* I q. 21 a. 1 ad 3): to form an army at all the individual soldiers must necessarily be ordered to each other, in good array, but this is for the purpose of

---

[42] See Aquinas, *Commentary on the Sentences* I d. 44 q. 1 a. 2; *STh* I q. 21 a. 1 ad 3; *STh* I q. 103 a. 2 ad 3.
[43] *STh* I q. 23 a. 7.

their ordering to the general who commands them and directs them to their ultimate end: victory. Nor does this necessarily presupposed ordering to the world as a whole deny the rational creature's special supernatural end of direct vision of the divine essence. Even those who receive that gift do not thereby cease being creatures, nor cease being component parts of a world order. Again there is no competition here, since the fundamental ordering to the world is for the sake of the ultimate ordering to God, just as ordering to God is ultimately, both structurally and providentially, by way of being ordered to other creatures and the created world as a whole.

Any attempt to determine whether God-ordination or world-ordination is "primary" simply falls into the competitive trap, since each is primary, albeit in different ways. The human being is indeed "primarily" created for the sake of knowing and loving God: namely, because this is the highest goal attainable by any conceivable creature, one that involves an actual participation in the personal relations constituting God's very being. In that sense, every other end for which a human being is created (i.e., any intra-worldly ordering or finality) is subordinate to that, the ultimate end. But there remains another mode of primacy: human beings are still finite creatures, and their ordination to fellow creatures within the world-order is "primary" in the sense that, as a prerequisite of their very being as creatures, it is likewise a prerequisite even for the beatific vision, and in fact would hold good even if God had not chosen to elevate human beings to personal participation in the Godhead. Finally, when it is said here or elsewhere in the chapter that the relation to the world "mediates" the relation to God, this does not rule out the fact that the creature's ultimate God-relations (saving grace and the beatific vision) are in their own right "immediate," both intentionally (for charity in this life as for vision in the next, God herself is the direct object) and causally (grace and beatitude are grounded in the creator's efficient power alone). This last point will receive further clarification below.

To sum up, the account of created being offered here, more fully congruent with Aquinas than Milbank's, assumes a structure that will become important for the following sections. Creatures "happen" according to a dynamic scheme that combines: (1) a relatively fixed pattern of differentiated and graded subsistents (the world order) that in itself is universal and "indifferent," bestowing places and ends on all; and (2) the temporal actualization or "application" of this order by the agents within it, wherein the ordered entities continually engage each other in constantly shifting configurations of causal action and reception. The universal order is "indifferent" in that it allows infinite combinations of concrete happenings without itself being directed to one as an end (the only end of the whole is God). Even the ultimate creaturely possibility of representing God, the *imago Dei*, "happens" as one of these concrete configurations; it is event, not structure, though it could not occur save within the "neutral" structure that defines its general possibility. So the world occurs via temporality or history, and this "via," this "by way of," will be decisive for the rest of the discussion.

One final point needs to be made before moving to the next section. The differentiated structure we have described requires a component of what might be called "mere being." By this is meant precisely the order of differentiation that itself is open to, but not defined by, the concrete, "local" (i.e., spatially and temporally specified) attainment of the triune image within created intentionality. Mere being, simply as created, is a *similitude* of the divine essence but is not fundamentally oriented toward the *vision* of God as triune interrelation; indeed it is opaque to it, constitutively so, with the exception of beings capable of universal intentionality, and even they as beings represent only the abstract possibility, not the actuality, of a created transparency to the Trinity. But for this latter reason mere being, though not *defined* by the beatific vision, is also constitutively *open* to it. Even so, the concrete possibility of this attainment can only "happen" within creation, as a concrete event in which the temporal, partially contingent development of the universal order allows human beings to occur and operate. Where and when such local possibilities remain unfulfilled, created being remains opaque to the Trinity.

This does not make creation as such "indifferent" to this end, however, only the fixed ontological *structure* as an abstract but essential feature of it. That order itself only attains concreteness as temporally operative, and under the direction of providence its processes are shaped toward just this supernatural goal. For Aquinas, every particular action, including every human action, is a result of the concrete totality of worldly relations, all prior and contemporaneous causes, aligning themselves at just the precise point, conjoining an agent's power, its current exertion of that power, and the presence of the susceptible object under the right enabling conditions. The entire cosmos must conspire in my slightest act. So the world is the organ of the ends God desires for creatures; it is animated by the divine providential governance that mediates every act of the entities within it, a notion Bernard Lonergan referred to as "universal instrumentality."[44] The hapless clerk Yepihodov (in the epigraph from Chekhov's play) is right: the meaning or destiny of the whole, "fate," can only be read from the specificity of events. Indeed, its supernatural meaning only "occurs" in these "signs" or concrete configurations of the otherwise opaque and abstract order of being. But for Aquinas "fate" is simply the name for providence as imprinted on creaturely history, both in its contingent and in its necessary developments.[45] Communion with God is thus a "local" possibility, an event apart from which the order of being reveals to intelligent inspection only an absolute cause, not an offer of friendship.

Since creaturely transparency to the triune divine being has been specified as the telos and meaning of grace, this point can be expressed in a different way, by appeal to Aquinas' stringent conditions for a possible intending of the eternal persons in God.[46] For although created being is indeed the revelation and representation of the divine power, it is constrained to offer only a glimpse of it, insufficient to disclose the divine essence in its Triune being. Based on rational observation and reflection of the created order as such, "it is impossible to attain to the knowledge of the Trinity of divine Persons," because we grasp creatures as effects of God and in this way "we can know of God that only which of necessity belongs to Him as the principle of all things," and this power is "common to the whole Trinity" (i.e., it fails to distinguish the persons). Created being as such reveals only the abstract

---

[44] Bernard Lonergan, *Grace and Freedom: Operative Grace in the Thought of St. Thomas Aquinas*, vol. 1 of *Collected Works of Bernard Lonergan* (Toronto: University of Toronto Press, 2000), 82–6.
[45] *STh* I q. 116 aa. 1 and 2.
[46] *STh* I q. 32 a. 1.

"unity" of the divine essence, not the concrete pattern according to which it is shared within God. Thus, the divine infinity or immensity retains the last word; God's being, even as participated, remains incommensurable with the world's being. The witness to this is the necessary, structural differentiation between "mere being" and concrete event. Only in the eschaton will being as such be transparent to the Trinity. Milbank's conception, it might be said, impatiently tries to anticipate that ultimate state of affairs; in attempting to indicate a "future Trinitarian metaphysic" has he allowed for just how distant that future is? Such a metaphysic resides in the absolute future of the new creation remaining unattainable (even by the recipients of revelation) in this life.

III. Mere Nature

De Lubac was just mixed up on the point.

Bernard Lonergan
Phenomenology and Logic

The very notion of "mere being," that is, being that is not always already defined, ontologically, by a destined communion with God or participation in the *imago Dei*, is stoutly resisted by Milbank. Indeed, the denial of any such possibility of a creaturely space somehow undefined or "neutral" in regard to the end of sharing or participating the triune divine essence itself, can be regarded as central to his entire project.[47] In the preceding section, the claims of Aquinas were developed into a quite different ontological picture than the one animating Milbank's work; in this picture just such a neutral or "indifferent" space turns out to be a necessary moment in the structure of created being. There must be a duality between general order and concrete or local application of that order, that is, event, and it is on the level of event, not of universal structure, that the possibility of imaging God occurs. In seeking to undermine any such duality, however, Milbank is not limited to the ontological considerations already discussed. Closer to the heart of his project, and far more systematically developed, is another set of considerations that focuses on the relation between human nature and grace.

If Milbank denies that any element of the created order is structurally undefined in regard to the vision of God or union with God, his primary rationale lies in his appropriation of certain claims associated with de Lubac.[48] De Lubac argued that according to Aquinas (along with the entire patristic and early medieval tradition), the human being is fundamentally oriented by God to union with God or the beatific vision. It is impossible for any creature to effect such a union by means of its own natural powers, so its occurrence requires some kind of aid or augmentation from

---

[47] The language here is deliberately chosen. As has been said, for Aquinas, all creatures, as such, participate the divine power and goodness and therefore represent or imitate the unique divine being. But what is in view here goes beyond that, since this universal representation does not attain to the divine triunity. See *STh* I q. 93 aa. 2 and 5.

[48] In the following discussion, no claim is made in regard to the accuracy of Milbank's (contestable) reading of de Lubac. The question of interpreting de Lubac, a large topic in itself, is irrelevant to the argument of this chapter.

God (grace) beyond the power of nature (hence "supernatural"). Now, the orientation to this union is innate in the human creature, taking the form of a "natural desire" for this naturally unobtainable, hence supernatural end. Milbank lays great stress on the paradoxical aspect of this natural desire for the supernatural; for him (and for de Lubac as he reads him), it demands a denial that the human subject or "spirit" in the present created order (in which grace occurs) could ever be purely or merely natural. If our humanity has been created precisely in view of an ultimate end of union with God, and if therefore our humanity has inscribed within its very nature the drive or aim toward this goal (as exemplified by the natural desire), then it seems as if it is somehow defined by that goal "already," even before the bestowal of saving grace as traditionally understood. The paradox celebrated by Milbank is that the end our nature could never attain on its own is somehow definitive of that very nature from the beginning.[49] Milbank develops this basic position by means of several different and often subtle claims, sometimes appealing to passages of Aquinas.

These claims are all concerned to stress how in Aquinas' universe nature, particularly human nature, is unintelligible apart from its defining orientation to supernatural beatitude; they cluster into three groups. First, Milbank emphasizes how grace is intrinsic to human being. For grace, according to Aquinas, "puts something in" the soul itself, and this bestowal is not miraculous. For Milbank, statements like these suggest that grace cannot be something extraneous "added to" an already complete nature by inexplicable divine fiat.[50] Second, Milbank sketches a complex scheme whereby the human soul as such is already, prior to the bestowal of saving grace, beyond any merely natural state due to the decisive intentional presence of God as the inchoate object of the natural desire for beatitude. The resulting "paradoxical" state means that the "natural" condition of human subjectivity or "spirit" is already, by anticipation, fully defined or constituted by its future graced state. Lest it be argued that this threatens the gratuity of grace by dissolving a preexisting natural endowment, Milbank claims that, because creation from nothing must constitute the very recipient of the gift of being, the logic of creation itself is already that of sheer gratuity, and thus disallows any contrast of natural obligation and gratuitous superaddition.[51]

In a third group of comments Milbank points to passages in Aquinas that he argues indicate the inherent deficiency, indeed incoherence, of a supposed "merely natural" condition of human being. For example, does not Aquinas say that the desire for assimilation to God that every creature displays in the fashion proper to it must, in the intellectual creature, take the form of a yearning for the supernatural end of a beatifying intellectual union with God? Further, Aquinas argues that the possibility even of merely natural justice in prelapsarian humanity already rested on a gift of grace to Adam; this strongly suggests the impossibility of a correct human stance before God apart from some gracious endowment. In yet a third passage, Aquinas can be read as asserting that a created intellect that lacked the supernatural orientation of

---

[49] Milbank, *Suspended Middle*, ix.
[50] Ibid., 22, 24.
[51] Ibid., 28, 36, 39–40, 43.

grace would not be "merely" natural, but would in fact be so radically deficient as to fall below the level even of irrational creatures.[52] All this constitutes evidence, for Milbank, of a covert but decisive Platonic or Neoplatonic orientation within Aquinas' hierarchical ontology, where what is most proper and characteristic of some lower level of being turns out itself to be "borrowed" from the higher level of being under the influence of which it exists.[53]

All of these readings of Aquinas, as will be argued, are open to serious criticism; the intent here, however, is not simply to deny Milbank's appeals to Aquinas, but to allow the interpretive debate over the latter to issue in a different construal of nature and its relation to grace. The picture that will emerge will turn out to be closely aligned with the results of the previous section. We begin by responding to Milbank's first group of claims. It can be argued that his stress on grace as intrinsic to nature is severely one-sided. Aquinas' denial of the miraculous character of grace rests not on the latter being *intrinsic* to human nature but rather on the fact that, as intellectual, that nature is *capable* of receiving grace.[54] Intentional being is not grace, but as intentional it is the fitting matter able to receive the formality of grace; as *imago Dei* (in the lowest grade) it is naturally *capax dei*.[55] This formality of grace is a created reality introduced into the soul; it is an accidental quality modifying the soul's substance.[56]

Beyond these details, however, the crucial point lies in the fact that for Aquinas grace involves two different kinds of divine effectivity: what is "put into" the soul is habitual grace, but this presupposes the providential constellation of natural and historical developments that dispose any given human being for this reception, and that actuate the choices and operations of that person to embrace the habit of grace and execute acts conditioned by the habits of faith and charity.[57] This is the "universal instrumentality" already referred to; when the divine *auxilium* required for any creature's act happens to enable human acts receptive to or preserving the state of grace, this providential aid, though in itself not at all distinct in mode from the other motions of providence, is "actual grace." Though conversion can on occasion be miraculous (as with St. Paul), the "common and usual course of justification" God employs involves the non-miraculous working of providence, whereby habitual grace is historically mediated by actual grace.[58]

---

[52] Ibid., 83, 98.
[53] Ibid., 101.
[54] *STh* I/II q. 113 a. 10.
[55] *STh* I q. 93 a. 8: "The image of God is found in the soul according as the soul turns to God, or possesses a nature that enables it to turn to God."
[56] *STh* I/II q. 110 aa. 1 and 2.
[57] *STh* I/II q. 111 a. 2.
[58] *STh* I/II q. 113 a. 10. This is another instance where the idea of mediation might prove troublesome: how can the gift of saving grace, which is nothing less than a participation in deity itself, possibly be reduced to an effect of created secondary causality, via providential direction? Does not this particular effect by its nature transcend any created cause? Some clarifications are necessary. First, even on the model laid out here God remains the only efficient cause of the gracious habit itself; a providentially arranged conjunction of worldly conditions and agents is only the dispositive cause, whereas, given the properly disposed matter, God directly creates the supernatural form. Second, the bestowal of the gracious habit upon infants through baptism might seem to undermine the stress here on the historical course of providential preparation of the free and rational soul for conversion

In contrast to Milbank's lopsidedly universalized and "ontological" picture of grace, Aquinas deploys a two-level, "ontic" mechanism for its selective distribution. Grace, in short, can only be "in" a human soul because it first "comes to" that soul via the workings of time and motion.

This sort of account is only reinforced by examination of Milbank's other two sets of arguments. The second group aimed at a theological anthropology in which the "natural" human spirit is always already surpassed, so to speak; it is intrinsically and essentially defined by the supernatural destiny of beatific union with God. But there are two significant obstacles in Aquinas for this extravagantly paradoxical reading. First, glorious as it is, Aquinas strongly distinguishes human intentionality (intellect and will) from the supernatural intentional operations of faith and charity enabled by grace. Human beings by their very nature have the capacity to understand and to freely will (thus they are *capax dei*); but only by grace can they come to know God as God, and love God as the perfect good; hence, only by grace are they justified, reckoned among the just (*justos*). The gap between these two states can only be bridged through a supplemental act of God via the world, for the simple reason that the operations of the latter state (knowing and loving God *qua* God) are actions proper to and natural to God alone.[59] Only God knows and loves God as God (and not merely as the first cause of creatures). God could not have made these operations "natural" to any creature, not even the mightiest angel.

This connects to the other obstacle to a paradoxical conjunction of nature and grace in humanity. Milbank appeals to the radical gratuity of creation itself as paradigmatic of divine grace: God's unsurpassable giving is such that he gives not just the gift, but the very recipient of the gift. But when Milbank tries to suggest that this unique logic of divine giving dissolves any order of obligation set up over against the gratuity of grace as its presupposition, he straightaway collides with Aquinas' entire manner of thinking. For the latter does indeed explicitly affirm two distinct logics: a logic of

---

and the infusion of faith. But for Aquinas there is no conflict, because the infant's reception of grace is only mediated by the actual faith of the community into which it is received (*STh* III q. 68 a. 9, cf. *STh* I/II q. 113 a. 3 ad 1). Finally, it might seem hard to credit that the bestowal of the supernatural form is not miraculous. But Aquinas (*STh* I/II q. 113 a. 10) distinguishes elements within any miraculous phenomenon. Like the act of creation itself, the bestowal of habitual grace is an act beyond any natural power; yet this does not mean it involves any disturbance in "the usual and customary order of causing an effect," as is common in miracles. The analog of the creation of the human soul is helpful here. God creates each individual soul directly at the moment of its infusion into the properly disposed bodily material, but Aquinas would hardly call this a miracle, since the natural order is not suspended (indeed, one could say it is precisely being upheld or preserved in each exercise of this direct divine efficiency). In both cases (the human soul, the supernatural habit), a formality arises within the created order that could only be due to the creator's "immediate" act, since it is beyond the power of any created cause. The reason is different in the two cases: a human soul must be directly created because it is subsistent form (*STh* I q. 90 a. 2), while the habit of grace must be directly created, even though it is not subsistent (being an accidental form in the category of quality), because even as "mere" quality it is absolutely supernatural, a deification or participation of divinity. So in insisting on the ordinary cosmic instrumentality of grace the point is the providential mutation that psychologically disposes the soul to its bestowal. The divinely guided worldly causes are indeed "media," means, but not in the sense that Aquinas is using when he denies mediation in the creation of the soul.

[59] *STh* I q. 12 a. 4 and a. 4 ad 3.

what is "owed" (*debitum*) to the creature, over against (though not in conflict with) a logic of free gift beyond what is owed.[60] Indeed, the former determines what Aquinas calls "nature"; nature for Aquinas thereby attains a distinctness and solidity within his metaphysical scheme that sharply demarcates it from Milbank's. God's justice demands that, if he create a world, it must display a variety, dynamism, and organic beauty, a limited perfection, sufficient to manifest (to a fitting degree) the divine perfection. This means, in turn, that the world must contain creatures of distinct kinds, each kind equipped by God with the array of capacities and parts necessary to fulfill its role within the overall world-system. Thus, in spite of the fact that God is in no way obliged to create, and hence creation is an act of free love and mercy, nonetheless if God does create, his own justice demands that she fulfill his twofold *debitum*: first, to herself, in arranging the perfection of the world; and second, to creatures, in supplying to them what he has herself ordained for them in pursuit of that overall perfection. The point is that creation involves the establishment of natures and a natural order that, *pace* Milbank, is indeed a realm of obligation that is contrasted by Aquinas with the supernatural gift of grace that, as already stated, cannot be natural to any creature, hence cannot be a *debitum*.

Milbank's final group of claims cited passages of Aquinas that seem to suggest the impossibility or incoherence of a "merely natural" intellectual nature; "spirit" simply must, on this reading, involve some definitive involvement with or conditioning by grace. The three passages in question, however, are susceptible of quite different (and arguably less forced) readings. In fact, the second passage is flatly misread: the "original" justice that Adam had does indeed require grace, but this justice is not "natural" justice, as Milbank claims, for the very passage he cites at *STh* I q. 100 a. 1 ad 2 explains that original justice in Adam was supernatural, a gift of sanctifying grace. The possibility of a merely natural justice is in no way denied. More complex is the third passage at *ScG* III 25 no. 5, which insists that the created hierarchy would be disrupted if the intellectual creature failed to attain God by its highest faculty, the intellect, for then it would fall back into the mode of attainment of unintelligent creatures. Several indications elsewhere in chapter 25, however, indicate that the attainment in question is not limited to its ultimate instance, the supernatural vision of God's essence; if lower modes of attainment are admitted here, then the argument that the human intellect could only subsist as oriented to the beatific vision fails.[61]

---

[60] *STh* I q. 21 a. 1 ad 3 and ad 4.
[61] In Milbank's discussion of *ScG* III 25 no. 5 (part of the long footnote at Milbank, *Suspended Middle*, 26), he goes beyond Aquinas' words by defining the attainment of God in question exclusively as the beatific vision. This ignores the clues elsewhere in chapter 25 which indicate that an intellectual grasp of God short of the beatific vision equally serves Aquinas' aims in the chapter, namely, to show that God himself is the ultimate goal of human intellects rather than separate substances or angels. For example, no. 9 and no. 11 are evidently referring to the possibility of philosophical knowledge of God or metaphysics as equally relevant arguments in favor of this claim. Likewise, no. 2 says that the divine substance is attained "when one knows something of the divine substance," a wording that strongly suggests that the divine end of the intellectual creature is in some degree (though not in the highest or last degree) attained even by merely knowing truths about the divine substance (for which the beatific vision is not necessary).

Most intriguing, however, is the first passage taken from *ScG* III 25 nos. 1 and 2 (but bolstered with other citations), which as Milbank reads it implies that the human creature's natural desire for God cannot itself be merely natural because it envisions, already from the beginning, that is, even as unfulfilled desire, a unitive grasp of the divine essence.[62] Any thorough reply to this reading would quickly lead into the interpretive morass created by the vast polemic literature surrounding de Lubac's *Surnaturel*. For the modest purposes of this chapter, all that need be said is that another reading of the natural desire in Aquinas is certainly possible than the one Milbank attributes to de Lubac, one that does not issue in his exorbitant appeal to a central, systemic paradox. The truly final or ultimate end of an intellectual creature, the highest possible to it in any universe, is the beatifying vision of the divine essence, the perfected and immutable grasp of God's being by the intellect and the loving will. De facto, in our own actual order of creation, this is the end destined for human being, presupposing the gift of divine grace. The prerequisite for this end, as has already been said, is intentionality (intellect and will). By its very nature, the intellect seeks to know the cause, the "why," of all classes of phenomena, but also, behind the totality of appearances, the cause of the universe itself. Thus, the human intellect naturally desires to understand the cause of all, which is God.[63]

But this is just where the dispute arises. The human seeks by nature to know God; *in fact* this knowledge is the beatific vision, but does that imply that the natural desire of the human intellect itself already aims specifically at that supernatural end? According to Milbank, in harmony with his interpretation of de Lubac, the answer is clearly yes; thus, human "nature" simply as such has always been an impossibility in the actual created order, since God has planted the supernatural end within it, as its fundamental orienting drive. No "mere" nature exists, for its purity was infected, as it were, from the beginning by the gracious call; nature is "already" grace: this is Milbank's great paradox. But perhaps Aquinas' own answer to the question of the natural desire for God is not so blunt as to result in paradox; we need, as he would say, to draw a distinction. Materially speaking, and factually, in desiring to know God the human intellect is indeed desiring the beatific vision; but formally speaking, in terms of the natural operative dynamic of human intellect, that goal is not specified and can only be specified through revelation. What drives the human being is the *eros* for universal being and its cause; it seeks the highest understanding of the first cause that is possible to it, which on the condition of supernatural grace becomes the vision of the divine essence that is impossible to any creature on its natural powers.

A natural desire whose scope can extend even to an end that transcends all nature: this is indeed a paradox, but strictly only for natural knowledge or philosophy. Milbank's scheme makes the irreducibility of this paradox foundational for theology itself, but on the reading suggested here theology begins from its resolution. The divine essence is in fact the material object of every human desire to know, but it only

---

[62] Milbank, *Suspended Middle*, 25–6, first part of footnote 10.
[63] *STh* I q. 12 a. 1, cf. a. 8 ad 4.

becomes the formal object under the individually granted gift of grace. An illustration used by Aquinas will help clarify matters.[64] I see someone approaching from a distance; it is Peter, though I cannot yet see who it is. Do I see Peter approaching? Yes and no. In fact the one I see approaching is Peter: he is the material object. But I do not see the one approaching *as* Peter: he is not (yet) the formal object of my vision. Human beings naturally desire knowledge of the ultimate as their final felicity, and in fact this knowledge is the supernatural vision of the divine essence. Do they naturally desire the supernatural? Materially yes, formally no.[65]

This account has been simplified and sidesteps the complications that have made this an issue of continued debate.[66] But the point has been made: a solid prima facie case can be made on Thomist grounds for an alternative understanding of nature and grace to that of Milbank, one that grants a role to "mere nature," that is, nature as not in itself defined by an orientation toward graced beatification. For even in the actual created order we live in, gifted with the call to supernatural beatitude, a proper, yet merely natural, orientation to God retains a structural role that would seem to be denied to it in Milbank's scheme. Aquinas calls this the natural love for God, a love whereby the unfallen human being would have loved God above all things, by limiting and shaping its desires in accord with the organic order of the cosmic totality, for the sake of loving the creator of that totality.[67] There are two sorts of objections to the invocation of this natural love as a genuine human possibility: first, it can be said that because such a love falls short of what is ultimately possible for human intellect and will (i.e., perfect felicity, the beatific vision), a universe in which human beings attained only this imperfect love would itself be inherently imperfect; second, it can be argued that at any rate this sort of love can play no role in the human telos defined for the

---

[64] *STh* I a. 2 a. 1 ad 1.
[65] Aquinas himself comes close to applying this same illustration to the issue of the natural desire. In *De malo* q. 5 a. 3 he uses it to argue that souls in limbo do not suffer from lack of the beatific vision. Why? "It pertains to natural knowledge that the soul knows it was created for happiness [beatitudinem] and that happiness consists in the attainment [adeptione] of the perfect good. But that that perfect good for which man was made is that glory which the saints possess is beyond [supra] natural knowledge." Lonergan invokes this very passage to forestall just the kind of reading of *STh* I q. 12 a. 1 that Milbank relies upon. Bernard Lonergan, *Early Latin Theology*, trans. Michael G. Shields, vol. 19 of *Collected Works of Bernard Lonergan* (Toronto: University of Toronto Press, 2011), 153.
[66] In my view, without claiming to have resolved the endless arguments over de Lubac, including the sub-debate over Milbank's appropriation of him, some treatment along the lines hinted at here comes closest to addressing both the dogmatic issues and the data of Aquinas' writings. Lonergan has worked out in more detail a version of this approach to the natural desire, one that utilizes his insightful notion of "vertical finality." For an excellent overview, with references to Lonergan's texts, see J. Michael Stebbins, *The Divine Initiative: Grace, World-Order, and Human Freedom in the Early Writings of Bernard Lonergan* (Toronto: University of Toronto Press, 1995), pp. 149–82. For similar appeals to Lonergan on this issue, see Raymond Moloney SJ, "De Lubac and Lonergan on the Supernatural," *Theological Studies* 69 (2008): 509–27; and Brian Himes, "Lonergan's Position on the Natural Desire to See God and Aquinas' Metaphysical Theology of Creation and Participation," *Heythrop Journal* 54 (2013): 767–83. Certain problems with Lonergan's approach have been suggested by Guy Mansini, "Lonergan on the Natural Desire in Light of Feingold," *Nova et Vetera* [English] 5 (2007): 185–98, seconded by Lawrence Feingold, *The Natural Desire to See God According to St. Thomas and his Interpreters*, 2nd ed (Naples, FL: Sapientia, 2010), 406, 437, 439. Again the matter is much too difficult to be entered into here, but I do not regard their objections as decisive.
[67] *STh* I/II q. 109 a. 3. Cf. *STh* I/II q. 62 a. 2 ad 3.

actual cosmos we live in, since this orientation has been displaced by the more radical end of charity enabled by grace.

The first objection does not hold, for it confuses two things that Aquinas keeps separate. "Perfect felicity" can mean the perfection of a *particular* nature's happiness, meaning the ultimate degree of happiness available to that natural kind, rational nature, for example. For perfection in this sense, only the beatific vision suffices, and all other happiness would be imperfect.[68] However, according to Aquinas, the perfection of the entire created order, nature *as a totality*, is quite compatible with, and might even require, defects and failures in particular natures. God's providence has primary concern for the whole of the created order, a principle Aquinas extends even to that part of providence concerned with the bestowal of grace, that is, predestination.[69] God still has in mind the perfection of the whole, even in a matter where the perfection in question completely surpasses the limits of nature, that is, a perfection that is supernatural not just with regard to human nature but absolutely. Aquinas affirms this in effect at *STh* III q. 1 a. 3 ad 2 (referring in this case to the incarnation, the universal root and cause of grace among human beings). Milbank, it seems, concludes to the impossibility of graceless nature *generally* from the admitted imperfection of a "mere" human nature *specifically*. But the point of Aquinas' comment here belies this: "It suffices for the perfection of the universe that the creature be ordained in a natural manner to God as to an end." A supernatural ordination is not requisite for cosmic perfection, even when rational natures are part of the cosmos.

But here the second objection is relevant, since it dispenses with such a hypothetical world to appeal to the world as it is, called to supernatural charity and beatitude. What place is there for the posited "merely natural" love of God within the order of grace? Aquinas, however, does not envision the sort of incompatibility between natural and supernatural ends that is implied by the question, indeed that is assumed by Milbank's entire "paradoxical" approach. In fact, as is generally the case, so here: supernatural charity perfects natural love, as grace always perfects nature. Indeed, it is dependent upon this already given structure of love. Natural love is perfected by charity.[70] Aquinas' discussion of how natural love works among the blessed angels clarifies the issue. If natural love did not love God above all things, it would be perverse and hence would be destroyed by (supernatural) charity rather than perfected by it.[71] The upshot is frankly stated by Aquinas: "There is a twofold ultimate perfection of rational or of intellectual nature," and even the perfection naturally attainable is "in a measure called beatitude or happiness."[72]

The contrast between this Thomist model and that commended by Milbank is neatly captured by their differing uses of tidal movement as an illustration. As Milbank describes the phenomenon, the ebb and flow so proper to and distinctive of the ocean cannot itself be traced to any inherent tendency or capacity of its constituent water

---

[68] *STh* I/II q. 3 a. 8.
[69] *STh* I q. 22 a. 2 ad 1; *STh* I q. 23 a. 3 and a. 7 ad 2.
[70] *STh* II/II q. 26 a. 3, cf. *STh* I/II q. 100 a. 3 and ad 1.
[71] *STh* I q. 60 a. 5.
[72] *STh* I q. 62 a. 1.

but results from its susceptibility to the influx of the moon's celestial potency. The dynamic is supposed to exemplify the Platonic-Proclean causal structure previously mentioned, where effects obtain their most characteristic features not from their immanent essences but "on loan" from higher, transcendent causes.[73] Aquinas' own explanation of ocean tides suggests a quite different causal arrangement, however. For him there is no "paradoxical" definition of lower beings through their "improper" appropriation of higher qualities; there is instead a dual, cooperative structure that requires the lower being to contribute its immanent potencies. As he explains at *STh* II/II q. 2 a. 3, wherever a lower nature is ordered to a higher one as its end, that is, is innately determined to a finality, the two natures work together to perfect the lower: a movement of the higher agent must combine with the lower agent's *proper* movement. He adduces the example of the tides, which rely not just on the moon's influence but on water's inherent gravity as well. He explicitly applies this dynamic to the instance of grace. Where the intellectual nature is ordered to the beatific vision, its immanent intellectual capacities will not be obviated by the supernatural aid of God, but will be supplemented by it.

So where does this leave the issue of "mere (human) nature"? De Lubac had claimed, particularly in the controversial concluding section to *Surnaturel*, that the natural human desire for supernatural beatitude creates an "exigence" for it, a just demand for its fulfillment.[74] Lonergan (among many others) argued that de Lubac had to be confused (if not guilty of loose usage of a technical term) because human nature, even as called by God to a supernatural end, simply cannot incorporate a demand that lays a claim on God's justice for fulfillment (this being the meaning of a natural "exigence," cf. above on *debitum*).[75] Milbank, however, appropriated de Lubac's claim and radicalized it, making it the central systemic instrument for his own project: if human being is concretely and fundamentally oriented toward the specifically Christian eschaton, the "secular," as a postulated zone of human theory and practice neutral in regard to the claims of the gospel, is rendered *de jure* heretical and *de facto* impossible. Milbank follows de Lubac in attempting to anchor this position in Aquinas, but the readings involved are far from cogent. Not only does a scheme like Lonergan's (differentiating formal and material aspects of the object of natural desire) satisfy the evidence, it is possible (as has been shown) to trace the outlines of a quite different understanding of nature in Aquinas, one in which nature is distinct from, and presupposed by, grace (these being the arrangements Milbank seeks to banish).

Grace cannot be nature, but it demands an already constituted nature, and it must "come to" it as a kind of divine application to or qualification of that nature, causally and temporally mediated through the causal history of the cosmos. Take each element of this sentence. First, supernatural grace cannot be nature. For Aquinas, to be "like" God in the proper sense cannot be "natural"; indeed this is pretty much the whole point of grace: the magnitude of this gift cannot be "naturalized." To know and love God

---

[73] Milbank, *Suspended Middle*, 101.
[74] Henri de Lubac, *Surnaturel: études historiques* (Paris: Aubier, 1946), 483–94.
[75] Bernard Lonergan, *Phenomenology and Logic*, vol. 18 of *Collected Works of Bernard Lonergan* (Toronto: University of Toronto Press, 2001), 350–1.

essentially, *qua* God (not merely *qua* ultimate cause) could only be natural to a being whose essence is existence, that is, only to God.[76] This is why grace must "recreate" the soul in the likeness of God (*deiformitas* = likeness to God, *STh* I q. 12 a. 5); grace "deifies," bestowing on nature that participation-by-likeness impossible to natural power.[77] (Since this is effectively the same as deiformity, even the graced in this life are already in some sense deiform, not just the blessed as the language of *STh* q. 12 a. 5 might suggest.) To be "like" God, deiform, cannot be natural for any creature, precisely because it is a sharing in the uncreated nature. Milbank's "paradoxical" collapse of these distinctions, insisting on "spirit" as "already" in some sense grace, short-circuits Aquinas' careful differentiations.

Second, grace demands already constituted nature. It does not itself constitute any nature but rather occurs within the framework of created nature. This is true in two senses. First, the bestowal of grace upon certain creatures does not disrupt their subordination to the cosmic ordering of the whole. Even though the arrival of justifying grace in a single creature is already the advent of a good greater than that of the entire natural cosmos, Aquinas asserts that God has ordained the rational creature for the good of that cosmos, especially the beatified rational creature.[78] Second, divine operations, as already said, cannot be naturalized in a creature; in particular, substance and operation are always bifurcated in the creature.[79] One upshot is that created grace cannot be a substance. It must modify an already constituted nature. Even the "entitative habit" of sanctifying grace that makes supernatural operative habits, and hence participative operations, possible, is just that, a habit or quality of created nature.

Finally, grace must "come to" nature. As already mentioned, Aquinas sees the giving of grace as a complex effect of God's simple act; it combines two distinct moments: actual grace and habitual grace. Actual grace operates by means of the same providential movements of nature through which God provides all natural goods, acts, and ends. Actual grace operates first, only in specific conjunctures triggering the arrival of the habit of grace (i.e., something actual in the created realm) that exceeds nature. But the distribution of the habit of grace, as a qualitative modification of intellectual creatures, occurs only by way of God's moving of the entire universe. Predestination or election is the plan of this distribution, and it "puts" nothing real into the elect creature; it is like providence in this regard, a relational pattern rather than an ontological inscription.[80] Whereas Milbank sublates the otherness of "mere" nature in order to avoid extrinsism, the scheme proposed here follows Aquinas' lead in giving actual grace its proper role, in cooperation with nature. Actual grace, operatively prior to habitual grace, is not

---

[76] *STh* I q. 12 a. 5 ad 3.
[77] *STh* I/II q. 110 a. 4, also a. 3; *STh* I/II q. 112 a. 1.
[78] On good greater than the cosmos, see *STh* I/II q. 113 a. 9.
[79] Aquinas' discussion at *STh* I q. 54 aa. 1 and 2 is particularly enlightening on this unbridgeable gap in the creature between its being and its immanent operation. No creature's operation can be identical with its substance, because all created action actualizes a potency, while the creature's very existence actualizes a substance or essence. And no human creature's highest (i.e., intentional) operations can be identical with its act of existence, because such operations (understanding or willing) are infinite of their own nature, while a creature's act of existence is always delimited as the actualization of that particular kind or species of creature.
[80] *STh* I q. 23 a. 2.

attached to created substances but "in between" them, in their providentially guided interactions. Grace must "happen" or "arrive," mediated by the temporal movement of the world's history. In this sense one might be tempted to say it is less metaphysics than physics.

Is the "mere" nature being proposed here the same as the much-disputed "pure nature"? No, the concrete cosmic order in which we exist is an order already determined in God's freedom to the beatitude of human beings. "Pure" human nature is a counterfactual hypothesis; but its reality can be denied, as here, without in any way implying a natural order, or individual human natures, *defined* (as human) by that beatific end or somehow "already" supernatural. Wherein lies the "impurity" of nature, its "infection" (as it were) by grace? For Milbank, it is on the level of ontology, as well as on the level of human "spirit" as such. On the alternative suggested here it is an ontic matter, or, better, it is "historical": it occurs on the level of individual natures, as determined by the providential impetus of history. For Aquinas, the "natural" end of human and of angel is to image God by possessing the potencies of intellect and will; to possess God intentionally, however, is something else, possible through a graced extension of the natural orientation that is not specified by the natural end. Even though that supernatural possession perfects its imaging of God, human nature is not already grace; it is *capax dei*, but not even inchoately deiform. The natural intentionality by which it images God also renders it capable of grace, via the inherently open-ended, infinite nature of the desire to know, and also via the ability of intellect to be "unhooked" from finitude: its ability to abstract from matter defines the natural entity that is susceptible to supernatural elevation.

What of the natural end of loving God and knowing God to the degree possible? Of course, there can be only one truly ultimate end, by definition, and in our world that end is the beatific vision. But God's concrete ordering of humanity to that end does not mean that the now surpassed (natural) end is simply dispersed into a hypothetical counterfactual as "pure nature." It remains in play, since the act that fulfills the natural love of God is ordered to, and integrated into, the further act of supernatural intellectual union with the divine essence. Like the virtual presence of the chess pawn in the third rank even though it has moved to the fourth, remaining "in play" there as subject to capture despite "really" being elsewhere, so the surpassed final end of nature remains virtually in play in the graced order, supernatural charity fulfilling the demand of "mere" nature "*en passant*." Considered from the other direction, the natural desire of humanity in this world is for both the natural end and the supernatural end; as an indeterminate but (through grace) real possibility in this present order, the supernatural end already conditions the impulse of natural desire, but beatitude remains an inchoate intentional presence in the will until specified by the gift of habitual grace. So then, the supernatural end is implicitly desired through naturally desiring the natural end, but even the natural end is fulfilled only in the fulfillment of the supernatural one. The continued virtual validity of the merely natural end is suggested in Aquinas by the fact that (counterfactually) a perfect world could be built around it; by the fact that supernatural charity does not replace but enhances it; and, perhaps, by the fact that it finds eschatological fulfillment in the gift (distinct from the intellectual vision of the divine essence) of bodily eyes enabled to see God's moving, animating presence in the world order.[81]

The alternate scheme of nature and grace developed here, then, leaves a place for "mere" nature without positing any actual zone of "pure" nature. If one considers the three different aspects of the created order that can be designated as "nature" or "a nature," none would lack the trace within it of the supernatural orientation. First, and obviously, individual human natures that receive habitual (saving or justifying) grace are no longer "pure" natures; the habit of grace "recreates" the human soul, granting it a new, divinized act of being (hence, the scholastics dubbed it the "entitative habit"). Second, on the cosmic level, the level of *rerum natura* (the totality of natures in their organic unity and concrete temporal extension), nature is not pure, since the entire causal machinery is providentially arranged by God to deliver the just described reception of habitual grace.

But what of the (third) level of human nature universally and as such, that which is identical in all humans and defines them as human ("spirit" in Milbank's parlance)? Here, it seems, is where Milbank (following de Lubac) would locate the "impurity" of nature, by paradoxically casting the natural desire for God (universal among human beings) as a defining, quasi-supernatural exigency inscribed within each nature simply as created, prior to the habit of justification. Would Milbank, faced with the alternative reading of the natural desire offered here (which reserves within the natural desire for God a certain "open neutrality" with regard to the supernatural end of beatification) not accuse it of, in effect, rendering humans after the fall, once original grace was lost, "pure natures"? That would be too hasty. This is where the "conditioning" spoken of in the previous paragraph comes into play, but on the historical, not the ontological level.

This conditioning of the natural by the supernatural can be theorized *historically* if the individuation of human souls that for Aquinas happens through embodiment and the accretion of habits in intellectual memory is extended (this would admittedly go beyond Aquinas) to the cultural formation that shapes each individual human being. This leads to a picture of both original sin and the history of grace that opens the possibility of denying "pure nature" even on the level of the human species, human nature in general. For as historical and cultural animals, each particular human will enter and dwell within a semiotic world shaped by the concrete, providentially directed histories of grace built up through the experiences and symbolizations of others. From this perspective, then, "human nature" prior to habitual grace is "pure" only in the abstraction of ontology; concretely, the living contours of human nature as animating any given individual are ceaselessly refined through the historical role of culture (within specifically human limits, i.e., ontologically determined by the soul's nature). In spite of the "neutral" ontology of each soul ("neutral" as not yet specified in regard to supernatural friendship with God, though, like every creature, still ontologically oriented to the natural love of God as first cause and apex of natural order), every actual human being inhabits a universe of meaning already determined by the universal history of sin and grace.

---

[81] *STh* I q. 12 a. 3 ad 2.

To conclude this section, it should be remarked that an overall picture of grace and "mere" nature has now been developed that harmonizes with the picture developed in the previous section of history and "mere" being. Once again, the influence of Aquinas suggests a double structure within the created cosmos. On the one hand, a fixed, differential order of defined substances woven into specified relational arrangements both "vertical" (ontological grades) and "horizontal" (active and passive potencies defining proper possibilities of efficient and final conditioning); on the other hand, the particular, partially contingent actualization of this scheme of possibility through the unfolding of interactive operations. The latter sphere is the concrete sphere of both cosmic and human history, governed by God's providential vision. This twofold scheme introduced in Section II repeats itself in Section III; the general structural role of "mere" being takes the specific form of "mere" nature, just as the outworking of actual grace with its concrete distributions should be seen simply as a privileged subset of the earlier section's universal providence. Milbank has served in both sections as a foil against which to define an alternative metaphysical architecture. The summary words from Section I can be recalled here. Milbank can be understood as seeking to render the transparency of creation to the Trinity as nearly as possible universal, essential (i.e., definitive of creatures), and intrinsic. The alternative model, following Aquinas, will cast this transparency as local, accidental, and (not truly extrinsic but) adventitious; it will be seen that the advent of God involves a gap or "play" between a defined created zone of structural or essential ambiguity vis-à-vis the divine gift on the one hand, and its localized mediation into transparency to that gift (i.e., the resolution of the ambiguity) by way of cosmic process or history: totality, temporality and contingency.

It was suggested that the discussions of both this and the preceding section can be connected to the overall structure of Aquinas' thought at two junctures. First, recall that grace qualifies the human soul, providing intellectual and volitional virtues enabling the intentional presence of God *qua* God, and thereby supernaturally augmenting the *imago Dei* in human beings. It will be remembered that this was the second of the three forms of the image of God in humans, and it directed the discussion toward this section's account of the relations of grace and nature. The groundwork has now been laid out for an alternative scheme of these relations than that offered by Milbank and his "radical" appropriation of de Lubac. Moreover, second, here at the conclusion of this section we can repeat the gesture made at the end of the previous section, connecting the points made with Aquinas' discussion of knowledge of the Trinity.

For once again *STh* I q. 32 a. 1 has, in a sense, anticipated our results. If, as Milbank suggests, no hard and fast line separates the natural and the graced aspects of human spirit; if, in fact, humanity as such is always already "in some sense" decisively defined by grace; and if, congruent with this vision, the triune being of God must "repeat" itself on lower creaturely levels in accord with a Neoplatonic scheme of causation: then human intelligence and desire must in principle, prior to any "external" revelation, proleptically envision the divine Triunity as structurally implicit within it. If as has been argued here, on the other hand, human nature is constitutively open to but not defined by the vision of the divine essence; if the gap between nature and grace remains historically open; and if created being as such can only reflect the essential unity of the

Godhead; then apart from some disclosive event within history human speculation should be simply incapable of rational inference to the eternal triunity from reflection on world or self. And so indeed it turns out to be. Aquinas insists (ad 1), in some tension with a tradition running back to Augustine, that even the most insightful Platonists grasped only the world's reflection in the unified creative intelligence. They called this eternal idea "the son," but they were alluding only to a common, essential attribute merely appropriated by Christians to the Son; of the Son, proceeding from and consubstantial with the Father, they knew precisely nothing. And this is the case with all reason or philosophy outside the horizon of revealed grace.

IV. Mere Culture

So I thought to myself, "What would God do in this situation?"

The Simpsons
"Two Bad Neighbors"

With the doctrinal ground now prepared, we are ready in the latter half of this chapter to turn back to the question with which we began. Given the doctrinal commitments of the Christian faith, and especially given the particular systematization and interpretive elaborations by which theology enables the church's appropriation of these doctrines for the present, it is both possible and desirable to derive from the resulting claims about God, Christ, and grace what seem the appropriate assumptions, expectations, and goals that should regulate Christian engagements with non-Christian (or even anti-Christian) social groups and their differing cultural understandings: an ideal model of the "stance" of the Christian believer toward "the world." The previous two sections have developed a systematic contrast between, on the one hand, the theological positions of Milbank on creation and being, human nature and grace, and, on the other, the outlines of a proffered alternative based on a fuller range of Thomistic commitments. It should now be attempted, albeit in a tentative and schematic way only, to delineate the respective cultural "stances" of Christian faith toward the world that readily arise from these divergent (though by no means diametrically opposed) theological frameworks.

A central emphasis characterizing both frameworks is that God's saving grace grants nothing short of a participation of human persons in the infinite triune essence of deity. Quite distinct inferences, however, are drawn from this common assertion of the immensity of the divine self-gift. For Milbank, this gift of deification involves a donation so in excess of God's primordial bestowal of creaturely existence that it (paradoxically) includes the latter.[82] This is shorthand for the Milbankian scheme outlined above: the orientation to deifying beatitude implies a bestowal upon the creature so radical that the mere possibility of such an end already, from the beginning, molds and decisively determines the very shape of created being generally, and human nature in particular. But, as has been suggested in the previous discussions, this speculative "outbidding" by

---

[82] Milbank, *Suspended Middle*, 46.

grace of the radicality of "mere" creation is neither required by the logic of grace, nor coheres with the thought of Aquinas.

On this question of creation and salvation, Aquinas, as always, prefers to make a distinction, in this case between two sorts of infinity. In terms of *what* is created, the intentional presence of the divine essence created by grace in the intellects and wills of deiform humans indeed lodges within the created order a good that infinitely surpasses it. However, in terms of the *mode* of divine action, God's calling of any creature from nothingness already infinitely surpasses in power the bestowal even of deifying grace on the sinning enemies of God, as the latter remains a transaction within an already constituted created order. Thus, to the question "What is God's greatest work?" there can be no less than two answers: the creation of the world and the justification of the sinner.[83] In other words, the self-donation of the divine immensity is exhibited in an *irreducibly* dual way, pointing to a different understanding of grace and creation than that of Milbank. Rather than grace circling back to ground and subsume creation, Aquinas maintains a tension between two stages or moments: the created universe, and the grace that comes to it, each maintaining its identity and integrity, even though the former, in God's unwarranted love, is ordered, destined to the latter. Grace comes to nature. This is the alternative that has been sketched in the previous two sections.

In laying out the ecclesial assumptions about, and approaches to, uncommitted or "worldly" culture that are connected with these two models, it will serve the purpose once again to begin with Milbank and then derive alternatives by way of critical contrast. Although Milbank offers no concentrated, systematic exposition of the cultural stance of theology, the seminal indications are to be found in *Theology and Social Theory*, mainly in the introduction and the final chapter. Retrieving and connecting some key passages of his discussion there will enable a reconstruction of what seem to be the basic assumptions of Milbank's approach. First, Milbank joins together two (conceptually distinct) claims. On the one hand, any social formation requires a shared and circulated ultimate rationale or "scenario," at least implicitly in the form of narrative(s), that explains and warrants the peculiar social practices and structures that identify that community, and encodes its ideal significance. On the other hand, Milbank shares with Rowan Williams (as discussed above) an understanding of the Christian community as itself a vehicle of ongoing, collective witness; as an extension or reconfiguring of God's elect "people" the ecclesial society through its unique institutions and social forms embodies or indirectly "displays" as a historical presence the identity of the redeeming God of Israel and Jesus. These two claims in themselves are unobjectionable for our purposes. What is critical, however, is the way these two ideas at Milbank's hands are fused together and undergo conceptual refinements that push them in a sharply uncompromising direction.

How does he make the two claims coalesce? On its self-understanding (the second claim) the church's social existence has the force or function of a unique and divinely constituted collective witness to the creator of all things, thus in some sense incarnating the final meaning of all creation. And (the first claim) every social unity

---

[83] *STh* I/II q. 113 a. 9.

generates and performs (usually implicitly though manifest at privileged moments) a founding "script," some symbolic scheme or narrative that connects the communal form and praxis to ultimacy or "transcendence" within a single story. Why not unify the two claims such that the founding script or "scenario" of the church itself shares in the latter's status as the unique and divinely constituted witness to the unique creator God?[84] The church's social script or founding mythos would become the story that in principle articulates everything and every other story, coordinating them critically with the church as its central protagonist of the human tale. Again, although this combination is not inherently necessary, and presents a bolder and more risky claim than either component would make taken separately, it might well be theologically attractive and defensible, at least in certain versions.

But Milbank goes farther. For Milbank, the social "script" the church articulates and embodies is an "ultimate" narrative, ultimate in an exclusive and exhaustive sense. That is, Christian discourse not only embodies claims about the most encompassing, humanly meaningful states of affairs, claims taken to be unsurpassable in their own terms (Lindbeck or Williams might well agree). Beyond this, the Christian community understands itself to be uniquely able to articulate the source of created existence and meaning, and the telos of all human action and history, such that it not only can but must also expose all alternative claims as false or meaningless. Christian claims are not only unsurpassable on their own terms; they implicitly rule out other narratives making true claims of equivalent scope, even if those claims do not directly falsify its own but merely supplement them or overlap with them via different concepts or language. How does the church come to be in possession of this "all or nothing" vision?

Christian faith according to Milbank seeks to elaborate a fully encompassing "logos," a scheme of practical and theoretical reason that is grounded in its particular culture but that is necessarily universal in its reach. Over against the now discredited universalizing schemes of modernity, it narrates a counter-history, embodies a counter-ethos, and pronounces a counter-ontology.[85] Taking each of these components in turn, the alternative "history" Milbank speaks of is still recognizably akin to Rowan Williams's idea that the church itself as the people of God bears witness to or displays God in history through its social and cultural forms. For Milbank, however, because the church is a direct extension of the incarnation of God in Christ, its self-narrative must also share in the privilege of that event. Hence, the narration of the origin and ongoing development of the church presents "the most fundamental of events," "the 'interruption' of history by Christ and his bride, the Church."[86] Thus, it is a "real" history but "has also an interpretative, regulative function with respect to all other history."[87]

---

[84] For the mutual articulation of the two assumptions, see, e.g., Milbank, *Theology and Social Theory*, 383, 388. Milbank agrees with Lindbeck that the Christian society's normative activities encode the imagined ultimate instance or authority ("God") to which the activities are in some way conceived as the response. But he goes on to insist that the communal imaginary must be rooted in an underlying scenario or narrative that expresses the "relationship pertaining between 'the absolute' and the [responsive] practice," indeed that only such a scenario or mythos "makes this response possible."
[85] Ibid., 381.
[86] Ibid., 388.
[87] Ibid., 387.

Note how two conceptually separable narrative functions are here run together. On the one hand, every religious practice involves a mythical scenario in which it is grasped; in the church's case the "mythos" would comprise the stories of Jesus, the apostles, and the founding of the church. But on the other hand, the religious community "reads" the actual, ongoing history of the world, situating itself within it. Now, for Milbank, the story of Christ and the apostles has no privileged narrative status apart from its initiating and exemplary function; it is integrated, without remainder as it were, into the ongoing story of the church. The meaning of Christ for humanity is exclusively incarnated, articulated, "performed" by the church.[88] Thus, when Christ is treated "as 'measuring' all reality, in the same way that God's generated wisdom, his word, is taken to do," this amounts to situating all human history within Christ's story, which is none other than the church's story.[89]

From this narrated history arises a counter-ethics. That is, this narration is socially lived and continually "interpreted" in the organs and practices of the collective Christian institutions for which it provides the rationale. Here it is strikingly clear how for Milbank the absolute status of the event of Jesus is directly translated into the absolute status of Christianity as a social practice. Criticizing as dangerously ahistorical Lindbeck's cultural-linguistic model of enduring ecclesial identity, where that identity is "defined in advance by the exemplary narratives of Jesus," Milbank offers a more "postmodern" understanding whereby the church's "response" to the story of Jesus is the insertion of itself into a narrative that extends "the 'original' story," becoming the universal (and different) realization of what is realized only in an exemplary way in Jesus's story.[90] But if Jesus's life is the humanity that measures and judges all other events, then the church must logically become the community that measures and judges every other form of human belonging.

Milbank insists on this repeatedly and energetically. Christian truth is fundamentally a social event, "able to interpret other social formations because it compares them with its own new social practice."[91] This comparison is emphatically, indeed essentially, *critical*; the very meaning of the existence of authentic community seems to lie precisely in its showing up the failure of authentic community in every other instance. As Milbank puts it, the passage from counter-narrative to counter-ethos is the necessary passage of the self-interpretive story of the church into "a 'Hegelian' … philosophy of history" where the ultimacy of the narrative can only be displayed as a continual "regulation" of every other social practice. From the beginning, Christianity existed "not simply as an 'identification' of the divine but also as a 'reading' and a critique-through-practice of all historical human community up to that point." As essential to

---

[88] The encounter between Milbank and Frederick Bauerschmidt is instructive in this regard. The former (his jibes about "pietism" aside) has the better of the exchange as far as his emphasis on the essential role of ecclesial interpretation in constituting the original and the ongoing identity of Jesus. Bauerschmidt's concerns, however, are dogmatically well grounded inasmuch as they protest against a functional absorption of the figure of Jesus into the church's identity, i.e., his instrumentalization. See Frederick C. Bauerschmidt, "The Word Made Speculative? John Milbank's Christological Poetics," *Modern Theology* 15 (1999): 417–32, esp. 426–8; Milbank, "Intensities," 486–7.
[89] Milbank, *Theology and Social Theory*, 383.
[90] Ibid., 385–6.
[91] Ibid., 388.

ecclesial existence this critique must ever continue, as became clear in the "universalist claim" of the Fathers that all salvation is through incorporation into the church, implying that "other religions and social groupings, however virtuous-seeming, were finally on the path of damnation."[92] "In this fashion a gigantic claim to be able to read, criticize, say what is going on in other human societies, is absolutely integral to the Christian Church, which itself claims to exhibit the exemplary form of human community."[93] This exemplary form is the counter-ethics, in which "Christianity starts to appear—even 'objectively'—as not just different, but as the difference from all other cultural systems, which it exposes as threatened by incipient nihilism."[94]

Milbank's discussion of these matters proceeds by means of a critical conversation with George Lindbeck. Indeed, Lindbeck's truth theory of communal "reference" to God is the conceptual link that enables Milbank to radicalize Williams's account of the ideal witness or "display" of God through the church's communal life into a "counter-ethical" account where the church's discursive "difference" comes to be sharply defined as an identifiable cultural practice that consummates the possibility of human togetherness. But the third moment, the turn to a "counter-ontology," marks a conscious departure from Lindbeck.[95] For Milbank, the church does not simply communally "display" the divine identity, the creator-incarnate-in-Christ, through its ethos; it reflectively grasps the logic or rationale of all being, including human being, from this uniquely privileged standpoint. In other words, the church is not only the history encompassing all history, and the communal practice exposing the inevitable sinful failure of all other communal projects; it must continually generate from within itself an ontology, an account of being that is supremely "authorized" by the signified presence within ecclesial practice of the Source of all being. Thus, the absolute status of the God of the universe migrates from Christ as God's self-disclosive word, to the communal human structures and practices enacting that word, and ultimately to an ontology that can be deployed or wielded by members of that community to anticipate and deconstruct (in principle) any other possible (non-Christian) account of being.

Due to the social nature of truth, Milbank insists, "it can *only* be through a claim to offer the ultimate 'social science' that theology can establish itself and give any content to the notion of 'God.'"[96] The force of the terms "social" and especially "ultimate" have now been made clear; the key point, however, is the non-optional character of that ultimacy: Christian theology has no choice, it is fated to rule or fail. "If theology no

---

[92] Ibid., 387–8.
[93] Ibid., 388.
[94] Ibid., 381.
[95] For Lindbeck, the privileged ecclesial locus of the divine or saving truth lies in the praxis of the church instantiating and performing the cultural-linguistic codes that identify or carry the original gospel message. This was expressly in opposition to attempts to find that locus in the propositional claims of the community's dogmas that (necessarily) indicate and encapsulate those original meanings. George Lindbeck, *The Nature of Doctrine: Religion and Theology in a Postliberal Age* (Philadelphia: Westminster John Knox, 1984), 63–9. Milbank in effect refuses this distinction, arguing that inherent within the communal practice itself is the articulation of those truth-claims; they lie implicit within the very narrative shaping the practice. As he sums up his position, "More place must be given to propositions, and so to ontology, than Lindbeck seems to allow" (*Theology and Social Theory*, 382). The entire discussion on pp. 382–8 is relevant.
[96] Milbank, *Theology and Social Theory*, 6.

longer seeks to position, qualify or criticize other discourses, then it is inevitable that these discourses will position theology."[97] Any theologian would agree on the right of theology to qualify or criticize other discourses; the key word here, rather, is "position." On the evidence of Milbank's rhetoric this goes well beyond ad hoc critique; it amounts to the denial *ab initio* and in principle of any possible counterclaim to the Christian theologian's assertions that she is bound to countenance. It is a pretension to be the single arbiter of final truth for all; should any other discourse be deemed valid, its truth value is treated as merely ceded to it by Christian theology, its "prior" possessor. Thus, the latter for its part cannot, in any *fundamental* way, be legitimately informed or challenged by a non-Christian discourse.

To name this transcendental discursive standpoint of theology or the Christian "logos" Milbank uses the term made current by Jean-Francois Lyotard: "metanarrative." He is careful to distance his own sense of this term from the latter's; after all, he shares Lyotard's "postmodern" suspicion of the modern metanarratives of universal reason and science.[98] But this gesture rather veils the similarity to those latter usages, which might be closer in Milbank's case than he wishes to acknowledge. The metanarratives of modernity functioned specifically to legitimate discourses and communal discursive practices, as does Milbank's. Indeed, though his does not "graft faith onto a universal base of reason," it still grafts faith onto a similar discursive claim to omnicompetence. The appeal to a universally *available* measure is dropped, but what remains is the pretended universal *scope*: arbitrator of all human meaning. The "postmodern" Milbank agrees with Lyotard that there is no universal reason any more, only particular narratives; but by means of the fusions and inferences described above he uses the Christian claim to uniquely authoritative revelation to guarantee that the church tells the one particular narrative that can authentically claim metanarrative status.

The reader should be cautioned at this point that nothing like a full-scale exploration of Milbank's discursive strategies and their theological rationale is being attempted here, much less a refutation of them. The goal of the account given in the last few pages has been to give an outline of the cultural "stance" that informs Milbank's project, briefly indicating the explicit warrants. This has been for the purpose of rendering clearer the shape of an alternative (yet to be delineated). Milbank's approach might be described as a bid for the discursive reinstatement of "Christendom," in lieu of its political or cultural actuality. This accurately captures, at least, the imperial status of theology among the world's discourses. Similarly, in terms of his preferred rhetoric Milbank at more than one point in his corpus harks fondly back to the uncompromising truculence of the Fathers. Contemporary theology, he thinks, desperately needs to recapture their aggressiveness.

At any rate, the "false humility" that he taxes modern theology with is not just a mistaken strategy; it is positively "fatal" to theology, which (as was stressed above) has no choice but to take up the role of supreme discursive arbiter, lest it fail entirely to exhibit its divine object in the fallen world.[99] This is even more true today in face

---

[97] Ibid., 1.
[98] Ibid., 381.
[99] Ibid., 1.

of the all-conquering counter-claim of secular humanism, which unfailingly reduces to nihilism: "*Only* Christian theology now offers a discourse able to position and overcome nihilism itself."[100] Milbank's stark dyad (either Christianity or modernity, i.e., nihilism), rooted in his reading of de Lubac ("[S]ecular humanism is the *absolute antithesis* of the gospel."[101]), heightens the stakes of theology's choice of the correct stance. But is his own recommendation unproblematic? Does it raise the specter of a performative contradiction within Christian theology? In so vigorous and systematic a turn away from "false humility" is theology heedlessly abandoning the real thing?

The remainder of this section will suggest, first, that these are indeed serious liabilities hidden within any theological "metanarrative" conceived on Milbank's lines; second, this will prompt the assembly of the theological claims developed in previous sections to develop, at least in outline, the contours of a different stance of faith toward the world, one at once more humane and more Christianly self-consistent. The initial critique of Milbank's metanarrative approach will draw heavily upon various observations of Williams that appeared around the same time as Milbank's *Theology and Social Theory* (though in most cases not referencing the latter). The dogmatic roots of the divergence between Williams's and Milbank's assumptions about the church and "worldly" culture will then be linked to the same Christological reflections of Cornelius Ernst discussed earlier in this chapter. The last part of the section will develop Ernst's brief suggestion in a much fuller way, using the insights about God, being, and nature presented in Sections II and III.

In articles written in 1989 and 1990, Williams makes statements that amount to principles for an incipient ethic of Christian cultural engagement. These principles are noticeably at odds with the assumptions that inform Milbank's own theorization of that engagement, though there is no evidence that Williams had Milbank in mind. In fact, in his 1992 contribution to a symposium on *Theology and Social Theory* he protests that his aim is not to weaken but to give more substance to the latter's metanarrative "project."[102] This emollient announcement belies, however, the weightiness of his objections there. For example, the early cultural engagements of the church "over against" Judaism and pagan society (which for Milbank are paradigmatic of its necessarily aggressive claim to embody the supreme societal form) were, Williams argues, far more nuanced, and involved more ambiguity and discursive give and take, than Milbank's schematic portrayal allows. Indeed, Williams challenges the very notion that ecclesial life can be profitably understood as the "negation" of other social forms. Williams also exposes the one-sidedness of any approach that is straightforwardly premised on the church's societal ethic as already "achieved" (i.e., readily available for deployment against rivals); this fails to take account of the vital yet complicating questions as to how such an ethic is, concurrently with its articulation, communally "learned ... discerned ... [and] risked" in social existence.[103]

---

[100] Ibid., 6. Italics added.
[101] Milbank, *Suspended Middle*, 9. Italics added.
[102] Rowan Williams, "Saving Time: Thoughts on Practice, Patience and Vision," *New Blackfriars* 73 (1992): 320.
[103] Ibid., 321.

As part of a symposium explicitly engaging Milbank's project, Williams registered these concerns with restraint, and at a carefully general level. If, however, his more detailed observations from the two earlier articles are read with Milbank in mind, a sharper picture comes into view of the kind of serious divergence merely gestured toward in the 1992 piece. We might suspect his 1989 critique of Lindbeck to be relevant given Milbank's avowed sympathies, and this suspicion is confirmed.[104] Even if Christian communities can today only persist as sociocultural enclaves, they nonetheless exist to present to the world (in terms it can assimilate) a vision and a possibility of global human community, else they risk degenerating into inert meaning-ghettoes.[105] Milbank might argue that such a bid for universal relevance is precisely what his metadiscourse offers, yet Williams gives us reason to doubt it. For the latter insists that Christians cannot truly engage the world by forcing its meanings into Christian categories. The church's traffic with worldly meanings must allow its judgment of the world, but it must equally allow the church to hear the world's judgment upon itself.[106] Above all, "in the world as it is, the right to be heard speaking about God must be earned." Citing Bonhoeffer, Williams here stresses how the schemes of Christian meaning cannot be heard *as gospel*, until and insofar as the church engages the public arena in ways recognizably redemptive on the world's terms.[107] Is this the "false humility" excoriated by Milbank? Say rather it is Williams's recognition that the pretensions of universal meaning will only be misheard until the Christian project can be seen as engaged in the cooperative struggle for a truly inclusive human community.

Similar notes are sounded in Williams's (already cited) 1990 reflections on confessing Christ's ultimacy within the world of interreligious encounter.[108] It is hard to read this essay without seeing in it repeated cautions or rejoinders to something distinctly resembling the metanarrative approach Milbank had been developing since "A Christological Poetics" (1982). Some such approach is arguably implicated under Williams's rejection of "strategies [that] assume that it is possible and proper to try and articulate a comprehensive account of religious meaning that somehow contains other meanings." Yes, the church bears God's final word, the word of Christ, in the world, and all human histories and their self-interpretive stories will converge upon Christ's judgment; but that convergence has *not yet* happened, and what it will concretely look like "can[not] be theorized in advance."[109] In the meantime, prior to the eschaton, the task of the church lies in continually discovering how that word can be made audible beyond its bounds. The Christian community's fidelity to God's unique and ultimate incarnation in Jesus does not put it in a position to "demonstrat[e] the comprehensive meaningfulness of Jesus," especially as this latter is "normally" reduced to the comprehensive meaningfulness "of the Church's language."[110]

---

[104] Rowan Williams, "The Judgment of the World," in *On Christian Theology* (Oxford: Blackwell, 2000), 29–43.
[105] Ibid., 36.
[106] Ibid., 39.
[107] Ibid., 40–1.
[108] Williams, "Finality of Christ," 93–106.
[109] Ibid., 94.
[110] Ibid., 100.

With that last remark, Williams broaches a particularly crucial point. He is alarmed by the fallacy of "identifying the 'meaning' articulated in the Christian institution with this fullness of meaning in Christ."[111] There is both a functional error here and a substantive dogmatic misunderstanding. The former threatens the church's witness with a lapse into performative incoherence. Williams warns Christians that the church's "foundational 'myths'" are not its legitimation but its agenda for dialogic encounter, specifically demanding its willingness to learn.[112] How can Milbank's cultural strategy avoid twisting witness into just the kind of communal self-legitimation rejected here? If the Christian intervention in the world is the proffer of the possibility (given by God in Christ) of universal human community beyond self-protective and self-justifying enclaves, then the truth of the story the church tells would be practically denied if that story were wielded as the guarantor of the church as an "ersatz universality," that is, as itself an "authoritative and comprehensive system of meaning." In this way the good news supposedly for all people hardens into "a large-scale tribalism."[113]

Otherwise put, granting the truth of the Christian self-narrative, it must still be protected from becoming a communal ideology, the legitimation of a certain social or cultural group over against others. The church has the news of God's ultimate Word, but this is no tool guaranteeing in advance that it is, even in principle, the exhaustive repository of social, ethical, or religious truth. Even for Williams, of course, the church is engaged in a process of encountering the world's meanings with what it affirms to be the "finality" of Christ; yet this encounter, even though necessarily critical, will still look less like an endlessly repeated triumph over contrapositions and more like the collaborative effort of building a common human language. The church will rightly understand this in terms of a kind of "conversion" of the world's truths to the truth of Christ, but it must always be on guard lest that truth become the self-authentication of "us" against "the rest." In short, in light of Williams's ruminations Milbank's rhetorical and argumentative moves seem insufficiently inoculated against the very real threat of turning the gospel into an ideology. The gospel's truth would not make its ideological effects any less pernicious.[114]

The Christian says every fallen community is a failure of inclusivity, a failure to be the community of all. But how to express this communally? How to be *evangelically* different? Milbank locates this difference in the church's capacity to tell a story that shows how every other community must necessarily fail (enabling the story's ideological

---

[111] Ibid., 96.
[112] Ibid., 95.
[113] Ibid., 100.
[114] It is incumbent upon theology to propose safeguards against this ideological temptation, to which the church has repeatedly succumbed. If Williams offers Christological and ecclesiological considerations as one such safeguard, Nicholas Lash provides more strictly methodological considerations toward the same end. Nicholas Lash, "Ideology, Metaphor and Analogy," in *Theology on the Way to Emmaus* (London: SCM Press, 1986), 95–119. In particular, Lash proposes the necessary role of transcendental reflection or "metaphysics" (construed broadly on p. 106 as "that branch of philosophy the logic of whose procedures focusses on analogical [conceptual] usage of unrestricted generality"), such as was practiced by Aquinas, as a vital curb on the too ready ideological "deployment" of theological (or even Biblical) language. The current chapter, likewise appealing to Aquinas but focusing on his more developed doctrinal claims, attempts to operates somewhere between, but still within the space marked out by Williams and Lash.

legitimation of the Christian community). But Williams locates this difference in the church's detachment of any legitimating function from its narrative of God, freeing it to become it a catalytic invitation to all other narratives. But that means ecclesial meaning will develop in unanticipatable ways, and non-ecclesial meaning will play an essential role in that, rendering the development never completely controllable. To put it briefly: the ecclesial account of "the way things are" cannot function metanarratively until the end of history. This is Williams's formal or methodological challenge to metanarrative.

But there is also a dogmatic issue raised by Williams that likewise throws a critical light on Milbank's approach. It was touched on above in treating Williams's reference to Ernst. Milbank's theorization of the church's truth as its possession in principle of an all-conquering "metanarrative" depends on accounts of the ultimacy of Christ, and of the relation of Christ to the church, that are called in question by Williams's appeal to Ernst. The pretension to metanarrative seems to rest on a specific way of connecting several claims.[115] First, every cohesive community shares a basic story or "scene," the collectively imagined narrative paradigm that encapsulates the origin, goal, and idealized career of its identifying institutions and practices. Second, the particular community called the Christian church is the elect vehicle of the creator-God's humanly decisive self-disclosure; its mode of sociality is the visible enactment in human history of the identity of the God of Israel and of his will for perfect human communion. Finally, since the divine disclosure involves the institution on earth of a perfected mode of human sociality, and since the telos of all human truth is precisely the realization of such a sociality, then this particular community's ongoing self-understanding must in principle usurp or negate every other human claim to collective human meaning. Its very style of social existence represents an implicit exposure of the self-deception and bias toward corruption at the heart of every other, non-redeemed social group or culture. So if this community is itself the revelation of the creator God, and if its social modality is accessible through its grasp of its basic scenario or grounding narrative, then the articulation of this narrative is itself the construction of a human story that legitimates its own unique claim while deconstructing every rival human story: a metanarrative. See what has happened: step by step, ultimacy has migrated from God's self-disclosive act, to the community bearing or embodying that disclosure, and finally (in principle, and subject to its proper and ongoing articulation and refinement) to the system or scheme of its own self-understanding.

Williams's brief but pointed appeal to Ernst's Christology has the effect of dismantling this metanarrative machine by interrogating the required connections. Ernst, in defining the ultimacy of Christ, speaks of him as the "meaning of [human] meaning"; in Williams's paraphrase:

> Jesus is God's participation in and ordering of the systems of human communication that constitute the unity, the possibilities of relation, the "sense" of human existence

---

[115] This paragraph synthesizes the discussion of Milbank's "metanarrative" above.

in the world, and is also our participation in the "communication" and relatedness that is the creative life of God.[116]

But Ernst goes on to add some critical stipulations. As the divine Word incarnate Jesus Christ is the "substance" of human meaning, the Word (as Williams put it) "through which human beings find a language for their common humanity." But this does not mean that as such Jesus supplies an "ontology" of human meaning, a linguistic or conceptual articulation of his own material significance. Hence, Ernst distinguishes his "substantive" meaning from his "ontological" meaning (described as "the thematizing of how the substantive significance of Christ works, and what are the conditions for it in the structure of reality"). For Ernst, such an ontological grasp of the total human significance of Jesus "would only show itself in the reality of a single—or better, a freely communicating—human culture" in which "the diversity of human experience and human struggle" could find full expression. Two implications of this division are noted by Williams. On the one hand, a fully adequate ontology of Christ must await the end of human history, since it can only be expressed and received within the consummate human community; to expect at present "a finished account of Christ as containing all meanings would make Christology non-eschatological." On the other hand, the distinction between Christ's substantive meaning and its possible communal thematization must seriously problematize any attempt to regard the church, which indeed culturally and really extends Christ's living body into human history, as in any way simply incorporating or absorbing or realizing his substantive meaning into its own. Thus, Williams's sharp warning, noted above, against identifying the meaning of Christ with the meaning of the communal institution that bears his living presence.

By appealing in this way to Ernst's Christological categories, Williams's discussion implicitly disrupts the metanarrative functioning envisioned by Milbank. Rendered in Ernst's terms, Milbank's scheme of cultural engagement involves, first, the church's ability to generate and deploy its own story in the form of an ontological scheme; the implication is that the church's grasp of Christ as the meaning of being guarantees its own ability to subsume or deconstruct all other narratives of human meaning. Second, the ecclesial availability of Christ's ontological meaning strongly implies the functional or effective subsumption of Christ's substantive meaning within the formality and ongoing history of the church.[117] Finally, this fusion, and the exploitable Christic ontology that flows from it, in principle *already* locate the totality of ultimate human meaning in the church; this arguably puts in question the real significance of the human historical struggle for encompassing community (and the church's role in it), as well as the eschatological deferral making that history possible. The point is that the questions put to Milbank's project from Williams's perspective are prompted not just by methodological considerations, but at least in part by a differing dogmatic

---

[116] This and the other quotations in the paragraph are Williams's descriptions of Ernst's position. See Williams, "Finality of Christ," 93–4.
[117] This was the question at issue between Bauerschmidt and Milbank. Some of Milbank's most audacious formulations, suggestive of such a subsumption, are found in John Milbank, "The Name of Jesus," in *The Word Made Strange* (Oxford: Blackwell, 1997), 145–68.

articulation of Christology and its relation to ecclesiology. For Williams, following Ernst, the church is not in a position to "operationalize" its own narrative in terms of an ontology; it cannot presume that its social form simply extends or incorporates the substance of Christ's meaning as God-man; and it must regard its own "finality" as the "form" of human community as for now merely fragmentary and anticipatory; it must await its unveiling at the consummation of the still unfinished human history it is helping to construct.

At this point we can return to the reflections developed in the previous two sections. Williams has provided the elements of a critique of Milbank's metanarrative project along with the outline of a different "stance" of faith toward culture, meaning different procedures and expectations in regard to the encounter between witness to Christ and the larger world of human meaning-making. It has already been seen that the points at issue cannot be confined to considerations of method but spill over into dogmatic contentions. Now the positions on God, creation, and grace developed earlier in this chapter as alternatives to Milbank's dogmatic emphases can also come into their own as an augmentation of Ernst and consequently as supportive elaborations of Williams's model of the cultural transactions of Christian witness. To see in brief how this is so, some of the implications of those earlier positions need to be extended into Christology, following lines already indicated by Williams's appeal to Ernst.

The basic understanding emerging from the earlier sections of this chapter can be summarized in this way. God's gracious act in and toward the world, the self-gift of the infinite Being, cannot be ontologized (i.e., made ingredient within the universal structure of created being), nor can it be naturalized (i.e., made into a definitive component of essential humanity). To be sure, created being and human nature are constitutively open to this infinite gift, but on their own terms they maintain a structurally ambiguous relation to it. God's gracious donation is the divinization of human beings, but their divinization is subordinated to and derivative of the perfect divinization of Jesus Christ, the paradoxical divine creature.[118] If this individual is the source of all grace, and grace relates to the total created order in the more open and ambivalent way just indicated (the Thomist alternative to Milbank developed in Sections II and III), then, to repeat a formula already used, grace must "come to" the world via the coming of Jesus Christ. Jesus will be the historical event of a human being (an animal possessed of intellective and volitional intentionality), subsequently disseminated into other intentional centers, all via a providentially guided but immanent historical causation. In a sense, it is due to the divine infinity that grace must come to the world in Christ, via the working of human history: this already suggests that grace as the final truth of being likewise must come in the course of history to the church, not apart from its own continuous traditions and institutions but not solely from them, because appropriated from outside of itself as well. The ecclesial community will never unlock the ontological meaning of Christ apart from the cooperative labor of human history.

---

[118] It would be too simple, but still not entirely misleading, to suggest that whereas Milbank expands paradox to cosmic proportions, the account here seeks to "contract" it, i.e., within Christ.

But that is not all. Further development of these ideas provides a theological rationale not just for the *advent* of Christ, but for the *ascension* as well. If the divinizing paradox had to come, there is a fitting necessity to the claim that it likewise had to go away. Of course, it is generally agreed that the church can be conceived as something like the communal and bodily extension in history of Jesus's incarnation. For Milbank, however, the unique status the community accords to Jesus comes close to being a projection backward onto its "founder" of the community's own claim to absolute difference. In eschewing such an identification Williams's conception leaves space for a fuller theology of Jesus's ascension. The significance of the withdrawal of the Resurrected is both negative, as the removal of his direct somatic presence within history, and positive, as the enthronement of his resurrected body, the body of the new eon. Functionally put, this frees Jesus to be more than just the founder, the organic "head" of his ecclesial body: he is its living judge as well. The corporality of Jesus is henceforth divided between transcendent (heavenly) and semiotic (ecclesial) bodies; the historically fluctuating gap between them measures the ongoing judgment of the former upon the latter. But what, finally, connects ascension to advent? Both Jesus's coming and his going preserve the integrity of the causal flow of finite history, protecting it from, on the one hand, irrelevance to the bestowal of infinite grace, and from, on the other, total subsumption into that bestowal. Just as the substantive meaning of Jesus (to recall Ernst's terms) had to arrive, so too it had to depart, in order to "leave time" for Jesus' ontological meaning to be worked out in history.

So the necessary delay of a Christic ontology proposed by Williams (after Ernst) is supported by the findings of Section II: God's gracious self-bestowal was there theorized less as a structural element of created being (á la Milbank) and more as an event continually arising through the interplay between structure and temporal development. In a similar way, the hiatus between Christ's enthroned and ecclesial bodies is undergirded by the third section's conclusion that grace is not "always already" ingredient within human nature but arrives within the open field of contingent human action. The foregrounding of time and history evident here connects in turn with the last of Williams's emphases: the deferral of the eschaton. Although the eschatological dimension as such has not been explored in previous sections, the stress on the ongoing and essential role of history points in and of itself to the still ongoing and unfinished nature of both church and humanity. The history of grace, and therefore human history generally, are still underway; hence the need for a continual caution against triumphal accounts of the ecclesial community and its knowledge.

Milbank's comments on eschatology are scattered throughout his oeuvre and not fully developed; however, the strict eschatological "hiatus" urged here between the historical body of the ecclesial community and the heavenly body of the risen Lord would seem to clash with his emphases. "Christ and his bride" are sometimes spoken of in a way that suggests their reduction to a single "social event."[119] The claim that Christ's body now *exists* "only as given, as eucharist," while capable of benign readings nonetheless gives one pause (and again recall the exchange with Bauerschmidt).[120] Most

---

[119] Milbank, *Theology and Social Theory*, 388.
[120] Milbank, "Enclaves," 342.

striking are the provocative assertions in the programmatic "Forty-Two Responses" from 1991, where the "real saving presence" of the resurrected Jesus lies (wholly?) in the church's fragmentary memory of "perfect community as once instantiated by the shores of Lake Galilee."[121] This apparent identification in response 25 of the living Jesus with "a new language of community" leads naturally into the metaphysically rather anemic account of his resurrection that follows in responses 26–28. The reader is ultimately assured (response 40) that for a "postmodern" theology, at any rate, debates over the historicity of the resurrection are pointless, once the "real" has come to be synonymous with "the cultural happening of 'meaning.'" Again there are theologically defensible construals of all this, but together Milbank's assertions point to a tendency, at least, that is quite at odds with the above insistence upon the church's eschatological proviso.

How does this third emphasis relate to the two previous Christological moments of advent and ascension? Jesus Christ as the substance of grace must come to the world, as an event of free human intentionality; he must leave the world, else the immensity of God in time would warp or "clog" the movement of history, arresting it prematurely. Hence the twofold character of Jesus's ascension: first he departs, then he is enthroned elsewhere, "in heaven." His Kingdom is for now hidden, withdrawn, leaving only his ecclesial body as a proxy or sign. (For his enthronement here would itself be the eschaton.) In Ernst's terminology, Jesus as the substantive meaning of humanity had to depart, because humanity's story is unfinished; he left to allow time for history, in which Jesus as the ontological meaning of humanity must be worked out. The very point of the ascension is eschatological deferral, and thus history; against the tendency in Milbank to make his semiotic body, the church, his only body, the eschatological proviso is the apartness of the two bodies until the end of history. Milbank speaks in the same sentence of Christians as "on pilgrimage" yet as "inhabitants of the *altera civitas*."[122] But by definition, it must be one or the other! The eschatological point is that one should rather say: citizens, yes ("Our *politeuma* is in the heavens." Phil. 3:20) but precisely *not* inhabitants. The sign body of Jesus, the unfinished historical proxy of his human meaning, is constitutively *on pilgrimage*. Only Jesus was at once *viator et comprehensor*; as his followers we remain only pilgrims awaiting their final arrival.[123]

Comprehensores is just what we are not: that is what must be stressed. Now we come full circle once again, back to Aquinas' threefold gradation of the image of God in human beings.[124] The first grade, the intentional capacity natural to all human beings, was connected (in Section II) with the necessity of temporal causality beyond the structure of "mere" being; the second grade, the gracious enhancement of natural intentionality by supernatural virtue, was linked (in Section III) to the necessary gap or "play" between "mere" human nature and grace. Here at the end of the fourth section, the third and highest grade of the divine image in humans, namely, the perfection "in glory" of the intellect's knowledge of God and the will's love of God, can serve to cast a

---

[121] Milbank, "Postmodern Critical Augustinianism," 225–37.
[122] Milbank, *Theology and Social Theory*, 380.
[123] On Jesus as pilgrim and beholder at once, see *STh* III q. 15 a. 10.
[124] *STh* I q. 93 a. 4.

backward light on the necessity of history. In other words, the deferred eschatological consummation of the *imago Dei* determines the shape of humanity's temporal career.

Two considerations are important here, drawn from Aquinas' theology of grace. If humanity's ultimate glorification is marked by the immutable vision of God, then the state prior to that highest exemplification of God's image is marked both by a lack of vision, and by an invincible mutability. First, lack of vision, because in the state of grace in this life a fundamental imbalance reigns; the will can be more perfectly attuned to God by the habit of charity than the intellect can be through the gracious habit proper to it.[125] Because the vision of God requires the reception of the divine essence as intellectual species, and this in turn demands a drastic recalibration of the interface between soul and body, the graced intellect is defined by "faith," not vision (in the state of faith we are, by charity, immediately "united to [God] as to one unknown," to use one of Aquinas' favorite phrases from Pseudo-Dionysius, e.g., *STh* I q. 12 a. 13 ad 1).

Second, invincible mutability, because Aquinas' discussion of the human conversion to the graced state indicates that, apart from special miraculous cases, God providentially assembles the external and internal (psychological) conditions via a process.[126] And even once grace is attained, it remains fragile, inherently vulnerable to possible disruption (mortal sin) in such a way that the whole process must be repeated.[127] Thus, in the "usual course" of things, human existence in this world is an adventure of imperfect conversion; only the eschaton ends this drama by closing the gap of history in the perfect stability of beatification. Another way of expressing this is to say that the infinity of God, and hence the infinity of the gift of participating God, demands an ontological transformation of the human order. Only the end of history allows the Triune image to be perfected in humanity; only when the human intellect truly beholds the Trinity is the divine being fully manifest in created being. But by divine decree what Herbert McCabe called the "revolution in our bodies," the resurrection of the flesh, presupposes the "long revolution" called history.

This in turn brings us back to our other touchstone from Aquinas, his discussion of knowledge in this life of the Trinitarian persons.[128] Section II concluded with his flat denial that the order of created being as such can possibly reveal the divine persons to human apprehension; this corresponded to the distinction between structural ontology and the order of event.[129] Section III recalled Aquinas' equally stubborn refusal to allow (even in the face of Augustine's assurances) that the *libri platonici* had in any way attained a glimpse of the Trinitarian Son or Word; this reinforced the integrity of the graced state and its cognitive achievement over against the capacities of "mere" nature. As the present section concludes, the focus is on Aquinas' reply to the second objection (ad 2): even as enlightened by grace, a rational demonstration of the divine Triunity is strictly impossible. The dialectical brilliance of earlier fathers

---

[125] *STh* II/II q. 27 a. 4.
[126] *STh* I/II q. 109 a. 6; q. 112 a. 2 ad 1 and ad 2; q. 113 a. 7 and ad 1; q. 113 a. 10.
[127] *STh* I/II q. 109 a. 10.
[128] *STh* I q. 32 a. 1.
[129] This does not deny that the "trace" of the creator's triunity is manifest in every creature to the eyes of faith; it simply reiterates Aquinas' point that the created "trace" images only the essential appropriations, not the personal distinctions themselves. *STh* I q. 45 a. 7 ad 1.

such as Richard of St. Victor notwithstanding, the most that can be achieved in this sphere is, on the one hand, a refutation of any pretended counter-demonstration (i.e., of the impossibility of the Trinity), and, on the other hand, a plausible rational account that "saves the appearances," casting the revealed data into a fitting order of reasoned interconnection. Even the most sophisticated exercise of the latter kind will never attain the unique necessity and validity of demonstration; and it will be, of its very nature, only one of several possible schemes. Thus, a repeated motif of Aquinas returns to view: the immensity of the absolute inhabits a height that cannot be humanly attained, even by grace. His final warning against any such pretention on the part of Christian faith to attaining a "god's-eye view" of matters is telling. Faith's attempt to appropriate knowledge that is reserved to God alone, and bring it to bear in the cultural encounter, will only awaken (and rightfully so!) the world's mocking laughter (*irrisio infidelium*).

V. Comme c'est drôle!

When [one] measures out the small world, as humor does, against the infinite world and sees them together, a kind of laughter results which contains pain and greatness.

Jean Paul
Vorschule der Aesthetik

Were you there when they crucified Jack Lord?

Michael O'Donoghue
Mr. Mike's Mondo Video

It is impossible even in a lengthy chapter such as this to do justice to John Milbank's monumental theological vision, brilliantly executed and exhilarating in its creativity, ambition, and depth. The task here has not been directly to dispute its founding insights or its many specific claims but rather to register a dissatisfaction with its presumed stance toward non-Christian culture, to trace how that stance possibly grows out of certain debatable details of his conceptions of creation and of grace, and finally to suggest (drawing imaginatively on Aquinas) an alternative approach. In light of the conclusion of the preceding section, it might be said that the Milbankian moves questioned here amount to an oblique attempt by ecclesial reason to "demonstrate the Trinity." (This rather abstract indictment acquires more literal force in view of the impatience expressed by Milbank in response to Aquinas' apophatic rigor concerning the Trinity.[130]) If that characterization of what is dubious about Milbank's project be admitted, then the alternatives proffered in this chapter amount to an elaboration of Aquinas' concern that our rational overreach needlessly provokes the derision of unbelief. The topic of humor, however, can be mined more fully in order to help draw

---

[130] For a discussion, see DeHart, *Aquinas and Radical Orthodoxy*, 171–8.

out some implications of the contra-Milbankian discursive stance delineated in the previous section. A full methodology of theological "humility" cannot be attempted here at the end of an already overlong chapter; but three dimensions of the humorous can serve as clues toward a fuller account: incongruity, slapstick, and irony.

One way of thinking about Milbank's metanarrative endeavor is to see it as an attempt to reestablish the cultural "stance" of Christendom, only now on a purely discursive (rather than social or political) basis. The thoughts developed above provide a dogmatic rationale for doubting the soundness of this attempt, but there are historical or sociological considerations found in the work of Michel de Certeau that equally suggest a performative self-contradiction within such a discursive Christendom. The forms of modern society have almost completely dissolved the earlier social body that generated and supported the discourse of Christian belief and action; the collective social form now locates and motivates cultural production and everyday practices along completely different lines, according to quite alien rules.[131] In other words, only the sociopolitical form of Christendom was capable of organizing Christian discourse on terms immanent to that discourse. It gave that discourse a public "place" at the center of collective consciousness. The breakup of this social formation is linked by Certeau with the rise of "mystical" speech; the latter responds to the new discursive marginalization of belief by attempting to reconstitute a new, "mystical" body whose bonds are no longer sociologically effective but rather derive from appeals to shared experience or sensibility.[132]

Indeed, Certeau came to question the very possibility that Christian practice could take form as a social body at all under modern conditions. It is arguable that so extreme a conclusion is unwarranted, that Christian discourse cannot be fully actualized save as integrated with a public, visible collective body, and consequently that social incorporation needs to be reimagined in (sociological and, in fact, metaphysical) forms distinct from those Certeau was prepared to entertain.[133] (In this matter Certeau and Erik Peterson represent opposed poles of a crucial debate on the modern ecclesial body. Justice must be done to the insights of both.[134]) Be that as it may, Certeau's prior

---

[131] For the crucial analyses of the social situation of Christian discourse, see Michel de Certeau, "Du corps à l'écriture: un transit chrétien," and "Autorités chrétiennes et structures sociales," in *La Faiblesse de Croire* (Paris: Seuil, 1987), 267–306 and 77–128.

[132] See the concluding discussion of Jean de Labadie in Michel de Certeau, *The Mystic Fable*, vol. 1, trans. Michael B. Smith (Chicago: University of Chicago Press, 1992), 288–93.

[133] For important critical remarks along these lines within an excellent overview of Certeau's thought, see Frederick C. Bauerschmidt, "The Abrahamic Voyage: Michel de Certeau and Theology," *Modern Theology* 12 (1996): 1–26, esp. 17–22.

[134] The theological reflections of both were rooted in their historical investigations; the different periods they specialized in had an outsized influence upon their ecclesiological proposals. Certeau, rooted in studies of spirituality in the sixteenth and seventeenth centuries, saw the church's social embodiment as a function of a European Christendom whose cultural decomposition in that period he analyzed (along with its byproduct, codified mysticism). Peterson, a historian of the first Christian centuries, became a theoretician of the pre-Constantinian ecclesial body, earthly outpost of the eschatological heavenly polis. Peterson's concern with the essential nature of the church as an identifiable communal organism occupying public and political space within the world emerges at various points within the essays collected in Erik Peterson, *Theological Tractates* [1951], trans. Michael J. Hollerich (Stanford: Stanford University Press, 2011), especially 1–15, 30–40, 102–14, 141–50. A most helpful synthetic account, drawing on published and unpublished sources, of Peterson's ecclesiological thinking and its close but critical relation to Carl Schmitt can be found

point loses none of its power: the discourse of Christendom cannot be deployed save from the site of Christendom, from a social corpus organized by a Christian imaginary. Certeau's distinction between strategy and tactics will help thematize the dilemma here.[135]

According to Certeau, a strategy is "the calculation (or manipulation) of power relationships that becomes possible as soon as a subject [i.e., some social collective or institutionalized practice] with will and power ... can be isolated." This demands "a *place* [a social site] that can be delimited as its *own* and serve as the base from which relations with an *exteriority* composed of targets or threats ... can be managed." By contrast, "a tactic is a calculated action determined by the absence of a proper locus." Lacking a determinate sphere of its own that is functionally integrated within the social whole, it likewise lacks "the condition necessary for autonomy." Thus, "the space of the tactic is the space of the other" because it can only engage its cultural setting parasitically. It cannot organize the symbolic media of communication solely according to its own immanent order of meaning, because its every significant gesture intervenes upon an already constituted semantic order that partially but unavoidably determines it. Because it cannot speak from its own place, Christian discourse can only be heard as it grasps alien semantic material and hijacks it, plays with it, improvises upon it. Thus, it speaks relative to its other, unable to freely constitute its own symbolic world: "it is necessary to open a space for speech and, to accomplish this, to make a cut in the social body."[136]

So the church's cultural ventures in conversion must carve out space within the world's symbolic traffic, but only at the cost of being (partially) appropriated by the world. The church, we recall, is the social exhibition of the living Jesus, the substantive meaning of humanity. But as Ernst and now Certeau tell us in their different ways, the categories the church wields, though implicitly universal in scope (Jesus *is* God), are in their actual application to human experience already interpreted through the imperfect and irreducibly multiple meanings of unbaptized semantic orders, resulting in a partial but ineliminable mismatch. They will only be fully "true" at history's consummation, finally matching up with the communal experience of a single harmonious human culture; until then, the categories of the Christ can only hope to catalyze the multiplicity of competing cultures and collectives toward that eventual (eschatological) harmony. How then should we name the "style" of this ecclesial engagement with the world? Perhaps its behavior is closest to what Jonathan Z. Smith calls "myth."[137] The universal scope and depth of potential meaning lodged in mythic stories and symbols is only released piecemeal, in their creative application, that is, their interpretive insertion into larger networks of everyday meaning.

---

in Barbara Nichtweiss, *Erik Peterson: Neue Sicht auf Leben und Werk* (Freiburg: Herder, 1992), 737–62.

[135] Citations in the following paragraph are drawn from Michel de Certeau, *The Practice of Everyday Life*, trans. Steven F. Rendall (Berkeley: University of California Press, 1984), 34–9.

[136] Certeau, Du corps à l'écriture," 279.

[137] For this view of myth I rely upon Jonathan Z. Smith, "Map is Not Territory," in *Map is Not Territory: Studies in the History of Religions* (Leiden: E.J. Brill, 1978), 299–309.

All myths, as such, claim and demand ultimacy in their designated sphere of application; that is their role, to tell the story that makes sense of reality. Of course, Christian faith holds that the Christian mythos is inexhaustible, and will at length make sense of every reality. God's word has been *uttered* as a human being, perfectly, once and for all; but it can only be *heard* imperfectly, fragmentarily, via the temporal, contingent "discourse" that is human history. The ultimacy of Jesus as God's word does not obviate this "detour" of history. As a word/sign, Jesus must be read or heard within the common language-structure that we call "the world," that is, the sphere of human meaning-making.

The conclusion here, to use Certeau's dichotomy, is that the church's engagement with culture is better understood as the tactics of myth rather than the strategy of metanarrative. The latter presupposes that the church is already in a position to straightforwardly out-narrate all rival realities; this would demand that the church occupy a social "locus" of its own from which it could organize its culture autonomously and then extend this organization indefinitely. But what if the eschatological hiatus is taken more seriously than that? It would mean that, short of humanity's final consummation, the church's word is unable to appropriate and "master" the world's meanings but must instead make its "cut" within them again and again. (Might we say the submission to Christ of the resistant body of the world's meaning is not a discursive conquest but death by a thousand cuts?) While the world endures this, the church, too, must endure the "play" between fit and lack of fit, the inability of its ultimate word to be fully and perfectly heard. What is this but a version of that "ordeal of incongruity" in the application of myth that Smith speaks of, structurally akin to the riddle and the joke?[138]

This requisite incongruity in the church's discourse is closely connected with a second comedic element, associated not so much with the church's sociocultural position as with the inherent character of its performance. Rowan Williams insightfully discusses this issue in his essay "Interiority and Epiphany," which at points reads almost like a rejoinder to Milbank's reading of Paul in "Enclaves."[139] Recall first the general terms of comparison used above to position Williams and Milbank. Both share an understanding of Christian performance as the exhibition of God in the world and the expression of the ultimacy of Jesus as God's embodied utterance; the difference of the church in communal-practical and hence doctrinal terms is fundamental to both this exhibition and this expression. However, the nature of this performative difference is understood in very distinct ways. Milbank insists that the church's discourse of non-mastery (ontological and hence social peace) can only relate to other discourses as a master discourse! So whereas Milbank understands ecclesial difference vis-à-vis the world in radically agonistic terms, Williams understands it in radically interrogative terms. As has been pointed out, Milbank is untroubled by this characterization and indeed adopts patristic rhetorical aggression as an admirable model; Williams suspects, on the other hand, a performative contradiction. His suspicion of the ideological

---

[138] Ibid., 309, cf. 301–2.
[139] Rowan Williams, "Interiority and Epiphany: A Reading in New Testament Ethics," in *On Christian Theology* (Oxford: Blackwell, 2000), 239–64.

function of ecclesial discourse has already been noted; the finality of Jesus the divine Word made flesh cannot be made a discourse of mastery but is rather only fittingly inhabited as a discourse of dispossession.

In "Interiority and Epiphany," Williams examines the theology of Matthew's gospel and of Paul's letters to demonstrate that "Christian behavior is to be interpreted in terms of the *manifestation* of God through Jesus Christ," but that "this manifestation is not restricted to *successful performance*: the comprehensiveness of the structuring vision emerges in the way in which failure, recognized and accepted as such, entails a 'dispossession' that itself mirrors the divine gift" in Christ.[140] For example, Paul's language suggests that his role as one who "handles or administers or conserves the narrative of the divine purpose" is most transparent precisely "when the apostle is dispossessed of … the kind of power that comes from the successful deployment of rhetoric." Indeed the "awkwardness" of his "voice" comes to be specially prized, such that Paul can be seen to be promoting an "'anti-rhetoric' of human inarticulacy."[141] For Williams, Christian persuasiveness must incorporate "the practice of penitent irony" and "a skepticism, both relentless and unanxious, about all claims to successful performance in our life and our discourse."[142] He is equally clear about what is to be avoided: the truth of Christ must not be "deployed."[143] It must never become "a form of religious persuasion that insists upon its right to possess or control its own outcome."[144] The Christian cultural intervention is true to itself "not by winning a succession of arguments that 'prove' the inadequacy of secularism, but in displaying at least the confidence that our theological discourse has the ability to promise human transformation."[145]

If Kierkegaard was right to remind us that "the human act of walking … is a continuous falling," this holds all the more for the church's historical and cultural performances.[146] "Who is sufficient for these things?" exclaims Paul (2 Cor. 2:16). The immensity of the treasure is only matched by the fragility of the vessels. As in slapstick, the necessitated display of ineptitude must be calibrated, becoming a skill in itself; failure before the world, precisely in Christ's name, is an essential element of the performance of Christ's dispossession. This is not the whole story, but it is a dimension that must not be suppressed in our theorizing of the church's cultural stance, for it is the mark of what was called above the historical adventure of imperfect conversion. If the church is the bodily repetition of Christ in human history, this cycle of pratfalls and renewals must be one mark of that distance from its Lord demanded by the deferral of eschatology. Marx's famous quip thereby attains a painful ecclesiological pertinence: "Hegel remarks somewhere that all great world-historical facts and personages occur, as it were, twice. He has

---

[140] Ibid., 254.
[141] Ibid, 256.
[142] Ibid., 257–8.
[143] Ibid., 259.
[144] Ibid., 257–8.
[145] Ibid., 253.
[146] Kierkegaard, *Philosophical Fragments*, 37.

forgotten to add: the first time as tragedy, the second as farce."¹⁴⁷ First Jesus, then the church.

Our first point was that the gospel's incongruous entry into each new cultural moment is something like a punchline; the second was that the ecclesial community's ham-handed reenactment of the Master's pattern must continually admit to merely an oafish mimicry of his self-emptying. But (our third and final comic aspect) the incarnation as God's final Word to the world incorporates its own high jest. We can see how this is so if we revisit some of the reflections above concerning the twofold composition of the created order, namely, as a meaningful expression (a similitude of the creator) incorporating both fixed form (ontology) and temporal process (physics). What does this mean but that, like Lacan's unconscious, the created cosmos itself is "structured like a language"? The ontological order of stable existents interrelated-through-differentiation functions like the semiotic code (*langue*), with the contingent unfolding of their particular interactions actualizing the code as the "utterance" of the world (*parole*). Contra Milbank's "postmodern" celebration of radical flux, we should think of finite subsistence and "merely" natural ordering as the relatively fixed structures off of which the divine intention of self-gift plays. Like the basso continuo where the melodic line is improvised over, against, but always with the bass line, these structures supply that disciplining of temporal flow which turns it into development, history; it is this interplay, this process, which, as Whitehead says somewhere, overcomes the emptiness of sheer difference.

So the world fashioned by God speaks its own similitude to the divine essence. But that is not all, for this created ordering, in turn, is the vehicle through which God gives what is beyond creation, namely, himself, in the form of grace, supernatural participation in the divine being. Creation simply as such, we have seen, requires more than the "postmodern" constitution of beings as sheer relations. It demands a process of ordered interagency, hence stably identifiable agents (substances) that enact and anchor the relations; this, in turn, demands regularized alterations (change, hence accidents) and time (for the reduction of potencies to acts). But the step from the creature as similitude of God to creature as "image" of God demands in addition a particular variation of this actualization, what has above been called "intentionality." Because only specific intentional operations of intellect and will (presupposing Aquinas' distinction of first and second act) allow the *imago trinitatis* to inhabit this world.

But if creation is God's language in this way, both for nature and grace, what should be said of the originating point of all saving grace in the world, namely, God's supreme self-utterance, the eternal Word incarnate as Jesus? This event is a very special instance of *parole*, a creative semantic bestowal of limitless significance upon a concrete sign; its dynamic is perhaps (at least partly) captured in the following description.

> [It is] the negation (*Aufhebung*) of the particular as particular in such a way that the conditions of finitude are at the same time respected (the particular is able to

---

¹⁴⁷ Karl Marx, "The Eighteenth Brumaire of Louis Napoleon," in *The Marx-Engels Reader*, 2nd ed., ed. Robert C. Tucker (New York: W.W. Norton, 1978), 594.

appear) and denied (the particular is negated). In this way the Romantic artistic device of irony reveals itself as the only conceivable solution of the contradiction involved in making that which is at the same time finite and infinite appear *within* finitude.[148]

A tentative and speculative sally, to be sure, but perhaps God's incarnate Word in the world is not just iconic (Balthasar) but also ironic, in the sense of Schlegel and the German romantics.

This still involves the "linguistic" form of created actuality, structure mediated into meaning-event. Once again there must be a defined zone within creation, a "code" that is structurally ambiguous toward God's self-gift, and hence that must be "read" by history, that is, played out in a certain way by contingent events, some of them free ones. But irony adds an additional margin of freedom. Irony plays in the gap between literal meaning and the user's intent. Note, irony depends on the literal meaning "working" and taking hold, even as its typical use is subverted. This is important for the conversation with Milbank: there is subversion of the created order, but not sublation. Just as metaphor depends on the implicit denial of literal truth, but not its negation, since it also relies upon the force of literal truth still embedded in the language used and hence "virtually" operative; and just as linguistic irony depends upon the virtual force of "literal" meaning; just so it is the "virtual" power of the natural (*en passant*) that is required for the supreme utterance of the supernatural. Created being, nature, the *saeculum*, these are the literal "texts" that God in the incarnation speaks ironically, requiring each precisely in its difference from divine being, grace, church.

The possibilities of this conceit, as well as its limitations, cannot be scrutinized here. But at least its relation to the alternatives under discussion can be indicated. The proper "stance" of witnessing faith to the world of human culture is seen in more "totalizing" or Hegelian terms by Milbank, more ironic ones by Rowan Williams, due to different emphases within the total picture of God's gracious meaning-making in the world and of the church's role in it. For Milbank ecclesial discourse, though eschewing universal foundations or fixed meanings, is still a continually self-grounding process (that is part of what its metadiscursive status means), and it requires the same questionable "border control" procedures posited by Lindbeck's "intratextuality."[149] Like Hegel's *Geist*, it is guaranteed beforehand to come out "right." But according to the alternative view developed here in dependence upon Williams, God's universal surplus of meaning is "given" to humanity only in Jesus Christ, whose human identity remains unfinished, that is, it is still being mediated by history. This means that the true "metanarrative" dwells only in the divine mind. God's truth within human minds continues to take on an unanticipatable shape, one that is never fully reducible to the meanings already generated within the community of faith and, hence, one that cannot be deployed for

---

[148] Manfred Frank, *Einführung in die frühromantische Ästhetik* (Frankfurt am Main: Suhrkamp, 1989), 311, quoted in Andrew Bowie, introduction to *The Subject and the Text*, by Manfred Frank, ed. Andrew Bowie, trans. Helen Atkins (Cambridge: Cambridge University Press, 1997), xxxiv.

[149] See the critical account in Paul DeHart, *The Trial of the Witnesses: The Rise and Decline of Postliberal Theology* (Oxford: Blackwell, 2006), 171–90.

mastery. To adapt Manfred Frank on Schleiermacher, the "style" of history as divine utterance will only be cognized in the eschaton: here and now it can only be "divined."[150]

In the meantime, unbeliever and believer alike remain confronted by the invincible irony of the divine self-utterance in Jesus, his history, and his ecclesial post-history. It is that irony of which Paul spoke when he disclosed the degradation and defeat of the cross as in fact God's triumph over the archons (1 Cor. 2:8). The grace of union with the infinite remains the last word, and yet it is a word spoken in the language of the world, a lexicon both of beauty and of continual brutality and loss that prima facie tells only of the indifference of the absolute. Faith in God's pure benevolence must often be the tenacious anticipation of an immense humor behind the devastating deadpan of history. As for faith's stance in and toward the world, the point is simply that the inscrutable infinity of the creator cannot be evaded given our temporal constraints, as if the revelation of Jesus put believers in possession of a knowledge beyond ambiguity. The best they can affirm is the divine irony, and this always involves that humor that, as the German novelist Jean Paul said, is the "inverse sublime," the partial but real truth of the insignificance of ourselves and our world when seen from the height of infinity.[151] Sublimity and its accompanying inverse sustain the faithful in the labyrinth of experience, especially when the creator of history can only be endured as the driest, or blackest, of humorists.

VI. Conclusion

The section just completed, drawing out some of the implications of Section IV, has begun, at least, to suggest a connection between a theological stance premised upon "winning a succession of arguments" and one unable to thematize the requisite ineptness of ecclesial performance. It is the same connection animating the agonized cry of C. S. Lewis's doomed painter in the passage opening this chapter: metanarrative conquest of "the world" is perhaps too grimly serious an affair, for the prospect of losing is "beyond a joke." An attempt has been made in this chapter to interrogate the metadiscursive stance of theology promoted by Milbank, and the interpretations about creation, nature, and grace that he draws upon to support such a stance, in light of a proposed set of alternative positions guided by Thomas Aquinas.

On the alternative model outlined here, God's self-gift involves, first, an interplay across a gap or interval of difference between defined, subsistent entities and a moving pattern of relations and operations, including contingent ones, in accord with an overall order; it also demands a similar interplay across a gap between nature and grace, habitual forms distributed via contingent motions by actual grace; and, third, it at least implies an interplay across a gap between (culturally speaking) "the world" as the total enterprise of human meaning-making and faith's critical collaboration-through-interrogation, undertaken while "on the way" through history, on pilgrimage.

---

[150] Frank, *The Subject and the Text*, 80.
[151] Johann Paul Friedrich Richter, *Horn of Oberon: Jean Paul Richter's School for Aesthetics*, trans. Margaret R. Hale (Detroit: Wayne State University Press, 1973), 88–94.

With Milbank and the whole ancient tradition it is affirmed that God does indeed give herself, but this gift occurs in, or rather takes place by means of, history as constituted by the gaps just enumerated, that is, the world of operations and final attainments (not without failures thereof), and imperfect conversions. All this takes time, the time of the church. As to "the world," because of the theo-ontological determinations of the first two gaps, that is, because being as such is opaque to God's self-relation, which cannot be inscribed within entities (and hence relies upon the *possibility* afforded by certain participative *operations*), and because nature can receive but not specifically anticipate grace, there is a residual theological space always present in culture (even within historical Christendom) called "the world." It is essentially ambiguous, compounded of moments of organized resistance to God alongside moments destined for redemption, yet always constitutively open to both.

What about the peculiarly modern moment of "the secular"? Secularism is not identical with "the world." It is the self-conscious affirmation and appropriation of the immanence afforded by God to creatures (bracketing or denying its giftedness), along with the cultural and sociopolitical arrangements justified in terms of that immanence. But because what it affirms remains an authentic aspect of creation, even the secular partakes of the essential ambiguity of "the world"; it cannot simply be identified in every case with the resistance of the world, though it most definitely can and does often take such a form. In itself, it continues to display that ambiguity vis-à-vis God's ends that all human culture, religious or not, shares. For Milbank, the secular, unlike pagan Greek thought or other premodern cultures, is *defined by* opposition to the Christian gospel. But another view is possible.

The secular is not the antichrist, even if it can at any moment become that, and sometimes does. It shares this characteristic with every pre-modern manifestation of fallen human culture. Indeed, in its best moments the secular strives to be not anti-Christian, because it seeks to define itself non-religiously. Hence it is arguable, regardless of its historical origins, that anti-Christianity is not its essence. It cannot be the antichrist because it cannot culturally nullify or negate incarnation. That is, in its self-affirming worldliness the world can only deny the God available to it; it cannot attain the dignity of a refusal of the Trinity. The secular is simply the world consciously and freely trying to ground itself in itself, which since the fall is what the world has always done, only unconsciously and willy-nilly. The proposal on the secular here is not unlike Karl Barth's position on unbelief, to refuse to take its pronouncements with such seriousness; the reasoning is analogous: God, the divine irony of providence and predestination, will always have the last word.[152]

However, Barth's theological ontology betrays an apparent insensitivity to this pneumatological irony not unlike that of Milbank's, and arguably for a similar reason. Milbank's radicalization of de Lubac, denying any dualism of nature and grace, is in a way formally analogous to Barth doctrine of election as the inner ground of creation: both represent the "inversion" or quasi-naturalization of God's self-gift.[153] In each case,

---

[152] Karl Barth, *Church Dogmatics I.1: The Doctrine of the Word of God*, trans. G. W. Bromiley and T. F. Torrance (Edinburgh, T&T Clark, 1975), 30–2.

[153] Karl Barth, *Church Dogmatics III.1: The Doctrine of Creation*, trans. J. W. Edwards et al. (Edinburgh: T&T Clark, 1958), 42–329.

creation and nature in their integrity are always already "sublated" by a gracious yet somehow overbearing divine decree of incarnation and redemption. The problem, from the standpoint developed in this chapter, is that neither Barth nor Milbank allow God's infinite gesture of creation itself its proper moment of balance over against God's free intent to elevate it. The space defined by this equipoise, that is, the historical field of divine irony, is thereby collapsed. But the imbalance is unwarranted, for grace is finally just as much a function of the universal instrumentality as nature is.[154]

There is, then, a Christian metanarrative, but only God can read it; it is the mystery of providence. Believers have been granted only a glimpse, not a sweeping view behind the ambiguities of history. For us the mystery of providence and predestination is irreducible. Christians have an inexhaustible theanthropic life mediated by the Word made flesh, and an indefeasible hope in the renewal of all things, but neither of these imply that they are in possession of "the history that [already] makes sense of all histories," nor that their cultural task is the grand strategy of meta-discourse. Of course, there are always convictions and practices in the world that they can and should, in piecemeal fashion, rationally refute or deconstruct. But as for their own most crucial affirmations (as Aquinas points out), they must play defense, settling for holding their own rather than conquering the field. The ever-present possibility (affirmed at *STh* I q. 1 a. 8) of a proof that the Christian position is neither irrational nor incoherent does not imply the ever-present possibility of a demonstration of the non-rationality or incoherence of the non-Christian position.[155]

It is imperative that the expectations and "stance" of the theologian reflect the unavoidable implication of the insights developed above: the field of struggle between Christian and non-Christian claimants is too topographically uncertain to allow many straightforward victories (or at least victories we can know to be such). It is not even so clear that the lines of friend and enemy are easy to draw. The situation is funnier than that, so to speak, because the world can never be reduced simply to the non- (or anti-) Christian; in every scene of contention between the gospel and its perceived enemy the world or culture is present as an ambivalent third, the "straight man," the unwitting recipient of faith's "cut."[156] As believer or theologian I can never stage an antagonistic confrontation without this ambiguous attendant showing up. The *saeculum* on this view looks less like the antichrist and more like Margaret Dumont. That's strange. And I can't think of anything else.

---

[154] *STh* I/II q. 109 a. 2.
[155] The theological overconfidence implicit in the metanarrative stance is quietly signaled when Fergus Kerr reports the upshot of *Theology and Social Theory*: "In contrast to all [sic] other views of the world, Christianity alone, properly understood, denies the ultimacy of chaos and conflict." Fergus Kerr, "Simplicity Itself: Milbank's Thesis," *New Blackfriars* 73 (1992): 310. In light of that eloquent little "sic," perhaps Kerr should be ranged alongside his fellow Dominicans Ernst and Pohier as a third witness to Thomistic sobriety.
[156] This at any rate avoids the temptation that plagues exercises in irrefutable Christian metanarrative, namely, to reduce the complex scene of faith's encounter with the world to the puerile ethical scenario of a movie like *Animal House*. In film critic Dave Kehr's acid summation (from a capsule review available at the website of the *Chicago Reader*): "In the world of *National Lampoon*, humanity is divided into two groups: Us and the Assholes. And guess what—we win!"

Part Three

Aquinas and God's Ideas: The Impossible Mind of the Creator

7

"Nothing in This Book is True, But It's Exactly How Things Are"

You had scrutinized my every action,
all were recorded in your book;
my days listed and determined,
even before the first of them occurred.

Ps. 139:16

This short transitional chapter develops no position of its own; it is intended only to introduce the last three chapters of the book, delineating their common theme. For Chapters 8, 9, and 10 were conceived and written in close connection with each other, and each extended in a particular direction certain reflections initiated by a particular, previously developed reading of Aquinas on the so-called divine ideas.[1] The larger problematic within which that reading was located was that of the divine ideas as essential to any account of God's timeless and totally efficient (i.e., creative) knowledge of the world. How to conceive of the relation of the ideas to the divine intellect: that is the point of contention with other readings of Aquinas. The particular interpretation defended in that earlier piece of exegesis of the medieval doctor laid special stress upon the inherent connection between the formal constitution of the ideas in the divine intellect and the concrete decision of the divine will to actualize a particular order of creation. The status and function of the ideas in this scheme turns out, upon consideration, to have departed sharply from the original idea model as developed in the Platonic philosophical tradition and absorbed within the mainstream of patristic and medieval Christian theology.

However, the peculiar orientation of Aquinas' idea theory does not seem always to have been sufficiently emphasized or acknowledged. This is true in discussions of Aquinas himself, as was directly suggested by the arguments with other Aquinas scholars in the earlier piece. But there is another way to look at the matter. The

---

[1] DeHart, "What Is Not, Was Not, and Will Never Be," 1009–58.

modifications to the status of God's ideas of the world that Aquinas (on my account) introduced were part of the conceptual outworking of his doctrine of creation; they represent safeguards against the various ways more traditional accounts of the ideas might undermine theology's hold on the absolute nature of the creative act. It is arguable that ignorance of, or failures to advert to, these modifications has led theology and philosophy, again and again, to reintroduce the ideas in their unadulterated Platonic form. Seeking thereby to solve perennial problems, it is nonetheless possible that by allowing God's ideas to reassume their ancient functions they introduced hidden contradictions into the Christian doctrine of creation. The exploration of these functions, and the exposure of these contradictions, is the task of the three remaining chapters.

Prior to Aquinas' adaptations, the divine ideas could serve epistemological functions (through a conjunction of human intellection with the divine archetypes of things, securing certain knowledge of those things); soteriological functions (through an aspiration or ascent of the soul to a participation of eternal ideals, even its own, in God's mind); and ontological functions (through an assertion of the eternal preexistence of determinate possibilities of "beings" as primordially inherent in the divine intelligence, in order either to ground creaturely differentiation in a prior multiplicity of "worlds" foreseen, or to concretize the hypostatic difference between Father and Son in the creative act). The point of the three chapters is to argue that, on Aquinas' assumptions, the divine ideas can no longer perform any of these functions; allowing them such scope inevitably disrupts the logic of creation *ex nihilo*. According to this logic, as the world's absolute ground, God is strictly incommensurate with it; no unit of meaning available to minds within the world can find adequate application in common to finite reality and God's reality. The problem with the three residually "Platonic" functions of divine ideas just enumerated is that they infringe on this limit; each in its way installs the divine idea as a common "measure" between God and world. The epistemological function assumes an effective coincidence between God's creative intuition of things and our cognitive judgments. The soteriological function assumes the possibility of our personal existence in its "actuality" or "truth" approaching or reaching the level of its supposed timeless ideal within God. The ontological function assumes that the specific concepts or essences of our world's realities are anchored eternally and, as it were, inevitably in the divine foreknowledge of possibility, and thus in the divine being itself.

But the divine ideas as envisioned according to my previously published exegesis of Aquinas would disallow these supposed overlaps between God's utterly originating vision of the finite order and the intelligent construals possible to even the most powerful cognitive agency within that order. In short, these ideas maintain the infinity and immensity of God.[2] How so? The following chapters provide the different

---

[2] In any class or category of beings that which is most simple and complete, and that which determines any other thing to exemplify more or less of the actuality of that kind of being as the other thing approaches it or recedes from it, is said to "measure" or to be the "measure" of all the beings in that class (Aquinas, *Commentary on the Sentences* I d. 8 q. 4 a. 2 ad 3). God is immense in the sense that God is in no class of being, hence God and created being can be subject to no common measure. True, God can be called the measure of everything in the broad sense that creatures possess more or

arguments in detail, but speaking generally, the best approach is perhaps through the utter metaphysical simplicity of God as the world's maker (and knower *because* maker). Theologians and philosophers in the classic monotheistic tradition all agree on this simplicity, as they do on God's complete and infallible eternal knowledge of all worldly reality. But how the supreme exactness of the knowledge is determined by the supremely pure unity of the knower is a nice question. For not even the infinite intricacy of "detail" encompassed within the former can disturb the latter in the slightest degree; this is what Aquinas seems to have seen.

We can explore this puzzle a bit further. The world as intentional object of the divine mind cannot differ *at all* from the world as it actually is. Yet, as inhabiting that mind, partaking of its simple immensity, its idea can never be attained by us. A memorable quote relayed by Rowan Williams suggests something of the paradoxical nature of this duplication: "There is another world, but it is the same as this one."[3] The paradox lies in the combination: the other world perfectly replicates ours, yet such is the nature of this replication that (due to its very perfection) it cannot be known or entertained as such. Extending Williams's creative appropriation, we can express this unity of replication and inaccessibility by tweaking the line again: "There is another world, but it is *exactly* the same as this one." The force of this "exactly" is expressed in one of the crucial insights from Kant's pre-critical period.

> Take any subject you please, for example, Julius Caesar. Draw up a list of all the predicates which may be thought to belong to him, not excepting even those of space and time. You will quickly see that he can either exist with all these determinations, or not exist at all. The Being who gave existence to the world and to our hero within that world could know every single one of these predicates

---

less of the act of existence as they are closer to or more distant from God in the hierarchy of being, but this sense of measure supposes no proportion, no common ratio, between God and creature (*STh* I q. 3 a. 5 ad 2). For God is the infinite cause of finite effects, and there is no proportion between infinite and finite (*STh* I q. 2 a. 2 objection 3 and ad 3). The divine form and created forms have no common ratio, no shared intelligibility, save the analogical relation between an essential existent and participatory existents (*STh* I q. 4 a. 3 ad 3). Hence, no proper proportion exists between God and any created intellect, only the relation of cause to effect and of pure, total actuality to partial actualization (*STh* I q. 12 a. 1 ad 4). God's intellect, for its part, cannot be actualized by any form, species, or intelligibility of any created thing; it can only know creatures through the virtual containment of their forms or species within the divine essence (*STh* I a. 14 a. 5 ad 2). Hence, divine ideas do not infringe upon, but rather participate fully in, the immensity of the divine essence itself. Created intellects may have knowledge of other creatures, but this does not involve a cognitive "sharing" in the divine idea, i.e., a common idea or ratio. For God knows the creature as only their omnipotent maker can know them: namely, (1) in every aspect, (2) as relationally implicated within the universal order, and (3) by way of knowing the infinite essence, as derivate from it.

[3] Williams, *On Christian Theology*, 201. This famous line has been widely cited in different versions. Williams was quoting it from another source, but can here be credited as a source for this particular form of it. Apparently working from memory, not only did he attribute it to the wrong Patrick White novel (it was an epigraph to *The Solid Mandala*, not *The Vivisector*), but he felicitously altered its wording. White's version reads: "There is another world, but it is in this one." White in turn credited the French poet Paul Eluard as the originator of the line. Others (including Williams on another occasion) attribute it to Rilke. The former seems more likely, but some obscurity remains. See John Llewelyn, *Margins of Religion: Between Kierkegaard and Derrida* (Bloomington: Indiana University Press, 2008), 452 n. 22.

> without exception, and yet still be able to regard him as a merely possible thing which, in the absence of that Being's decision to create him, would not exist. Who can deny that millions of things which do not actually exist are merely possible from the point of view of all the predicates they would contain if they were to exist. Or who can deny that in the representation which the Supreme Being has of them there is not a single determination missing, though existence is not among them, for the Supreme Being cognizes them only as possible things. It cannot happen, therefore, that if they were to exist they would contain an extra predicate; for, in the case of the possibility of a thing in its complete determination, no predicate at all can be missing.[4]

Kant's point is that the creator's combination of infallible knowledge and absolute power means that the divine idea of the creature cannot fail to be perfectly and exactly replicated by the creature's actuality. The very point of the divine ideas within a tradition of monotheistic creation is precisely this total absence of interval between the two worlds; omnipotence means the world is exactly as it is (divinely) known. God makes what God knows, and nothing can intervene or hinder; that is the meaning of omniscient omnipotence.

Kant correctly saw in this perfect union of cognitive and productive power the hallmark of the creator; he elsewhere dubbed this unique capacity *intuitus originarius*. However, Kant famously draws from this example the conclusion that existence or being cannot be a real predicate. The existence of any thing is a determination of human empirical judgment, the simple categorical registration of its presentation to sense intuition. Being remains outside the concept proper of the real thing; it is not among the innumerable possible predicates whose "complete determination" is the mark of the actual individual. Granted this confined role of "existence" in human reason, it is not surprising that God as the "ideal of reason" must for Kant be conceived as the *ens realissimum*, the synthesis of what is real in all possible predicates. The difficulties in this conception have been noted by commentators,[5] but the particular problem of interest here is that the divine essence is thereby conceived (though never given) as the paramount object-as-such, the projected idealization of the human

---

[4] Immanuel Kant, *The Only Possible Argument in Support of a Demonstration of the Existence of God* [1763], in *Theoretical Philosophy 1755–70*, ed. David Walford (Cambridge: Cambridge University Press, 2002), 117–8. Julius Caesar had no doubt for some time been a stock character used in philosophical arguments, a stand-in for "human being" or "historical figure." It is nonetheless fascinating to find Leibniz seventy-seven years before, in introducing the concept of what he would later call a "monad," exemplifying the divine idea using the complete "notion" of Julius Caesar as containing the entirety of his properties and historical predicates. Kant apparently could not have known the passage, as the text in question was only published later in the nineteenth century. G. W. Leibniz, "Discourse on Metaphysics," in *Philosophical Texts*, edited and translated by R. S. Woolhouse and Richard Francks (Oxford: Oxford University Press, 1998), 64–5.

[5] For an excellent discussion, see Allen W. Wood, *Kant's Rational Theology* (Ithaca: Cornell University Press, 1978), 25–78. As Bernard Lonergan points out, because Kant holds this reference to experience to be "as such the source of the concept of being," the real must be "confined to the field of possible experience." Lonergan, *Verbum: Word and Idea in Aquinas*, vol. 2 of *Collected Works of Bernard Lonergan* (Toronto: University of Toronto Press, 1997), 57. The upshot is that the actuality of the *ens realissimum* can never be rationally affirmed; it must remain an "idea" of reason in Kant's sense.

subject's thing-judgments. The resolution of our paradox, the perfect semblance yet incommensurability reigning between God's idea and our world, will not be found on this path.

Thomism takes a different theistic course. It roots the divine *intuitus originarius* precisely in being as the ultimate predicate. Being, the act of existence, is the final actuality within every particular actual, the most formal of realities; God is pure being, identified not as this or that existing thing but as the sheer subsistent act of existence containing every defined, lesser act of entity as its ground of possibility. On this all Thomists would agree. But the paradox of exactitude and incommensurability only becomes visible, along with its resolution, when Aquinas' insistence upon the utter lack of composition in God, the divine simplicity, is pressed to its limit. This is one way of understanding the "voluntarist" reading of ideas (contested by some Thomists) presented in my specialized essay on the divine ideas. The simplicity of the divine being is finally what demands the immensity of the divine idea of the world, in spite of its exact duplication of the world.

So from a certain perspective, what ties together the reading of Aquinas animating the three following chapters, and links them to the previous article on voluntarism and divine ideas, is the extension or radicalization of divine simplicity. This move exploits what seem to be the logical pathways opened up by several Thomist interpreters. The divine simplicity, which Aquinas asserted with as much vigor as anyone, involves affirming the highest degree of metaphysical unity and identity over against any conception of composition or juxtaposition within God's being, or within the intellect and will that are identical with that being. The applications of this principle that lie behind the approach chosen in these chapters were inspired, for example, by Etienne Gilson. His interpretation of the identity of existence and essence in God emphasized the primacy of the former as infinite act, surpassing and subsuming any differential determination of essence. Rudi te Velde for his part stressed the total unity of the act of creation; not the divine will's secondary bestowal of existence upon a range of supposedly prior essences (foreknown in the divine intellect), creation is at one and the same time the origination of finite essences with their finite existential acts. Bernard Lonergan was another impetus, dismissing any model of divine intellection as visualization, a confrontation with objects; for Aquinas, the act of understanding is naturally the metaphysical identity of knower and known. Understanding achieved, the rational integration of data into a higher, formal unity, provides our closest conceptual approach to the unimaginable unity of created multiplicity in God's grasp of her own essence.

The key to divine idea theory in its more Platonic modes is a questionable differentiation between knowledge and will in God. First, the story goes, God sees all finite possibles, discrete and already determined, within the divine power; in a second moment, God sifts this naturally, nay inevitably, viewed array for a select group voluntarily chosen for actualization. In response to this, my original piece on ideas in Aquinas resumes the dismantling of composition in God, extending the line plotted by the interpreters enumerated in the foregoing paragraph but particularly informed by James F. Ross. The result is, in effect, another simplification: the forced confrontation within the creator of knowledge and will demanded by Platonic ideas is not a satisfactory way to interpret Aquinas. Another collapse of differentiation within God is demanded: in knowing the things of the created world *as such*, God only knows what God is going to do; to know ideas and to will them are ultimately the same act. But accepting this account has further implications; in following their lead, the final three chapters of this book show how the just-described insistence upon divine simplicity as the very cause and mode of the exactitude of divine knowledge must lead to the immensity of God's ideas, and hence to the abandonment of their classic Platonic-Christian functions.

The account laid out in my article on Aquinas is admitted to be inferential. Yet, though it was never fully or explicitly presented by Aquinas himself, echoes of its concerns and emphases could be heard among some later scholastics (especially Dominicans). Even the ingenious Nicholas of Cusa, who is often numbered among medieval Platonists, reveals at several points in *On Learned Ignorance* (1440) a good "feel" for the position Aquinas arrived at. The diversity of creatures as such has no positive cause in God (contrary to the ever-renewed attempt to locate Triune distinction as the eternal root of finite differentiation).[6] It is rather due to the "contingency" or deficient cause of not being God; as Rudi te Velde argues, created being must of necessity involve differentiation.[7] But since the divine essence is the one exemplar imaged in countless varied ways by creatures, each of these is a finite reception of infinity, a created or "occasioned" god.[8] The point of these metaphors is that every creature positively imitates God's being; their gradations and limits and differences are not positive imitations in themselves but wisely variegated modes of deficiency or failure of imitation. Cusa's point is partly to preserve the idea that God's own being as exemplar is itself always one and identical with itself; there is no array of ideas lodged in the divine essence.

In a remarkable anticipation of James Ross's "W.C. Fields" simile (see the conclusion to Chapter 10 that follows), Cusa argues that different creatures should not be understood as replicas of different eternal exemplars but as graded approximations of a single exemplar.

---

[6] Nicholas of Cusa, *Selected Spiritual Writings*, trans. H. Lawrence Bond (New York: Paulist Press, 1997), 131–2. Rather than seeing the eternal Word in its differentiation from the Father as the source of creaturely otherness, Cusa sees the Word as the absolute upper limit of replication, perfect identity with the imitated Father (*aequalitas*), and hence the eternal principle of created (finite or "contracted") form in its limiting or *adaequatio* of created potentiality. From perfect equality descends its imperfect approximations, i.e., otherness lies in the descent from unity; it is an artifact of the passage from God to creature (ibid., 145). This is one of the key emphases of Rudi te Velde's book referenced in the following note. (It must be admitted that the early Aquinas dallied with a Trinitarian grounding of creaturely diversity, but arguably it never attained significance for his mature thinking.)

[7] Rudi A. te Velde, *Participation and Substantiality in Thomas Aquinas* (Leiden: E.J. Brill, 1995), 200–14.

[8] Ibid., 134. An *occasio* is a cause *per accidens* (the "contingency" Cusa refers to). Every natural cause "intends" or aims at the fullest possible replication of itself in its effect. An "occasionated" effect means an effect that fails in certain respects, due to conditions extraneous to the causal power itself, to replicate its cause in some significant aspect or other. These deficiencies are "outside the intention" of the cause.

> God is in all things that which they are, like the truth in an image. Suppose a face were present in its own image, which, according to the image's multiplication, is either a distant or a close multiple of the face; I do not mean according to spatial distance but according to progressive distance from the true face, since the image cannot be multiplied in any other fashion. Then, the one face ... would appear in different and multiple ways in the different images multiplied from it.[9]

For Cusa's theory of ideas, this means an open and surprisingly forceful departure from Platonism. God's being is the absolute quiddity of each thing but cannot contain the contracted quiddity, that is, the quiddity as differently "cut down" and proper to each thing.[10] There is no transcendent Platonic "container" of distinct forms, not even in God. "It is only in their contracted existence that the forms of things are distinct; as they exist absolutely they are one indistinct form, which is the Word of God."[11] Again: "Between the absolute and the contracted there is no intermediate ... Forms, therefore, actually (*actu*) exist only in the Word *as Word* and in things as contracted."[12] The differentiation of exemplars derives not from an eternal differentiation in God's mind but from their different created exemplata: "When ... we say that God created the human being by one essence (*alia ratione*) and stone by another, this is true with respect to things but not with respect to the Creator."[13]

The same theoretical instincts animating Cusa's remarks pervade the three final chapters in their attempt to draw out the implications of the version of Aquinas I originally presented in "What Is Not, Was Not, and Will Never Be." According to Chapter 8, this world as eternally foreknown in God's idea (God's "book," as the Psalmist has it) is known precisely as the intended object of omnipotent creation. As ingredient within a mode of act for which our knowledge can have no adequate concept, the ideas are never accessible directly and as such by human intelligence. As divinely (indeed contingently) willed, the ideas are not essential to the eternal generation of the Word, they possess no timelessly distinct formal or semantic act of being within God, and (particularly in tension with Christian Platonism) as differentiated from the divine essence they do not "illuminate," secure, or serve as truth-makers for human cognition. As the creator's ideas they are so exact as to be incommensurable with our concepts: God's book is unreadable by us. We cannot know that "other" world, which

---

[9] Ibid., 137.
[10] Ibid., 139–40.
[11] Ibid., 153.
[12] Ibid., 155 (italics added).
[13] Ibid., 154. This can be read, in agreement with my article on Aquinas' ideas and "voluntarism," as grounding the formal differentiation of exemplars exclusively in their respective entities as actually created by God, rather than supposing omnipotent possibility itself as "already" differentiated from eternity into distinct possible *rationes*. This stress on the divine will as differentiator is related to that same article's emphasis on the fitting of the actual variety of created beings to the particular concrete universe God intended to create. The same logical priority of created whole over created part appears in Cusa: "Just as in the design (*intentio*) of an artisan the whole exists before the part ... so, because all things have come forth into being from God's design (*intentio*), we say that the universe appeared first and all things subsequently" (ibid., 139). (The priority here is logical, not temporal.)

is our world as infinitely and exhaustively known in the deity, hence it cannot possess the truth we can and do know.

Chapter 9 moves from Platonic-style epistemologies to ethical or soteriological uses for divine ideas. There have been different attempts to construe salvific elevation or moral attainment in terms of a kind of approximation or approach to one's "ideal" self as it dwells in eternal unity with God. (Meister Eckhart is an especially profound example, representing an entire late medieval mystical tradition trading on this motif.) However, if the Thomist reading offered here is accepted, this notion makes no sense. First, while the ontological status of the idea is indeed higher as identical with God, its formal content is keyed exclusively to the creature-to-be-created. That creature's proper life and existence, the fruition of the idea, is found here in the created order and not in God. Second, as the foreknowing of what omnipotence accomplishes, there can be no difference at all between my actual being and God's idea of it. Hence, there can be no approach to it; it is another world, yet the same as this one. Once again it turns out that my duplication in God's mind is too exact; as God's pattern for my creation, it cannot be my "true" self in any other sense. The truth of my salvation is to be found in my temporal existence as created, not in an eternal ideal foreknown in God's "book."

If in this chapter the practical or spiritual implications of Aquinas' idea-theory are central, the vital conceptual consequences for the doctrines of God and creation are to be found in Chapter 10. It argues in effect that the ideas not only cannot instantiate the truth of my life, they cannot be the truth of God's life either. The willed character of the ideas is the stress here, which leads to consequences already enumerated. The willed creation is the formal constitution of the ideas themselves, not the actualizing of a selection of "already" known essences populating God's awareness. The divine intelligence of realizable finitude, that is, of actual things in concrete relations within a determinate world order, can never be played off against the divine will in this way. Finally, God's necessary willing of himself, of her own being, can in no way be equated with the contingent divine will-to-create. This means that the execution of the world can never be the fulfillment or realization of God's identity; God is as God can only be, and the positing of finitude is in no sense a moment of God's life. If the ideas are the signs or semantic units in which the book of the world is written, they are unique to its contingent constitution; they are formally adequate to worldly meaning, not a common measure of finite and infinite being. Their truth is not found in their determinate inscription as such, but only in the abyss of divine reality from which they are willed, and in the actuality of the world which they intend.

"Nothing in this book is true, but it's exactly how things are."[14] The purpose of the rather impressionistic summaries just provided is only to set forth the thematic unity of this book's three final chapters, not to present their arguments. Each chapter pursues in a different way the paradoxical unity of exactitude and incommensurability

---

[14] I must give all credit for this magnificent line to Bob Frissell, the title of whose 1994 book (Berkeley, CA: Frog Books) I have borrowed to name this chapter. As for the burden of that work, which concerns (among other things) the transcendental spiritual significance of certain sacred monuments located on the planet Mars, my only comment will be to refer the reader first to Mr. Frissell's book itself, to be followed immediately by a careful audition of the 1974 Firesign Theatre album "Everything You Know Is Wrong."

implied within Aquinas' account. The uncanny property of God's creative idea, the universe's *doppelgänger*, is captured in Magritte's well-known painting *La reproduction interdite*: viewing the canvas we appear to stand behind a figure, looking over his shoulder as he gazes into a mirror; but instead of seeing his face in the mirror we see, impossibly, the precise image of the back of his head. The "reflection" he sees is of our view, not his. This is a parable of the practical issue of the ideas: though the beatific vision is the telos of all prayer and all action in this life, this hoped-for suffusion of our awareness with the light of the creator's mind does not involve any direct mediation of the divine ideas in our sanctification.

The truth of our existence in God cannot be found in the ideated world in any way prior to or apart from our existence itself. Even though that world does indeed contain my own idea, the latter perfectly duplicates my life here in each of its moments and choices, and is as such inaccessible via those moments and choices. As Kierkegaard argued (see Chapter 3), it is the reflection of our acts in eternity, blown up to enormous proportions so to speak (like Lewis's chess players[15]) but always the expression of our unfolding existence in this world. Hence Kierkegaard's famous conclusion: my idea cannot be recollected, only repeated. Even if we could know the divinely ideated world, we could not strive to live in it; it is always too late for that, it has already been given to us as our own world. We would see ourselves looking, not back at ourselves as in a mirror, but ahead of us, toward the selves we must continue to create.

---

[15] Lewis, *Great Divorce*, 130–1.

8

Eclipse of the Divine Mind: The Divine Ideas as Anti-Platonic Epistemology

Science and mathematics
Run parallel to reality, they symbolize it, they squint at it,
They never touch it: consider what an explosion
Would rock the bones of men into little white fragments and unsky
the world
If any mind for a moment touch truth.

Robinson Jeffers
"The Silent Shepherds"

I. Platonic Ideas and Christian Theology

A centuries-long theological tradition running back at least to Origen baptized Plato's "ideas." The transcendent archetypes were eventually taken to be God's eternal thoughts of the cosmos and were invoked to account for human cognition of both God and creation. Augustine, especially influential for the early medieval continuation of this tradition, insisted upon an ontological kinship between the human intellect and that of the creator that enabled the former to grasp truth in its timelessness, a kinship mediated by the eternal *rationes* in God's mind.[1] Beginning around the middle of the thirteenth century, this venerable tradition suffered a series of wrenching changes in reaction to Amalric of Bene on the one hand and the Arabic metaphysicians (Avicenna and Averroes) on the other.[2] Under these new pressures, the issue of the divine ideas had to be thought through anew, from the ground up. The focus shifted from their role

---

[1] Vivian Boland OP, *Ideas in God according to Saint Thomas Aquinas: Sources and Synthesis* (Leiden: E. J. Brill, 1996), provides a useful account of the larger tradition. For medieval theology, the *locus classicus* in Augustine for his doctrine of ideas was *De diversis quaestionibus 83*, no. 46.
[2] Helmut Meinhardt et al., "Idee," in *Historisches Wörterbuch der Philosophie* (Basel: Schwabe, 1976) 4: 81–2; Maarten J. F. M. Hoenen, *Marsilius of Inghen: Divine Knowledge in Late Medieval Thought* (Leiden: E.J. Brill, 1993), 239–40.

in human knowledge to their role in God's. In particular, any theorization of the ideas now had to allow for their perfect cognitive scope, accounting for divine apprehension of all particularity and distinction; yet it also had to explain how they could be actually one with the divine essence (since what is not God can only be created) without in any way undermining the metaphysical simplicity of God by introducing a kind of composition in God's being. Different thinkers responded in different ways to this conundrum. Thomas Aquinas did so in a particularly elegant way, but the unavoidable result of his solution was to overthrow the long-standing conviction that fully adequate human knowledge or science can only be accounted for by granting some kind of explicit connection between our minds and the ideas in the creator's mind. Aquinas' theory of the ideas thus implied, strikingly, a refusal of epistemic Platonism. In the Platonic theory, ideas are the source and medium of true human knowledge; in the anti-Platonic theory, ideas are not only unknowable as such but are also systematically distanced from any positive role in human cognitive accomplishments. After Aquinas has finished, the luminosity of the ideas is occulted, as it were.

Thus, Aquinas offers (in some ways intentionally, in others implicitly and in effect) a uniquely "anti-Platonic" theorization of ideas in their epistemic role. The thesis of this chapter is that the real implications of Aquinas' position (which itself is arguably a necessary response to the stringent conceptual demands of the doctrine of creation from nothing) can only be grasped and appreciated negatively, drawing them out in light of a survey of some later discussions in which theologians and philosophers fall back in various ways into the Platonic gravitational field of classical idea theory. Section II will provide a brief, far from exhaustive account of Aquinas on the ideas; it will concentrate on the outlines of his reconciliation of perfect divine knowledge of creation with perfect divine simplicity of being. The remaining sections will examine several later medieval and modern discussions to unfold three consequences of Aquinas' position, hinting as well at the troubles arising from failing to advert to them. The first such consequence (Section III) was the most quickly grasped, namely, the near impossibility of accommodating Aquinas' idea theory to the ancient tradition that understood the achievements of human understanding as effected by God's ideas "illuminating" the human intellect. The second anti-Platonic epistemic consequence of Aquinas' ideas (Sections IV and V) results from his insistence that the ideas are in no sense bearers of distinct acts of existence proper to them but rather are identical with the one act of divine existence itself. The third consequence (Section VI), contrary to a hallowed tradition going back to the Fathers (and often revived since) that closely associates ideas and the eternal Word, was that idea theory in fact needs to be disentangled in principle from theories of the eternal generation of the Son as Word.

II. Thomas Aquinas and the Reconfiguration of Idea Theory

For Aquinas, all creaturely reality, distributed in its varied kinds, consists in nothing but deficient reflections or repetitions of, "participations in," the utterly unique but infinitely rich and absolutely perfect act of divine existence itself, God's act of being God.[3] Not just individual creatures in themselves, but also their relations and differentiations, all are part of the distributed balance and order that God bestows on the universe; hence, even their collective unity of distinction and interconnection itself is a participation of the divine unity of perfection. The result is that the world and all in it, in their diminished and diversified ways, infinitesimally replicate the content, so to speak, of God's own identity or essence; they are, individually and collectively, acts of being-like-but-therefore-not God's act of being God. Nothing real about them results from anything extraneous to the creator (say from subordinate makers or intransigent matter). And hence God can know all that they are simply by knowing herself, his own essence. This addresses initially the issue of God's omniscience. But for any thinker of this period, knowledge involves the presence, in some manner, of a resemblance or likeness of the known in the mind of the knower. This is true both for sensible knowing as well as for that higher form of knowledge shared by God, angels, and humans, which is called understanding or intellection. How, then, can the divine intellect know all these creatures and not be diversified in some way by the multiplicity of their ideas existing in it?

Aquinas begins to answer this question by specifying two different modes in which the likeness of a thing can be in the intellect that understands it. The first points to that aspect shared by all kinds of knowledge, one that was stressed by Aristotle, namely, that knowing occurs as the knower actually takes on a formal similarity to the known. The second points to something unique to intellection, which might be called the self-transparency of intellect and of the intelligible. According to the first mode, the form of the thing understood, that is, its identifying and actualizing principle, comes to be shared with the intellect that knows it. Intellection, in other words, primarily presupposes not two things, say subject and object, but one thing: the unified actuality in which both the understanding and the understood merge or coincide in an identity of form. Aquinas means this quite literally. The intellect is not simply activated by contact with intelligible form (often called a *species*); rather, that form or *species* becomes the form itself that actualizes the intellect. As he puts it, the intellect in the act of understanding something "actually exists through the *species* [of the thing understood] as through its own form." When this happens, the intellectual knower is said to be actually understanding.[4]

To the degree that intellect is not understanding, but has to be brought into union with the understood thing, it is passive, that is, it is in a state of potentially understanding until unity with the *species* occurs. However, properly speaking, intellection in itself is not a mere passive capacity but a kind of activity that Aquinas calls immanent action or operation; that is, the intellect, actualized by its formal identity with the understood thing, exercises itself in accord with this actualization, not by effecting change outside

---

[3] The fundamental treatments of divine knowledge, ideas, and providence upon which the discussion in this section is largely based can be found in Aquinas, *ScG* I 47–54 and 66, and *STh* I, qq. 14, 15, and 22. Boland, cited above, provides a thorough overview of Aquinas' various discussions of these topics. As has been said, the reading of Aquinas laid out in the following paragraphs is not a straightforward summary but is very much a synthetic interpretation along the lines developed in detail in DeHart, "What Is Not, Was Not, and Will Never Be."
[4] *ScG* I 53 no. 2.

the knower but by augmenting or perfecting the knower from within. Like any operation, the act of intellection has an object or terminus, a goal or resultant within the knower that occurs in immediate association with the act of unity with the understood object. The result is that the object, already present in the first mode of unity, must also be realized as present in another mode. This is where the metaphor of intellectual transparency might be helpful. To put it crudely, formal union with the thing known just is the state or activity of understanding it, but the awareness or grasp of the internal presence of the thing as of something understood is a discernibly different aspect of the event, the result of that state of understanding. As present in the intellect, indeed as form of the intellect, the thing must also, in a different mode, be present as grasped and understood; it is not lodged within as adventitious or opaque but is discerned in its true nature, structure, and relations. In short, the dynamics of intellect demand two different (but intimately connected) ways of looking at the presence of the known in the knower. In Aquinas' terms, the thing understood is "inside" the intellect not only as species activating and forming the intellectual faculty (i.e., as *quo intelligitur*, that by which the event of understanding as union occurs); it is also "inside" as the result or quasi-effect of the event (i.e., as *intellectum*, the thing *qua* understood, the "intellected" resulting from "intellection").[5]

There is one more relevant aspect of understanding. For Aquinas, the world is not an agglomeration of things but is an intricate structure in which different kinds of things are stratified in their interactions according to their location on a scale of relative operative strength and scope. If things are identified and actualized according to their respective forms, those forms themselves are not randomly differentiated but form a hierarchy, such that as the scale is ascended, higher forms incorporate in a unified way the different capacities dispersed among lower forms. This is important for understanding intellect, for, as was said, intellection is an assimilation of form. As the intelligent knower shares in the *species* of the known, it grasps in a single view, so to speak, all the intelligible content of that form. And just as forms in nature are measured by their greater or lesser inclusion and integration of lower grade realities, so too the *species* or forms that actualize intellect are measured by the degree to which they afford insight into a richer and broader range of reality. This is crucial, because for Aquinas, following Aristotle, it is of the very nature of the event of understanding that it involves a single, penetrating apprehension of multiple actualities, precisely not as multiple but as implicates or organic elements within some higher and more ontologically intense structure. They become secondary objects, ordered facets of intellect's primary object. The more powerful and encompassing the intelligible species, the more universal is the swath of reality taken in, and at the same time the more fine-grained the resolution of secondary layers. The unity of the event, and of its primary object, is the point here. The secondary objects are grasped simultaneously with, and as concomitant with, the primary object; they are "there" in the object precisely as understood, like unavoidable inferences from a premise or the range of a function, yet they need not be resolved as objects of attention in their own right.[6]

---

[5] ScG 51–2.
[6] ScG I 54–5.

Enough has been said now of intellection generally in Aquinas, but the final piece he uses to solve the puzzle of divine ideas still remains: for what is an idea? As Aquinas specifies, an idea is a form that serves as the exemplar according to which some other formality is shaped. It serves this function intentionally, that is, it is reducible to neither natural causality nor accidental resemblance but is intended as an exemplar by some intelligent agent. This last point is significant. To have an idea is the prerogative of intellect; consequently, the just-discussed dynamics of the intellectual act come into play with regard to ideas. An idea is intended for some kind of formal replication, and hence some aspect of its formal content or intelligibility must be grasped as such. Aquinas gets at this in an uncomfortably brief passage that easily confuses unless it is read as a highly compressed recapitulation of earlier more-detailed descriptions. An architect is just like anyone else with intelligence in that she can understand a house as a house, that is, she can by a cognitive act mentally capture and integrate the extended presentation in her sensible field in terms of its components, structure, and intentional function. But in so doing, she does not have the idea of the house, even, remarkably, if it is a house she herself designed. (I take this subtle implication to be the reason Aquinas took for his illustrative example specifically the mind of an architect.) Something else is needed for her to have the idea of a house, whether one already built or not yet built. She must advert to its formal presence within her as the intelligible product of her own act of understanding. It must be "considered" or "observed in itself" (*speculatam*) precisely as an intelligible mental content. This is a way of saying that an idea, as an intelligently intended exemplar, is present in the mind not simply as the actualization of formal unity with something understood. It is more than what enables the act of understanding or causally constitutes the state of understanding (the *quo intelligitur*) but must be the product of such understanding (the *intellectum*). This is why Aquinas says that in having the idea of the house the architect does not just understand it, she understands that she understands it. The idea depends upon the transparency of intellection, for it is the advertence of the intellect to the product of its own intelligent act, as such a product.[7]

All the preceding elements fall into place as we attempt to apply the image of the architect to God as creator. For unlike a human maker, God in addressing herself to the act of creating cannot have anything "in mind" as a form for intentional replication except himself, for literally nothing else exists. The only possible "idea" for creation is God herself, the divine essence or what-it-is-to-be-God. More than this, the idea is not the essence as such, but as perfect act of intelligence and hence perfect intelligibility, as Aquinas signals by the striking (and eerily prescient: think artificial intelligence) example of a craftsman who wished to fashion an artifact in imitation of her own intellect.[8] Now by definition the divine essence could never be perfectly replicable, but as infinite it is open to an unlimited number of imperfect replications. Any such incomplete replication will be in fact nothing but the divine essence, shorn of *precisely almost* all of its unimaginable intensity of content, leaving as residue the specific shape of some exceedingly feeble and infinitesimal reflection of that content. Hence, God's

---

[7] *STh* I q. 15 a. 2 and ad 2.
[8] *De veritate*, q. 3 a. 2.

considering the idea of the creature is nothing but God intelligently considering his own essence drastically cut down to an indigent replication of itself. Such ideated replications, even if multiplied, add nothing real whatever to God; as a function of God's self-intelligibility, the resulting cloud of deficient self-relations are only "relations of reason." Nor is any multiplication or composition introduced, and here returns the issue of primary and secondary objects, capping things off neatly. For according to Aquinas it is precisely the achievement of intellect that it comprehends the multiplicity of implicit content in its unified entertainment of the higher object.[9] In God's case, it is precisely in the single act of self-consideration that all adjunct "not-Gods" are captured, and not by any (impossibly) "subsequent" act of divine cognition.

III. The End of Illumination

Given our distance from his intellectual milieu, it might easily appear that in the moves just described Aquinas has simply incorporated the grand tradition of divine ideas into his own system, adding a few characteristic flourishes and some technical detail. But the appearance deceives; his account in fact hides within itself any number of consequences that fundamentally destabilize the tradition of Christian Platonism. Yet it is true that these consequences were not immediately evident in their variety; as noted in the introduction, they (and their different anti-Platonic implications) must be drawn out in light of later discussions. Especially in view will be the ways in which Aquinas' conclusions were resisted, evaded, or ignored in later centuries, and the consequences for the doctrine of creation. The first and most obvious consequence is with regard to the supposed role of the ideas in enabling human intellection. Aquinas' new systematic approach to God's ideas confronted many established models that posited a functional, "illuminating" connection between those ideas and human epistemic success, putting such models under a terrible strain. If Aquinas in these discussions tends to muffle his departures from tradition in benign and rather innocuous rhetoric, many in his immediate wake were under no illusions. In a well-known and often-cited letter, John Peckham, the Franciscan archbishop of Canterbury, fulminated in 1285 against a teaching that has arisen "within the last twenty years" that has had the effect, among others, of "destroying with all its strength what Augustine teaches concerning the eternal rules and the unchangeable light."[10] "Illuminationism" had its roots in Augustine's teachings; variations in detail notwithstanding, it basically had two components. First, the human mind's grasp of eternal truth was held to be impossible using its natural powers, instead requiring a direct influx of God's own intelligible light; as Aristotelian notions began to be better known, God in many illuminationist schemes (such as that of Albert the Great) functioned as the sort of separated agent intellect postulated by some of Aristotle's

---

[9] *STh* I q. 85 aa. 3 & 4.
[10] Etienne Gilson, *History of Christian Philosophy in the Middle Ages* (London: Sheed and Ward, 1955), 359.

interpreters. Second, scientific certainty concerning the created order meant in effect some kind of contact, via the illuminating process, between the human mind and the eternal ideas or "intelligibilities" (*rationes*) of created things present in God's mind. While Augustine and later thinkers were careful not to posit a direct inspection of the ideas by our minds in this life, their functional proximity was necessary to explain the highest human cognitive achievements. This long-standing complex of ideas in fact received its most splendid articulation at the hands of Aquinas' contemporary, the Franciscan Bonaventure.[11]

Peckham and many other champions of what they took to be a key teaching of Augustine were dismayed at Aquinas' acceptance of a largely Peripatetic epistemological scheme, one that left no role for illumination as they understood it. The consequence of Aquinas' bold appropriation of Aristotle's noetic was an understanding of intellection in which God's ideas were left without much to do.[12] The discussion at *ST* I, q. 84 a. 5 makes this evident. Aquinas apparently affirms, with Augustine, that the human intellect knows things "in the eternal intelligibilities," but by the end of the article the reader discovers just how attenuated the role of the intelligibilities as such really is. After a curiously cautionary-sounding stipulation that Augustine was "steeped" (*imbutus*) in the doctrines of the Platonists, Aquinas proceeds to explain his language of knowledge "in" the intelligibilities or ideas. They do play a role as causal principles in our knowing. But how? We participate in them. But in what sense? The final step of the argument more or less gives the game away: the actual participation in question is that of the power of our naturally endowed agent intellect, understood as a kind of created intelligible "light," participating (like all creaturely perfections) in the infinite power of God's intellect as in an uncreated "light." And the latter, after all, "contains" the ideas. This conclusion slips by so quickly that its upshot is easily missed: any functional contiguity between divine ideas and our cognitive processes has been more or less abandoned, leaving only the hazy connection afforded by their presence generally speaking in the light of uncreated intelligence, the created replication of whose power is the natural light of human understanding.[13]

How, then, does human intellectual knowledge actually occur for Aquinas? Famously, and scandalously for those sympathetic to the epistemic models of Plato and Augustine, he took with the strictest seriousness Aristotle's empiricist insistence that all human understanding originates in sense awareness of material realities. Direct causal impingement of the concrete object upon the external sensory equipment is processed via internal cogitative sense powers into a unified intentional presentation (the "phantasm"). The human intellective power (in its role as "agent intellect") then illuminates within the phantasm the element of universal structure, detaching and projecting this strictly intelligible aspect upon its own receptive potency (in its role as

---

[11] Peckham, Bonaventure, and other theorists of illumination are fully treated in Steven P. Marrone, *The Light of Thy Countenance: Science and Knowledge of God in the Thirteenth Century, Volume I: A Doctrine of Divine Illumination* (Leiden: E. J. Brill, 2001).

[12] Gilson, *History of Christian Philosophy*, 377 and 382 connects Aquinas' rejection of illuminationist theories with his equally anti-Platonic insistence on the human soul as the unique substantial form of the human being.

[13] For a more detailed discussion, see DeHart, *Aquinas and Radical Orthodoxy*, 135–8.

"possible intellect"). Thus, it is the "light" of the agent intellect inherent as a power of the human soul, as was said in the previous paragraph, that does the actual abstraction of universality from concrete particularity and hence can, in a fashion, be said to partially replicate the light of God's absolute intellection, which is the source of God's idea. But clearly for Aquinas the divine idea as such is neither object, nor medium, nor agent of human intellection; its role is only virtual and analogical.

But it is not just that the divine ideas were idled in Aquinas' account of human knowledge; they were already made unavailable due to his account of divine knowledge. After all, the primary role of the ideas in Aquinas' thought is to register God's awareness of the creature as product of her will and infinite power, and this in itself renders them simply incommensurate with our modes of cognition. For God is not the creator only of "essences" but also of matter, of time and relations and contingency. What God makes, God understands, intimately and perfectly, individually but also as part of the ordered whole, the cosmos and its history. The contrast with the lower-grade human intellect is total: at best it can just barely attain to universal formalities by clearing them of that mass of concrete conditions and interrelations of which it can make nothing. Divine understanding of the world, however, is attuned quite differently, geared as it is to the production of the concrete singular on the one hand, and to the total ordered ensemble of things and their temporal career on the other.

In a superb essay Mark Jordan lays out the implications. The ideas of God demand both "the radical intelligibility of the singular" and the concrete situation of the singular in the providential order, which is "deeply obscure" to us. As a result, "the mode of truth in the human mind is entirely different from the mode of the original truth in divinity."[14] Nor is the deeper irony of this result lost on Jordan. What Aquinas has done with his theory of divine ideas is "to explain [the world's] intelligibility only to remove it from human power ... The intelligibility is surely there, but not for human minds as naturally active."[15] In view of the epistemic pretensions of Christian Platonism, Aquinas' account of ideas is radically deflationary. Human intellection, magnificent as it is when compared with lower levels of knowing, is nonetheless humiliated before the divine understanding, groping in the dim, participated light of the agent intellect to piece together this or that generalized structure.

IV. Ideas as the Divine Essence or Ideas as "Objects"?

Although illuminationist theories did not long survive Aquinas' death, his position on the ideas was vigorously resisted, giving rise to developments that by the early modern period would render visible another aspect of that theory's counter-Platonic occlusion of the ideas from human knowledge, distinct from its problematizing of illuminationism. The aspect in question results from the radical unity between the act of existence (*esse*) of the divine idea, and the act of existence of the divine essence. In

---

[14] Mark D. Jordan, "The Intelligibility of the World and the Divine Ideas in Aquinas," *Review of Metaphysics* 38 (1984): 17–32 at 24.
[15] Ibid., 30.

the medieval discussions after Aquinas (topic of the present section) that unity was rejected or undermined in different ways; in baroque scholasticism (treated in section V) this rejection eventually supported a firm reconnection between divine ideas and human knowledge. This reconnection, in effect Platonic, was quite different from the old illuminationist scheme, but no less than the latter it was only possible as a total refusal of the ontological status of divine ideas in Aquinas, that is, of their radical identity even as ideas with the divine act of being.

Such a refusal is implied because the "reconnection" in question means the direct securing or anchoring in God of selected aspects of claims to truth in human cognition, and that in turn will require the positing of some definite proper act of existence possessed by God's ideas, formally distinguishable from the divine act of existence as such. Consequently, the present section will discuss how ideas, contrary to Aquinas, came to have their "own" being. The medieval scholastic discussion of ideas after Aquinas is exceedingly complex, and what follows schematizes that discussion in a particular way but hopefully does not distort it. Roughly speaking, the first step was Henry of Ghent's bold new account of the ideas as essences, self-consciously harking back to specifically Platonic motifs. Next, Duns Scotus, reacting partly against Aquinas but even more against Henry, formulated yet another account of the ideas as the "being-known" of actual or possible creatures; the powerful influence of this account (enhanced by William of Ockham) on later discussions, contributed to the eventual marginalization and disappearance of divine ideas among many late scholastics. What binds together Henry and Scotus, however, in spite of their differences, is the "objective" ontological status they grant to the ideas. The stage will thus be set for Section V, in which it will be suggested that the extremely influential baroque metaphysician Francis Suarez recaptures aspects of the different anti-Thomistic ideas theories of Henry and Scotus in order to construct a renewed quasi-Platonic role for God's ideas as direct, truth-making counterparts to human propositions.

The essence of Aquinas' position on the status of the ideas in God is that his knowing anything not herself is integral to the single act of knowing his own essence, and that what is so known is known perfectly in the utter transparency or intelligibility of that essence. In God, to be is to be both the total act of intellection and total openness to that act at once; in God, unlike any creature, *esse intelligible* is *esse naturale*, and vice versa.[16] Henry of Ghent finally cannot countenance this radical unity of knower and known, a unity not just real but formal as well. He did not believe God could know creatures in their distinctness immediately, by knowing the divine essence; God had to know creatures mediately, that is, by means of the ideas, and God's apprehension of these latter required a logically distinct act of derivation or production in the divine mind.[17] Otherwise put, unlike Aquinas for whom God knows her modalities of imitability in the very act of knowing his essence, Henry believes he can detect a sort of process in God whereby she engages in logically distinguishable stages of deeper

---

[16] *ScG* I 47 no. 5.
[17] Meinhardt et al., "Idee," 4: 93–4; Carlos Steel, "Henricus Gandavensis Platonicus," in *Henry of Ghent and the Transformation of Scholastic Thought*, ed. Guy Guldentops and Carlos Steel (Leuven: Leuven University Press, 2003), 18–21.

reflective penetration, over the course of which the creaturely possibilities of imitation resolve themselves, so to speak, detaching themselves to confront the divine gaze.[18]

Crucially, this reflective "production" bestows upon the ideas a peculiar ontological status. No longer reducible, as with Aquinas, to the implicit modalities of God's self-relation, ideas in fact are the essences of created things. Tellingly, Henry expressly invokes Plato's notion of ideas as his inspiration here.[19] While still really identical with God's act of being, conceived as essences Henry's ideas acquire something else that, formally speaking, is not God's act of being. He avails himself of a threefold classification of modes of being for essences that derives in the main from Avicenna. The dual presence of essences both within things and within the minds that know the things demands a third, logically prior mode of "essential existence" that is theirs absolutely; it is quite their own, apart from their presence in mind or thing.[20] In effect, then, Henry roots the accord between mind and thing (truth, in other words) not, as with Aquinas, in the act of existence (*esse*) of the concrete entity in formal unity with the intellect's act of existence, but rather in the hypostasization, so to speak, of the abstract essence in itself: the famous *esse essentiae*. Thus, although ideas-as-essences are really identical with the divine act of existence (God's *esse existentiae*), they must be the bearers, in addition, of a rather mysterious formal mode of existence all their own. And so on the one hand the idea in God's mind can no longer be simply identified with God, but on the other hand it is now freed to be identical with the essence of some created thing. Even though Henry does not make a point of this in his argument, we might suspect that this exact identity of essences straddling the divine-creature divide has the function of securing, in good Platonic fashion, the stability and identifiability of created objects for the infallibility of human science.

To account for this "new" act of essential existence in God, Henry rejects Aquinas' position that ideas are the implicit contents of God's unique act of self-regard, fracturing the latter into a series of moments and clearing a special zone "within" the divine being for eternal essences. These in turn stand "between" the divine essence itself and creatures; instead of God knowing the creature immediately through his essence, these derivative "essences" serve her as cognitional media. This scheme very soon suffered a withering critique at the hands of John Duns Scotus, a critique that in its point of departure resonates with Aquinas' position but which nonetheless breaks with the latter on formal identity and so, remarkably, remains in tacit agreement with Henry on the crucial issue: at base, what is the divine idea primarily an idea *of*?

Scotus attacks Henry's conception on a couple of points that might put Scotus in proximity to Aquinas' account. He firmly rejected the notion that God's ideas are means or instruments enabling God's knowledge of creatures. Like Aquinas, although for different reasons, Scotus insists that God knows creatures immediately, in knowing

---

[18] Maarten J. F. M. Hoenen, "Propter Dicta Augustini: Die Metaphysische Bedeutung der Mittelalterlichen Ideenlehre," *Recherches de Théologie et Philosophie Médiévales* 64 (1997): 245-62 at 257.
[19] Steel, "Henricus," 19-20.
[20] Theo Kobusch, "Heinrich von Gent und die Neuplatonische Ideenlehre," in *Néoplatonisme et philosophie médiévale*, ed. Linos G. Benakis (Turnhout: Brepols, 1997), 198-9.

the unique divine essence itself.[21] Also, Scotus pointed out that "essential existence" is a form of real being; it is not purely formal and always accompanies "existential existence." The upshot is that if God's act of knowing in itself bestowed "essential existence" on all possible creatures, then their actualization would no longer be strictly a creation "from nothing."[22] But in spite of these astute points, Scotus has another criticism that, to his way of thinking, invalidates not only Henry's theory of ideas but Aquinas' as well.

Both Henry and Aquinas, albeit in distinct ways, rely on the notion that ideas are basically ideated (not real but merely rational or notional) relations of imitability, that is, God's intellectual grasp of ways in which his essence can be differently refracted in creatures.[23] For Henry, this notion gives ideas a priority in God's mind to the actual creatures themselves, thus ensuring that the former can be means for God to know the latter. For Aquinas, the relative status of ideas functions rather differently, to clarify the way in which God's single act of self-understanding can also encapsulate an unlimited range of implicit secondary objects. The proviso that these are only notional, "relations of reason," means that they do not multiply realities in God. But Scotus objects to this approach with the axiom that the being of a relation presupposes the prior being of its extremes or *relata*. Against Henry, this means that God's relations to created things cannot be media for knowing them, because God must know the created term of the relation prior to knowing the relation. Against Aquinas, it means that relations of imitability cannot themselves be objects of God's knowledge and yet remain merely relations of reason.[24] Bernard Lonergan locates the kernel of Scotus's objection: "The object [of knowledge] precedes the knowing, and relations that precede knowing are not notional but real." Lonergan's retort in Aquinas' name is important because it points toward a crucial presupposition that, surprisingly, is shared by both Henry and Scotus but not by Aquinas: "The argument [of Scotus] does not touch Aquinas' real position, which is that the object as known is not prior [i.e. to the act of understanding] and that the relations pertain only to the object as known."[25]

For Aquinas, what God knows in an idea is a relation of imitability implicit in the act of understanding the divine essence itself; as a secondary object the relation presupposes only the being of the primary object, the divine essence, and the understanding of that primary object is itself a function of the intelligible identity of knower and known in the understanding act. There is simply no need to posit any "prior" act of proper existence in the object *qua* understood because, as Lonergan repeatedly argued, intellection for Aristotle and Aquinas is first and foremost union and not, as in the Platonic tradition, the contiguity of dual realities, knower and known, subject and object. On the latter understanding, knowledge (whether sensible or intellectual) is always akin to "looking

---

[21] Hoenen, *Marsilius of Inghen*, 78–9.
[22] Ibid., 131–2.
[23] For Aquinas, the different ideas are nothing but the differently understood proportional relations of creaturely perfection to the one divine perfection (*De veritate* q. 3 a. 2). For Henry, the ideas are not the relations as such but rather emerge as products of a logically posterior stage of divine self-reflection. See Steel, "Henricus," 19–20.
[24] For an outline of Scotus's argument see Hoenen, *Marsilius of Inghen*, 78–84.
[25] Lonergan, *Verbum*, 19.

at" something, and consequently the authenticity of knowledge will be guaranteed by the coordinate "reality" of what is being observed. The basic opposition of the two points of view is already in place in Aquinas' construal of human intellection and its natural object, the form embedded in the material singular. Whereas Aquinas, following Aristotle, can construe the similitude of mind and thing in terms of a mental event of intelligible coincidence enabled by selective illumination of the sensible presentation ("abstraction"), Plato had to assume that the universal and immutable form "seen" by intellect in things must in fact involve the contemplation of a form that exists in itself, universally and immutably: a Platonic idea.[26]

There is no need to enter here into the epistemological debates themselves. The point is rather that the Platonic scenario of a confrontation of subject and object implied, as Lonergan suggests, in Scotus's objections uncovers a deep connection between Scotus and Henry that sets both of them over against Aquinas with regard to the ontological status of the divine idea. Both find it necessary to distinguish between the being of the idea (which is identical with the being of the divine mind) and the being of the "information" or signification carried by the idea. That is, both Henry and Scotus readily associate the intelligible content of the idea with its own distinct act of being "within" God. As was just seen, Scotus rejected Henry's identification of this distinct act of being with *esse essentiae*, but he still insisted that ideas have a special, diminished act of existence (*esse diminutum*) as the distinguishable contents of God's cognition. For Scotus, ideas are not prior to creatures as known relations that mediate God's knowledge; rather, they are posterior, arising as a result of the prior act of God's essential, immediate knowing of the possible or actual creature. The idea, then, is just the "being known" of the creature (*esse cognitum*), the internal presence of its content as an object of cognition (*esse objectivum*).[27]

In an important essay the Dutch medievalist Lambertus de Rijk perceived that Henry and Scotus, in spite of the latter's critique of the former, share a remarkable new orientation in their approach to the divine ideas. Against the Thomist view of them, "with Henry of Ghent ... a substantial change of view-point came in," and the view of Scotus is "substantially the same": divine ideas are "*objective* contents of God's knowledge."[28] We can go further. It is to be expected that any hangover of Platonic epistemology, for which the paradigm of intellection is not the identity of intelligible act but rather the abutment of dual actualities, will bring in its wake the endowment of these objective contents with their own peculiar acts of being. And so it turns out: "The Platonist assumption that knowledge involves confrontation led later Scholastics to attribute to the ideas an *esse objectivum*," an "error" from which "Aquinas was

---

[26] *ST* I q. 84, aa. 1 & 2.
[27] Armand Maurer, "Ens Diminutum: A Note on its Origin and Meaning," *Mediaeval Studies* 12 (1950): 216–22 at 221–2.
[28] Lambert M. de Rijk, "Quaestio de Ideis: Some Notes on an Important Chapter of Platonism," in *Kephalaion: Studies in Greek Philosophy and its Continuation offered to C. J. de Vogel*, ed. J. Mansfeld and L. M. de Rijk (Assen: Van Gorcum, 1975), 208–9. For a more detailed discussion centering on Henry, see Lambert M. de Rijk, "Un Tournant Important dans l'Usage du Mot Idea chez Henri de Gand," in *Idea: VI Colloquio Internazionale del Lessico Intelletuale Europeo*, ed. M. Fattori and M. L. Bianchi (Rome: Edizioni del Ateneo, 1990), 89–98.

free."²⁹ The divergence of the two positions on ideas can be presented succinctly by posing the question: primarily speaking, what is the divine idea an idea *of*? While Henry, Scotus, and a host of later Scholastics will say that the idea is primarily God's idea of the creature, Aquinas' position (as we have already seen) is that the idea is primarily God's idea of God, of the divine essence.

V. The Early Modern Revenge of Platonism: Ideas as Uncreated

Scotus's extensive critiques of his predecessors on the divine ideas proved hugely influential, but they did not triumph completely, not even among those of his own school.

Francis of Meyronnes argued that there had to be ideas in God's mind because they are the eternal ground for the truth of our necessary propositions. Their truth is grounded in the formally distinct act of being that the idea possesses within God.³⁰ That is, the contents of the divine ideas must maintain even in God's intellect an ontological status sufficiently defined and robust as to enable them to bear the modal properties that guarantee the integrity of our necessary inferences. Henry of Ghent had already linked the formal being of ideas with their possession of a modal status, namely, that of possibilities. *Esse essentiae* is precisely the property borne by ideas insofar as they could be granted actuality by God, as opposed to mere chimeras.³¹ Indeed, contradicting his master Scotus, Francis strikingly insists on the "essential being" (*esse essentiae*) of the ideas, rejecting Scotus's critique of Henry in order to return to a position on ideas not unlike the latter's. In fact, Francis joins Henry in identifying ideas with the quiddities or essences of things.³² Francis's quasi-revival of Henry, intended or not, was not especially influential in the medieval centuries, but in the long run it proved prophetic. A cloud no bigger than a man's hand, with the advent of a later Francis, the famous early modern metaphysician Suarez, the position that God's mind is a repository of truth-makers for human modal propositions, and the related Avicennist reading of essences as direct links between the divine mind and ours, assumed a position of fateful importance for the history of philosophy. The following section will say a bit more about this forward influence of Suarez, but the point at present is to show how his position looks backward, in that it signals once again the refusal of Aquinas' revolutionary account of ideas in favor of yet another return, in a new key, to their "Platonic" role in human cognition.

For Aquinas, divine ideas are a way of treating God's knowledge of the world. The reasons Suarez gives for his dissatisfaction with Aquinas' position go far beyond a

---

²⁹ Lonergan, *Verbum*, 202.
³⁰ Hoenen, *Marsilius of Inghen*, 133–4. See also Egbert Peter Bos, "The Theory of Ideas according to Francis of Meyronnes: Commentary on the Sentences (Conflatus), I, Dist. 47," in *Néoplatonisme et philosophie médiévale: Actes du colloque internationale de Corfu* (Turnhout: Brepols, 1997), 211–27.
³¹ Hoenen, *Marsilius of Inghen*, 131.
³² Ibid., 133–4.

technical dispute, revealing instead that his own appeal to that tradition is driven by the completely different concern evinced earlier by Francis of Meyronnes.[33] Having argued that the being of essences (*esse essentiae*) is only real in existents as actual, he is deeply repelled by the consequence some thinkers have drawn that true essential predications (e.g., "A human is rational") are only true supposing the actual existence of the things they are about. Suarez wants to affirm strongly that essential predications, as necessary truths, have timeless or eternal validity. If they did not, then they would in fact be contingent, and human scientific knowledge would cease. Now Suarez is quite aware that Aquinas argued against the inherent eternity of any truths about creatures; apart from the actuality of the creatures, whatever "eternal" truth they may have is simply their truth in the divine intellect. But this is just unacceptable to Suarez. This kind of "eternity" is simply identity with the divine being itself, and that eternal status would hold just the same whether a given truth about a creature were necessary or contingent.[34] Suarez obviously regards himself as under an imperative to secure the basis of the human knowledge of necessity; a position like Aquinas' is intolerable, because it means that the divine mind simply does not acknowledge the utter necessity of an essential predicate in the same way that a human mind must.

Faced with this affront to the modal status of true human propositions, Suarez does not hesitate to invoke a distinct ontological realm of absolute truth that God eternally confronts rather than willingly creates. On the one hand, he follows the lead of Henry of Ghent and Francis of Meyronnes in asserting that unlike "imagined and impossible things such as a chimera," some objects of divine omnipotence are genuine possibilities and hence are lodged, so to speak, in the divine power from all eternity as "real" essences.[35] Even as a mere possibility, such a "real" essence, say "human being," bears within itself the necessity of all possible true propositions premised upon it, such as "is rational." Even if its terms "human being" and "rationality" do not exist, and never will, their necessity of connection eternally presents itself to the divine mind, as the possible essence (for "the truth of an essence is really nothing else than the essence itself"). This recrudescence of Henry's Platonist essentialism is based, however, on a Scotist account of "objective being." The *esse objectivum* of a really possible essence is not real being, and yet this does not affect the "reality" of its essence![36] If we speak of a divine idea or exemplar at this point, we must repeat Scotus's position that it is nothing but the "being known" of the (possible) creature, and any necessity of truth that the "objective being" of the exemplar bears is actually derivative, arising from the necessity of the object itself, the possible creature's definition or essence.

---

[33] Francisco Suarez, *On the Essence of Finite Being as Such, on the Existence of that Essence, and their Distinction. Metaphysical Disputation XXXI*, trans. Norman J. Wells (Milwaukee, WI: Marquette University Press, 1983), 199–201

[34] Ibid.

[35] It is a mark of the confusion on these issues that plagued the later followers of Aquinas that Suarez can summon up support for this quintessentially non-Thomist position by appealing to the so-called prince of Thomists John Capreolus. Suarez, *On the Essence of Finite Being*, 58–9. For an excellent discussion of the fundamental opposition between Aquinas and Suarez on the ontological status of eternal truth, see Armand Maurer, "St. Thomas and Eternal Truths," *Mediaeval Studies* 32 (1970): 91–107.

[36] Suarez, *On the Essence of Finite Being*, 63.

With such an account of God's ideas we find ourselves in an altogether different conceptual world than that of Aquinas. Suarez's forceful formulae bear witness to this. The eternal truths of essences are not true because they are known by God but rather are known by God because they are true.[37] Indeed, the necessity they bear ontologically means God "must" necessarily know them to be true, just as we do. In another statement reminiscent of Scotus's critique of Aquinas, Suarez says that God's speculative intellect presupposes the truth of its object, it does not produce it. So the divine ideas are the "objective" presence in God of the essences eternally possible for her, and these have inherent in them an eternal truth "not only as they are in the divine intellect but also in themselves and prescinding from it."[38] As Armand Maurer points out, for Aquinas, the fundamental "truth-maker" for propositions about created things is the act of existence inhering in those things. God's creative knowledge of them, however, grants them that act of existence.[39] With Suarez at the turn of modernity a strikingly different scheme is perfected, one where the truth-maker for human propositions about things is the eternal being of those things in God (agreeing with Henry of Ghent), and that eternal being itself is that of a truth not "granted" by God but necessarily acknowledged by him. Such truth is, in fact, uncreated.[40] For Plato and his followers, human science is guaranteed by epistemic ascent to the divine ideas. Aquinas' idea theory demolished any such possibility, but the dream died hard. With Suarez, it returns in a new guise, as the modal necessity of our logical and essential predications puts us in direct touch with the necessity of the exemplars impelling the divine mind itself.

VI. Aquinas contra Suarez: Marion's Interpretation and the Question of the Trinity

Aquinas resolutely reduced the existence of the divine ideas to the one intelligent existential act of the divine essence itself; the claims of Suarez depended ultimately upon the refusal of this reduction. This opposition has been noticed before. In the third chapter of his magisterial work on Descartes's "white theology," Jean-Luc Marion mounts a splendid investigation of some of the key issues just treated, albeit with a slightly different set of concerns and motives. Marion's starting point is the Cartesian demand that even what human reason rightly discerns to be necessary or "eternal" truth must not be conceived as anything imposed upon or given to the divine mind; no creaturely truth could confront the divine intellect as a kind of "fate" to which God had to submit. In other words, Descartes asserted that eternal truths were created by God.[41] In a series of penetrating discussions, Marion has explored the way in which this radical position of Descartes provides a standpoint from which to explore many of

---

[37] Ibid., 200.
[38] Ibid., 200–1.
[39] Maurer, "St. Thomas and Eternal Truths," 94–6.
[40] For Suarez, the existence of necessary truths about creatures falls quite outside the creative will of God. Indeed, such truths have no efficient cause at all. Suarez, *On the Essence of Finite Being*, 201. See also Maurer, "St. Thomas and Eternal Truths," 92–3.
[41] Marion, *Sur la théologie blanche*, 27–31.

the key thinkers and debates of early modern philosophy, especially the consequences of evading or ignoring the Cartesian position (which was the tactic of most of the influential figures).[42] One of the main issues of concern for Marion is what he calls the "march of univocity," the way in which seventeenth- and eighteenth-century philosophers undertook to discourse on the divine with little regard for, or even comprehension of, the centuries of accumulated philosophical wisdom concerning the sharp limitations encumbering any application of human language and concepts to God. Foregoing the technical safeguards developed in the scholastic tradition that attempted to shunt any claims about God away from their literal and ordinary ranges of meaning into "analogical" predication, most philosophers extended their definitions and inferences directly into the sphere of transcendence with little epistemological restraint. This implies that the ideas, propositions, and truths entertained by human reason appear to hold "univocally" for God, without significant qualitative shifts for the divine reason (however they may fall short quantitatively, so to speak, of the unlimited mass of "information" available to omniscience).[43] Marion's assessment is that, even though Descartes hardly differs from other early modern innovators in having little use for the classical apparatus of analogy, his explosive claim about the creation of truth represented a radical refusal, at once insightful and potentially fruitful, of the constellation of modern metaphysical assumptions.

Of particular importance to the present discussion is Marion's disclosure that the Cartesian claim of eternal truths as divine creations was not snatched from thin air. It was in fact a counter-position, an explicit rejection of what he took to be the "scholastic" position but which turns out more precisely to be the position we have just examined: that of Francis Suarez. As we have done, Marion, too, juxtaposes the position of Suarez on eternal truth with that of Aquinas. Marion argues that Suarez's account of truth in God's mind leaves the door wide open to the kind of univocal identity between divine and human notions (e.g., the necessary truths derived from "essences") that directly encouraged modern theistic speculation. He rightly discerns the way such an account of truth posits an ontological gap between the divine essence and the formal content of divine ideas, a gap that the account of Aquinas does not allow. For the latter, "the relation of the divine essence to its ideas does not arise from representation (knowledge by objects), but from expression (by *exemplares*), and thus from a play of God with himself."[44] The summation states in different language the point made in the section above: God's ideas of creatures are implicit in the known self-relation of the divine being, rather than "objective" entities serving as representative media for God's knowledge of the world.

Marion's exploration is profound and affords many insights not touched on here. However, at a crucial point his analysis takes a turn that must be interrogated in light of the "anti-Platonic" reading of Aquinas being developed in this chapter. Right

---

[42] See, e.g., Jean-Luc Marion, "Creation of the Eternal Truths: The Principle of Reason—Spinoza, Malebranche, Leibniz," in *On the Ego and on God: Further Cartesian Questions*, trans. Christina M. Geschwandtner (New York: Fordham Univ. Press, 2007), 116–38.
[43] Jean-Luc Marion, "The Idea of God," 265–304.
[44] Marion, *Sur la théologie blanche*, 39.

after the passage quoted above, Marion asserts that Aquinas' position on the ideas is incomprehensible in merely philosophical terms; the true nature of exemplars or ideas in his thought can only be grasped and defended on theological, specifically Trinitarian, grounds. He maintains it would be paradoxical to assume that the exemplars, as direct expressions of the unified and simple divine essence, could, "on their own" as it were, sustain the differentiations that define their similitude to the varied creation. Instead, God is said to arrange a place for created otherness within herself, so to speak. That God can do this in turn presupposes that the divine unity is not an inert self-enclosure; the relation "other than God" must itself already subsist within the divine, an essential self-differentiation within self-relation. This "internal alterity" is, of course, the generation of the eternal Son or Word.[45] In short, Marion insists that a true understanding of ideas in Aquinas can only occur when one identifies their emergence within God as a particular aspect or dimension of God's primal self-utterance. That God understands the temporal world is rooted in the eternal speaking of the Word. However, two things must be said in reply. First, what Marion attributes to him here is not, indeed cannot be, Aquinas' position. Second, Marion's Trinitarian claim in regard to Aquinas' ideas can be regarded as yet another dubious attempt, ironically contrary to Marion's own intent, to "re-Platonize" them.

That Marion's reading is unacceptable can initially be argued based upon an examination of Aquinas' actual arguments for divine ideas. The detailed account at *Summa Contra Gentiles* Bk. I chs. 51–4 is especially informative. Chapter 51 lays down as the basic constraint Aquinas' position on the radical unity of existence between God and the ideas: there are many things understood by God (*intelligibilia*), but they cannot have distinct acts of existence (*esse distinctum*) in God else his essence would be composite, nor can they be added like accidents. The solution begins in chapter 53. Aquinas is clear that the key to resolving the issue is simply "how things understood exist in the intellect." He means in intellects generally, not just in God's intellect, and the ensuing discussion begins with the analysis of human intellection (*ab intellectu nostro*) already summarized at the beginning of this chapter. He distinguishes two aspects or moments of the act, which I have dubbed unity and transparency, or metaphysical formality and intelligibility (*quo intelligitur* and *intellectum*). Now Aquinas does indeed apply this account to the case of God, specifying that the *quo intelligitur* in God, the formal unity enabling understanding, is the one divine essence; likewise, there is the equivalent in God of our *intellectum* (what he here calls an "*intentio intellecta*"), namely, the eternal Word, that is, the Son. In the context of the problem Aquinas is addressing, this might immediately suggest that the solution to the problem of multiple ideas is indeed to be found in positing the eternal generation of the Word in God. But there are strong reasons to doubt this.

First of all, the introduction of the eternal Word as "*intentio intellecta*" does not in itself solve the problem of multiple ideas at all. Quite the contrary: the upshot of the discussion is precisely that just as there is only one divine essence through which God knows all, so there can be only one divine Word expressing the content of that

---

[45] Ibid., 39–41.

intellective act. The actual solution occurs in chapter 54, and is entirely in terms of the divine essence: to repeat, God in the one act of knowing her essence knows at the same time all the grades of partial participation in his essence. The discussion of the Word in the prior chapter merely sets the stage for this solution. Intellection involves not just metaphysical unity but the richness of intelligible content rendered transparent in the unification. God's essence is not just utterly one, it is also the unimaginable concentration of all meaning. It is precisely this rendering in chapter 53 of the dynamic aspects of intellection that prepares the discussion in chapter 54 of primary and secondary objects of understanding that provides the actual solution to the problem of multiple objects of understanding, that is, why this multiplicity nonetheless does not disrupt the unity of the act of understanding itself, the act that God is. There seems to be no ground here, or for that matter in any other discussion of ideas to be found in Aquinas, for the conclusion of Marion that the multiplicity or "alterity" of ideas of creatures can be reasonably supported only on the supposition of Trinitarian procession.

But there is a second issue. Aquinas, as is well known, draws a sharp distinction between truths that can be demonstrated by human reasoning alone, as opposed to truths that can be acquired only on the premise of some special disclosure from God. Aquinas is emphatic that the Trinity, that is the presence of eternal processions in God, is completely unavailable to any reasoning that begins with the natural knowledge of creation.[46] However, there is not the slightest indication in his multiple arguments about ideas that they rest on anything but that latter, naturally based kind of reasoning. Indeed, the chapters of the *Summa Contra Gentiles* just examined are found in the first book of that work, where Aquinas is at pains (putatively for apologetic purposes) to rest his positions on rational arguments available to all, apart from special revelation.[47] But what, then, accounts for the explicit mention of the divine Word at the end of chapter 53? Does it not suggest, in its context, that something like an eternal intellectual procession in God is, in fact, a conclusion justifiable simply on the assumption that God is intelligent and knows what she creates? And does this not, in turn, give support to Marion's contention of an intrinsic, necessary connection between exemplars and the generation of the Son? I do not think so. Aquinas will naturally affirm, as a Catholic Christian, what the church knows by revelation, namely, that there is indeed an eternal generation in God. He also follows Augustine in applying the so-called psychological analogy to this revealed datum, using the instance of the production in human intellectual acts of the *intellectum* or intelligible word as a conceptual model able to illuminate in a limited way the intelligibility of the divine generation. These commitments appear in the wording of the conclusion to chapter 53, but the crucial point is that, as has been shown, the logic of his argument about ideas does not at all turn on affirming the eternal utterance of the Son in God. It rests simply on an understanding of the nature of intellection in itself.

To be sure, the distinction just mentioned of the two aspects or moments of intellection is central both to the solution to the problem of God's simple knowledge of a

---

[46] *STh* I q. 31 a. 1.
[47] *ScG* I 9.

complex creation and to the psychological analogy of the Trinity. But close examination of Aquinas' argument for the former will reveal that he makes no demonstrative inference from his affirmation of the second moment (that of *intellectum*) in God to the kind of generation or production of an interior word that necessarily characterizes that second moment in human intellectual acts. In human beings, the two moments, the information of intellect by the species and the resulting production of the concept or judgment, are separate, really distinct acts. In us there must first be actualization of intellect (*intelligere* proper); now activated, the intellect, in a second step (*dicere*), "speaks" the *intellectum*, what has been understood.[48] The notion of an interior word requires two notes: it must be understood (*intellecta*), but it must also expressed from another (*ab alio*), and the latter implies a genuine duality. But in our rational affirmation of intellection in God no necessary ground can be found for this note of "expression from another," hence for a similar separation of *intelligere* and *dicere*.[49] There is no inherent necessity that in an intellectual act *quo intelligitur* and *intellectum* must "confront" one another, though de facto that is what happens in us. To repeat yet again, Aquinas' position is that God knows the other (derivatively) in the simple act of knowing himself (primally), and thus that "by which" God knows can be assumed to be identical with "what" God knows.

Thus, in Aquinas' argument about ideas, all that is required is to affirm the two aspects of intellection as such. Once attention has been directed to the intelligible aspect of the divine self-presence, what might be called its transparency or (to recall the language in the *Summa Contra Gentiles* of *intentio intellecta*) its character as intelligently intended, the groundwork for the argument about ideas is complete. Any mention of the Word as a real procession in God is a fitting but (*pace* Marion) logically superfluous allusion to the mental word's analogical propinquity to revealed truth. We might venture further. Here quite possibly is the reason for the remarkable redactional history of *Summa Contra Gentiles* chapters 51–54.[50] In earlier drafts of this material Aquinas continued and extended the language found in his earlier detailed treatment of ideas at *Disputed Questions on Truth* question 3: he spoke of a "twofold form" in the understanding mind, one being the actualizing species, the other the object as understood, the *intellectum*.[51] This required him to say that the intellect, formed by the species, now acts to form .... yet another form, that of the *intellectum* or *ratio* or interior word. What is striking is that for his final version of the discussion in the *Summa Contra Gentiles*, Aquinas went through these chapters and either redrafted them or carefully excised passages in order to completely delete this characterization of the second element in intellection as an intelligible "form." Nomenclature for the latter is restricted to *intentio intellecta* or *ratio*, while form-terminology regards either

---

[48] Lonergan, *Verbum*, 135–6.
[49] *De veritate* q. 4 a. 2 and ad 5.
[50] The suppressed drafts of *ScG* I 51–54 upon which the following comments are based can be found in volume 13 of the Leonine edition of Aquinas' works: Thomas Aquinas, *Summa Contra Gentiles*, vol. 13 of *Sancti Thomae Aquinatis doctoris angelici Opera omnia iussu Leonis XIII. P. M. edita*, cura et studio fratrum praedicatorum (Rome: Typis Riccardo Garrone, 1918), 19*–22* (appendix).
[51] Cf. *De veritate*, q. 3 a. 2.

Platonic "separate" forms or the intellectual species as form of the intellect (i.e., in the first moment of intellection).

It is possible that his motive in this expurgation was to enhance understanding of the distinct role of the *intellectum* aspect in the act of understanding while warding off any hint that the production of the latter need be thought of as a metaphysically differentiated event, a diversification implied by the presence of rival forms.[52] In us, no doubt, we must speak in terms of such a real production, a kind of formal doubling; but for Aquinas we are in no position to claim this for God's understanding. In the rational analysis of our intellectual act, an internal *dicere* is the literal and argumentatively necessary concomitant of *intelligere*. In God, we affirm intelligence with equal rational necessity, but if we speak of an intellectual *dicere* we merely venture a fitting analogy, and that only on the basis of revelation. This is to reaffirm the careful arguments of Lonergan, who some time ago concluded rather forcefully that a proceeding intellectual word in God is not demonstrable on the basis of her understanding of the world, and consequently that the association in Aquinas' discussions of divine ideas with the eternally generated Word is not intrinsic to his argument but simply a nod to custom.[53] And it honors the distinction Aquinas himself drew between the Word "in the beginning" mentioned in "the books of the Platonists" (*in libris ... Platonicorum*) and the Trinitarian Word disclosed in Jesus. The latter is the "person born within Divinity," known only to faith; the former notion, attained by the philosophers, is merely the "ideal *ratio* through which God founded all things."[54] The disjunction Aquinas intends could not be clearer: the creative intellect knows what it creates, because it knows its essence as exemplar, hence as exemplars or ideas; this "word" is properly just the divine intelligence, an essential property that is (Aquinas is careful to note) only "appropriated" to the Son.

For all the penetration of Marion's discussion, he unaccountably misses the import of this disjunction. More than that, this Trinitarian misstep threatens, quite against Marion's own intentions, to precipitate us back into that world of traditional Christian Platonism that actually cannot accommodate divine ideas as Aquinas has come to understand them. Marion recognizes, with Aquinas, that the ideas are not objective "representations," and he is not promoting an illuminationist epistemology. But Aquinas knows something more: the "eternal word" in the divine intellect of the creator must never be confused with the generated Son, even though no less an authority than Augustine promoted just this conjunction, famously claiming it was already to be found in the "books of the Platonists" (*Platonicorum libros*).[55] (The phrasing is discretely but unmistakably echoed in the Aquinas passage above.) When Marion suggests that

---

[52] Some of this squeamishness disappears in the more curtailed treatment in *Summa Theologiae*. But a similar motive perhaps lies behind the compressed passage already referred to above (*STh* I q. 15 a. 2 and reply to second objection), where a different image is employed, that of the self-reflection of intelligence, but with the same intention, to specify the dynamic involved precisely as a function of intelligence and not simply of the generic metaphysics of formal causality.
[53] Lonergan, *Verbum*, 201–4.
[54] *STh* I q. 32 a. 1 ad 1.
[55] Augustine, *Confessiones*, ed. Pius Knöll, Corpus Scriptorum Ecclesiasticorum Latinorum, vol. 33 (Vienna: F. Tempsky, 1896), 154 [Bk. 7, ch. 9].

only the "distance" between Father and Son can support an eternal divine knowledge of creaturely difference, he is repeating the Christian Platonic gesture whereby the "logos" in God is posited as the "place" of the ideas, since the latter in their ontological multiplicity and distinctness are seen to require a special "zone" or "receptacle" within the divine being.[56] Indeed, Lonergan correctly warned of the link between this kind of Trinitarian move and the Platonic assumption that ideas require a special "*esse objectivum*," the position on ideas discussed in the previous section.[57] The irony, then, is that Marion's insightful critique of "objectivism" and "representationalism" in Suarez's idea theory rightly bids farewell to just that assumption (born of the Platonic demand for a necessary "confrontation" between knower and known) but then lingers perilously in its vicinity in his insistence that, logically, the intelligibility of creatures is invincibly multiple not merely for our understanding, but must be the transcription or "expression" of an "alterity" in the divine being itself.

VII. Conclusion

This chapter has explored three stances on ideas, namely, their integration into a functional role in human cognition, the ontological discontinuity of their semantic content with God's very act of being (in Henry's *esse essentiae*, Scotus's *esse cognitum*, or Suarez's amalgamation of both), and finally their incorporation within the intra-divine procession of the Son as Word. It has been our task to show that all three of these conceptual maneuvers are forbidden in light of Aquinas' rethinking of divine ideas. Moreover, it has been the intention here to assemble the different discussions involved, in spite of their broad chronological spread, in order gradually to reveal the deep antagonism between Aquinas' theory of ideas and that orienting of the ideas toward human epistemology that characterizes the Platonist tradition. In fact, it could be argued that just these three interdicted moves (the ideas as illuminating, as "objective being," and as segregated within the eternal "logos") together form the complex of Christian Platonism in its noetic aspect. Each had to be affirmed in order to rescue even within the trajectory of Jewish monotheism the possibility, still inspired by Diotima's oracle to Socrates, of an aspiring ascent to cognitive communion with that timeless realm to which the demiurge looks in fashioning our world. The tradition runs back to Origen, himself inspired by Philo.[58]

---

[56] Marion, *Sur la théologie blanche*, 39–42.
[57] Lonergan, *Verbum*, 202.
[58] There is indeed such an ascent of the created human subject to God. But our basic orientation toward God, our constitutive *eros* for the divine, is to be found in the implicit direction of our acts of intellection toward their own perfection as acts. Lonergan's *Insight* and Farrer's *Finite and Infinite* have laid the fundamental groundwork here. See Bernard Lonergan, *Insight: A Study of Human Understanding*, ed. Frederick E. Crowe and Robert M. Doran, vol. 3 of *Collected Works of Bernard Lonergan* (Toronto: University of Toronto Press, 1992); and Austin Farrer, *Finite and Infinite: A Philosophical Essay*, 2nd ed. (London: Dacre Press, 1959). For some time these texts, along with Blondel's *Action*, have appeared to me essential building blocks in the development of a metaphysic that properly connects a theism of creation *ex nihilo* with a theological anthropology of the subject. See the brief suggestions in DeHart, *Aquinas and Radical Orthodoxy*, 194–9. The perspective of this book is in complete harmony with these approaches, albeit with a central incorporation of

This centuries-old line of speculation, haunted by Plato's dream of a certain kind of liaison between God's mind and ours, Aquinas' theory of ideas quietly demolished. Thus, our title speaks of an eclipse of the divine mind, meaning the occlusion or blockage of its ideas from our view. This finding is significant not just for intellectual history but for theistic theorization as well, whether in philosophy or theology. For the obverse of the negative, anti-Platonic aspect of Aquinas' position is its positive, systematic recalibration of the relations between omnipotent creator and human knower. In fact, his theory of the ideas interlocks logically with the centerpiece of the classic monotheistic inheritance, namely, creation *ex nihilo*; their eclipse before our minds is the mere drawing out of the strict implications of such a monotheism for human cognition. To conclude, we will briefly reiterate each of the three aspects of the "anti-Platonic" noetic encapsulated in Aquinas' theory of ideas in order to highlight the connection to his doctrine of creation.

First, the mode of God's knowledge of the world is estranged from our own because it tracks exactly with the mode of his production of the world. This was the main point brought out so effectively by Mark Jordan; its damaging implications for illuminationist accounts of God's ideas as mediators of our grasp of worldly truth is readily apparent from his discussion. God understands creatures uniquely, as their utter and unfathomable source; the divine intellect (unlike the human or angelic) neither abstracts their identifying formality nor, indeed, grasps them as implicates of higher and more general layers of created causality. What is understood is at once, totally and precisely, what the creature is: there is no bracketing of background contingency, no disengagement from its cocoon of conditions and relations. There is no opaque residue, no "noise." Every aspect of creation is known identically within the total willed product. The divine idea encompasses in a higher mode all that created intellects could know, and more; the creator's idea is intimately inside the creature's idea, but the creature's idea is quite outside the creator's. As in the Borges parable ("*Del rigor en la ciencia*"), God's idea is the resolution of all created detail; the scale is 1:1, a map unreadable by us. The ideas are occulted by transcendence, the barrier interposed by that scarcely thinkable "from nothing."

Second, we have shown why the ideas suppose no ontological "space" for created truths as such in the creator's being. All creaturely meaning, the infinite shortfall of the divine totality of meaning, is understood in the act of God knowing herself, which itself in turn is just the act of God being God. The actuality of creaturely being apart from God is known as willed by God, but as virtual or possible it has no defined presence in God that "meets" him from within. God, in Kant's excellent phrase, is *intuitus originarius*; to that intelligence, nothing that is not God could ever possibly be presented, nothing is "given," not even from inside God's self-knowing. Nothing definite is given materially (as a real actuality), nor formally (as an intelligibility, a meaning, a truth). The world, the determined creature as such, in its determined act as simply not-God (as opposed to its infinite act as the indeterminable range of God's

---

Kierkegaard's account of the dynamic of subjectivity. At any rate, the consummating union with God is to be understood not in terms of the Platonic rendezvous with the realm of ideas but rather along the lines laid out in Chapters 3 and 9 in this book.

imitability), is not given *to* God's knowledge but is rather given, in its execution, *by* God's self-knowledge. So the truth of the creature in God has no being private to itself but is known only as an implied distance from God's own truth. That is why the created truth we apprehend is rooted in the creature itself, and truth-making for our intellects is finally a world-immanent affair. For Henry of Ghent, God's ideas make things true; for Duns Scotus, things make God's ideas true. Aquinas' position denies both: there is no direct verificational traffic between the truth of ideas and the truth of things; it is instead mediated by the participatory act of being granted by the divine intent to create.

Third, since the ideas in their difference are the entertainment by God of her willed product, they are not implicated in God's natural product, the eternal Son. Though there reigns between them that quasi-aesthetic resonance that Aquinas calls "fittingness," the two enigmas of alterity, intra-divine and creaturely, are of quite different orders, and one should not, with Marion, make one the explanatory ground of the other.[59] The Trinitarian otherness is the mystery of a production or "coming forth" whose absoluteness is paradoxically marked by a total unity of product and origin. The otherness of creatures, by contrast, is the automatic result of the contrast between the unity of identity and actuality in God's being, and their being poised against each other in the creature. As Rudi te Velde has emphasized, it is just this diremption of essence and existence, the creature's very "outsideness" to God's being, that immediately demands a multiplicity of differentiated creaturely identities.[60] And this otherness of creatures themselves is the direct ground of the otherness of their respective divine ideas. To be sure, the human act of intellection provides Aquinas a model for both intra-divine (Trinitarian) and extra-divine (created) difference, but the same aspects of that act are not relevant in the two cases. The analogy for God's eternal generation is found in the interior unity of *intelligere* and *dicere*, while the multiplication of ideas in God's self-regard is accounted for by means of the mutually illuminating interpenetration in all human understanding of more general and more particular elements, of prime and subordinate objects captured in the single glance.[61] The riddle of differentiation among divine ideas is unimaginable, but unlike that of personal distinction in God, it presents itself readily to natural reflection on the very idea of creation, and is solved by appeal

---

[59] The issue is too large to argue here, but I am not convinced by the claims of the formidably learned Gilles Emery, among others, that the revealed doctrine of the divine persons is truly foundational for the notion of creation in Aquinas. That grasping the full depth and scope of the latter requires Trinitarian insights I do not doubt, but in Aquinas' mature works the Trinitarian dimension of creation habitually reduces to appropriations of intellect and will to the proceeding persons. It is telling that a large proportion of the material upon which Emery depends in his argument for a fundamental logical interdependence of the two doctrines is drawn from Aquinas' *Sentences* commentary. It should be borne in mind that Aquinas hardly elaborated upon many of these early claims, and often failed even to mention them, in his later work. See Gilles Emery, "Trinity and Creation," *The Theology of Thomas Aquinas*, ed. Rik van Nieuwenhove and Joseph Wawrykow (Notre Dame: University of Notre Dame Press, 2005), 58–76.

[60] Te Velde, *Participation and Substantiality*, 128, 221.

[61] See *ScG* IV 11 for the claim that the unity of Father and Son in God is to be understood on the analogy of the perfected identity of knower and known that is the pinnacle of intellection. The most complete procession is precisely where the emergent remains utterly one with its origin.

to our own self-awareness as intellectual. The two mysteries, creation and Trinity, have each their own province, and Aquinas' ideas theory avoids any Platonic merging of them as "logos."

In sum, God's ideas of our world, first, cannot themselves light up our minds nor make our notions their ectypes, for God's ideas originate in his incomprehensible creative gesture, utterly estranging them from our own. Second, as not-given they have no act of being but God's, so their mode of "carrying" truth is too foreign for them to be the direct guarantee of even our necessary judgments. Finally, as the definitively not-given notions of what is not-God, they cannot be included within or reduced to the eternal giving of God to God in the Triune life. The divine idea is too infinitely precise to provide a verifying counterpart to our merely "correct" judgments; its concentrated precision would overwhelm even the angelic intellect. Thus, for Aquinas, even though worldly intellects work by catching a glint of the infinite understanding, they never overtake the creator's act at its origin. So, too, we are never "contemporary," so to speak, with the being, which is the immediate effect of that act, not even with the being of ourselves; thus, even our most successful and rigorous diagrams of worldly process remain conjectural, albeit asymptotic, exercises. *Pace* Plato (and science's mathematical enthusiasts from Galileo to Einstein), the world architect's original schematic is indecipherable. We can say more. Created truths are only sustained in their "impossible" separateness from God as a sort of negative exposure; in their origin, then, at the blinding core from which the universe radiates, they cannot maintain their own truth against God's. "My thoughts are not your thoughts" (Isa. 55:8). Our minds read truth by the flickering glow of the proper beings of things in their distinctness. But from a divine perspective these "lights" are really more like shadows, cast by the selective interpositions of God's creative will against the vast solar glare of the divine being itself.

9

The Creature Makes Itself: The Divine Ideas as Anti-Platonic Soteriology

Since at least the third century CE many Christian theologians have employed the notion of divine ideas, that is, the contents of the divine mind in its timeless knowledge of temporal creatures. The continuity of the usage is deceptive, however, for it is not clear that they have all been talking about the same thing. In particular, it is arguable that Thomas Aquinas developed a notion of the divine ideas that marked a revolutionary break with their original, Platonic orientation.[1] Aquinas, in attempting to square God's perfect knowledge of creatures with the strict implications of creation *ex nihilo*, reconceived the ideas in terms of a double identity: ontologically, ideas are identical with the divine essence itself; cognitively, in terms of their epistemic content, ideas are identical with the creatures to which they respectively correspond.

Now, in their original Platonic milieu, and in most of their subsequent reappearances in Patristic and early Medieval theology, the divine ideas could serve an epistemic function (i.e., mediating the human grasp of eternal truth), an ontological function (i.e., anchoring the diversity of creaturely kinds and attributes as immutable expressions of the articulated structure of being itself), and/or a salvific function (i.e., providing an ideal realm, contact or conjunction with which constitutes human beatitude or communion with God).[2] It appears, however, that Aquinas' version of the ideas, with their double identity, plays havoc with the first two of these functions. As ontologically identical with the divine essence, the ideas turn out to be perfectly unattainable, cognitively speaking, for human beings in this life and hence cannot provide an epistemic medium. And as identical in cognitive content with the actual creatures God creates, the ideas are completely bound up with the concrete divine will

---

[1] The repeated usage in what follows of the (admittedly provocative) phrase "anti-Platonic" should not be misunderstood. The reader must take care always to relate the postulated opposition of Aquinas to "Platonism" strictly to the theory of ideas and its explicitly discussed implications. There might be, and are, any number of other facets of Aquinas' thought that could deservedly be labelled "Platonic" from our perspective, nor is the claim being made that he necessarily understood even his theory of ideas explicitly in terms of an opposition to the Platonic tradition.

[2] No source with which I am familiar tells this entire story in detail. To reference it again, there is the selective but useful overview provided by Boland, *Ideas in God*, 17–192. The philosophical side of these developments is helpfully canvassed in Meinhardt et al., "Idee," 61–102.

to realize this universe out of a potentially infinite number of worlds; the ultimately unfathomable contingency of this divine choice means that even God's eternal knowledge of creatures is chosen, not necessary, and hence the map of species with their "necessary" attributes cannot be projected onto being itself, that is, God herself, as an immutable feature.[3] But what about the third Platonic function of the ideas? In light of Aquinas' revolution, can the ideas continue to play an ideal role for human striving? And if they cannot, if the divine ideas as he conceived them are truly anti-Platonic in all three senses, does that leave them any role in human salvation at all? Are they functional only for divine knowledge, while humanly irrelevant?

In the following I will argue two connected theses. First, Aquinas' ideas are indeed anti-Platonic in the third sense, which means that if we accept creation *ex nihilo*, connection with God's ideas is no longer a meaningful role for human attainment: they are "de-idealized." Second, however, I will also suggest that divine ideas can still play a vital role in how we construe anthropology and soteriology, but that in order to see how, and thus to realize the full theological significance of Aquinas' position, it is necessary to go beyond him, to develop (with the aid of later thinkers) the implications of his new departure into a kind of "existential" ethic, built around the ontological and ethical primacy of the concrete human individual. The first section sketches the problem confronting Aquinas (that of reconciling divine knowledge and creation *ex nihilo*) along with his solution via the double identity of the divine ideas, and then shows how one side of the double identity, the perfect intentional or informational identity between the creature and God's idea of it, makes the divine idea an impossible ideal for the creature's attainment or even approximation. The second section begins with the other side of the double identity, the fact that the idea is not itself a creature but is identical with God's being, and goes on to show that by this move Aquinas has de-idealized the ideas in a further, deeper sense: not only is the idea not an ideal for attainment, it is not even (in Platonic fashion) a higher, "ideal" form of the creature; rather, it is itself instrumental to the divine intention of realizing the creature's individual existence and agency.

Thus, for reasons having to do with the metaphysics of divine knowledge and the act of creation, Aquinas asserted both the unattainability of the divine idea and the divinely intended pragmatic primacy of the real creature over its ideal representation in God's mind. But he did not fully unfold his position on the ideas by systematically extending their anti-Platonic implications into the realm of ethics and theological anthropology. The remainder of the chapter turns to develop the possibility that Aquinas' account of the ideas gestures toward but that he chose not to exploit, tentatively and briefly sketching the implicit, proto-existentialist ethic of subjectivity that might consolidate the anti-Platonic dimension of his thought. The necessity of such an explicitly anthropological development will be shown in the third section: the remarkable vision of Meister Eckhart shows that even full acceptance of Aquinas' metaphysic of divine ideas in itself (i.e., the double identity), without a sensitivity to their implied anthropological orientation, can result in a view of human salvation almost completely

---

[3] I argue in Chapters 8 and 10, respectively, for the anti-Platonic epistemic and ontological implications of Aquinas' account of divine ideas.

at odds with that of Aquinas. Eckhart's stress on the creature's ideal preexistence in God undermined Aquinas' emphasis on the creature's own real existential agency, thereby allowing Platonism to return by another route.

If the example of Eckhart shows the necessity of anthropologically extending Aquinas' anti-Platonism, the fourth section turns to Søren Kierkegaard to show the possibility of such an extension. He both (unwittingly) diagnoses the Platonic malady of Eckhart's scheme and offers a positive alternative, one that understands the eternal truth of the creature in God (a close analog to Aquinas' divine idea) to be an integral component of an existential ethic of human freedom. The final two sections attempt to bolster, ontologically, this possibile Kierkegaardian extension of Aquinas. Kierkegaard's ethic of selfhood, foregrounding freedom and "local" self-transcendence, presupposes an ontologically robust sense of the self that might seem ripe for deconstruction; post-structuralist critics have inferred from the inextricably cultural and linguistic embeddedness of the self to its metaphysical exiguity as an unstable and partially illusory byproduct of impersonal symbol systems. To forestall this criticism, the fifth section draws on the German hermeneutic philosopher Manfred Frank to show how the possibility of linguistic use and interpretation itself presupposes the prior ontological reality of the individual self as creative agent. Finally, the sixth section shows how the irreducibly concrete *individuum* demanded by Kierkegaard and defended by Frank is not, as Frank thinks, an impossibility within Aquinas' "scholastic" metaphysics but is rather affirmed at the highest level: as the original divine intention in creation. Thus, by the end of the chapter, the deep significance of Aquinas' anti-Platonic turn in divine idea theory will have come to light, thanks to the suggested actualization of its anthropological potential.

I. Aquinas and the Unattainability of the Ideas

The critical intellectual situation in which Aquinas creatively had to appropriate the long-standing affirmation of divine ideas was shaped by two developments. The first can be traced all the way back to maybe the most original Patristic theorist of the divine ideas (or *logoi* to use his preferred term): Maximus the Confessor. Although for Maximus the multiple ideas may be said to preexist in God's knowledge in a simple or virtual, unified form, it appears that he assigned them a different ontological status in their willed diversification by God, pursuant to his act of creation. Perhaps motivated by an anti-pantheistic urge to uphold the distinct and positive existence of the world over against God, Maximus did not identify the being of the diverse *logoi* with the essential being of God.[4] In an indirect way, this decision helped precipitate centuries later the new discussion of eternal ideas in which Aquinas participated. For Maximus's position, differentiating the being of the idea from the being of God, was boldly developed by Scotus Eriugena; and the obscurities of the latter still later got caught up in the anti-pantheist controversy touched off by Amalric of Bene. The upshot was a

---

[4] Lars Thunberg, *Microcosm and Mediator: The Theological Anthropology of Maximus the Confessor*, 2nd ed. (Peru, IL: Open Court, 1995) 73, 77.

firm ecclesiastical consensus by the early thirteenth century that the eternal ideas must be ontologically identical with the divine essence.[5] The other key development that influenced Aquinas was a powerful wave of Arabic philosophical speculation sweeping into the Latin Christian discussion along with the flood of newly available Aristotelian writings. In different but analogous ways Avicenna and Averroes developed an account of creation that stressed its necessity rather than its willed character, and that called into question the need or the possibility for divine knowledge of particular entities of the lower order. The Christian scholastic theologians were united in repudiating these notions as incompatible with the tradition of a free and intentional creation.[6] Aquinas' new account of God's eternal ideas arose in response to these two developments and in so doing distanced itself from its Platonic antecedents. It should be noted in this connection that although the basic inspiration of the Arabic schemes was Aristotelian, they were nonetheless suffused with Platonic elements, including a stress on general forms or essences as ontologically basic, rather than particular individuals. While many Christian critics viewed the Arabic threat in terms of its Aristotelianism, the striking thing about Aquinas' own use of idea theory against that threat was that it salvaged the Aristotelian elements of the idea tradition and instead dispensed with the venerable Platonic framework of the theory.

Aquinas deployed the notion of God's eternal ideas of things in order to ensure, in opposition to the Arabic philosophers, that the created order is fully intended by God, both in the sense that it is perfectly foreknown and in the sense that it is freely willed. However, the earlier decisions against Amalric also demanded that in any account these ideas must be identical with God's own essence. On the one hand, they cannot be contingent accidents added to the divine substance; on the other hand, if they are substantively one with the divine essence, their multiplicity cannot be allowed to disturb the absolute metaphysical simplicity of God. The details would require much longer treatment, but briefly, Aquinas' doctrine of ideas can be seen as a brilliant response to these converging pressures.[7] God knows all creatures through perfectly understanding, in one eternal intellectual act, her own total perfection; any non-divine entity is thus always already known because it is itself an imperfect, participatory act expressing God's unified excellence in some partial way. However, this unified grasp does not mean that God's mind has always been populated with an infinity of determinate "possibles" as cognitive objects. God's grasp of mere possibilities is virtual, a single continuum of intelligibility; only the decision to constitute a particular cosmos, a beautifully ordered and interlocking pattern of necessary and contingent causality, "resolves" the continuum of intelligibility into a particular range of discrete exemplars, the intentional units of this freely elected world. As I discuss in the two

---

[5] For Eriugena and these complex developments in his wake, see Meinhardt et al., "Idee," 68–72, 81–4.
[6] Ibid., 81–2; Hoenen, *Marsilius of Inghen*, 239–40.
[7] The elements of Aquinas' mature account of divine knowledge, ideas, and providence can be found in ScG 1 47–54 and 66; and STh I qq. 14, 15, and 22. Boland, cited above, provides a thorough overview of Aquinas' various discussions of these topics. Aquinas specialists are again to be reminded that the reading of Aquinas laid out in the following paragraphs is not a straightforward summary but depends on the detailed (and disputable) interpretative hypothesis laid out in DeHart, "What Is Not, Was Not, and Will Never Be."

chapters linked with this one, Aquinas' reconfiguration of eternal ideas as components of a strict doctrine of creation from nothing brings in its wake two remarkable consequences. First (see Chapter 8), any functional role of the ideas within human cognition is effectively eliminated. Second (see Chapter 10), the articulation of being into differentiated multiplicity is no longer an ultimate ontological feature, as it was for Platonism (the intelligible cosmos as the demiurge's "plan") and for the Arabic schemes of emanation (the "essences" necessarily preexisting in God's intellect); that differentiation is rather an inevitable by-product, contingent upon the divine wisdom and volition directed to expressing God's perfection in this particular universe.

For the purposes of this chapter, however, attention must center on yet another consequence of Aquinas' notion. Once the eternal ideas in God assume the systematic position he assigns them, any remnant of the older expectation that these archetypes can be goals or ends for human aspiration or salvation must simply be abandoned. This is not only because, as has already been mentioned, the ideas in Aquinas are no longer functionally necessary, nor even available, to account for the human intellect's grasp of truth. The deeper reason is that Aquinas' dual identification of the ideas, ontologically with God and intentionally (i.e., in terms of information or cognitive content) with creatures, prompts a new understanding of the relation of ideal exemplar and real creature that de-idealizes the former. There are two senses of "ideal" at stake here; the idea can be an ideal either as an object of creaturely attainment, or as a kind of higher reality of the creature itself, an ideal existence of which the creature is but a lower grade reflection. On either understanding, assigning an ideal role to the Aquinas' version of divine ideas no longer makes any sense.

The first reason for this lies in what I have been calling the intentional identity of God's idea and its connected creature, by which I mean the utter exactness with which the creature matches God's eternal knowledge of it. Aquinas was committed fully to creation from nothing as an intelligent act of God. This means that all that exists in any way in the created realm has its source in God's creative act; it also means that, because God knows perfectly his own act, God perfectly knows all its effects, down to the minutest detail. But the eternal idea is God's knowledge of the creature as a willed and enacted participation of God's own being. And because God's omnipotent will cannot be hindered it is perfectly effective. The upshot of all these points is this: the creature replicates the eternal idea, or rather the informative content of the eternal idea, with absolute fidelity. If it did not, that would mean that God's power had somehow failed to create what God's intellect had intended, and that is impossible. But if this is the case, then to speak of any kind of "convergence" between a creature and God's idea of the creature is meaningless, since God's creative idea already perfectly coincides with God's creative effect, that is, the creature itself. There is no gap, no room for "play" or "adjustment" between a creature and its idea. The creature always already is everything its idea determines it to be. If it were not, it would not be at all. It does not help to assume, with Maximus and with many scholastics still influenced by Plato's privileging of universals or essences, that the convergence is between the creature and its essence or specific identity. For Aquinas, a dog could not fail to share the species "dog." True, a given instance of that species might exhibit more or fewer of the ideal qualities of the species; but at this point one would have to speak of a kind of providentially intended divergence between the idea God has of the species "dog" and the ideas God has of the individual substances, the dogs, that instantiate the species. Given Aquinas' clear assertion that the intended target in God's creative causality is not the universal form but the being of the individual substance, it is hard to see at any rate how the idea of one's species could function as an eternal ideal that preempts, as it were, the concrete idea that corresponds to one's individual being.[8]

II. Aquinas and the Pragmatic Primacy of Created Existence

On the other side of his double identification, Aquinas' theory of ideas identifies them ontologically with God's being, and that disrupts the other possibility for their ideal status mentioned above. Though (as has just been seen) their intentional or informational content is identical with the respective creatures to which they correspond, because the being of the eternal ideas is identical with that of the divine essence their ontological status is not creaturely at all. All that is in God, is God; what God knows (*qua* known) is God, even when God knows what is not itself God. Hence, the being of the ideas is one with the unique divine act of existence, and shares its attributes: eternal, immutable, simple, and so on. At first sight this seems to open up space for another, obvious sense in which ideas might be ideals for creaturely attainment. Even if their intentional content differs in no way from their respective creaturely counterparts, their mode of existence surely does. Perhaps, then, one might say that the salvific ideal is to attain the timeless and unchanging status of the realm of ideas. Indeed, this is an integral part of the ancient Platonic ideal; the height of wisdom is precisely to rise in theoretic contemplation of the ideas to share their life, so to speak, a kind of homecoming achieved by a human intelligence purified of the encumbrances of embodiment and passionate attachment to ephemeral worldly goods. Indeed, this tradition received fresh impetus from the Platonized Aristotelianism of the Arabic philosophers. From Al-Kindi and Al-Farabi onward, an influential tradition saw human beatitude to consist in an intellectual apprehension, through theoretic discipline, of the pure, higher life of the creative archetypes contained in the single agent intellect illuminating all human beings, or even in the higher separate substances.[9]

Aquinas thoroughly refutes the notion that human beatitude lies in union with anything but God herself,[10] but there is another difficulty with the fundamentally Platonic notion that sets the higher life of ideas as a human ideal. Briefly, once Aquinas reconceived eternal ideas, their possible status as a "higher" form of creaturely life suddenly looked problematic, and in more than one way. First, when it comes to the ideas generally, Aquinas does not see them substituting for or even mediating the beatific union with God to which human beings are called. He is careful to note that

---

[8] *STh* I q. 45 a. 4.
[9] Lenn E. Goodman, "Happiness," in *The Cambridge History of Medieval Philosophy*, ed. Robert Pasnau (Cambridge: Cambridge University Press, 2010), 465–9.
[10] *ScG* III 26–63.

the quasi-angelic illumination by infused species that human souls separated from their bodies can experience is not in fact a view of the ideas.[11] And even in the beatific vision, it is the direct union with God and the Word that mediates any awareness of the ideas, not vice versa.[12] Second, built into Aquinas' theology is a broader metaphysical bias against the very notion that the eternal idea of a creature is a kind of better or truer version of that creature. Insofar as the idea is immutable, eternal, and so on, it is not the creature at all, but God. And insofar as it contains the complete truth of the creature, it is not thereby "more true" than the creature itself. For the truth that is genuinely proper to the creature itself is not its truth in God's mind but the truth connected to its inherent act of creaturely existence, given by God.[13] Finally, there was a tradition based on Jn 1:4 ("that which has been made was life in him [i.e., the Word]") that spoke of the creature's preexistence in God's Word as a higher and better form of life than its being as created. This immediately introduces the old conundrum mentioned above: if better versions of creatures already exist in God, then why are actual creatures produced at all? Aquinas' reading of the John passage reframes the issue in a fascinating way. Yes, the idea is "higher" and "life" compared to the creature, but only because it is causally prior with respect to the creature. Neither its divine mode of existence nor its perfect cognitional content are the proper grounds for comparison to the creature; rather, it is its exemplary effectiveness that counts.[14] But that means, in fact (and this is the point of the "voluntarist" note in his theory), that the whole point of the eternal idea is to result in the actual creature. Just as the divine exemplar is not the creature's proper "truth," so the divine exemplar is not the creature's end. In fact, one could even say, speaking very loosely, that the creature is the "end" intended by the divine exemplar! "Pragmatically" speaking, that is in regard to God's will to create, it is the existence of the creature that has primacy even vis-à-vis the divine being of its discrete exemplar.

God fully intends the created individual, willing its actual concrete existence as a substance relationally intertwined with the universe of other substances: this, and nothing else, is the meaning encoded in its divine idea. This means that the ideas cannot be the "forms" or "essences" of things, as a number of Christian theologians even in Aquinas' day and beyond had taught, perpetuating the Platonic scheme where ideas are the true entities somehow dispersed and vitiated by their multiple instantiation in matter. This connects closely with a characteristic element of Aquinas' anthropology, the subject (in its day) of bitter controversy. Gilson has shown how many of the tenets that most disturbed the more traditionalist scholastics of his period can be traced back to his insistence that it is essential to the human soul to be the substantial form of a body. Indeed, it is the sole substantial form of the integral person.[15] William de la Mare's notorious set of "correctives" to Aquinas, required reading among Franciscans, pointed out the scandalous consequence of this unicity of substantial form: since the form actualizes, gives existence to, what it informs, then in the human being one and

---

[11] *Quaestio disputata de anima*, a. 20 ad 9.
[12] *STh* I q. 12 aa. 8–9.
[13] Maurer, "St. Thomas and Eternal Truths," 94–6.
[14] Boland, *Ideas in God*, 245.
[15] Gilson, *History of Christian Philosophy*, 361–2, 376, 381.-3.

the same form would give existence to both spiritual and bodily components.[16] It is difficult to appreciate how absurd and indeed revolting a conclusion this was to many, perhaps most, a register of how deeply embedded Platonist assumptions still were in theology. The archbishop of Canterbury, a Franciscan, angrily denounced the Thomist deviations as showing contempt for the Fathers;[17] within a few years of his death many were convinced his characteristic teachings were under an ecclesiastical ban. But Aquinas, true to Aristotle, maintained the metaphysical privilege of the concrete substantial individual as an integrated actuality (and agent) and firmly pursued the logic of this position right into anthropology. He dismissed the still reigning Platonic dualism, where the human soul is a substance in its own right adventitiously yoked to a second substance, the material body. Against the Arabic interpreters of Aristotle, he dragged the agent intellect down from an illuminating heaven to become the individuated and most personal possession of each individual human, its cognitive antenna tuned specifically to the likewise materially embedded universal. Finally, he located the peculiar dignity of the created order in the reality of its particular agents and their acts, each of them intended as an imitator of the God who is totally act.

It is understandable that many scholastics saw in all this a reckless abandonment of a hallowed Patristic inheritance. Aquinas' contemporary, the great Bonaventure, was at the very same moment giving to this inheritance a brilliantly elaborated and systematic form. The key to it all was once again ideas in the Platonic sense, which for Bonaventure (similarly to Maximus) provided the ontological joint connecting the light of human intellects, the cosmos of creatures as signs turned toward God, and the eternal Word of the creator as the receptacle of infinite possibilities.[18] For him, to deny the ideas was to deny the Son. In Aquinas' writing, by contrast, the connection of eternal ideas with the Word is affirmed but hardly developed; it appears customary and vestigial rather than necessary and systematic.[19] For all his enormous debt to Augustine in so many areas, in idea theory Aquinas went his own way. He gladly took the basic point necessary to secure a creation as an intelligent act, but he quietly let the Platonic husk of the theory fall away. Their role in human illumination, their necessity as a divinely envisioned world of infinite possible items, their incorporation within the theory of Trinitarian generation: all these themes traceable back to Augustine were laid aside. And with them, too (to return to the special concern of this chapter), disappeared the apparatus of traditional contemplative and even soteriological or eschatological positions that were built around the divine ideas. For Aquinas, our higher life is not to be sought there. Salvation cannot fundamentally turn on the ontological harmony between disembodied souls and a heaven of paradigms. The point of connection is rather the personal impetus of desire, drawing the individual as knower and as willing agent through the humanity of the incarnate Son into a face-to-face encounter with

---

[16] Ibid., 731 n.60.
[17] Ibid., 359.
[18] Two older but still very useful discussions are Jean-Marie Bissen, *L'Exemplarisme Divin selon Saint Bonaventure* (Paris: J. Vrin, 1929), especially 19–99; and Chapter Four of Etienne Gilson, *The Philosophy of St. Bonaventure*, trans. Frank J. Sheed and Illtyd Trethowan (New York: Sheed & Ward, 1938).
[19] This was argued some time ago (1949). Lonergan, *Verbum*, 202.

the Father. In that beatifying communion, the world-creative thoughts of God are at best secondary objects seen in the Son and only insofar as they pertain to the identity built up in one's particular personal history.[20] If Aquinas, recasting the eternal ideas to fit them into the demanding framework of creation from nothing, finds that he has de-idealized them as well, then this turns out to harmonize nicely with his anthropological and soteriological emphasis on the drama of personal agency. For Aquinas, the ideas cannot be imitated or attained, nor are they a higher version of the creature, but are rather God's cognition of his own will to realize actual creaturely existence. But the anti-Platonic impulse revealed in these positions remained, in Aquinas' writings, restricted mostly to discussions of the divine knowledge. In particular, Aquinas did not give greater play to that impulse by developing a systematic connection between the nonideal divine exemplar and the crucial agency just sketched of the human sojourner it creates. The wager of the remainder of this chapter is that without a fuller and more systematic extension into anthropology or soteriology the full scope of Aquinas' departure from Platonism will remain veiled. That the suggestive outlines of such a connection might appear in later thinkers is therefore the possibility to be explored in the remaining sections.

III. Eckhart and Aquinas' Ideas: Re-Platonizing the Double Identity

To recapitulate: responding with other scholastics to the dual threat of Amalrician pantheism and Arabic emanationism and necessitarianism, Aquinas had developed a position that insisted upon a double identity within the divine idea. On the one hand, the divine idea is ontologically identical with God or the divine essence; on the other hand, the divine idea is intentionally or informationally identical with its respective created reality. Any wavering on these identifications leads the theologian into the forbidden zone of a *tertium quid* between God and creature. It has been seen that the latter identity eliminated in principle any possibility that its own divine idea might serve the creature as a kind of ideal. There is no room for a replay of Platonic aspirations; the idea in God's mind cannot be approached, converged upon, or "lived up to" by the creature, since the latter is already its perfectly effected product. Does this mean that the divine idea had to become a purely technical notion? The solution to a systematic theological problem that had no direct relevance for the understanding or living of Christian life? Meister Eckhart provided perhaps the first and certainly the most influential attempt to recreate the spiritual or ethical role that ideas had played in Platonic tradition, only now under the conditions mandated by Aquinas' double identity theory. But it will be claimed here that, though adopting the theory itself, he allowed his anthropology to remain untouched by its anti-Platonic subtext and so could not protect the deeper meaning hidden in Aquinas' theoretical turn.

---

[20] Boland, *Ideas in God*, 283; *STh* III q. 10 a. 2.

The broader roots of Eckhart's teaching lie in a particular tradition of reflection on spiritual praxis, and especially in a theme developed among a series of Beguine authors, beginning with Hadewijch of Antwerp. That God has eternally foreknown me, along with all other creatures, is of course a centuries-old theme in Christian spirituality, closely related to the divine idea tradition. It seems that around the middle of the thirteenth century certain circles of female contemplatives began to reflect in profound and daring ways upon this timeless presence of the creature with God. Combined with related themes from the tradition, such as the human being's status as image of God, and the classic Pauline stress on the Christian's unity with Christ or her true life in Christ, the powerful notion of an existence of the human person within God's being, apart from and prior to her existence as a creature ("outside" of God), helped to bring about a new epoch (as Bernard McGinn has argued) in Western contemplative practice.[21] The older masters of the spiritual life had spoken of a spiritual unity with God, a state that is for the most part only rarely and fitfully experienced, but to which the practitioner aspires through prayer and discipline. The new emphasis on the believer's exemplary or eminent unity with God pointed to a state of affairs that has always obtained, and that is a fact regardless of one's own striving (though one must nonetheless struggle to realize the truth or effects of this state of affairs in one's own thoughts and actions). Above all, it pressed beyond the idea of a mere spiritual unity or identity of will between God and believer, to speak of a unity of complete identity, a unity without distinction. My reality, my true identity, is my utter unity with the eternal being of the creator.

With his university training, Eckhart was able to take up this theme and give it a more systematic and conceptually precise treatment. The still ongoing discussions around divine ideas proved a particularly fruitful avenue for this. In such a context, Eckhart must have recognized the spiritual potential of the double identity (i.e., with God and with the creature) contained within the divine idea insisted upon by his famous predecessor in the Dominican Order. He casts the double identity as a paradox; the resolution of this technical paradox leads directly to the essence of his theory of contemplative praxis.

> Things themselves and their forms are not in God, but the ideas of things and of forms. God is the Word, that is, the Logos, which is the Idea ... But nothing is as equally similar and dissimilar as the idea of something and the thing itself, for an idea is not truly and affirmatively predicated of a thing ... unless it is similar to it ... But on the other hand, what is as dissimilar as the eternal uncreatable and the temporal created?[22]

---

[21] McGinn discusses this motif and its influence in several places in his history of mysticism. See especially Bernard McGinn, *The Flowing of Mysticism: Men and Women in the New Mysticism—1200-1350*, vol. 2 of *The Presence of God: A History of Western Christian Mysticism* (New York: Crossroad, 1998), 214–6.

[22] Meister Eckhart, *Meister Eckhart: Teacher and Preacher*, ed. Bernard McGinn (New York: Paulist Press, 1986), 83.

The true depth of Christian existence is only realized with the total awareness, the full acceptance in and through each conscious moment, that my truth, my actuality, my being, thanks to its eternal presence in God's intellect, just is God's being. That is, in the true depth of the self the dissimilarity is already overcome: I am my divine idea. The theorization of this state of affairs is worked out in concentrated form in a few paragraphs from Eckhart's *Commentary on the Book of Wisdom*. A creature has no formal existence of its own in God, only virtual or causal existence, identical with God's own being. Hence, only its formal existence is mutable, or even creatable. Formal existence (*esse*) marks the creature's similarity (as effect) to the creative causality of the divine essence, an act common to the three divine persons just as the divine existence is common to them; but it also marks its separateness from God, indicated by its remaining "external" to the interior life of God, the Trinity. The idea of a creature, however, is not and cannot be created. And in the Son or Word, the primal idea, I (i.e., in my idea) am life and intellect beyond all being.[23] To use the language of Eckhart's sermons, when I have cultivated utter detachment from all created difference, I become one with my own uncreated reality (the "ground" or "spark" of the soul) and thereby "break through" beyond creation, into the uncreated realm of inter-trinitarian relations.[24] When this happens, what can be said of Jesus can and must equally be said of me. The Son is truly born (temporally) within me, because his divine generation is (eternally) equally my own. "We should never rest until we become that which we eternally have been in [the Son]," for then "my body and my soul are more in God than they are in themselves."[25]

This is only the briefest outline of a multilayered complex of thought that shifts its terminology with disconcerting ease, but already it is clear how it could find expression in controversial and easily misunderstood utterances. Even so, it represents a brilliant incorporation of Aquinas' post-Platonic theory of ideas into a highly charged and insightful theorization of prayerful existence. Yet it cannot be denied that Eckhart's appropriation of Aquinas is selective and somewhat disorienting. In fact, several points of tension indicate the way in which Eckhart has forcibly wrenched Aquinas' revisionary stance on ideas out of its broader metaphysical and anthropological context. It is of course no secret that Eckhart can hardly be called a Thomist. The very real debts he bears to Aquinas are more than balanced by his deep alignment with the peculiar conceptual lineage of the German Dominican houses, where sympathies with Albert the Great remained strong and Latin translations of Neoplatonic sages were eagerly studied. The broadly differentiated orientations are nicely summarized by McGinn: "Unlike Thomas Aquinas, for whom formal existence was essential for giving creatures a reality of their own, Eckhart's attention focused on the virtual, true, that is, the 'principial' existence of things in God."[26]

---

[23] Ibid., 148–9.
[24] Bernard McGinn, *The Harvest of Mysticism in Medieval Germany*, vol. 4 of *The Presence of God: A History of Western Christian Mysticism* (New York: Crossroad, 2005), 149–50.
[25] Eckhart, *Preacher and Teacher*, 298, 261.
[26] McGinn, *Harvest of Mysticism*, 145.

This critical shift in overall emphasis plays out in more specific displacements, such that Aquinas' theory is apparently accepted but its meaning is turned on its head. First, Eckhart has no patience with Aquinas' careful distinctions between natural philosophy, metaphysics, and revealed doctrine. Indeed, it is one result of his continual stress on the eternal Word as the specific site of the creature's virtual pre-existence that the natural, creaturely world of "formal existence" is seen less as a distinct realm with its own integrity than as merely an illustrative extension of the higher dynamics of soteriology. Thus, the Gospel of John is mined for "truths of natural principles, conclusions and properties"[27]: "The Word universally and naturally becomes flesh in every work of nature and art ... [T]he incarnation itself exemplifies the eternal emanation and is the exemplar of the entire lower nature."[28] This merging of natural and supernatural somewhat tips the ontological scales in favor of the "higher" preexistence of the creature. The trend is exacerbated on the anthropological level, where a genuinely Aristotelian and Thomist celebration of the immediate identity of intellect with its cognized object is used, in a very un-Thomist way, to denigrate the role of willing. For the will's desire for God grasps her under the aspect of the good, a stance that interposes between me and God a defined medium that separates. Unlike the will, the intellect "is not satisfied with goodness or with wisdom or with truth or with God himself [i.e., as differentiated in any way from me] ... [I]t bursts into the ground from which goodness and truth come forth ... [It] enters in and pierces through to the roots from which the Son pours forth."[29] Finally, Eckhart's stress on "my own" idea in God is not as intimate or personal as one might think, for he returns to the old Platonic theme of the idea as primarily the universal, the general definition or species. This fits his spirituality exactly, since the individual person is called to the deepest embrace of that lack of differentiation which characterizes the unified preexistence of creatures in the Word.[30] Paradoxically, unification with one's idea in the Word is the eradication of its separate identity: "Abandon yourself, all things, and everything you are in yourself, and take yourself according to how you are in God."[31]

The mutation that Aquinas' vision undergoes at Eckhart's hands is striking. The concentration of the former on the creature's own inherent act of existence is dissipated. The tenacious focus on the individual human substance and its freedom, its self-creative agency by which repeated choices build up decisive dispositional inclinations within the self, all this is outweighed by detachment, a letting go of personal identity and of intelligent desire in a spirituality of radical unity with God. Aquinas' compelling embrace of the reality and dignity of creaturely causality as the very rationale of creation has receded from view in Eckhart, allowing the old question to return: if I am "already" God, why is there a "lower" reality at all? In comparison with the creature itself, Aquinas limited the superiority of the creature's idea to its exemplary causality,

---

[27] Meister Eckhart, *Meister Eckhart: The Essential Sermons, Commentaries, Treatises and Defense*, ed. Edmund Colledge and Bernard McGinn (New York: Paulist Press, 1981), 123.
[28] McGinn, *Harvest of Mysticism*, 154.
[29] Eckhart, *Preacher and Teacher*, 315.
[30] Ibid., 157.
[31] Ibid., 285.

thus circumventing the idealization of the idea. In a remarkable turn, the very same notion in Eckhart ushers in a re-idealization of the exemplar.

> Where man still preserves something in himself, he preserves distinction. This is why I pray God to rid me of God, for my essential being is above God insofar as we comprehend God as the principle of creatures. Indeed, in God's own being, where God is raised above all being and all distinctions, I was myself, I willed myself, and I knew myself to create this man that I am.[32]

For Aquinas, the drama of my existence is my willed self-creation in time; for Eckhart, my self-creation has always already happened. This reversal constitutes impressive evidence for the necessity of exploring how the anti-Platonic turn implicit in Aquinas' theory of divine ideas might play a fuller and more explicit role in theological anthropology; failing that, the technicalities of Aquinas' position on ideas in themselves (the double necessity) can, as Eckhart shows, be accepted but yoked with an anthropology that neutralizes their deeper meaning.

IV. An Eschatology of Existence: Kierkegaard

This is very far from the last word to be said on Eckhart, a conceptual enthusiast and a fearless cartographer of far reaches within the realm of prayer. Two cautionary points in face of the above positioning of Eckhart against Aquinas: first, some recognition is in order of the different modes of existence traditionally labelled the "active" and the "contemplative" life; second, the success of Eckhart's schematization of human existence as an account of graced, "supernatural" life within the Triune deity must be balanced against any apparent distortions of the basic architecture of "natural" created human agency. That being said, with Eckhart it looks as if Aquinas' anti-Platonic revolution has been turned against itself, his ideas forced back into a broadly Platonic conceptual frame that no longer really fits them. A structurally analogous diagnosis, that of a return, supposedly in the name of Christianity, to a pagan or Greek frame of mind that secretly undermines faithful existence animates the writings of Søren Kierkegaard. For in his case, too, the divine idea in something like its Thomist guise, with its dual identity, plays a (disguised) role, but the result is an entirely different sort of self-creation than Eckhart speaks of. He will provide a model for the genuine anthropological and ethical theorization of Aquinas' post-Platonic divine idea.

Kierkegaard's fierce indictment of his age, in both its political and intellectual manifestations, was that it sanctioned a massive evasion of the fundamental human task, that of thinking and acting fully into one's own finite individuality as a self-choosing agent. The success of Hegelianism and its variants in Denmark was the presenting symptom. For Hegel, individual decisions and acts in history acquire their ultimate

---

[32] Bernard McGinn, "Meister Eckhart on God as Absolute Unity," in *Neoplatonism and Christian Thought*, ed. Dominic J. O'Meara (Norfolk, VA: International Society for Neoplatonic Studies, 1982), 135.

meaning only within the ongoing unfolding of collective social and cultural forms; this unfolding follows the dialectic of intelligence whereby the multitude of phenomena is progressively ordered by the logical movement of concepts toward ever greater scope, richness, and interconnection; finally, this dialectic in nature and history is deciphered by philosophy as also the life of infinite spirit, the concrete realization of the absolute or God. This scheme was intolerable from Kierkegaard's point of view. First, it invited a stance toward one's own historical and existential position that was finally "objective," that is, impersonal and contemplative; my finite standpoint, and hence my limited agency, is completely relativized within a necessary play of cumulative masses. Second, it disastrously blurred any boundary between the temporal and transtemporal spheres of reality. Not only did it wrongly submit the transcendent complex of eternal truth, the divine mind, to a kinetic process, a falsely "mobilized" logic, but it also presented the ideal human relation to the divine as participation via philosophical intellection, rising to share the adventure of concepts; the ultimate aspiration was thus to a view from nowhere, divorced from the passion of living here and now. For Kierkegaard, even if pure thought could relate to the absolute through thinking itself, "I" cannot, no actual human individual is capable of this. Each is ceaselessly confronted with the unfinished task of being herself, in a particular way, in the next moment.

In one respect, Kierkegaard saw this intellectual development as a falling away from ancient wisdom.[33] The Greeks at least never forgot that the philosopher was first and foremost a living person; ideas were passionately appropriated to the sage's own existence, they were only real as suffered and lived into. But in another respect, Hegelianism rejoined Greek thought, or at least its essence as distilled by Platonism, at just the point at which it had been forever surpassed by the Christian revelation of sin, redemption, and eschaton. Due to the close kinship between the human intellect and the divine realm of changeless truth, the realm of ideas, the Platonic counsel of wisdom lay in withdrawal from the myriad snares of worldly desire and active involvement with lower diversity, to seek theoretic reconnection with the soul's eternal homeland. Kierkegaard was struck by the way in which Hegelian philosophy aligned itself with this older Platonic ethos; the supposedly Christian idealist philosophy actually entered into a secret compact with paganism to sap and scatter the concentrated energies marshalled by the living individual faced with choosing her path through life, and taking total responsibility for her self-formation (and de-formation). Platonic and idealist wisdom presumes that the ultimate truth about oneself has always already been decided. But the essence of the Christian message, as Kierkegaard saw it, was precisely the opposite: my fate, the authentic definition of myself that will persist beyond temporal flux, can only be worked out in my own individual agency. God has put my soul, as a task, into my hands.

Kierkegaard discovered this opposition between the ancient and modern views of life partly through reflecting on a classic conundrum: if deity, or the unbreakable chain of causes, has already determined the future, what meaning is there in my own choices or acts? The answer lay in the recognition of one's own necessary participation as a free

---

[33] Detailed argumentation and citations for the account which follows can be found in Chapter 3.

agent in the causal nexus; wise choice is causally efficacious and is ingredient in the determined complex of future effects. This solution struck Kierkegaard as paradigmatic of the Christian belief in human beings as free creatures of an omnipotent, providential creator. Yes, God has eternally foreseen, in her idea of me, all that I will do. But the intention of that idea is precisely my creaturely agency; it incorporates my free and contingent acts, the very acts that I, and only I, can and must freely perform. (The resonance with Aquinas here should be evident.) So both Greek and Christian / modern orientations understand the final verdict on a human's temporal career to lie in a transtemporal or eternal truth; but for the Greek the key is to "recollect" that truth as something already finished and behind me, as it were, while for the Christian the eternal idea of myself must be "repeated" forward by my full engagement in the temporal progress of existing.

The metaphysical scheme underlying Kierkegaard's anthropology of freedom demands a maximum both of proximity and of tension between the human self's temporal dimension (centered on the will and its repeated finite choices, each one reshaping the psychological context of later choices), and its transcendent dimension (centered on intellect's grasp of truth in the medium of thought, though always from the ever-shifting standpoint of existential commitment). Selfhood is precisely the paradoxical unity-in-opposition of time and the timeless; the flaw of both paganism and Hegelianism lies in their false reconciliation ("Better well hanged than ill wed!"[34]), a merely notional arrangement that volatilizes the individual's essential temporality and lifts the weight of eternal consequence from the self-shaping process of freedom. The tension of time and eternity is not a problem to be solved by a philosophy of finite spirit or by mythmaking about a semi-divine soul. Only the passion of existence ("earnestness") repeatedly brings time and timeless into fruitful union in the chosen act; the opposed stance, which passively cultivates the variety of experience, and toys with selfhood rather than committing oneself to it, Kierkegaard calls the "esthetic" stage of existence. Its pessimistic maxim is a version of the older sophistry: Why do anything? (Get married: you will regret it. Don't get married: you will regret it.[35]) Genuine selfhood only commences with the full realization of itself as its own most basic task, that is, with submission to the claim (as a commission from the absolute) upon every moment of my life of the universal idea of the human person (the "ethical" stage). Yet for every individual this awareness always comes too late, by which time freedom has already crippled itself by its previous failed decisions. There remains only faith, the religious, which suspends the ethical relation to the absolute in the name of that very relation. In faith, the individual faces the divine directly, no longer mediated by the universally human. Only in this way can I as an existing subject truly access the eternal, always beginning anew from total indigence and total forgiveness, to take on my own eternal idea in God as my endless responsibility.

The paradox of the dual identity in the divine idea, already noted by Eckhart, finds resolution as a practice, necessarily repeated: the constant, free elaboration of one's identity through chosen responses to one's living context must be continually,

---

[34] Kierkegaard, *Philosophical Fragments*, 3.
[35] Kierkegaard, *Either/Or, Part One*, 38.

consciously embraced rather than evaded. As the self struggles to find the path that allows continued openness before God, it "repeats" its idea. Recall the paradox. Each of the two identifications found in Aquinas' divine idea, taken by itself, presents an unanswerable question. If the exemplar in God's mind codifies to the least detail the shape and the course of the creature, then why does God create anything? If my entire progress is already enclosed within my eternal exemplar, then why do anything? In Kierkegaard's theory of personhood before God, the answer to both questions turns out to be the same. God creates that we might act, that is, God is (now ... and now) creating our act precisely as ours, so that there can be agency beside God's. Created agency is what the creative exemplar intends, and what complements it. But the profundity of this answer is only realized in the living practice of selfhood, only as the two questions are continually connected to each other in the subject's repeated exercise of its freedom. Though he could not know it, Kierkegaard's theological anthropology was actuated by the same Thomist premise as Eckhart's: the de-Platonized, that is, de-idealized yet eternal exemplar of myself in God. But he arrived at an ethos of the idea that was very different. Everything turns on the shift in grammatical mood. In place of Eckhart's indicative ("You are your idea."), Kierkegaard supplies an imperative: "Be your idea!"

V. The Linguistic Self as Ontologically Irreducible

If Eckhart shows the necessity of extending the anti-Platonism of Aquinas' idea theory into anthropology, Kierkegaard shows its possibility. But is Kierkegaard's position itself possible? Two obstacles present themselves. First, is his anthropology of subjective freedom not highly vulnerable to the post-structuralist reduction of selfhood to a derivative and largely illusory effect of language? Second, even if the metaphysical irreducibility of selfhood implied by Kierkegaard's theory can be sustained, can this quintessentially modern emphasis on individuality be reconciled with the ancient and medieval metaphysical assumptions of Aquinas? Full discussion is impossible, but the remaining two sections will suggest ways around these obstacles. First the problem of the compatibility between the self's linguisticality and its irreducibility.

Over the course of his authorship, Kierkegaard's ethic of free subjectivity was supported by philosophical reflections on the shape of the self and the nature of its relations to world and God. The roots of human freedom lie in the person's dual structure, a tense unity of opposition between the organic body and the "soul" as its actualizing or animating formal principle, continually requiring mediation by a third principle that actively rebalances and reconnects the two unstable components. This rather precarious structure that must consciously negotiate the potentially explosive instability of its own dynamic elements is what Kierkegaard calls "spirit," and its unique natural status is marked by its temporality, that is, the disclosure within itself of time-succession as such. The task of self-construction that arrives with self-awareness implies that something has levered the human subject out of mere psychic unity, out of an animal totality of presence, and precipitated it into "the present." The present, in turn, only appears as the rolling point of connection between an internally sedimented past and an array of projected futures.

As many philosophers besides Kierkegaard have remarked, it is the projection of possible futures that makes human selfhood a free venture, indeed an exercise in constructive self-interpretation. Since his time, however, there has also been the gradual discovery (already adumbrated, to be sure, in some of the German romantic thinkers) of the key role of language in enabling the increment of local transcendence that marks human selfhood and freedom. Such a discovery is not necessarily incompatible with Kierkegaard's insights. In fact, his stress upon the founding dialectic of mind and flesh at the basis of spirit is only enhanced by the realization that the interpretive construction of self-presence occurs by means of a traffic with signs in their concrete, material opacity: semantic bodies. But, as is well known from the philosophical history of the previous century, a number of influential theories have arisen that begin from this linguistic insight in order to demote or abandon the ontological solidity of selfhood. Theorists of this bent have often begun from a certain reading of the Swiss linguist Ferdinand de Saussure, who argued that sign-systems only work by the simultaneous opposition of each semantic element to every other one, thereby making a language equivalent to an achronic chain that is in principle endless. The conclusion drawn from this has often been that, since the self can only mediate its own identity through meaning-complexes that are in fact interminable and shifting, then something like self-presence is endlessly deferred, and thus the subject itself is reduced to an ideal that is impossible in fact.

The issue is too enormous to explore here, other than to assert that the matter is far from settled. One philosopher in particular, the German hermeneutic theoretician Manfred Frank, who has offered powerful analyses of these claims (in discussions of Foucault, Derrida, Lacan, Deleuze, etc.), has vigorously and convincingly argued the incoherence of this reduction of the subject, and for the continued viability, and indeed inevitability, of real subjectivity.[36] Two theses are basic to his argument. First, he completely affirms the material mediation of self-presence by means of an endless commerce in signs; but he argues that the supposed disruption by meaning deferral of all subjective stability is a false inference, based upon an inherently defective model of perfect self-presence grounded in a primordial "reflection." Frank, working from the earlier research of Dieter Henrich, has shown how the post-structuralist reduction of the subject rests upon an uncritically assumed account of subject-formation that was in fact exposed as flawed as early as Fichte and Novalis. Frank's second thesis is based on his rejection of the widespread assumption that linguistic interpretation is analogous to decoding, the substitution of meaning units according to a fully rule-determined and (in principle) calculable procedure. Against this "code-model" he argues for the indispensably creative moment in all interpretation. The interpreting subject in every act of linguistic understanding infinitesimally extends the semantic chain in a new direction, not determined in advance by the existing stock of shared meaning, and thereby recreates the entire complex of signs, incarnating it anew.

---

[36] Manfred Frank, *What is Neostructuralism?* trans. Sabine Wilke and Richard Gray (Minneapolis: University of Minnesota Press, 1989). This work offers a marvelously lucid and fair-minded treatment of the family of (largely French) deconstructions of selfhood, even while exposing (in light of his own case for its irreducibility) their shared, questionable assumptions.

In other words, there is no getting "behind" the hermeneutic subject, as if it were an already completed ideal linguistic system that "utters" selves, speaks through them, creating the subject as a mere effect (as argued by post-structuralist reductionism). Frank shows the subject to be *"unhintergehbar"*; it is living human language-users and the ongoing events of communicative creation they enable that first realize the abstract sign system, temporalizing the achronic chain of signs, constituting language as speech. For Frank, the seminal theorist of the irreducible hermeneutic subject was Schleiermacher. It was Schleiermacher who accurately formulated the relation between the interpreter and the linguistic system, and who realized the unique ontological status of the former. As the site and engine of the irreducibly new semantic realization, each particular subject continually constitutes itself as an utterly unique configuration, an impenetrable kernel of reality rather than an "instance" of a set or a "construct" of overlapping, more general categories: a precipitate of the hermeneutical event, it is *individuum*, in a technical sense, incommensurable with other individuals.[37] One purpose of pointing to Frank's discussion in this context is to suggest that his retrieval of Schleiermacher's irreducible hermeneutic self is an effective commentary upon and elaboration of Kierkegaard's existential self, helping to situate the psychological and metaphysical structures explored by the latter with respect to cultural processes. Kierkegaard and Frank share a common perspective: the ontological unity and identity of the individual subject is never simply given but is an achievement, bought at the price of a restless need for the self to actualize itself by freely interpreting itself into its world. If Kierkegaard's "repetition" provides the better attempt to capture the ethical implications of Aquinas' post-Platonic divine idea (as opposed to Eckhart's almost perfect anticipation of what Kierkegaard calls "recollection"), then Frank's discussion helps to alleviate the suspicions likely in our contemporary intellectual setting that the Dane's ontology of the subject can be dismissed as an obsolete holdover of idealism or "logocentrism."

VI. Reconciling Frank and Aquinas on Individuality

In resisting a powerful contemporary trend, Frank and Aquinas might thus find themselves on the same side. The human self is indeed finite: situated, in transit, multiply and uncontrollably conditioned, continually subject to contingent deformations. It does not, however, thereby forfeit a certain ontological priority, a unity and solidity of being; it is not a mere derivate, an epiphenomenon, not a necessary fiction, not an effect thrown off from more basic impersonal structures. But one problem remains to trouble this proposed liaison between the free subject and Aquinas' world of thought. Frank names Aquinas specifically as a prime representative of the dominant Western

---

[37] Ibid., 438–49. Manfred Frank, *Die Unhintergehbarkeit von Individualität* (Frankfurt a. M.: Suhrkamp, 1986), especially 116–31. Manfred Frank, "The Text and its Style: Schleiermacher's Theory of Language," in Frank, *The Subject and the Text*, ed. Andrew Bowie, trans. Helen Atkins (Cambridge: Cambridge University Press, 1997), 1–22. Manfred Frank, "Style in Philosophy: Part I," in *Metaphilosophy* 30 (1999): 145–67.

misunderstanding that has always diluted the status of the authentically individual to a mere "particular."

> Humboldt's and Schleiermacher's concept of individuality is noticeably at odds with a far more powerful tradition … [For this tradition] the peculiarity of the individual cannot only be reached by a categorical leap from the general but can be derived by continuous transitions from the universal. This means of course that the "incommensurability" of individuals in relation to each other is limited; they are—according to the unanimous teaching of, say, St. Thomas Aquinas and Leibniz——centred toward God and can also communicate with one another through him——through shared participation in the "esse commune" … This is the thesis of the sameness in kind [*Gleichartigkeit*] between the general and the individual.[38]

In suggesting that Kierkegaard's philosophical anthropology is a de facto extension of certain insights of Aquinas on divine exemplarity, am I falsely yoking his own thesis of incommensurable individuality to the kind of standard ontology that, Frank says, refuses this ultimacy of individuality?

There are telling indications that Frank's rather casual mention of Aquinas too hastily assimilates the latter to an undifferentiated "scholastic" consensus. In fact, as several scholars of medieval philosophy have suggested, Aquinas' metaphysical stance is markedly accommodating to just the sort of "individuality" Frank seeks to secure. Anton Pegis had already seen that for Aquinas, God's essence "is compared to the essences of things, not as the general to the particular, but as a perfect actuality to imperfect actualities" and that "the individual, existentially considered, contains a uniqueness and an incommunicability which no Platonic method of unlikeness will ever produce," that is, "the reality of the singular cannot be derived by the method of contracting universals."[39] Edward Booth, likewise, pointed out that the way Aquinas radically unites divine ideas in the divine essence allows him to make divine creative act terminate directly in the individual existent; the "individuation of God's activity with regard to each individual" (a rejection of his teacher Albert's mediation of creation through radiated universal forms) means that the concrete individual is the intent of the divine exemplar, not the species.[40] Nor is Frank's reading of the role of "being in general" (*esse commune*) correct, for the latter is an abstraction and not the divine plenitude; it is not a common ontological formality in which creatures commensurably participate. As Rudi Te Velde shows, it is the realm of shared non-divinity (where ontological difference reigns of necessity), a complex of mutually overlapping and negating limitations of the divine perfection whose pattern is no direct "derivation" from God but is specific to this created order.[41] Finally, a close examination of the

---

[38] Manfred Frank, "The Entropy of Language: Reflections on the Searle – Derrida Debate," in Frank, *The Subject and the Text*, 178–9.
[39] Anton C. Pegis, "The Dilemma of Being and Unity: A Platonic Incident in Christian Thought," in *Essays in Thomism*, ed. Robert Edward Brennan (New York: Sheed & Ward, 1942), 178, 166–7.
[40] Edward Booth, *Aristotelian Aporetic Ontology in Islamic and Christian Thinkers* (Cambridge: Cambridge University Press, 1983), 235, cf. 264.
[41] Te Velde, *Participation and Substantiality*, 128.

voluntarist distinction Aquinas makes between God's ideas as "intelligibilities" and as "exemplars," the latter emerging only with the willing, in infinitesimal providential detail, of the actual universe, suggests that Aquinas saw in divine creation itself the ground for Frank's proposed "categorical leap" (rather than a "continuous transition") from universal to individual.[42]

Schleiermacher made it a mark of the individual that it cannot be encompassed in a concept; Kierkegaard drew the theological correlate, that God "has no concept" but knows the created individual directly, with no created generic conception as medium; and Aquinas agreed when he argued that God knows every created event the way any casual observer might, through direct inspection, and not like an Avicennist "scientist," through accumulated generalities.[43] And as God knows, so God creates, for God creates as (in Kant's phrase) *intuitus originarius*, simply through knowing what he wills. And what God knows and wills, God's creative idea, is first and foremost the individual substance, albeit as thoroughly embedded in its world's causal grid. The marvel of Aquinas' theory of divine ideas, as I have tried to suggest in this chapter and its two companions, is its escape from a perennial dilemma: on the one hand, the theory accepts the tradition of the divine and eternal exemplar but voluntarizes it (i.e., de-Platonizes it) and thereby allows the individual creature a kind of metaphysical ultimacy; on the other hand, it retains the eminence of all created truth and meaning in the divine intellect, instead of resorting to the "blank" God of Ockham's voluntarism.[44] On Aquinas' conception, creatures add nothing to God's being, since they are merely contingently ordered decompositions and complex negations of the simple divine fullness; yet they have their distinct reality and do not occur via a "straight" descent by piecemeal deletions of that fullness, as if particulars could be defined simply by piling up a big enough selection of generalized attributes. In short, Aquinas views the production of creatures not as an incremental, rule-bound exhibition of instances of a preexistent set but rather as more akin to a unique, imaginative articulation of infinite possibility, an act of divine self-interpretation even. For this reason, there is room also among creatures for the acts of human meaning-creation that constitute freely existing subjects.

In Chapters 8 and 10 I suggest that the significance of Aquinas' departures from earlier notions of God's ideas was masked not just at first; consideration of philosophical and theological theorizations of divine creation across subsequent centuries seems to reveal that its full implications have still not been absorbed. An anti-Platonic time bomb, one might say, lay hidden in the thought of this medieval man, and its slow-moving shock wave is still rumbling toward us. If in the present chapter plausible use has been made of Kierkegaard and Frank to help register its full existential force, perhaps that is further testimony to its delayed impact. The keynote of Aquinas' revision of the theory of exemplars is divine voluntarism, a specifically Thomist voluntarism

---

[42] For the significance of this distinction, see DeHart, "What Is Not, Was Not, and Will Never Be," 1020–2, 1031–8.
[43] Frank, *Unhintergehbarkeit*, 115; Kierkegaard, *Philosophical Fragments*, 41; Aquinas, *De veritate*, q. 2 a. 5.
[44] Pegis, "Dilemma of Being and Unity," 169–71.

that integrates divine will and intellect, rather than the rival "Franciscan" voluntarism that pitted will against intellect. The final lesson of the present discussion is that the spiritual and anthropological response to this divine voluntarism is a similar fusion of intellect and will in the human self, a shift in the impetus of Christian life toward free, self-shaping existence.

The Platonic consensus on ideas tended to equate discernment of the universal and necessary structures of physical and moral reality with an ascent to union with God's mind. Aquinas' alternative disrupts that elevation which read the created order as a direct expression of the divine being. On this alternative, the sheer freedom with which the exemplars arise in God points to the contingency of the world's "style"; as beautiful the world is certainly not arbitrary, it is a genuine participation of divine perfection, but still as just *this* participation it is accidental, one of an infinity. There could have been another beauty. With this in mind, the focus of existential discernment must accordingly shift, from universal structure to providential unfolding; the balance tips away from the ancient contemplation of interlocking orders, microcosmic and macrocosmic, and tips toward the navigation of history. Worldly things are no longer to be understood as "signs" of God in any straightforward sense. On the old Platonic model the analogy of human and divine intellect meant that God's disclosure in the world was really more akin to a single mind speaking to itself. But with the more voluntarist cast given to creation, something like a real labor of aesthetic or artistic interpretation is required in "reading" the world. The obstacle to our grasp of the creator's mind is no longer our material embodiment or even our sin; it is the very fact of creation as an act of will, as like a work of art rather than a selective transcription of God's eternal thoughts.

Kierkegaard offers the fitting ethical extension of Aquinas' revised idea theory. The human ideal ("repetition") is not to merge with the realm of the static and universal "thought." Each person is rather assigned one divine idea, one eternal exemplar to concern her ultimately: that of herself. It is not to be contemplated (it is actually unknowable by us) but is rather to be "operated" by the self, through the interpretive labor of existing freely, the work of interpreting myself and my situation in each new moment in order to create my next act, and thereby my next self and my next situation. In other words, for Kierkegaard, the effect of God's creation of myself is nothing other than my cumulative creation of myself. The very meaning of human existence, its authentic maneuver through the world through free self-interpretation, must be differently symbolized in light of this shift from the more ancient Platonic model. We might image the displacement of categories required here as a move from a "linear dynamics," which saw the hermeneutic of existence as like a decoding of the world, to a "chaotic dynamics," where the world confronts the self in the radically unanticipatable form of history. Reading the world in that form is a creative act of free interpretation, not the implementation of a program. And this ongoing creativity of existence is only possible, as Frank indicates, because of the reality of the subject as irreducible, as individual, as agent; it is due to the primordial relation of the free self, in its ontological priority and density, to the linguistic order "upon which" it moves. What Aquinas and his theory of divine ideas adds to this is an encompassing and rigorously consistent metaphysical scheme: that of the creator God who in her fullness affirms a world of diverse creatures who make things happen. In this way the mystery of otherness within the world is divinely grounded. Yet, crucially, it turns out not to spring from some differential negation within God's being but rather from an erotic positivity; the world of individuals who act, and of some who create themselves, is the voluntary overflow of God's desire (in Jacques Pohier's words[45]) "not to be everything."

---

[45] Jacques Pohier, *God—in Fragments*, trans. John Bowden (New York: Crossroad, 1986), 266–70.

10

Improvising the Paradigms: The Divine Ideas as Anti-Platonic Ontology

*Rien n'est, du moins rien n'est absolument
(dans le domaine linquistique)*

Ferdinand de Saussure

Dans la langue il n'y a que des différences

Ferdinand de Saussure

*Deus ... scit enuntiabilia non
per modum enuntiabilium*

Aquinas

The Platonic philosophy of eternal ideas was for centuries gladly appropriated by Christian thinkers. Famous warnings about gift-bearing Greeks should perhaps have been heeded, however, since this particular Trojan horse smuggled into the being of the monotheistic creator a pernicious multitude, akin to a viral infection. The logic of the Platonic position time and again has invited theologians to locate the archetypes of created things as distinct existences "within" God's own understanding, but in a way utterly detached from the creative will of God. Hence the problem: if the creature's free determination by God from nothing is precisely the mark of its creation *ex nihilo*, yet its proper creaturely identity is already a predefined feature of God's own being, then either it cannot really be created in the full sense of that word, or else in some sense it always already has been! The considerations that follow will address this conundrum by suggesting that Thomas Aquinas' rethinking of the creative role of the divine ideas moves in a decidedly more voluntarist direction, extricating them from Platonist ontological assumptions. The examination in that light of some different accounts of creation over the centuries will suggest that there is a way, inspired by Aquinas, of relating divine ideas and divine will that can isolate the different "Platonic" diseases afflicting these accounts, that perhaps even should have prevented them. The following section (I) will attempt in very brief compass to suggest the voluntarist dynamic implicit in Aquinas' discussion of divine ideas. The remaining sections will progressively explore what seem to be the unavoidable and unfortunate consequences of ignoring this dynamic: an impossible disruption of the creative act into "stages" (II), an impossible bifurcation of intellect and will in the simple creating agent (III), and an impossible incorporation of the created world into the divine life itself as a necessary ingredient (IV). After suggesting three contemporary theological echoes of this last deviation (V), a concluding section (VI) will schematize the results.

I. Aquinas' Voluntarism of Creation

It may as well be admitted: Aquinas' writings are frustratingly obscure on the detailed relationship between the divine ideas and the divine creative will.[1] We can, however, make an initial approach to the riddle of how God's will connects with God's knowing of creation by posing this question: granted that God perfectly knows not only what is not God (i.e., actual creatures) but also all that is not God and that could exist but will not (i.e., possible but never realized things, non-actuals), is that knowledge, materially speaking or in terms of its content, the same in kind? Otherwise put: granted that God's ideas of (non-divine) things are always secondary terms contained within God's perfect knowledge of her own essence (i.e., as ways in which that essence can be deficiently imitated or participated), is there nonetheless anything to suggest that ideas of non-actuals (shorthand here for "mere" possibilities, i.e., what could exist but never has or will) have a cognitive status distinguished in principle from the cognitive status of ideas of creatures (meaning here actual creatures)? It is crucial to see that the distinction in cognitive status at issue here is in material terms, that is, it is specifically directed to the non-divine content as cognized. Of course, God will know that ideas of creatures, unlike ideas of non-actuals, are ideas of what God actually wills to exist. All would agree to that. But the key issue is this: can the difference of known content between ideas of creatures and ideas of non-actuals be restricted to divine awareness of the decision to create or not (a kind of extraneous detail, as it were), or does the noetic differential extend beyond the divine option itself to condition as well what is known about the very creature or non-actual respectively? Crudely: does an idea of a creature "look (to God's knowledge) like" an idea of a non-actual? If God's decision to make a creature translates into a greater determinacy of known content in that creature's idea, then clearly for Aquinas God's creative act involves something more, well, "creative," more voluntarist, than is assumed by those interpreters who think Aquinas basically extends the Platonic lineage of the ideas. I will point out two kinds of evidence implying that Aquinas on further consideration did indeed settle upon a more voluntaristic

---

[1] As noted in previous chapters, Boland's *Ideas in God* provides a thorough survey of Aquinas' doctrine of ideas and references much of the secondary literature. Aquinas' mature position on divine knowledge, divine ideas, and divine will is essentially laid out in *ScG* I 47–54 and *STh* I qq. 14 and 15. As will become clear from the following discussion, the earlier discussion of ideas in Aquinas' *De veritate* represents what I regard as a transitional and more problematic treatment specifically where the question of the divine will to create is concerned. A final reminder: the reading of Aquinas offered in the following paragraphs, like that of the two preceding chapters, is fundamentally based on the account given in DeHart, "What Is Not, Was Not, and Will Never Be."

reading of ideas: first, a progressively stabilized and careful distinction between ideas as intelligibilities (*rationes*) and ideas as exemplars; and second, the pivotal role assigned to providence in the divine envisagement of non-divine possibility.

Cutting a long story short, in regard to the first point it seems Aquinas made an important decision soon after the *Disputed Questions on Truth*. In that work he had recognized a distinction between ideas in a more proper and limited sense, which are God's practical knowledge of things properly producible in themselves, and ideas in a broader and vaguer sense, which denote any intelligible aspect (actual or possible) of the non-divine realm that can fall within God's speculative cognition.[2] The idea properly speaking is of what stands and independently exists as such, that is, the substance; but are there such ideas of never-to-be-created substances? I would argue that Aquinas abandoned an earlier position that defined the proper idea from what was producible as such (regardless of the divine intent to produce) and which thus identically encompassed both created and non-actual substances. By the time of the *Disputed Questions on the Power of God*, his position is that ideas in the proper sense are practical not because they are geared to the producible but because they incorporate a willed determination to execute their creation (*per voluntatem ad opus ordinatam*); so non-actuals do not have ideas in the full sense.[3] His commentary on Pseudo-Dionysius's *Divine Names* supplies a straightforward rejection of his own earlier reading of that author, where the "practicality" of ideas properly speaking meant only "potential" practicality; now, proper ideas are of what God actually intends to create.[4] In the *Summa Theologiae* he terminologically fixes the now stabilized distinction; God's ideas, properly speaking, are exemplars, and are of actual creatures, while his knowledge of non-actuals demands only ideas in the vaguer sense of intelligibilities (*rationes*).[5] A late disputed question confirms the mature position: an idea means a form according to which an agent actually intends to make something.[6]

The question as to where non-actuals "belong" within God's knowledge evidently struck Aquinas as of sufficient importance to warrant careful thought and a definite resolution. Such resolve would hardly seem justified if the divine fiat had no other relevance to God's cognition of some participant in her being than a shift of title, as if creation means an intelligibility simply "becomes" an exemplar by being "selected," so that, unchanged in itself, it is shifted into a subset of actualized intelligibilities called exemplars, as an accountant moves a number to a new column. But intelligibilities are not only of non-actuals, and this already suggests that the difference between intelligibility and exemplar might be of greater cognitional import. For it is noteworthy that Aquinas implicitly assigns God's knowledge even of non-actual *substances* to the same cognitional category as his knowledge of matter in itself, or of genus, or of property, which are realities that in themselves are abstractions and can only truly

---

[2] *De veritate* q. 3 aa. 3, 5, and 7.
[3] *De potentia* q. 1 a. 5 ad 11.
[4] *In De divinis nominibus*, chapter 5, lectio 3. The rejected earlier interpretation is found at *De veritate* q. 3 a. 3 ad 3.
[5] *STh* I q. 15 a. 2.
[6] *Quodlibet* IV q. 4 a. 1 ad 1.

exist as elements within some more metaphysically fundamental whole.[7] Is there, then, some sense in which the merely possible substance even as substance is known by God as inherently lacking in some degree of concreteness or determinacy, as devoid of some constitutive context? A further indication pointing in this direction is the important discussion in the *Summa Contra Gentiles* where Aquinas elaborates on the traditional distinction between God's "simple knowledge" (i.e., of all possible to her, including non-actuals) and God's "knowledge of vision" (i.e., of what he actually creates). Aquinas defines the difference by the fact that in the latter God knows the acts of existence proper to the creatures, while in the former things are known only "in" God's power and not "in themselves."[8]

What does it amount to, then, this distinction made by Aquinas between a divine idea as the intelligibility of a non-actual and a divine idea as the exemplar of a creature? The way God knows anything is always the same, by knowing her own essence; such knowledge is always necessary; and in accordance with Aquinas' most basic metaphysical assumptions, what is known, that is, what makes knowledge true, is ultimately the act of existence (*esse*) of the known. Now, in the act of knowing his own perfect act of existence God also knows every intelligible participation thereof, that is, every imperfect act of existence. This field of intelligibility is infinitely, if arbitrarily, divisible; hypothetically, any non-divine actuality that might have been given can be said to have its "own" intelligibility (*ratio*) in God.[9] This is God's "simple knowledge." But, uniquely, in knowing actual creatures, God is no longer knowing simply her own act of existence, but also their own, just as the contingent effect of her free will. But what "more" is thereby known? After all, as Kant long ago saw, God perfectly envisions the creature, including its existence, so it seems that God could know nothing different of the creature than he could know of a non-actual: "mere" existence adds nothing.[10] But this conclusion will not harmonize with the evidence adduced above. God's actual willing of a creature must "put something into" it that cognitively differentiates it, something that amounts to a meaningful distinction between its "own" act of existence and its virtual presence "in" God's power. The answer is already suggested in the just cited discussion from *Summa Contra Gentiles* chapter 66, where Aquinas stipulates that, in contrast to her knowledge of non-actuals, in his "knowledge of vision" God sees creatures in their proper causes. That knowing their proper acts of existence also involves knowing their causal interactions with other creatures sounds like the constitutive context we were seeking. This is the point of our second kind of evidence, namely, Aquinas' doctrine of providence.

---

[7] *STh* I q. 15 a. 3 ad 3 and ad 4.
[8] *ScG* I 66.
[9] Note that the virtual status of distinction among the intelligibilities of mere possibles, i.e., their indeterminacy in terms of a lack of a fixed or discrete content does not amount to the claim that God's knowledge is in any way indeterminate. Since it is precisely the mark of the non-actual that it has no proper act of existence (unlike the creature), then its only act of existence is that of the divine being and power as such. And God's perfect grasp of his own perfection is no more indeterminate than the divine act of being itself.
[10] Kant, *Only Possible Argument*, 117–18. Cf. Chapter 7 of this book.

As is clear from *Disputed Questions on Truth*, q. 5, a. 1 (and replies), there is only a "world," that is, a combination of many different kinds of creatures into a causally interconnected whole, due to the providential ordering of God. But this work of disposing means ordering specific things to their ends, and the world as a whole to its end; the only end outside the world is God's own goodness, God's own ultimate end (i.e., herself), and only the actual act of creation is the willing of such a disposition.[11] In other words, there is no merely speculative aspect to providence as with the "intelligibilities" among ideas; there is no such "idea" of a world because a world as a system of ends is not merely entertained by God: all subordinated ends fall into position only in view of the end of participating God's being, that is, of being created.[12] Thus, the total range of causal interconnections that enters into the concrete actuality of any individual creature is already part of the envisioning of the total end of creation. We might venture further. Some passages strongly suggest that the ensemble of different things and kinds to be found in creation are themselves artifacts of the particular providential world order intended by God.[13] Aquinas' language here does not suggest that God simply stocks a world with a selection (off the shelf) of "potential" creatures already given in some determinate way. Rather, the divine wisdom "thinks out" the order of the universe that itself partially consists in the distinguishing of the things that populate it. Hence, God does not just actualize preexisting distinctions but rather distinguishes in making. Not just multitude but differentiation are "*ex intentione*": they are intended together, as subordinated to the intention to create itself. I am suggesting that it is just this enormous range of information that derives from God's actual will to create, that concretely renders actual creatures only within the concrete context of an intended cosmos, and therefore that constitutes the surplus of cognitive content signaled by the "proper being" and "proper causes" distinguishing God's ideas of creatures from his ideas of non-actuals.

So, combining the evidence of the intelligibility/exemplar distinction and the role of providence, the results are: first, that there is indeed a material contrast among ideas between intelligibilities (*rationes*) and exemplars; second, that in the latter God's essence is known as participated in a more concretely determined mode; and third, that this gain in definition springs from the actual creature's exhibition within the intended totality or world, for only this bestows upon substances the living fullness of actuality (accident, relation, condition, reciprocal order). This reading harmonizes with Aquinas' metaphysical system, where the privilege of reality is granted not to "essences," the differentiated formal identities, but rather to the act of existence (*esse*). So intelligibilities and exemplars are not simply two classes of Avicennian essences, merely externally denominated as unactualized or actualized as the case may be. Only exemplars envision creatures in their fullness, while the virtual multiple of intelligibilities signals only the general truth that every "aspect" of the non-divine abstractable from the concrete order of things in relation, must equally be rooted in God's knowledge of her own complete perfection. In fact, the establishment of a technical distinction

---

[11] Cf. Aquinas, *STh* I q. 22 a. 1.
[12] *STh* I q. 19 a. 3: *alia autem a se Deus vult, inquantum ordinantur ad suam bonitatem ut in finem*.
[13] *STh* I q. 44 a. 3 and q. 47 a. 1.

between intelligibilities and exemplars indicates that Aquinas' mature position on ideas is a hybrid: as intelligibilities the ideas protect God's full knowledge of created detail and possibility against Arab necessitarianism; the privileging of exemplars over intelligibilities in turn reflects the ontological priority of the actual over the possible and maintains the centrality of free willing in the creative act. Only the concrete will to create this world resolves the infinite divine potency into multiple definite forms, mediated by the wisdom that envisions a cosmos.

Here we can sum up the way in which Aquinas' "voluntarist" theorization of the ideas is attuned to his doctrine of creation from nothing, the consequence of which is the denial of their customary Platonic status. Creation is not the selection of a pre-assembled world from an infinite series of worlds, nor is it even the assembly of a world from a chosen menu of pre-given "possibles." There is no continuous logical or deductive path leading directly from intelligibilities to exemplars, as if God merely adopted some of the latter as already substantially defined, and then added judicious touches of relationship and incidental detail. The move is not from already definite intelligibilities to added determination. In fact, to imagine the relationship more adequately one would do better to begin from the concreteness of exemplars and move backwards from them, not to a larger set of equally definite "exemplars-in-waiting," but rather into the background field of God's perfectly understood potency. The divine comprehension of that field as the virtual ground of all viable modes of participation is captured by the notion of the "intelligibilities," a kind of *Restbegriff* necessitated by the special status of exemplars.

As theorized by Aquinas, in neither of their aspects can the divine ideas play the role demanded for them by Platonism, that is, as the ultimate formal constituents of being itself, its necessary articulation. Intelligibilities are too vaguely evanescent, too "perspectival," too virtual to serve the turn, while exemplars are only necessary as elicited or "called forth" on the divine hypothesis of a concretely intended world. The remaining sections of this chapter will turn to various (mainly later) deviations from Aquinas' position on the ideas. In each case, the result will be some erosion of the integrity and radicality of God's creative act; the diagnosis of these consequences will enable us by the end of the chapter to see how Aquinas resolves the subtle pattern of relations connecting God's knowledge, God's will, and the created cosmos, untangling the conceptual snarl introduced by residual Platonic assumptions.

II. Dissolving the Unity of the Creative Act

If the above reading of Aquinas is accurate, then the lineaments of a radically non-Platonic and voluntarist doctrine of ideas can at least be glimpsed in his writings. It is hard to claim more than this. After settling his mind on exemplars and providence, Aquinas chose not to develop the scheme further. Perhaps this was because the sphere of counterfactual possibility in itself failed to hold his interest, no doubt due to his metaphysical commitment to the primacy of the actual. Then, too, he could hardly have foreseen the sensational metaphysical exploitation of this realm lying just around the corner with Duns Scotus and its later investiture by Suarez. Yet these developments can be seen as a kind of flowering of decisions surrounding the divine ideas made by Aquinas' great colleague in Paris, the Franciscan Bonaventure. Indeed, in the later medieval period, wherever the reality of divine ideas continued to be maintained, something akin to Bonaventure's notion of them, rather than Aquinas', appears to be the received wisdom. Besides, that Aquinas' brief comments on divine ideas concealed a radical departure was usually missed; on the one hand, his metaphysical vision was mostly contested and/or misunderstood, and, on the other hand, the role he envisioned for the divine will in the constitution of the ideas was obscure in its specifics. In the long run, the alternative line on the divine ideas had the advantage of clearer exposition and a readier connection with older traditions. As I will show in this section, however, its embrace of the "Platonism" that Aquinas' ideas avoid leads directly to problems for the doctrine of creation.

The venerability of this alternative line hit close to home for Aquinas, for his own teacher Albert the Great stood under its influence. I cite two interpreters of Albert to capture the nature of the opposition between the dominant trend in idea theory and Aquinas' minority position. The divine ideas in Albert, reflecting the influence of Avicenna, are "an introduction of the Platonic Forms into the divine intellect as an order of essences, really distinct from the divine essence and really distinct in their essential being."[14] In contrast to Aquinas, because Albert "did not give the same fundamentality to *esse*, the divine rationes, whilst making up a unity in God, are not expressed as they are in Thomas as being 'non secundum aliquam diversitatem.'"[15] Albert's Platonist assumption remained the default position of most later scholastic discussions of the ideas: the archetypes of created things and of non-actuals must somehow preexist in God's self-understanding with equal determinacy, comparable to that of creatures themselves. However, the more detailed and generative formulation of this position probably lay not with Aquinas' mentor but, as already mentioned, with the latter's counterpart in the Franciscan chair at Paris.

Just as with Aquinas, one of the prime motivations for Bonaventure in taking up the tradition of divine ideas was to resist the reduction of creation to a kind of necessary and "blind" emanation of the world. In face of this kind of scheme, associated with the powerful Arabic interpreters of Aristotle, Bonaventure like Aquinas resorted to an exact knowledge of creatures in the divine intelligence. And, again like Aquinas, Bonaventure understood the ideas as the different relations of participation or imitability rooted in God's knowledge of his own essence. But there is a fateful shift in emphasis. To Bonaventure's way of thinking, the best way to insure God's exhaustive knowledge of ideas is to construe that perfection of intellection as the presence in God's mind of exact similitudes of all things that are not God.[16] Bonaventure grounded truth

---

[14] Pegis, "Dilemma of Being and Unity," 175.

[15] Booth, *Aristotelian Aporetic Ontology*, 232.

[16] "Because [God] expresses [sc. the *rationes aeternae* or *exemplares*] inasmuch as he is the supreme light and pure act, therefore he expresses most brilliantly, most articulately [*expressissime*], most perfectly, and through this equally and by intention a similitude in no way diminished; and hence it is that he knows all things most perfectly, most distinctly, and most integrally." Bonaventure, *Quaestiones disputatae de scientia Christi*, in *Opera Omnia*, vol. V, ed. the Fathers of the College of St. Bonaventure (Quaracchi: Collegium S. Bonaventurae, 1901), 9.

not, like Aquinas, in the identity of knower and known, that is, Peripatetically; truth rather consists, Platonically, in the mental observation of objective likenesses ("*Eo similitude, quo veritas.*").[17] The totality of these similitudes constitute the simultaneous articulation of God's comprehension of her own infinite power. Thus, the truth about God is "expressed" in God's mind in the form of this multitude; because the divine power is infinite, the multitude of similitudes is likewise infinite. And, finally, because the eternal Son or Word is the direct expression of God's self-knowledge, then the ideas, too, are eternally expressed in the eternal utterance of the Word.

What seems a displacement of detail is actually of great moment. In Bonaventure's approach to the divine ideas, their connection with the willed act of creation itself has been almost completely set aside. The systematic distinction between intelligibilities and exemplars that Aquinas thought it necessary to work out is absent in Bonaventure. And no wonder: there is no constitutive difference for him between ideas of creatures and of non-actuals. All that is not God, actually created or not, has the same cognitive status in her; they are the product of a single mechanism, the "expression" of divine truth: ideas are the infinity of "possibles." More than that, this expression is an essential aspect of God's eternal self-expression in the Son. Hence, component within the necessary Triune identity lie the countless forms of non-divinity in their discreteness: God's own life includes their inevitable articulation. The role of the electing will of God in the constitution of creaturely identities has been rendered invisible. This aspect of the difference between Aquinas and Bonaventure is encapsulated in their rival readings of a passage from Anselm.

In discussing God's eternal knowledge of creatures, Anselm (*Monologium* ch. 32) had said, "There can be no word of what was not, is not, and will never be." On its face, such a dictum seems to imperil God's knowledge of what he could but does not create. The way Aquinas interprets this utterance in the *Disputed Questions on Truth*, even though he had yet to firm up his position, already shows his characteristic sensitivity to the connection of idea, will, and actual creation. Instinctively, he sees something true in Anselm's statement. To the eternal Word is appropriated the content of the divine knowledge and wisdom; but though the Word expresses the Father's total knowledge, it only "speaks" actual creatures, that is, the Word is only "of" creatures, not of "possibles."[18] This in turn affects the way he reads the traditional claim (based on Jn 1:4) that all creatures were eternally "life" in the Word.[19] Does this include non-actuals? Only insofar as all possibility is understood and hence is identical with the Word's own life (which itself is an act of understanding). But only what God will actually produce is alive in the Word with, in a manner of speaking, its own life; its idea (which Aquinas will later call an exemplar), unlike a mere "possible," is productive of the created thing, the principle of its movement, its life.

---

[17] Bissen, *L'Exemplarisme Divin*, 29–31. For the quoted phrase, see p. 30 fn. 4. Bernard Lonergan repeatedly opposed Aquinas' model of knowledge by identity to the Platonic model of knowledge by "confrontation" favored by medieval Augustinians. Lonergan, *Verbum*, 85, 192–3, 196, 197, 202, 225–6.
[18] *De veritate* q. 4 a. 7.
[19] Ibid., a. 8.

It is completely characteristic of Bonaventure that he must simply reject this kind of reasoning, and with it Anselm's claim. There is no basis in his scheme of ideas for even this relative privileging of the actual over the non-actual. He refutes the reasoning of those who link life in the Word to its actual "utterance," its production of creatures. The divine ideas are primarily to "express" the fullness of the Father's knowledge, hence Augustine's authority must trump Anselm's. Augustine called the Son the Father's "art, full of all the living intelligibilities," and since the Father's knowledge is infinite, the Word as "art" must contain infinite intelligibilities, and that means all the possibles.[20] In effect, the systematic demands of Bonaventure's construal of the constitution of ideas in God means that he cannot countenance the kinds of distinctions demanded by Aquinas' quite different construal: between intelligibility and exemplar, and between the Son as "art" of the Father (i.e., reflecting all her knowledge) and the Son as "word" of the Father (i.e., particularly connected with the actual "speaking" of creatures, their creation).[21]

We may sum up the comparison as follows. Both Aquinas and Bonaventure faced the same problem: to defend creation from nothing and providence against the schemes of necessary and mediated emanation propounded by Avicenna and Averroes. Both saw that "ideas," God's intimate foreknowledge of his own creative act, were the key. But Bonaventure, immediately associating ideas with Plato, made Aristotle's rejection of them the *proton pseudos* from which Arab necessitarianism flowed. He saw only the Arab alliance with Aristotle and pitted it against the alliance of Plato and Augustine.[22] By insisting that the ideas of all possible creatures are eternally expressed in the Son as the necessary fullness of the Father's truth, Bonaventure disregards the divine will, in effect baptizing the Platonic notion of a "logos" in God as the requisite eternal receptacle of the necessarily defined array of archetypes. The irony, from the perspective of this chapter, is that the "expression" of ideas understood in this way is arguably simply an internalized form of necessary emanation. Aquinas drew different lessons from the threat of Arabic philosophy, namely, the need for a deeper exploration of Aristotle and also the need for a more profound probing of the meaning of creation as the shaping of a complex of imperfect acts of existence into the reflective shadow of the perfect act. Non-actuals can thus remain "dissolved" as it were in the single divine potency, reserving full exemplar status only to those ideas mediated by the divine will to execute. Where Bonaventure chose more Plato, Aquinas chose more will.

The continuing intuitive allure of the Platonic scheme is such that a number of learned and authoritative scholars have, it would appear, even interpreted ideas in

---

[20] Bissen, *L'Exemplarisme Divin*, 76–7.
[21] Aquinas' line of interpretation is discussed in Boland, *Ideas in God*, 243–5. The discussion reveals the distinction presupposed by Aquinas' reading of Anselm: the Son as "art" must be distinguished from the Son as "word" because "speaking" implies disposition, i.e., actual creation. A comparison of Boland's analysis of Aquinas on p. 244 with the quote from Bonaventure's *Commentary on the Sentences* to be found in Bissen, *L'Exemplarisme Divin*, 76 fn. 7, will make it evident that the interpretation of Anselm adopted by "some" and rejected by Bonaventure is identical with the line of reasoning adopted by Aquinas, though Bonaventure need not have had Aquinas in mind.
[22] Gilson, *History of Christian Philosophy*, 404.

Aquinas himself along quintessentially Bonaventurian lines.[23] They found grounds for this in one of the most characteristic of his teachings, that of the distinction in all creatures between two principles that are identical in God: "essence" and "act of existence" (*esse*). Now, does not Aquinas famously assert a "real" distinction between essence and act of existence? Does he not speak accordingly of their union in creatures as a kind of "composition"? Finally, does he not image this composition as a kind of "reception" and "limiting" of the act of existence by the essence? All this naturally suggests that essence somehow possesses an independence, in fact a kind of prior reality over against the act of existence such that it can serve as its limiting receptacle. This in turn implies that the essence and the act of existence require quasi-distinct "moments" within the constitution of the unified creature. There follows all too readily from this an account of creation whereby God simply bestows the act of existence understood as sheer undifferentiated "actuality" upon already differentiated essences of creatures. What more natural (i.e., Platonic) than to assume these essences to be a selection from the infinity of foreknown "possibilities" eternally present in God's self-knowledge? The awkward supposition, however, is that such essences have somehow already been constituted, before the act of creating them. But what else can creation be than the constitution of a creature (i.e., a defined form of imperfect or non-divine entity)? One of these interpreters rather gives the game away when he says that "every essence … is created as potency to be actualized by the participated *esse* which it receives."[24] But if actualization by a creaturely act of existence can also scarcely be called anything but creation, then the logical moments assumed in the language here make for a curious picture: the essence is first created in order subsequently to be … created!

Of course, this crude summary can only do limited justice to the different accounts in question. But the point for now is that the basic approach to Aquinas upon which all of them are based has been subjected to a convincing critique by Rudi te Velde. Louis Geiger, for example, conceives the composition of essence and act of existence on the model of the union of subject and form construed Platonically, as "an accidental union between two principles which are foreign to each other." But while Aquinas proposes this composition itself as an ultimate fact accounting for the constitution of the creature's metaphysical structure, the attempt to juxtapose the principles in this extrinsic and dualist way vitiates its intended finality; the rival principles themselves now require ulterior, and indeed separable, explanatory principles in God.[25] Cornelio Fabro, in response, insists upon a double creation: essence springs from God's fullness of perfection, act of existence from God's purity of actuality. Te Velde comments,

---

[23] These interpreters have offered distinct but structurally similar proposals concerning the nature of participation in Aquinas and the relation of the act of existence to essence in creatures. Louis B. Geiger, *La participation dans la philosophie de saint Thomas d'Aquin* (Montreal: Institut d'Études Médiévales, 1952). Cornelio Fabro, "The Intensive Hermeneutics of Thomistic Philosophy: The Notion of Participation," *Review of Metaphysics* 27 (1974): 449–91. John F. Wippel, "Thomas Aquinas and Participation," in *Studies in Medieval Philosophy*, ed. John F. Wippel (Washington, DC: Catholic University of America Press, 1984), 117–58.

[24] Fabro, "Intensive Hermeneutics," 474.

[25] Te Velde, *Participation and Substantiality*, 147, cf. 88–9.

Authors [like these] feel compelled, in one or another way, to assume a double participation, one according to which essence has actual being, and another which accounts for the formal determination of the created essence in itself as a partial likeness of the divine essence … [But] one cannot tacitly presuppose a (possible) essence in the creature, which is subsequently constituted into a relation with God as origin of being … Creating does not simply mean the actualization of a possibility; creation denotes the origin of things according to their entire being.[26]

Te Velde's verdict seems unavoidable: this whole approach denies "the unity of the act of creation."[27]

In reply, Te Velde consistently argues for a reading of Aquinas on creation that avoids from the outset any dualism of essence and act of existence; such a dualism automatically generates false dilemmas. Essence and act of existence are in fact mutually co-constitutive principles, and cannot be separated. The specific nature just is the determinateness existence acquires in what "receives" it; one must not be captivated by the image of existence being "limited by" essence since one could equally say that the limited essence itself is nothing but the product of the contraction of the act of existence.[28] The creature "receives" being as already specifically differentiated by divine wisdom; there is no need for a prior act that extrinsically limits an otherwise undifferentiated act of being.[29] The key point Te Velde accuses his opponents of missing is that for Aquinas the single fact of difference from God, the inherent deficiency of the non-divine existent, already implies and demands the composition within it of essence and act of existence. These are not two principles requiring differentiated modes of explanation, as if the imperfection of created essence were logically distinct from its relation to the act of being.[30] To be "not-God" means to be distinct from others that are also "not-God" and therefore to share a common being with them, that is, the common "being-not-God" (*ens commune*).[31] For Te Velde, in short, the formal differentiation of essences is identical with the diversity of relations that creaturely being bears to God's being. Created existence cannot be construed as a second moment of creation, extrinsic to the constitution of essential differentiation.[32] The distinction of essence and act of existence is dialectically related to the sharing of non-divine status; they are two sides of the one state of affairs that is being a creature.

Unsurprisingly, Te Velde's critique has not been without answer, and the details of his full argument cannot be entered into here. But I believe the essential points of his interpretation of Aquinas to be profoundly insightful. For the purposes of our discussion, the consequences for the way divine ideas are understood will be readily drawn. God's essence is the one exemplar of all as diversely imitable, so the ideas are not "possibles" or mental pictures of essences. The idea as determined to creation

---

[26] Te Velde, *Participation and Substantiality*, 147.
[27] Ibid., 90–1.
[28] Ibid., 152.
[29] Ibid., 107–8.
[30] Ibid., 95.
[31] Ibid., 128.
[32] Ibid., 110.

already implies composition of essence and act of existence. Exemplarity and efficiency must be seen not as two different modes of divine causality but as together making up the one creative act.[33] Any other picture of the ideas is a form of "essentialism" that leads immediately to the disruption of the unity of the creative act that Te Velde's entire discussion is directed against. Traces of such a conception are to be found in Aquinas' earlier works, but he gradually works his way out from under the influence of Avicenna's existentially "neutral" essences as the implications of his own focus on the act of existence work their way into all aspects of his thought. Essence cannot be thought apart from the act of existence whose specific determination it is, since potency as such can in no way be neutral toward its own act.[34] Nor has Te Velde been the only one to notice this fatal conjunction of essentialist idea theory and flawed conceptions of creation. Harm Goris likewise complains of the "essentialism" of a view on ideas like that of John Wippel (grouped in Te Velde's critique alongside Geiger and Fabro): "It is not as if there were a given number of logically possible things and events from which God were to choose some to exemplify and to grant them actual existence. Such a view was held by Scotus [but not Aquinas]."[35]

The mistake of the accounts under criticism is to allow the genuinely Thomist insight of the composition of essence and act of existence to be skewed in an Avicennist direction and thereby to falsely inflect Aquinas' view of divine ideas. It was Avicenna who famously regarded existence as related quasi-accidentally to essence, and who also posited the equally influential threefold scheme of universals whereby the universal essence subsists prior to (and existentially indifferent to) its mental and real (creaturely) modes, as an idea in God's mind.[36] But for Aquinas, the pivotal image for the metaphysical relation of essence and existence is not the extraneousness of substance and accident but rather the intimacy of potency and its proper act. Consequently, creation cannot be the "attachment" of existence to a separately ideated essence. Yet these Avicennist themes were hard to resist in Aquinas' era; his own unique perspective was chronologically bracketed by imposing elaborations upon them, in the persons of his teacher Albert the Great and of Henry of Ghent, who came to prominence after his death. Edward Booth describes in great detail how Aquinas broke with the Avicennian bent of Albert (who understood creation as a multiple, staged flux of universal formalities). But Aquinas "insist[ed] on the simplicity of the divine communication in its unmediated directness to each created thing": "He differs from Albert in insisting on the singleness of God's creative action in terms of *esse*."[37] Anton Pegis diagnoses in Henry of Ghent a similar disruption of the unified act of creation by a flawed idea theory. In fact, he sees Henry and Albert as equally victim to

---

[33] Ibid., 113–15.
[34] Ibid., 68.
[35] Harm Goris, *Free Creatures of an Eternal God* (Leuven: Peeters, 1997), 273.
[36] See Gilson, *History of Christian Philosophy*, 421–2, for the relation of essence to existence. For a sketch of the origins and influence of the threefold scheme, see Kobusch, "Heinrich von Gent und die Neuplatonische Ideenlehre," 200–2. Aquinas did, as Kobusch indicates, invoke the scheme on occasion; but he does not allow it the crucial metaphysical role granted to it by others. For a good discussion of its limited use in Aquinas, see Maurer, "St. Thomas and Eternal Truths," 99–103.
[37] Booth, *Aristotelian Aporetic Ontology*, 228. For Albert's understanding of creation as emanation, see p. 175.

the same Avicennist deviation in their account of divine ideas. The result: "When we turn to creation, Henry therefore argues that there is first a *production* of the *essential* being of creatures in the divine intellect which is followed by an external production of their *existential* being."[38]

This forced doubling of creation strikingly foreshadows the interpretations of Aquinas put forward by Geiger, Fabro, and Wippel. That it is a result, in Henry, of "an enormous Platonism," namely (to repeat Pegis's indictment cited at the beginning of this section), "an introduction of the Platonic Forms into the divine intellect as an order of essences ... really distinct in their essential being," is precisely why we must remain highly suspicious when the attempt is made to read Aquinas along such lines. Aquinas' theory of ideas is anti-Platonic, in that it does not depend upon this dubious importation into God's self-knowledge of an "ideal world" of dispersed and discrete possibles. This section has delineated the initial and most straightforward form of departure from his insights, that of the alternate scheme initiated by Bonaventure and yet also, even to this day, attributed to Aquinas himself. The impact of this deviation upon the conception of creation is immediate and impressive: the bifurcation of God's unique creative command into distinguished stages or moments. The next section will show that this bifurcation allowed by forsaking Aquinas' insights on divine ideas can have even more serious consequences than the splitting of the divine act, namely the splitting of the divine being itself.

III. Dissolving the Unity of the Creative Agent

Although his essay is concerned with medieval philosophy, Pegis affords the reader a momentary glimpse of the larger historical implications of rejecting Aquinas' anti-Platonic ideas in favor of injecting "the multiplicity and the atomism of the Platonic Forms" into the divine intellect:

> Within the order of creatures there is an order of essences which requires only the gaze of the human intelligence in order to declare an independence from sensible being which will make the Christian soul dream, however fugitively, of some of the privileges of a Platonic god. ... But ... however exciting it would be to tell the story of this Greek god seeking to recapture his lost divinity in a Christian world, it remains that for St. Thomas Aquinas the Christian world yields no such message.[39]

One part, at least, of this "exciting" historical story passed over by Pegis has, in fact, found another narrator, one of rare gifts: Jean-Luc Marion. In a series of erudite and powerful publications, Marion has argued: (1) that developments in late medieval thought eroded the necessity for analogical displacement that safeguarded the distance between God's ideas of the cosmos and our scientific knowledge; (2) that

---

[38] Pegis, "Dilemma of Being and Unity," 175.
[39] Ibid., 176.

René Descartes, though lacking the scholastic tools of analogy, protested against this assimilation by asserting the willed creation of "eternal truths" (e.g., of mathematics, logic, or essential predication); and yet (3) that the other key figures of early modern philosophy evaded or rejected the radicality of this protest, thus allowing the "march of univocity" in Western metaphysics to continue.[40]

The kinship between the apophatic spirit animating Descartes's intervention and the anti-Platonic thrust of Aquinas' doctrine of ideas is noticeable at once. Indeed, Marion himself shows at length how it was the rejection of Aquinas' position on eternal truth in God by the line running from Scotus to Suarez that enabled the triumph of univocity.[41] But in spite of the great debt owed by scholars to Marion for his investigations, there is something not quite right in the way he reads Aquinas, and this means that the way he traces the consequences of the departure from Aquinas in the modern period largely misses a crucial dimension of the story, namely, the role of the divine will in the constitution of the ideas. In his discussion of Aquinas, Marion virtually ignores the crucial distinction of exemplar and intelligibility (*ratio*) and thus construes the ideas simply in terms of the self-expression of divine cognition in isolation from the voluntary intent to create.[42] Moreover, he insists that the expression of the ideas in Aquinas is only comprehensible when situated within the space opened up by the eternal generation of the Son.[43] As will be clear from the discussion above, these are the hallmarks of a divine idea theory that is not that of Aquinas; it remarkably resembles that of Bonaventure.[44] The objections we have already outlined against the latter will apply equally to Marion's reading of Aquinas, but the issue of interest here is the way this skews his narrative of modern metaphysics. I will suggest in this section that Marion's resolute focus on the issue of analogy versus univocity, encapsulated in Descartes's opposition to Suarez on the creation of the eternal truths, partially obscures the older and more basic opposition in divine idea theory between Aquinas and the inheritors of Bonaventure. Taking up and combining the two disputed points (i.e., the disconnect between the ideas and the divine will on the one hand, and their conjunction with the Trinitarian processions on the other) will show where we must augment Marion's story of the moderns. A further increment of insight into our own problem of creation from nothing will thereby be attained. For both these points are instances of that Platonism that Aquinas' ideas forbid, but that reaches an illustrative culmination, fateful for later philosophical developments, in Leibniz.

How the marginalization of the divine will is an intrinsic feature of what we might call the "Franciscan" account of the ideas can be quickly sketched. In spite of considerable overlap between their respective treatments of divine ideas, comparison with Aquinas reveals Bonaventure's characteristic emphasis to be that the ideas emerge as distinct cognitive entities immediately, concomitant with the natural outflow of

---

[40] See especially Marion, *Sur la Théologie blanche*, 9–139; Marion, "The Idea of God," 265–304; Marion, "Creation of the Eternal Truths," 116–38.
[41] Marion, *Sur la Théologie blanche*, 70–109.
[42] Ibid., 36–9.
[43] Ibid., 39–43.
[44] Indeed, Marion speaks of a "direct complicity" between Aquinas and Bonaventure on the doctrine of ideas. Ibid., 37.

divine truth and light. As cognitive expressions of God's perfection, they must all naturally possess, even as merely possible, the full determinacy of the created actual; unlike the exemplars of Aquinas, these ideas, as such, require nothing from the divine will.[45] For all the genuine diversity amid Bonaventure's many successors, this particular aspect will come to seem almost axiomatic. Henry of Ghent shifts the emphasis from God's "expressibility" to God's "reflexive" capacity, elaborating multiple stages within God's self-comprehension as a kind of progressive discovery by God of her own imitability.[46] But the whole point is precisely that this imitability is captured in its determinate completeness by the reflective process itself, apart from the divine will. Scotus criticizes Henry lavishly, and yet a central plank of his own alternative argument about the divine ideas is the affirmation that "the ideas in God are antecedent to the act of will."[47] Scotus's follower Francis of Meyronnes even resurrected Henry's "essential being" (*esse essentiae*) in order to secure the "truth of [our] necessary propositions" as formally distinct acts of being necessarily lodged within God's self-understanding.[48] This entire trend of thought achieved authoritative formulation in early modern continental metaphysics through Francis Suarez, who does not shy away from the bold implications. Necessary propositions about creatures

> are not true because they are known by God, but rather they are known because they are true; otherwise no reason could be given why God would necessarily know them to be true. For if their truth came forth from God himself, that would take place by means of God's will; hence it would not come forth of necessity, but voluntarily ... [I]n regard to these enunciations, the divine intellect is related as purely speculative, not as operative.[49]

Nor, for Suarez, can the necessity of our demonstratively or definitionally true predications about creatures have their source in the creature's divine exemplar. This is Aquinas' position, subordinating the modal properties of created things and truths fully to the divine will to create this world. Suarez rejects it out of hand: "the divine exemplar itself had this necessity of representing man as rational animal ... this necessity arises from the object itself [i.e., the essence "human being"] and not from the divine exemplar."[50]

What is remarkable about this trend of thought is not just the focus on the divine intellect but rather the accompanying pressure actually to pit it against the divine will. The arguments continually turn on juxtaposing God's knowledge and volition, dividing them. This tendency received further impetus by way of the second divergence from

---

[45] See the old but still valuable treatment by Bissen, *L'Exemplarisme Divin*, especially 29–31, 58–9, 76–7.
[46] Hoenen, "Propter Dicta Augustini," 256–8.
[47] Hoenen, *Marsilius of Inghen*, 128. Gilson remarks, "There is no trace of voluntarism in [Scotus] even with respect to the essences of creatable beings" (*History of Christian Philosophy*, 460).
[48] Hoenen, *Marsilius of Inghen*, 133–4.
[49] Suarez, *On the Essence of Finite Being*, 200. Marion demonstrated that it was exactly this position of Suarez to which Descartes opposed his own assertion of the creation of the eternal truths. But he fails to highlight the role of the will, to which Suarez explicitly alludes.
[50] Ibid., 205–6.

Aquinas of the Bonaventurian idea theory, namely, the conjoining of the expression of the ideas of creatures and the generation of the Son or Word. One might think that assigning a Trinitarian role to the ideas would provide a countervailing pressure against the wedge being driven between intellect and will in God. After all, classic Trinitarian discourse emphasizes the perfect unity of God as triune. But the "disintegrating" effect on the divine being could in fact be reinforced, not restrained, by this association with Trinitarian procession due to a noteworthy trait of the Franciscan tradition of theorizing the Trinity. Working from a detailed comparative analysis of (broadly speaking) "Dominican" and "Franciscan" currents of Trinitarian speculation, Russell Friedman shows how an early Franciscan propensity to ground the differences of Son and Spirit on their differing modes of origin or emanation (in contrast to the Dominican tendency, seen in Aquinas, to focus on relations of opposition) eventually resulted in a literalization of the psychological analogy. Aquinas was careful to root the two processions of Son and Spirit in the single divine essence, and to stress the limited, analogical nature of the claim that the Son proceeds "in the mode of intellect" while the Spirit proceeds "in the mode of will."[51] But the characteristic Franciscan emphases were taken in a contrary direction, in a line beginning with Henry of Ghent and further elaborated by Duns Scotus.[52] The Trinitarian processions came to be directly linked to intellect and will as distinct divine powers. Whereas Aquinas had laid great weight on the ultimate identity of intellect and will within the divine simplicity, for the later Franciscan theorists the revealed distinction of Son and Spirit feeds back into the construal of divine understanding and will, solidifying their "opposition" as modes in spite of the acknowledgement of their unity. As the scholastic legacy filtered into early modern philosophy, it is at least arguable that this tradition, once its built-in apophatic safeguards were forgotten, led to a hardening of the analogical predications of divine intellect and will into quasi-"faculties." The door was open for a kind of divine "psychology" that Aquinas would never have countenanced.

Leibniz glaringly illustrates the profound distortion introduced into the doctrine of divine creation by the combined impact of these two related developments (the exclusion of will from the constitution of the ideas, and the divine "psychology" of opposed knowing and willing faculties). As Aquinas and Bonaventure were confronted by the Arab philosophers, Leibniz was similarly confronted by Spinoza with a powerful conceptualization of the world as a necessary emanation from God. In his response he, too, turned to the discourse of the divine ideas, only now in an atmosphere conditioned by the later medieval dualisms we have identified. The result was a scheme in which Leibniz sought to affirm creation, on the one hand, as free, avoiding the Spinozist vision of a cosmos unintelligently emergent, springing directly and "blindly" from the divine nature, but equally, on the other hand, as not merely arbitrary, for that would mean the exciting new scientific truths currently unveiling the beauty of the physical order rested upon the mere meaningless fiat or whim of the creator. To avoid

---

[51] Russell Friedman, *Intellectual Traditions at the Medieval University: The Use of Philosophical Psychology in Trinitarian Theology among the Franciscans and Dominicans 1250–1350* (Leiden: Brill, 2013), I: 337–40.

[52] Ibid., I: 256–7, 388–9, 391–2.

these extremes he posited an infinite series of potential creations (now aggregated into "possible worlds," a post-medieval touch) eternally and necessarily presented to the divine understanding, from which God voluntarily chooses the uniquely best to actualize.[53] This account had the advantage of preserving divine freedom (the divine will is in no way compelled) while nonetheless assuring us that God has deliberately created our world as the best one (hence "optimism" in the technical sense); the divine choice is not coerced, but it is necessitated by a "moral necessity."[54] But the cost of this maneuver is high when judged against the doctrine of creation from nothing as Aquinas has taught us to think about it. An array of entire prepackaged "worlds" accost God from within, residing in his self-understanding quite apart from any intention; thus, in creation the divine will is reduced to the role of a "selector" of "options." The entire scheme rests upon a juxtaposition of intellect and will in God as extrinsic to one another; it is quite doubtful that the divine unity, the classically asserted absence of metaphysical composition that in Aquinas is the direct counterpart of created multiplicity, can escape intact from this "*Streit der Fakultäten*."

In his famous letters to Mersenne from 1630, Descartes (in direct opposition to Suarez, as Marion showed) asserted the creation of the eternal truths by God. Although he does not name him, it was Suarez who said, as we have seen, that "the truth of something precedes God's knowledge of it." What must not escape our notice, though, is that for Descartes this is not just a philosophical mistake but a blasphemy, for "in God willing and knowing are a single thing."[55] As Marion notes, Descartes drew from this the conclusion (a correct one from the Thomist perspective) that God creates the creature's essence as much as its existence; but when Descartes says that "by the very fact of willing something, [God] knows it" (*ex hoc ipso quod aliquid velit, ideo cognoscit*), he perhaps peers even more deeply into the issues under discussion in this and the previous section.[56] Both essence and existence arrive together, products of a single act of creation that springs from a profound unity between God's knowing and God's willing. Marion followed Gilson and Gouhier in seeing the "revolutionary" nature of Descartes's break with the picture of a "world of ideas" eternally situated in the divine understanding,[57] but when he presents the foregone option of Aquinas in terms of an "expression" of all possibility in the eternal Son, he comes perilously near the Suarezian birfucation of divine intellect and will that Descartes instinctively avoided. It is our examination of Leibniz that has enabled us to recognize this danger.

But there is an ambiguity here, for Leibniz can retort that it is actually Descartes who is wrongly separating divine will from understanding. Leibniz regularly defended his unfashionable indebtedness to the scholastics, notably the "profound" Suarez.[58] In a

---

[53] For sample remarks on God's knowledge of possible worlds, see Leibniz, *Theodicy*, 127–9, 151 (encompassing sections 7–9, and 52).
[54] On moral necessity, see ibid., 228–9 and 282 (sections 168, 282).
[55] Descartes, *Philosophical Writings*, III: 24. The three letters, found at III: 20–6 of this edition, date from April 15, May 6, and May 27, 1630.
[56] Ibid. For Marion's discussion, see Marion, "The Idea of God," I: 273–4.
[57] Meinhardt et al., "Idee," 101–2.
[58] G. W. Leibniz, *New Essays on Human Understanding*, ed. Peter Remnant and Jonathan Bennett (Cambridge: Cambridge University Press, 1996), 431.

letter from 1680, Leibniz's hostility to Descartes's "most strange" doctrine that the good or evil of created things depends upon the divine will is explained in terms strongly reminiscent of Suarezian reasoning: if Descartes is right, "the good cannot be a motive of [God's] will, being posterior to his will. His will, then, would be a certain absolute decree, without any reason."[59] As will be seen in the conclusion, Aquinas offers a way to resolve this issue such that both perfect wisdom and radical contingency unite in God's willing of the world. This dissolves the Leibnizian fear of creation as an act of naked arbitrariness but without yielding an inch to Leibniz's own solution: yet another attempt to foist Platonic ideas upon God as an infinite set of distinct possibilities eternally fixed before the divine understanding. At the conclusion of his *Theodicy*, Leibniz symbolizes his position by imagining the creator as Jupiter, dwelling in an immense palace whose halls comprise all the possible worlds, rising pyramidally to a summit, the unique, best world that Jupiter's wisdom cannot avoid selecting.[60] From the perspective on creation being developed in this chapter, indeed in this book as a whole, it is hard to see in this parable (no doubt intended as a retort to Descartes) anything but an unintentional confirmation of Descartes' complaint that denying God's will a role in creating all ideal possibility is "to talk of him as if he were Jupiter ... and to subject him to the Styx and the Fates."[61]

This section has tried to portray another kind of impairment of the doctrine of creation that results from forsaking Aquinas' approach to the divine ideas. Both the Franciscan tradition and its renewal in Leibniz preserve the Platonic necessity of ideas only at the cost of playing God's mind and God's will off against one another. At stake here is the disruption of the unity not just of the divine creative act, as in the previous section, but of the divine being itself. We may decide that Descartes's dismissal of ideas was an overreaction, but in its context it showed a healthy refusal of late medieval divine psychodynamics in favor of an embrace of God's absolute simplicity.

IV. The World as God's Inner Life

Guided by our reading of divine ideas according to Aquinas, namely, as voluntarily elicited exemplars, we have pursued the more Platonic counter-tradition over the centuries in order to uncover what appear to be the serious problems for theorizing creation to which it gives rise. A final efflorescence of this unhappy legacy remains to be delineated before in the conclusion we return briefly to Aquinas to set out the logical pattern relating divine will and creation that would forestall all the Platonic aberrations discussed. We have already seen how construing God's knowledge of creation (the ideas) along the lines of a Platonic aggregation of discrete possibles can result, first, in the problem of a double constitution of the creature, and, second, in the more serious problem of an extrinsic relation of divine knowledge and will. The

---

[59] G. W. Leibniz, *Philosophical Papers and Letters*, 2nd ed., ed. Leroy Loemker (Dordrecht: D. Reidel, 1969), 273.
[60] Leibniz, *Theodicy*, 369–73 (sections 413–17).
[61] Descartes, *Philosophical Writings*, III: 23.

problem under investigation now is the gravest of all: identifying God's self-knowledge with the knowledge of the ideas. This is one way of deciphering the real meaning of the speculative Trinity in German idealism, but variants of this theme appear among Christian theologians as well. This move, though not as a rule recognized as such, represents the most daring culmination of the Platonic idea tradition, the annexation of the divine self-cognition by the paradigms of non-divine being. God's freedom and true otherness vis-à-vis the creature is vitiated, and the divine majesty is compromised if its fullness of intelligible content is reduced to the collected patterns of worldly realities, even if these latter are infinite in number.

The roots of such a position can once again be traced back to the different decisions of Aquinas and Bonaventure. In response to the Arab thinkers it was recognized by all that God's ideas of the world must formally encompass all worldly minutiae and yet ontologically be identical with the divine essence. But with this development a decisive reckoning with the Platonic idea tradition became most urgent; that this happened in Aquinas yet failed to happen in Bonaventure and his lineage marked the parting of the ways in divine idea doctrine. Without the introduction of divine willing into the constitution of the ideas, the influence of Avicennian essentialism combined with the inclusion of the "possibles" in the natural (nonvoluntary) generation of the eternal Son to populate God's intellect with a necessary, determinate multiplicity. In other words, the failure to purge the divine ideas of the remnants of their Platonic origin left the door wide open to a fusion between God's self-contemplation and God's detailed apprehension of this (or of any possible) world. It was left to the late eighteenth and early nineteenth centuries, to G. E. Lessing and those inspired by his daring Trinitarian speculations to draw the forthright conclusion: the created order as divinely known is an inherent and essential dimension of the eternal divine identity. The great Christian confession (shared with Jews and Muslims) of a free creation from nothing was completely and consciously overthrown. The role of the divine ideas is an indispensible part of this story, as is shown by the inspiration Lessing drew from his illustrious predecessor as ducal librarian at Wolfenbüttel: Leibniz.

The suggestions Lessing took from Leibniz are clearest in his early, posthumously published writings. There he argues that what Christian tradition calls the Son is actually the result of God thinking her own infinite perfection in discrete, separated form, as an unlimited plurality of distinct degrees and modes of perfection. But since God's thinking is most perfect, this multiplicity, capable in itself of infinite variety since infinite perfection is subject to a limitless variety of arbitrary analysis, takes on the single most harmonious and continuous arrangement. The echo of Leibnizian "moral necessity" is clear. But not only is the choice of this world necessitated, its production is as well, since "every thought for God is a creation" and "the concepts which God has of real things" are "these real things themselves."[62] Here, too, Leibniz shows the way, for Lessing seems to have grasped that Leibniz's fundamental substances or monads are in fact the old divine ideas now transformed

---

[62] G. E. Lessing, *Philosophical and Theological Writings*, ed. H. B. Nisbet (Cambridge: Cambridge University Press, 2005), 27, 31.

into cosmic constituents. Leibniz perhaps even suggested the Trinitarian force of this "naturalization" of creation within God by referencing (albeit with disapproval) thinkers like Lull and Keckermann, at whose hands the old psychological analogy is literalized and becomes a quasi-proof that God's self-knowledge rationally requires an eternally generated Son.[63] All these basic elements remain in the famous later passages from *The Education of the Human Race* where Lessing rationally "decodes" the ancient dogmas of the Trinity and of Christ's satisfaction: the Son is the substantial duplication within God of God's perfections as represented, and individual human moral failings drop from God's sight when situated within the cosmic context of the Son's generated plenitude, allowing divine justice to be satisfied with the incremental improvement of the race in history.[64] The key to it all is a replay of the archetypal Platonic scenario: Lessing has transformed God's self-knowledge into a cosmic order (our own) that is necessarily and eternally ingredient in God, that indeed simply is God's own being, thought discretely. Thus, divine idea theory became the midwife of German idealism, as Leibniz quite unwittingly communicated the dangerous "Franciscan" variant of that theory to Lessing, thereby shaping the ferment of German speculation about God and world in his wake.

Schelling in his turn invoked Lessing even as he knowingly took a step beyond him. While Lessing blurred the distinction between the Son's generation and creation, for Schelling creation is actually the deciphered meaning of the dogma of incarnation; the reality of the world marks a genuinely new stage in which God's eternal self-apprehension takes on a reality over against the Father as finitude and history, marking a breach within divinity itself that requires reconciliation.

> The eternal Son of God, born of the essence of the Father of all things, is the finite itself, as it exists in God's eternal intuition; this finite manifests itself [i.e., in a distinct, second moment] as a suffering God, subject to the vicissitudes of time, who at the culmination of His career, in the person of Christ, closes the world of the finite and opens the world of the infinite, i.e. the reign of the Spirit.[65]

Finally, Hegel accepted this basic framework but went further still. God as "spirit" necessarily posits its own "other."

> The other grasped in the pure idea is the Son of God, but this other in its differentiation is the world, nature and finite spirit: the finite spirit is thus posited as a moment of God. Hence the human being is itself contained in the concept of God.[66]

---

[63] H. B. Nisbet, "The Rationalisation of the Holy Trinity from Lessing to Hegel," *Lessing Yearbook* 31 (1999): 67–8.
[64] Lessing, *Philosophical and Theological Writings*, 234–5.
[65] F. W. J. Schelling, *On University Studies*, trans. E.S. Morgan, ed. Norbert Guterman (Athens: Ohio University Press, 1966), 91.
[66] Nisbet, "Rationalisation of the Holy Trinity," 80.

By now it should be clear that this is no eminent containment, as in Aquinas, but a true coincidence of created reality and divine idea. Moreover, the implication of finite with infinite spirit extends to their exemplifying an identical spiritual or conceptual logic. The discursive rhythm that rationally conducts human thought from one concept to another replicates the unfolding of God's very actuality. As Lonergan saw, here the Platonic epistemology of objective ideas fully triumphs over Aristotle's intellect-as-unity, as the latter's self-contemplating deity becomes a "thinker," a developing entrainment of multiple, interrelated "thoughts."[67] As a constituent of God for both Schelling and Hegel, creation might seem to be exalted; but in fact instead of the world Aquinas saw, the harmonious refraction of divine perfection, it has become a "fall" into finitude, a tragic but necessary rupture in reality whose otherness demands rectification. The Platonic idea-world, after centuries of dwelling in God's mind like a dormant virus, eventually displays its true virulence.

V. Lingering Consequences

It has been the repeated contention of this chapter that, *contra* Aquinas' more voluntarist appropriation of the divine ideas, the Platonic model introduces the worldly modes of multiplicity and formal differentiation as a necessary and ultimate feature of being into God himself. The speculative Trinity of German idealism pursues the logic of this misstep to its fateful end: the idea of the world has become, in the most real sense, God's inner life. While this conclusion may seem remote, confined to the thinnest upper atmosphere of speculation, in fact variations on this theme keep cropping up, wittingly or not, among respectable Christian theologians. I can do no more in the space remaining than suggest three examples in more recent theology that take on a dubious appearance in light of the standpoint of Aquinas and divine ideas as I have sought to define it. The need for haste means that full justice cannot be done to them here, but at least the question must be sharply put: are the following proposals ultimately compatible with the transcendence of the creator God as Aquinas' ideas elucidate it?

In his great posthumously published work *The Bride of the Lamb* (1945), Sergei Bulgakov proffers a "sophiology" to overcome the spectre of arbitrariness that he thinks has tainted theological conceptions in the West. Unfortunately, in attempting to use Aquinas on the divine ideas as a prime exhibit of the malaise he subjects that thinker to a nearly perfect misreading. On all the key points—God's "simple knowledge," the relation of intelligibilities to exemplars, the preexistence in God of creative possibility (not, *pace* Bulgakov, "possible worlds")—where we have argued Aquinas is signaling his voluntarist bent, Bulgakov stubbornly insists on reading him against the grain, in fact attributing to him just that opposition of necessary intellect to capricious will that Aquinas' account enables theology to avoid.[68] In the name of Pseudo-Dionysius

---

[67] Lonergan, *Verbum*, 196.
[68] Sergius Bulgakov, *The Bride of the Lamb*, trans. Boris Jakim (Grand Rapids, MI: Wm. B. Eerdmans, 2002), 22–6.

he denigrates ideas in Aquinas for being merely cognitive, failing to see the hybrid aspect of Aquinas' account that, faithful to Pseudo-Dionysius, builds willed intention into the exemplars. In the end, Bulgakov complains that the ideas of creation are left arbitrary and extrinsic in relation to God. Failing to detect Aquinas' solution to this problem, Bulgakov offers his own. Unfortunately, "sophia" as the perfect preexistence of the unique cosmos in God, the necessitated expression of the divine perfection, looks like an instance of fleeing Scylla only to fall into Charybdis. When he rules out the notion that God could create a better world, or that God knows a field of possibility beyond her willed act, he adduces as a principle that in God "all is equally necessary and equally free."[69] But for Aquinas, this would be little more than a confusion of the ontological status of exemplars as sharing God's act of being (and consequently God's transcendence of worldly modal categories) with their intentional content (which is inevitably contingent by comparison). As a result, for Aquinas Bulgakov's talk of "the uniqueness of the ways of God [in creation] … that excludes all other unactualised possibilities" would be incoherent.[70] Yes, God's way in this world could only be God's way, but this world need not be the only one. We cannot get back behind the willing of this world to find some deeper, "natural" grounding in God's being that determined this world as the uniquely possible "shape" or externalization of God. Indeed, sophiology, adopting the position of German idealism that makes our cosmos both uniquely preexistent in God and necessarily emanated, opens an ontological space that looks very much like the halfway house between God and creature that Bulgakov says he wishes to avoid.

For Aquinas, our creation is contingent not as arbitrary but as one of the innumerable harmonious reflections sustainable by God's essence. No created world could fail to be an imitation of the divine being and goodness, perfect in its own unique order. But because the distance between perfection and imperfection is infinite, there could always be other likewise perfect worlds, and no single one could be "best." The lesson to be drawn from Bulgakov for a doctrine of creation is that the freedom of God vis-à-vis the creation must be a freedom of choice (though not of fixed options necessarily pre-given). But also to be noted is the way God's act, as God's being, modally transcends the modal categories of its effect. This leads to our second example, Karl Barth's doctrine of election, especially as interpreted by Bruce McCormack.[71] Barth radicalizes the central Reformed notion of eternal election, making it in effect God's choice, "prior" to all creation, of his own identity, her existence in an eternal covenantal commitment to humanity incarnated in creation as Jesus Christ. The many interpretive difficulties that attend this notion cannot be entered into here, but what is important is to see the way in which Barth has taken the contingent choice of God to create just this world as the context for his incarnation and projected that choice backward into God's own eternal self-relationship, such that God's very identity is conditioned upon

---

[69] Ibid., 31.
[70] Ibid.
[71] Bruce McCormack, "Grace and Being: The Role of God's Gracious Election in Karl Barth's Theological Ontology," in *The Cambridge Companion to Karl Barth*, ed. John Webster (Cambridge: Cambridge University Press, 2000), 92–110. Whether the position outlined is genuinely Barth's or is rather confined to McCormack is immaterial to my criticism here.

a "prior" decision. For Aquinas, the sheer impossibility, not to say absurdity, of this act of divine self-creation is plain: as the perfection of total actuality God has no "other" way to be God, no variety of "identities" to select from or fashion. God's being is the chosen "means" to nothing; it is simply and supremely encompassed end. "Choice" or "election" apply only to God's will to create a particular world; this creative will is an impassable barrier: no defined creature, and thus no definite relation of God to creature, can be prior to it, nor can any modality of God's infinite being be located posterior to it. Indeed, the will to elect humanity in Jesus Christ cannot be prior to the will to elect this world because this world is precisely the world in which God's Word is incarnate as Jesus, and there is no other. *De facto* there is no other world, and *de jure* there is no other God: any variable disposition of God to the world is a feature of the world, not of God. If the creation of this world is contingent, and in no way a matter of God's eternal constitution, then her identification with Jesus of Nazareth is utterly contingent in exactly the same way. God must love, but not necessarily in this way. The field of choice is the range of possible effects of the creative act, that is, it opens out "in front of" God and not "in" him. It is impossible to miss once again the strong whiff of German idealism in Barth's account: yet another attempt is being made to inscribe the contingent cosmic order into the divine being as an essential, identifying component of God. Stipulating that God freely "chooses" this identification really does not mitigate the problem; the complete freedom God enjoys in being God simply excludes the very notion of self-election with its impossible implication of alternative options for divinity.

So if we follow Aquinas on divine ideas, then creating a world, any world, including this world into which God projects herself in solidarity with humanity, is not a different way of being God. God is already the only way to be God. The lesson to be learned from this example is that some kind of absolute distinction must be made in the mode of free divine willing depending upon its object: God's being, or the world's. God is God freely, but God is not free to be God differently, as that could only be freedom to be worse than he is, that is, it is no freedom at all. The concept of "choice" supposes the presentation of differentiated opportunity, hence an articulation of divine self-knowledge that, as we have argued, is only intelligible within the intending of what is not-God, and which cannot be a necessary imprint upon God's essence. This question of articulation introduces our last example. In a brilliant stroke of speculation, John Milbank seized upon the classical Augustinian language of the Son as the eternal "word" and "art" of the Father in order to apply a rigorous analogy with human artistic production.[72] Thus, the Son is not just the reflection of the Father's knowledge but a shaping and particularizing concretion of that knowledge as a quasi-poetic "utterance." This move presumes Gadamer's attempt to make language itself, as "infinite" concept-formation, a kind of transcendental perfection. This in turn enabled Milbank to secure a necessary speculative role for the Spirit by employing Hans Robert Jauss's theory of interpretive reception: just as the work of art only "exists" as fulfilled in the achieved event of its receptive interpretation, so too the Spirit is the co-primordial principle that

---

[72] For what follows, see John Milbank, "The Second Difference," in *The Word Made Strange*, 171–93.

"reads" the eternal Word "back" to the uttering Father, the indispensable co-enabler of the eternal "art." This is exhilarating stuff, but by equating the utterance of the Son with the emergence in God's intellect of a constitutively new concrete artifact, a particularized act of "meaning," it has once again summoned up the ghost of Plato's "cosmos" of ideas within God. Against this, for Aquinas as we are reading him the determination of exemplars, the "articulation" of divine knowledge, is not in any way a natural, unelected emergence, and hence the natural procession of the Son simply cannot be represented as itself the artistic determination of the Father's knowing (a quintessentially Bonaventurian move). Besides, the ancient metaphor of the Son as "art" has here been surreptitiously modernized; for practical capability has been substituted the creative self-concretion of the romantics. Therefore, it seems that Milbank's ingenious "semiotic" model, where the Trinity is an eternal circuit of utterance-sign-interpretation, is finally compatible neither with Aquinas, nor with creation from nothing. The willed event of producing what is not God can be the only "articulation" of God's eternal self-apprehension; hence, the latter cannot be a constitutive moment within God's being. This is the force of the distinction Aquinas draws between what is "known" in the Son (the unified fullness of God's self-knowledge) versus what is "spoken" in the Son (the chosen complex of participations that reflects that fullness from an infinite remove).[73]

VI. Conclusion

As with all of the previous non-Thomist approaches we have examined, each of the three theological proposals just canvassed bears one or both of the marks of the "Franciscan," that is the Christian-Platonic, idea tradition: an eternal pre-presence in the divine essence of articulated or differentiated being and an entanglement of the production of exemplars with Trinitarian procession. We have been suggesting all along that Aquinas' opposed conception has something in it that neutralizes these Platonic elements, something we have been crudely labelling his "voluntarism." The time has now come to see whether a final clarification can be achieved from Aquinas' writings as to how the divine will provides the key concept that polices the boundary between divine and worldly being and prevents the subtle coalescences of the two that threaten the very notion of creation classically conceived. For Aquinas, not just the actualization but also the formal constitution of the world must be freely willed, or else creation simply is not creation, and God is not God. We have seen that the Platonic prioritization of divine ideation over divine willing (sometimes abetted by its "naturalization" as a Trinitarian event), left unexposed, has led in the history of ideas to the splitting of the singular creative act (Section III), the degrading of divine simplicity into dueling "faculties" (Section IV), and finally the fraudulent elevation of the world into the very mystery of God's life (Section V). All of this can be prevented if, with Aquinas, God's exemplary causality in creation is fully united with the willful

---

[73] *De veritate* q. 4 a. 7.

intention of this world, without at the same time confusing that intention with God's free embrace of her own necessary goodness. The elements needed for making the requisite distinctions are available in Aquinas' theory of the will.

But before turning to that theory and some concluding comments, it is important to assert the peculiar importance of the more rigorous theorization of creation that Aquinas' idea theory enables. The religious imagination chafes at the way this rigor blocks and channels its exercise; then, too, the most suggestive and exciting speculative avenues (a sophiology; a God who freely elects his own identity; a semiotic Trinity) are shut off. But such constraints are in fact precious, and necessary. The living traffic with deity in worship and prayer can only take shape via a traditional stock of vital and indispensable images and ideas, but a second-order conceptual discipline is required to keep the embedded meanings and claims coherent with each other. Theology's role is to provide this discipline through some kind of transcendental reflection.[74] This is the interpretive work by which, in Ricoeur's words, the symbol gives rise to thought.[75] This cannot occur when the symbols of worship and the narratives of confession are simply pressed into service as ersatz thoughts, so theology, when it remembers what it is about, always includes demythologization, that is some sort of processing of religious expressions through a conceptual machine that detaches, preserves, and purifies their residual semantic core for experimental deployment in propositional terms. Not even the most meticulous restatements of the kerygma can do without the abstract discipline of self-consistent transcendental reflection. Trying to ground theology exclusively in "revelation" does not succeed in avoiding speculation; it only results in undisciplined speculation, which is just another form of mythology. I would suggest there have been at least four great eras of fruitful demythologization that remain living resources today: the third and fourth centuries CE, with the conciliar definitions as high points; the great period of mature scholasticism, with Aquinas as a high point; the post-Kantian ferment in Germany, with its resulting technical sophistication in idealism but especially with the anti-speculative, even apophatic protest of romantic thought (Schleiermacher and Kierkegaard); and finally so-called dialectical theology in twentieth-century German Protestantism, with its twin giants Barth and Bultmann.[76]

All four of these great epochs arguably in their critical projects employed a similar conceptual machinery: the most careful thinking through of God as absolute source, absolute origin. But unlike the devices of dialectical theology, which turned for their anti-mythical protocols to a foundational *Offenbarungstrias* on one side (Barth), and to a phenomenology of *Dasein* on the other (Bultmann), it was the classical dynamic of creation *ex nihilo* that motivated the first two epochs, and, perhaps in a way, the

---

[74] Lash, "Ideology, Metaphor and Analogy," 95–119.
[75] Paul Ricoeur, *The Symbolism of Evil*, trans. Emerson Buchanan (Boston: Beacon Press, 1967), 236–7.
[76] For the Nicene Creed as demythologization, see the tantalizingly brief remarks in Rowan Williams, "The Nicene Heritage," in *The Christian Understanding of God Today*, ed. James M. Byrne (Dublin: Columba Press, 1993), 45–8. On German idealism the remarks of Gilson are apt: "Kant [is] the first [modern] philosopher who, after a long interlude of brilliant amateurs, has claimed for philosophy the right to a 'scholastic' method of exposition. … [T]echnically speaking, the doctrines of Kant, of Fichte and of Hegel belong in the same class as the most perfectly elaborated Scholastic philosophies and theologies of the Middle Ages." Etienne Gilson, *Being and Some Philosophers*, 2nd ed. (Toronto: Pontifical Institute of Medieval Studies, 1952), 113.

third as well. Theorizing creation in a conceptually precise way is, I would maintain, a metaphysical transcription of Israel's *shema*: a way of confessing the one source of all, whose *kabod* can only be aniconic, and who foments an implacable revolution against the world of gods.[77] Only the patient working out of all this in thought can show that calling God creator "from nothing" is not the result of minds dazzled by the *doxa* (both glory and traditional communal opinion) into paying God empty "metaphysical compliments," as the great Whitehead believed.[78] Against the latter it should be said that God is not the highest "instance" of any principle, nor the coordinator of the most general elements of organic process. God is the fecund abyss of all principle, the free fountainhead of all formed actuality. Followers of Aquinas in particular will want to insist that the notion of creation from nothing, *pace* Whitehead, is no myth, but in fact our most important conceptual safeguard against the uncritical absorption of myth into our theological thinking. Undeterred by German polysyllabics, let them cry: creation *ex nihilo* is our *Entmythologisierungsprogramm*!

With these general remarks in mind, it is time to conclude with a specification of Aquinas' voluntarism of creation. It is an ontological axiom for Aquinas that nothing is indifferent to its own act of existence; part of what it means for anything to be is to display some kind of impetus toward its own persistence and completion, its own formal actuality. When this drive is an unconscious causal weight or instinct, it is natural appetite. But intellectual existence is formally perfected by union with the intelligible; the impulse toward this union with the understood, whether the latter is possessed or sought, is intelligent appetite or will.[79] It is another given for Aquinas that perfection or goodness seeks to propagate itself beyond its possessor, which is the deep metaphysical significance of causality and its replication in effect; hence, it is fitting for God, too, to disperse her own goodness as creatures. But as the simple totality of all perfection he can only will the good of creatures as partakers of that totality, and because the diffusion of the totality is variable without limit, creatures can only be willed as contingent means to the necessary end of all ends, herself.[80] But this introduces a crucial distinction: a gap like that between heaven and earth yawns between God's self-will or self-appetite or self-love and his willing of creatures: God necessarily wills herself as the perfect intelligible good, but no creature is an indispensable means to that end, so God can only will any creature contingently. And as befits will as intellect's appetite, this distinction in willing follows from the different cognition of end and means. But really there is but one act of cognition with two objects, for God knows the creature in knowing himself.

> Hence, as in God to understand the cause is not the cause of his understanding the effect, for he understands the effect in the cause, so, in Him, to will an end is

---

[77] It was the often repeated message of Herbert McCabe that Jewish monotheism was a cultural and ethical upheaval with the most profound historical consequences, overthrowing the domination of humanity by "gods." See, e.g., Herbert McCabe, "Trinity and Prayer," in *God Still Matters*, ed. Brian Davies (London: Continuum, 2002), 54–63.
[78] Alfred North Whitehead, *Science and the Modern World* (New York: Macmillan, 1925), 179.
[79] *STh* I q. 19 a. 1.
[80] *STh* I q. 19 a. 2.

not the cause of his willing the means, yet He wills the ordering of the means to the end.[81]

In other words, God's necessary self-willing does not compel the creation, but the willing of creation is a contingently intended ordering known virtually in the cause.

The lesson learned from Aquinas' anti-Platonic stance toward the ideas, that is, their voluntary elicitation, is that God's intellect can never be played off against her will, but rather God knows as he wills and wills as she knows. But then for saving the logic of creation "*ex nihilo*" everything turns on rightly unifying the two different intellectual objects (himself and creatures) with proper and coordinate modes of God's willing act. Contrary to a perennial confusion, free willing is not identical with choice. The will's freedom to choose is always grounded in a prior deep orientation toward its own fulfillment, its one inalterable desire for its good. As the very nature of desire, this is no coercion; the usual opposition of natural and voluntary is here transcended, for this ingrained impulsion toward perfection is the quintessence of the voluntary.[82] But when the good is not perfectly possessed, or when some free play of its dispersal, its overflow, is sought, then the logically derivative question of choice first arises. Hence, Aquinas demands a sharp distinction in voluntary acts, calling upon the ancient distinction between *boulesis* and *thelesis*, between will as such (*velle*) and choice (*eligere*).

> On the part of the appetite to will implies the simple appetite for something; hence the will is said to regard the end, which is desired for itself. But to choose is to desire something for the sake of obtaining something else, and so, properly speaking, it regards the means to the end.[83]

So the unity of knowing and willing presupposed by Aquinas' idea theory demands the correct alignments: God self-willing is a dynamism of enjoyment, in unity with his cognitive act of sheer self-transparency; but God's willing of the creature must be an election, an exercising of one among a virtually unbounded range of options, concretized in the elicitation of the ideas, that is, a single, defined articulation of her power or essence. Steady attention to this alignment inoculates theology against the Platonic maladies that have attended idea theory from its origination. Contrary to the spurious symmetry of idealistic speculation, for God to know ideas (as exemplars), even an infinity of them, is not to know himself, though to know herself is to know an infinity of ideas (as intelligibilities). And contrary to the Franciscan or Christian-Platonic scheme that some interpreters still attempt to foist on Aquinas, the only necessity that attaches to the intentional content of exemplars is hypothetical necessity, and this is exclusively annexed to the creative act itself. That is, proper ideas or exemplars are not a necessary, fixed, and pre-given array but derive their only necessity from the supposition of the act of creative will.

---

[81] *STh* I q. 19 a. 5.
[82] *STh* I q. 82, a. 1.
[83] *STh* I q. 83, a. 4.

Given the intimate and necessary relation in God of will to intellect that Aquinas insists upon, a certain nicety in the correct connecting of intellectual objects and volitional ones is just what we should expect. On the other side, in one way or another, the serial mutations of the doctrine of creation that have passed in review above have involved some breach of these rules of connection; at the basis of these breaches has been one or another attempt to equip possible non-divine entities, "creatables" so to speak, with an intra-divine necessity that did not befit their status as ultimately contingent objects of divine will. Pegis has perfectly captured the ontological vision of Platonism that underlies this perennial impulse within theism.

> Being in its ultimate nature is an organized whole of distinct and hierarchically arranged Forms. Each Form is the same as itself and different from all others; each Form introduces into the very heart of being that character of sameness and difference which is necessary to the preservation ... of the intelligibility of Forms ... By nature being is, therefore, a system of determinate essences. By nature being is possessed of what may be called the principle of interior diversification or otherness.[84]

Pegis calls this Platonic ontological prejudice, where "non-being [i.e., otherness, difference] is the mysterious co-principle of [the] interior intelligibility" of being, the "alphabet theory of reality." We are struck by the similarity to Saussure's insight: linguistic systems are reducible to an ensemble of signs poised in patterns of mutual differentiation or exclusion. But for Aquinas, "in the unity of a God Who is Being we have transcended the reign of *otherness* and *difference* within being."[85] Otherwise put, Aquinas' doctrine of ideas enables us to see that only created being is "linguistic," while being as such is just God.

Aquinas' God is infinite actuality, that is, God knows all ways of existing because God is the perfect act of existence. Only this "existentialist" approach will avoid the "essentialist" importation of multiple differentiated essences into God. God's essence relates to created essences not as general to particular but as perfect act to imperfect acts. One who knows the more perfect act knows the less perfect.[86] James F. Ross unforgettably described the results of this for divine ideas: God knows creatures by knowing herself, just as anyone who recognizes W. C. Fields perfectly by that very act also implicitly recognizes every imitation of Fields.[87] Thus, God's perfect knowledge of creatable possibility in no way requires an infinite "set" of determined others as cognitive objects, nor as the perfect idea of all things does his essence resolve itself into such a set. This is why the knowledge of creatures, even in their concrete actuality as the world, adds nothing to God; they are all decompositions and complex negations of

---

[84] Pegis, "Dilemma of Being and Unity," 156.
[85] Ibid., 183.
[86] Ibid., 178.
[87] James F. Ross, "Aquinas's Exemplarism, Aquinas's Voluntarism," *American Catholic Philosophical Quarterly* 64 (1990): 186.

the simple fullness of God. And their exemplars in God are voluntarily elicited from this fullness, not eternally fixed and "installed" in an intellect divided against will.

In this way, Aquinas came to abandon the traditional but impossible marriage between Platonic ideas and monotheistic creation. The argument of this chapter has been that a rigorous conceptualization of creation has been undercut over a period of centuries by repeated attempts to revive that marriage. With Aquinas' purge of Platonism, the mode of God's freedom in creating is harder for our imaginations to come to grips with; this, as was suggested above, is the price of demythologization. Even so, we are not totally bereft of an analogy for that supreme freedom. In God there is no mere assemblage of givens, no timeless reservoir of homogenous possibilities, and hence creation is basically neither externalization nor replication. The emergence of the features of this world is more like a deep chess problem: not simply unpredictable in advance but incalculable in principle. There is no algorithm moving from primitive principles to the final total order; instead, logically prior fields of possibility, as they come into willed focus, give rise to posterior fields whose range cannot be fully fixed in terms of the earlier domain. So from our perspective there is an infinite discontinuity between (using Aquinas' terms) ideas as intelligibles and ideas as exemplars, as in the latter a cascade of defined possibility and ramified relation is instantaneously realized. The "fact" of exemplars in God (though it "adds" nothing to his being) is only and could only be a divinely willed fact, and for this fact (identical to the "Let there be …") the best, albeit distant, analogy we have is the flash of artistic insight, the mysterious intuition that pounces on us from nowhere and tells us, "This is the way to do it." Furnishing God with Platonic ideas invites us to imagine creation as a selection, a deduction, a derivation; Aquinas invites us to see it as more akin to a stroke of genius, a coup, a feat of legerdemain. Or, perhaps, it is an improvisation, indeed the grandest of improvisations: the theme is the variation and the variation is the theme. Like a perfect artwork, its immanent necessity (how could it have been other than it is?) remains, mysteriously, a freely expressed contingency. Thus, the abyss of freedom from which God first snatches our cosmos gives beings a depth even beyond their beauty and sublimity. It is that uncanny halo of the aleatory that plays along the edges of all things, the surprise that jolts the metaphysician awake.

Works Cited

Aquinas, Thomas. *Summa contra Gentiles*. Vol. 13 of *Sancti Thomae Aquinatis doctoris angelici Opera omnia iussu Leonis XIII. P. M. edita*. Edited by members of the Leonine commission. Rome: Typis Riccardo Garrone, 1918.
Augustine. *Confessiones*. Edited by Pius Knöll. Corpus Scriptorum Ecclesiasticorum Latinorum vol. 33. Vienna: F. Tempsky, 1896.
Augustine. *De diversis quaestionibus 83*. Edited by Almut Mutzenbecher. Vol. 44 of *Corpus Christianorum, Series Latina*. Turnhout: Brepols, 1975.
Balthasar, Hans Urs von. *The Realm of Metaphysics in Antiquity*. Vol. 4 of *The Glory of the Lord: A Theological Aesthetics*. Edited by Joseph Fessio, S.J. and John Riches. Edinburgh: T&T Clark, 1989.
Balthasar, Hans Urs von. *The Realm of Metaphysics in the Modern Age*. Vol. 5 of *The Glory of the Lord: A Theological Aesthetics*. Edited by Joseph Fessio SJ and John Riches. Edinburgh: T&T Clark, 1991.
Barth, Karl. *Church Dogmatics I.1: The Doctrine of the Word of God*. Translated by G. W. Bromiley and T. F. Torrance. Edinburgh, T&T Clark, 1975.
Barth, Karl. *Church Dogmatics III.1: The Doctrine of Creation*. Translated by J. W. Edwards, O. Bussey, and Harold Knight. Edinburgh: T&T Clark, 1958.
Bauerschmidt, Frederick C. "The Abrahamic Voyage: Michel de Certeau and Theology." *Modern Theology* 12 (1996): 1–26.
Bauerschmidt, Frederick C. "The Word Made Speculative? John Milbank's Christological Poetics." *Modern Theology* 15 (1999): 417–32.
Bissen, Jean-Marie. *L'Exemplarisme Divin selon Saint Bonaventure*. Paris: J. Vrin, 1929.
Boland, Vivian, OP. *Ideas in God According to Saint Thomas Aquinas: Sources and Synthesis*. Leiden: E. J. Brill, 1996.
Bonaventure. *Quaestiones disputatae de scientia Christi*. Vol. 5 of *Opera Omnia*. Edited by the Fathers of the College of St. Bonaventure. Quaracchi: Collegium S. Bonaventurae, 1901.
Booth, Edward. *Aristotelian Aporetic Ontology in Islamic and Christian Thinkers*. Cambridge: Cambridge University Press, 1983.
Bos, Egbert Peter. "The Theory of Ideas according to Francis of Meyronnes: Commentary on the Sentences (Conflatus), I, Dist. 47." In *Néoplatonisme et philosophie médiévale: Actes du colloque internationale de Corfu*, 211–27. Turnhout: Brepols, 1997.
Bulgakov, Sergius. *The Bride of the Lamb*. Translated by Boris Jakim. Grand Rapids, MI: Wm. B. Eerdmans, 2002.
Burrell, David. *Aquinas: God and Action*. Notre Dame: University of Notre Dame Press, 1979.
Burrell, David. *Faith and Freedom: An Interfaith Perspective*. Oxford: Blackwell, 2004.
Burrell, David. *Freedom and Creation in Three Traditions*. Notre Dame: University of Notre Dame Press, 1993.
Burrell, David. "Review of *Beyond the Necessary God*, by Paul J. DeHart." *Theological Studies* 62 (2001): 207.

Caputo, John D. "Kierkegaard, Heidegger, and the Foundering of Metaphysics." In *International Kierkegaard Commentary: Fear and Trembling and Repetition*, edited by Robert L. Perkins, 201-24. Macon, GA: Mercer University Press, 1993.

Certeau, Michel de. "Autorités chrétiennes et structures sociales." In *La Faiblesse de Croire*, 77-128. Paris: Seuil, 1987.

Certeau, Michel de. "Du corps à l'écriture: un transit chrétien." In *La Faiblesse de Croire*, 267-306. Paris: Seuil, 1987.

Certeau, Michel de. *The Mystic Fable*. Vol. 1. Translated by Michael B. Smith. Chicago: University of Chicago Press, 1992.

Certeau, Michel de. *The Practice of Everyday Life*. Translated by Steven F. Rendall. Berkeley: University of California Press, 1984.

Chomsky, Noam. *Syntactic Structures*. The Hague: Mouton, 1957.

Dalferth, Ingolf. *Gott: Philosophisch-theologische Denkversuche*. Tübingen: Mohr Siebeck, 1992.

DeHart, Paul. *Aquinas and Radical Orthodoxy: A Critical Inquiry*. New York: Routledge, 2012.

DeHart, Paul. *Beyond the Necessary God: Trinitarian Faith and Philosophy in the Thought of Eberhard Jüngel*. Atlanta: Scholars Press, 1999.

DeHart, Paul. "Farrer's Theism: *Finite and Infinite*." In *Austin Farrer for Today: A Prophetic Agenda*, edited by Richard Harries and Stephen Platten, 98-110. London: SCM Press, 2020.

DeHart, Paul. "Quaestio Disputata: Divine Virtues and Divine Ideas of Virtues." *Theological Studies* 81 (2020): 467-77.

DeHart, Paul. "*Ter mundus accipit infinitum*: the Dogmatic Coordinates of Schleiermacher's Trinitarian Treatise." *Neue Zeitschrift für Systematische Theologie und Religionsphilosophie* 52 (2010): 17-39.

DeHart, Paul. *The Trial of the Witnesses: The Rise and Decline of Postliberal Theology*. Oxford: Blackwell, 2006.

DeHart, Paul. "What Is Not, Was Not, and Will Never Be: Creaturely Possibility, Divine Ideas and the Creator's Will in Thomas Aquinas." *Nova et Vetera* 13 (2015): 1009-58.

De Lubac, Henri. *Surnaturel: études historiques*. Paris: Aubier, 1946.

Dempsey, Michael T., ed. *Trinity and Election in Contemporary Theology*. Grand Rapids, MI: Eerdmans, 2011.

De Rijk, Lambert M. "Quaestio de Ideis: Some Notes on an Important Chapter of Platonism." In *Kephalaion: Studies in Greek Philosophy and its Continuation offered to C. J. de Vogel*, edited by J. Mansfeld and L.M. de Rijk, 204-13. Assen: Van Gorcum, 1975.

De Rijk, Lambert M. "Un Tournant Important dans l'Usage du Mot Idea chez Henri de Gand." In *Idea: VI Colloquio Internazionale del Lessico Intelletuale Europeo*, edited by M. Fattori and M. L. Bianchi, 89-98. Rome: Edizioni del Ateneo, 1990.

Descartes, René. *The Philosophical Writings of Descartes*. 3 vols. Translated by John Cottingham, Robert Stoothoff, Dugald Murdoch, and Anthony Kenny. Cambridge: Cambridge University Press, 1984-91.

Descartes, René. *Œuvres de Descartes*. 13 vols. Edited by Charles Adam and Paul Tannery. Paris: Vrin, 1964-76.

DeSpain, Benjamin. "Quaestio Disputata: Aquinas's Virtuous Vision of the Divine Ideas." *Theological Studies* 81 (2020): 453-66.

Duquoc, Christian. "Le théologie naturelle. Son enjeu dans le débat ouvert par la Réforme." *Lumiere et Vie* 32 (1983): 75-88.

Eckhart, Meister. *Meister Eckhart: The Essential Sermons, Commentaries, Treatises and Defense*. Edited by Edmund Colledge and Bernard McGinn. New York: Paulist Press, 1981.
Eckhart, Meister. *Meister Eckhart: Teacher and Preacher*. Edited by Bernard McGinn. New York: Paulist Press, 1986.
Emery, Gilles. "Trinity and Creation." In *The Theology of Thomas Aquinas*, edited by Rik van Nieuwenhove and Joseph Wawrykow, 58–76. Notre Dame: University of Notre Dame Press, 2005.
Eriksen, Niels Nymann. *Kierkegaard's Category of Repetition: A Reconstruction*. Berlin: Walter de Gruyter, 2000.
Ernst, Cornelius, OP. *Multiple Echo: Explorations in Theology*. Edited by Fergus Kerr OP and Timothy Radcliffe OP. London: Darton, Longman & Todd, 1979.
Fabro, Cornelio. "The Intensive Hermeneutics of Thomistic Philosophy: The Notion of Participation." *Review of Metaphysics* 27 (1974): 449–91.
Fabro, Cornelio. "Kierkegaards Kritik am Idealismus: Die metaphysische Begründung der Wahlfreiheit." In *Der Mensch vor dem Anspruch der Wahrheit und der Freiheit: Festgabe, Johannes B. Lotz S.J. z. 70. Geburtstag am 2. August 1973 gewidmet*, edited by Josef de Vries and Walter Brugger, 151–80. Frankfurt a. M.: Knecht, 1973.
Fabro, Cornelio. *Participation et Causalité selon S. Thomas d'Aquin*. Louvain: Publications universitaires de Louvain, 1961.
Farrer, Austin. *Finite and Infinite: A Philosophical Essay*. 2nd ed. London: Dacre Press, 1959.
Feingold, Lawrence. *The Natural Desire to See God According to St. Thomas and his Interpreters*. 2nd ed. Naples, FL: Sapientia, 2010.
Frank, Manfred. *Die Unhintergehbarkeit von Individualität*. Frankfurt a. M.: Suhrkamp, 1986.
Frank, Manfred. "Einleitung des Herausgebers." In Friedrich Schleiermacher, *Dialektik*, edited by Manfred Frank. Vol. 1, 10–136. Frankfurt: Suhrkamp, 2001.
Frank, Manfred. "The Entropy of Language: Reflections on the Searle – Derrida Debate." In *The Subject and the Text*, edited by Andrew Bowie, translated by Helen Atkins, 123–89. Cambridge: Cambridge University Press, 1997.
Frank, Manfred. "Style in Philosophy: Part I." *Metaphilosophy* 30 (1999): 145–67.
Frank, Manfred. *The Subject and the Text*. Edited by Andrew Bowie. Translated by Helen Atkins. Cambridge: Cambridge University Press, 1997.
Frank, Manfred. "The Text and Its Style: Schleiermacher's Theory of Language." In *The Subject and the Text*, edited by Andrew Bowie, translated by Helen Atkins, 1–22. Cambridge: Cambridge University Press, 1997.
Frank, Manfred. *What is Neostructuralism?* Translated by Sabine Wilke and Richard Gray. Minneapolis: University of Minnesota Press, 1989.
Frei, Hans W. "Niebuhr's Theological Background." In *Faith and Ethics: The Theology of H. Richard Niebuhr*, edited by Paul Ramsey, 9–64. New York: Harper & Row, 1957.
Friedman, Russell. *Intellectual Traditions at the Medieval University: The Use of Philosophical Psychology in Trinitarian Theology among the Franciscans and Dominicans 1250–1350*. 2 vols. Leiden: Brill, 2013.
Frissell, Bob. *Nothing in This Book Is True, but It's Exactly How Things Are*. Berkeley, CA: Frog Books, 1994.
Geiger, Louis B. *La participation dans la philosophie de saint Thomas d'Aquin*. Montreal: Institut d'Études Médiévales, 1952.

Gilson, Etienne. *Being and Some Philosophers*. 2nd ed. Toronto: Pontifical Institute of Medieval Studies, 1952.
Gilson, Etienne. *History of Christian Philosophy in the Middle Ages*. London: Sheed and Ward, 1955.
Gilson, Etienne. *The Philosophy of St. Bonaventure*. Translated by Frank J. Sheed and Illtyd Trethowan. New York: Sheed & Ward, 1938.
Goodman, Lenn E. "Happiness." In *The Cambridge History of Medieval Philosophy*, edited by Robert Pasnau, 457–71. Cambridge: Cambridge University Press, 2010.
Goris, Harm. *Free Creatures of an Eternal God*. Leuven: Peeters, 1997.
Grimsley, Ronald. "Kierkegaard and Leibniz." *Journal of the History of Ideas* 26 (1965): 383–96.
Hannay, Alastair. *Kierkegaard: A Biography*. Cambridge: Cambridge University Press, 2001.
Heidegger, Martin. *Identität und Differenz*. Pfullingen: Neske, 1957.
Heidegger, Martin. *Nietzsche, Volume IV: Nihilism*. Edited by David Krell. Translated by Frank Capuzzi. San Francisco: Harper & Row, 1982.
Himes, Brian. "Lonergan's Position on the Natural Desire to See God and Aquinas' Metaphysical Theology of Creation and Participation." *Heythrop Journal* 54 (2013): 767–83.
Hoenen, Maarten J. F. M. *Marsilius of Inghen: Divine Knowledge in Late Medieval Thought*. Leiden: E.J. Brill, 1993.
Hoenen, Maarten J. F. M.. "Propter Dicta Augustini: Die Metaphysische Bedeutung der Mittelalterlichen Ideenlehre." *Recherches de Théologie et Philosophie Médiévales* 64 (1997): 245–62.
Johnson, Junius. *Christ and Analogy: The Christocentric Metaphysics of Hans Urs von Balthasar*. Minneapolis: Fortress Press, 2013.
Jordan, Mark D. "The Intelligibility of the World and the Divine Ideas in Aquinas." *Review of Metaphysics* 38 (1984): 17–32.
Jüngel, Eberhard. "The Dogmatic Significance of the Question of the Historical Jesus," In *Theological Essays II*, translated by J. B. Webster, 82–119. Edinburgh: T&T Clark, 1995.
Jüngel, Eberhard. *Entsprechungen: Gott—Wahrheit—Mensch. Theologische Erörterungen*. Munich: Christian Kaiser, 1980.
Jüngel, Eberhard. *Ganz Werden: Theologische Erörterungen V*. Tübingen: Mohr Siebeck, 2003.
Jüngel, Eberhard. *Gott als Geheimnis der Welt: zur Begründung der Theologie des Gekreuzigten im Streit zwischen Theismus und Atheismus*. 6th ed. Tübingen: Mohr Siebeck, 1992. Translated by Darrell L. Guder under the title *God as the Mystery of the World*. Grand Rapids, MI: Eerdmans, 1983.
Jüngel, Eberhard. *Gottes Sein ist im Werden: Verantwortliche Rede vom Sein Gottes bei Karl Barth—Eine Paraphrase*, 4th ed. Tübingen: Mohr Siebeck, 1986. Translated by John Webster under the title *God's Being Is in Becoming: The Trinitarian Being of God in the Theology of Karl Barth—A Paraphrase*. Edinburgh: T&T Clark, 2001.
Jüngel, Eberhard. *Unterwegs zur Sache: Theologische Bemerkungen*. Munich: Christian Kaiser, 1972.
Jüngel, Eberhard. "Von der Dialektik zur Analogie: Die Schule Kierkegaards und der Einspruch Petersons." In *Barth-Studien*, 127–79. Gütersloh: Gerd Mohn, 1982.
Jüngel, Eberhard. *Wertlose Wahrheit: Zur Identität und Relevanz des christlichen Glaubens. Theologische Erörterungen III*. Tübingen: Mohr Siebeck, 1990.

Kant, Immanuel. *The Only Possible Argument in Support of a Demonstration of the Existence of God* [1763]. In *Theoretical Philosophy 1755–1770*, edited by David Walford. The Cambridge Edition of the Works of Immanuel Kant. Cambridge: Cambridge University Press, 2002.

Keller, Catherine. *The Face of the Deep: A Theology of Becoming*. New York: Routledge, 2001.

Kerr, Fergus. "Simplicity Itself: Milbank's Thesis." *New Blackfriars* 73 (1992): 305–10.

Kerr, Fergus. *Theology after Wittgenstein*. Oxford: Blackwell, 1986.

Kierkegaard, Søren. *The Concept of Anxiety*. Vol. 8 of *Kierkegaard's Writings*. Edited and translated by Reidar Thomte. Princeton: Princeton University Press, 1980.

Kierkegaard, Søren. *The Concept of Irony with Continual Reference to Socrates*. Vol. 2 of *Kierkegaard's Writings*. Edited and translated by Howard V. Hong and Edna H. Hong. Princeton: Princeton University Press, 1989.

Kierkegaard, Søren. *Concluding Unscientific Postscript to "Philosophical Fragments."* Vol. 12 (2 books) of *Kierkegaard's Writings*. Edited and translated by Howard V. Hong and Edna H. Hong. Princeton: Princeton University Press, 1992.

Kierkegaard, Søren. *Early Polemical Writings*. Vol. 1 of *Kierkegaard's Writings*. Edited and translated by Julia Watkin. Princeton: Princeton University Press, 1990.

Kierkegaard, Søren. *Either/Or, Part One*. Vol. 3 of *Kierkegaard's Writings*. Edited and translated by Howard V. Hong and Edna H. Hong. Princeton: Princeton University Press, 1987.

Kierkegaard, Søren. *Fear and Trembling / Repetition*. Vol. 6 of *Kierkegaard's Writings*. Edited and translated by Howard V. Hong and Edna H. Hong. Princeton: Princeton University Press, 1983.

Kierkegaard, Søren. *Journals EE–KK*. Edited by Niels Jørgen Cappelørn, Alastair Hannay, David Kangas, Bruce H. Kirmsme, George Pattison, Vanessa Rumble, and K. Brian Söderquist. Vol. 2 of *Kierkegaard's Journals and Notebooks*, edited by Bruce H. Kirmmse and K. Brian Söderquist. Princeton: Princeton University Press, 2008.

Kierkegaard, Søren. *Notebooks 1–15*. Edited by Niels Jørgen Cappelørn, Alastair Hannay, David Kangas, Bruce H. Kirmmse, George Pattison, Vanessa Rumble, and K. Brian Söderquist. Vol. 3 of *Kierkegaard's Journals and Notebooks*, edited by Bruce H. Kirmmse and K. Brian Söderquist. Princeton: Princeton University Press, 2010.

Kierkegaard, Søren. *Philosophical Fragments/Johannes Climacus*. Vol. 7 of *Kierkegaard's Writings*. Edited and translated by Howard V. Hong and Edna H. Hong. Princeton: Princeton University Press, 1985.

Kierkegaard, Søren. *The Sickness unto Death*. Vol. 19 of *Kierkegaard's Writings*. Edited and translated by Howard V. Hong and Edna H. Hong. Princeton: Princeton University Press, 1980.

Kierkegaard, Søren. *Søren Kierkegaard's Journals and Papers*. Edited and translated by Howard V. Hong and Edna H. Hong, assisted by Gregor Malantschuk. 7 vols. Bloomington: Indiana University Press, 1967–78.

Kierkegaard, Søren. *Søren Kierkegaards Skrifter*. Edited by Niels Jørgen Cappelørn, Joakim Garff, Jette Knudsen, Johnny Kondrup, Alastair McKinnon, and Finn Hauberg Mortensen. 55 vols. Copenhagen: Gad, 1997–.

Kierkegaard, Søren. *Works of Love*. Vol. 16 of *Kierkegaard's Writings*. Edited and translated by Howard V. Hong and Edna H. Hong. Princeton: Princeton University Press, 1995.

Kobusch, Theo. "Heinrich von Gent und die Neuplatonische Ideenlehre." In *Néoplatonisme et philosophie médiévale*, edited by Linos G. Benakis, 197–209. Turnhout: Brepols, 1997.

Lacan, Jacques. "L'instance de la lettre dans l'inconscient ou la raison depuis Freud." In *Écrits*, 493–528. Paris: Editions du Seuil, 1966.
Larmore, Charles. "Hölderlin and Novalis." In *The Cambridge Companion to German Idealism*, edited by Karl Ameriks, 141–60. Cambridge: Cambridge University Press, 2000.
Lash, Nicholas. *The Beginning and the End of "Religion"*. Cambridge: Cambridge University Press, 1996.
Lash, Nicholas. "Ideology, Metaphor and Analogy." In *Theology on the Way to Emmaus*, 95–119. London: SCM Press, 1986.
Lash, Nicholas. *Voices of Authority*. London: Sheed & Ward, 1976.
Leibniz, Gottfried Wilhelm. "Discourse on Metaphysics." In *Philosophical Texts*, edited and translated by R. S. Woolhouse and Richard Francks, 53–93. Oxford: Oxford University Press, 1998.
Leibniz, Gottfried Wilhelm. *New Essays on Human Understanding*. Edited by Peter Remnant and Jonathan Bennett. Cambridge: Cambridge University Press, 1996.
Leibniz, Gottfried Wilhelm. *Philosophical Papers and Letters*. 2nd ed. Edited by Leroy Loemker. Dordrecht: D. Reidel, 1969.
Leibniz, Gottfried Wilhelm. *Theodicy: Essays on the Goodness of God, the Freedom of Man and the Origin of Evil*. Edited by Austin Farrer. Translated by E. M. Huggard. 1951. Reprint, La Salle, IL: Open Court, 1985.
Lessing, Gotthold Ephraim. *Philosophical and Theological Writings*. Edited by H. B. Nisbet. Cambridge: Cambridge University Press, 2005.
Lewis, C. S. *The Great Divorce*. New York: Macmillan, 1946.
Lewis, C. S. *The Problem of Pain*. New York: Macmillan, 1943.
Lindbeck, George. *The Nature of Doctrine: Religion and Theology in a Postliberal Age*. Philadelphia: Westminster John Knox, 1984.
Llewelyn, John. *Margins of Religion: Between Kierkegaard and Derrida*. Bloomington: Indiana University Press, 2008.
Løkke, Håvard, and Arild Waaler. "Gottfried Wilhelm Leibniz: Traces of Kierkegaard's Reading of the *Theodicy*." In *Kierkegaard and the Renaissance and Modern Traditions, Tome I: Philosophy*, edited by Jon Stewart, 51–76. Farnham: Ashgate, 2009.
Lonergan, Bernard. *Early Latin Theology*. Translated by Michael G. Shields. Vol. 19 of *Collected Works of Bernard Lonergan*. Toronto: University of Toronto Press, 2011.
Lonergan, Bernard. *Grace and Freedom: Operative Grace in the Thought of St. Thomas Aquinas*. Vol. 1 of *Collected Works of Bernard Lonergan*. Toronto: University of Toronto Press, 2000.
Lonergan, Bernard. *Insight: A Study of Human Understanding*. Edited by Frederick E. Crowe and Robert M. Doran. Vol. 3 of *Collected Works of Bernard Lonergan*. Toronto: University of Toronto Press, 1992.
Lonergan, Bernard. *Phenomenology and Logic*. Vol. 18 of *Collected Works of Bernard Lonergan*. Toronto: University of Toronto Press, 2001.
Lonergan, Bernard. *Verbum: Word and Idea in Aquinas*. Vol. 2 of *Collected Works of Bernard Lonergan*. Toronto: University of Toronto Press, 1997.
McCabe, Herbert. *God Matters*. London: Geoffrey Chapman, 1987.
McCabe, Herbert. "The Trinity and Prayer." In *God Still Matters*, edited by Brian Davies, 54–63. London: Continuum, 2002.
McCormack, Bruce. "Grace and Being: The Role of God's Gracious Election in Karl Barth's Theological Ontology." In *The Cambridge Companion to Karl Barth*, edited by John Webster, 92–110. Cambridge: Cambridge University Press, 2000.

McCormack, Bruce and Thomas Joseph White OP, eds. *Thomas Aquinas and Karl Barth: An Unofficial Catholic-Protestant Dialogue*. Grand Rapids, MI: Eerdmans, 2013.

McFague, Sallie. *The Body of God: An Ecological Theology*. Minneapolis: Augsburg Fortress, 1993.

McGinn, Bernard. *The Flowing of Mysticism: Men and Women in the New Mysticism—1200 1350*. Vol. 2 of *The Presence of God: A History of Western Christian Mysticism*. New York: Crossroad, 1998.

McGinn, Bernard. *The Harvest of Mysticism in Medieval Germany*. Vol. 4 of *The Presence of God: A History of Western Christian Mysticism*. New York: Crossroad, 2005.

McGinn, Bernard. "Meister Eckhart on God as Absolute Unity." In *Neoplatonism and Christian Thought*, edited by Dominic J. O'Meara, 128–39. Norfolk, VA: International Society for Neoplatonic Studies, 1982.

Mansini, Guy. "Lonergan on the Natural Desire in Light of Feingold." *Nova et Vetera* [English] 5 (2007): 185–98.

Marion, Jean-Luc. "Creation of the Eternal Truths: The Principle of Reason—Spinoza, Malebranche, Leibniz." In *On the Ego and on God: Further Cartesian Questions*, translated by Christina M. Geschwandtner, 139–60. New York: Fordham University Press, 2007.

Marion, Jean-Luc. *God without Being: Hors-Texte*. Translated by Thomas A. Carlson. Chicago: University of Chicago Press, 1991.

Marion, Jean-Luc. "The Idea of God." In *The Cambridge History of Seventeenth-Century Philosophy*, vol. 1, edited by Daniel Garber and Michael Ayers, 265–304. Cambridge: Cambridge University Press, 1997.

Marion, Jean-Luc. "Is the Ontological Argument Ontological? The Argument According to Anselm and Its Metaphysical Interpretation According to Kant." *Journal of the History of Philosophy* 30 (1992): 201–18.

Marion, Jean-Luc. "Metaphysics and Phenomenology: A Relief for Theology." *Critical Inquiry* 20 (1994): 572–91.

Marion, Jean-Luc. "The Saturated Phenomenon." *Philosophy Today* 40 (1996): 103–24.

Marion, Jean-Luc. *Sur l'ontologie grise de Descartes: Savoir aristotélicien et science cartésienne dan les Regulae*. Paris: Vrin, 1975.

Marion, Jean-Luc. *Sur la prisme métaphysique de Descartes*. Paris: PUF, 1986. Translated by Jeffrey L. Kosky under the title *On Descartes' Metaphysical Prism*. Chicago: University of Chicago Press, 1999.

Marion, Jean-Luc. *Sur la théologie blanche de Descartes: analogie, création des vérités éternelles et fondement*. 2nd ed. Paris: Quadrige/PUF, 1991.

Marrone, Steven P. *The Light of Thy Countenance: Science and Knowledge of God in the Thirteenth Century, Volume I: A Doctrine of Divine Illumination*. Leiden: E. J. Brill, 2001.

Marx, Karl. "The Eighteenth Brumaire of Louis Napoleon." In *The Marx-Engels Reader*. 2nd ed., edited by Robert C. Tucker, 594–617. New York: W.W. Norton, 1978.

Maurer, Armand. "Ens Diminutum: a Note on its Origin and Meaning." *Mediaeval Studies* 12 (1950): 216–222.

Maurer, Armand. "St. Thomas and Eternal Truths." *Mediaeval Studies* 32 (1970): 91–107.

Meinhardt, H., G. Schrimpf, Chr. Knudsen, G. Wieland, G. Jüssen, and W. Kluxen. "Idee." In *Historisches Wörterbuch der Philosophie*, vol. 4, edited by Joachim Ritter and Karlfried Gründer, 62–93. Basel: Schwabe, 1976.

Milbank, John. "Can a Gift Be Given? Prolegomena to a Future Trinitarian Metaphysic." *Modern Theology* 11 (1995): 119–61.

Milbank, John. "A Christological Poetics." In *The Word Made Strange*, 123–44. Oxford: Blackwell, 1997.
Milbank, John. "Enclaves, or Where is the Church?" *New Blackfriars* 73 (1992): 341–52.
Milbank, John. "Intensities." *Modern Theology* 15 (1999): 445–97.
Milbank, John. "The Name of Jesus." In *The Word Made Strange*, 145–68. Oxford: Blackwell, 1997.
Milbank, John. "'Postmodern Critical Augustinianism': A Short *Summa* in Forty-Two Responses to Unasked Questions." *Modern Theology* 7 (1991): 225–37.
Milbank, John. "The Second Difference." In *The Word Made Strange*. Oxford: Blackwell, 1997.
Milbank, John. *The Suspended Middle: Henri de Lubac and the Debate concerning the Supernatural*. Grand Rapids, MI: William B. Eerdmans, 2005.
Milbank, John. *Theology and Social Theory: Beyond Secular Reason*. Oxford: Blackwell, 1990.
Milbank, John. *The Word Made Strange: Theology, Language, Culture*. Oxford: Blackwell, 1997.
Moloney, Raymond, S.J. "De Lubac and Lonergan on the Supernatural." *Theological Studies* 69 (2008): 509–27.
Mooney, Edward F. "*Repetition*: Getting the World Back." In *The Cambridge Companion to Kierkegaard*, edited by Alastair Hannay and Gordon D. Marino, 282–307. Cambridge: Cambridge University Press, 1998.
Moore, Sebastian. "Some Principles for an Adequate Theism." *Downside Review* 95 (1977): 201–13.
Nicholas of Cusa. *Selected Spiritual Writings*. Translated by H. Lawrence Bond. New York: Paulist Press, 1997.
Nichtweiss, Barbara. *Erik Peterson: Neue Sicht auf Leben und Werk*. Freiburg: Herder, 1992.
Nisbet, H. B. "The Rationalisation of the Holy Trinity from Lessing to Hegel." *Lessing Yearbook* 31 (1999): 65–89.
Pascal, Blaise. *Pensées*. Translated by W. F. Trotter. 1932. Reprint, London: J. M. Dent & Sons, 1956.
Pegis, Anton C. "The Dilemma of Being and Unity: A Platonic Incident in Christian Thought." In *Essays in Thomism*, edited by Robert Edward Brennan, 151–83. New York: Sheed & Ward, 1942.
Peterson, Erik. *Theological Tractates* [1951]. Translated by Michael J. Hollerich. Stanford: Stanford University Press, 2011.
Peterson, Erik. "What is Theology?" In *Theological Tractates*, translated by Michael J. Hollerich, 1–14. Stanford: Stanford University Press, 2011.
Pohier, Jacques. *God—in Fragments*. Translated by John Bowden. New York: Crossroad, 1986.
Reimer, Louis. "Die Wiederholung als Problem der Erlösung bei Kierkegaard." In *Materialien zur Philosophie Søren Kierkegaards*, edited by Michael Theunissen and Wilfried Greve, 302–46. Frankfurt: Suhrkamp, 1979.
Richter, Johann Paul Friedrich. *Horn of Oberon: Jean Paul Richter's School for Aesthetics*. Translated by Margaret R. Hale. Detroit: Wayne State University Press, 1973.
Ricoeur, Paul. *The Symbolism of Evil*. Translated by Emerson Buchanan. Boston: Beacon Press, 1967.
Ross, James F. "Aquinas's Exemplarism, Aquinas's Voluntarism." *American Catholic Philosophical Quarterly* 64 (1990): 171–98.

Rousselot, Pierre. *Intelligence: Sense of Being, Faculty of God*. Translated by Andrew Tallon. Milwaukee: Marquette University Press, 1999.
Schelling, F. W. J. *On University Studies*. Translated by E. S. Morgan. Edited by Norbert Guterman. Athens: Ohio University Press, 1966.
Schleiermacher, Friedrich. *Der Christliche Glaube. Nach den Grundsätzen der evangelischen Kirche im Zusammenhange dargestellt. Zweite Auflage (1830/31)*. Edited by Rolf Schäfer. Vol. 13 of *Kritische Gesamtausgabe, Erste Abteilung: Schriften und Entwürfe*. Edited by Hermann Fischer, Ulrich Barth, Konrad Cramer, Günter Meckenstock, and Kurt-Victor Selge. Berlin: Walter de Gruyter, 2003. Translated by D. M. Baillie, W. R. Matthews, Edith Sandbach-Marshall, A. B. Macaulay, Alexander Grieve, J. Y. Campbell, R. W. Stewart, and H. R. Mackintosh under the title *The Christian Faith*. Edinburgh: T&T Clark, 1928.
Sløk, Johannes. "Die griechische Philosophie als Bezugsrahmen für Constantin Constantius und Johannes de Silentio." In *Materialien zur Philosophie Søren Kierkegaards*, edited by Michael Theunissen and Wilfried Greve, 280–301. Frankfurt: Suhrkamp, 1979.
Smith, Jonathan Z. "Map is Not Territory." In *Map is Not Territory: Studies in the History of Religions*, 299–309. Leiden: E.J. Brill, 1978.
Sokolowski, Robert. *The God of Faith and Reason*. Notre Dame: University of Notre Dame Press, 1982.
Stebbins, J. Michael. *The Divine Initiative: Grace, World-Order, and Human Freedom in the Early Writings of Bernard Lonergan*. Toronto: University of Toronto Press, 1995.
Steel, Carlos. "Henricus Gandavensis Platonicus." In *Henry of Ghent and the Transformation of Scholastic Thought*, edited by Guy Guldentops and Carlos Steel, 15–39. Leuven: Leuven University Press, 2003.
Stolina, Ralf. "'Ökonomische' und 'immanente' Trinität? Zur Problematik einer trinitätstheologischen Denkfigur." *Zeitschrift für Theologie und Kirche* 105 (2008): 170–216.
Suarez, Francisco. *On the Essence of Finite Being as Such, on the Existence of that Essence, and their Distinction. Metaphysical Disputation XXXI*. Translated by Norman J. Wells. Milwaukee, WI: Marquette University Press, 1983.
Tanner, Kathryn. *Christ the Key*. Cambridge: Cambridge University Press, 2010.
Tanner, Kathryn. *God and Creation in Christian Theology: Tyranny or Empowerment?* Oxford: Basil Blackwell, 1988.
Tanner, Kathryn. *Jesus, Humanity and the Trinity: A Brief Systematic Theology*. Minneapolis: Fortress Press, 2001.
Te Velde, Rudi A. *Participation and Substantiality in Thomas Aquinas*. Leiden: E. J. Brill, 1995.
Thunberg, Lars. *Microcosm and Mediator: The Theological Anthropology of Maximus the Confessor*. 2nd ed. Peru, IL: Open Court, 1995.
Tonstad, Linn. *God and Difference: The Trinity, Sexuality, and the Transformation of Finitude*. New York: Routledge, 2016.
Ward, Graham. "John Milbank's Divina Commedia." *New Blackfriars* 73 (1992): 311–18.
Weinandy, Thomas. *Does God Suffer?* Edinburgh: T&T Clark, 2000.
Whitehead, Alfred North. *Science and the Modern World*. New York: Macmillan, 1925.
Williams, Rowan. "Balthasar and Rahner." In *The Analogy of Beauty*, edited by John Riches, 11–34. Edinburgh: T&T Clark, 1986.
Williams, Rowan. "The Finality of Christ." In *On Christian Theology*, 93–106. Oxford: Blackwell, 2000.

Williams, Rowan. "Interiority and Epiphany: A Reading in New Testament Ethics." In *On Christian Theology*, 239–64. Oxford: Blackwell, 2000.
Williams, Rowan. "The Judgment of the World." In *On Christian Theology*, 29–43. Oxford: Blackwell, 2000.
Williams, Rowan. "The Nicene Heritage." In *The Christian Understanding of God Today*, edited by James M. Byrne, 45–8. Dublin: Columba Press, 1993.
Williams, Rowan. "On Being Creatures." In *On Christian Theology*, 63–78. Oxford: Blackwell, 2000.
Williams, Rowan. *On Christian Theology*. Oxford: Blackwell, 2000.
Williams, Rowan. "Saving Time: Thoughts on Practice, Patience and Vision." *New Blackfriars* 73 (1992): 319–26.
Williams, Rowan. "Trinity and Ontology." In *On Christian Theology*, 148–66. Oxford: Blackwell, 2000.
Wippel, John F. "Thomas Aquinas and Participation." In *Studies in Medieval Philosophy*, edited by John F. Wippel, 117–58. Washington DC: Catholic University of America Press, 1984.
Wittgenstein, Ludwig. *Tractatus Logico-Philosophicus*. Translated by D. F. Pears and B. F. McGuiness. London: Routledge & Kegan Paul, 1961.
Wood, Allen W. *Kant's Rational Theology*. Ithaca: Cornell University Press, 1978.
Wood, Charles M. *The Formation of Christian Understanding*. Philadelphia: Westminster, 1981.
Žižek, Slavoj. *The Ticklish Subject: The Absent Centre of Political Ontology*. London: Verso, 1999.

Index

absolute creator 1, 23, 126; *see also* creator
absolute dependence 8, 41–53
   consciousness 46–47, 50
   self-consciousness 46
absolute interest 47
absolute metaphysical axiom 4
absolute superiority 30, 34
active consciousness 51; *see also* consciousness
actual grace 11, 146, 153, 156, 179
agnosticism 107–108
Albert the Great 229, 252
allegorization 125
altera civitas 170
Amalrician pantheism 227
Amalric of Bene 195, 221
analogia fidei 36
Animal Crackers (film) 126
anthropology 50, 91, 220, 227
   cultural 97
   Greek 71
   theological 88, 119, 147
anti-Cartesian 34
anti-Christian 180; *see also* Christian
anti-Christianity 180
anti-Platonic 196, 210, 216, 219–220, 227, 231, 253
anti-Platonism 221, 234; *see also* Platonism
aporia 23–25, 34, 37, 119
aptness 90, 95
Aquinas, T. 4–7, 133, 136, 144–145, 147, 151, 154, 156–158, 165, 172, 196–203, 209–215, 219–220, 236–240, 253, 262
   agnosticism 108
   anti-Platonic stance 267
   Bonaventurian idea theory 256
   Christian metaphysical theism 105
   construal of human intellection 206
   created existence 141
   description of analogy 107

   Disputed Questions on Truth 213, 243, 245, 248
   divine ideas 185
   doctrine of ideas 254
   fittingness 217
   framework of creation 227
   hierarchical ontology 146
   human action 143
   idea theory 209
   ocean tides 152
   pragmatic primacy of created existence 224–227
   Pseudo-Dionysius 107–108
   re-Platonizing the double identity 227–231
   revised idea theory 239
   Summa Contra Gentiles 15, 211–213
   theology 171, 225, 261
   theory of ideas 205, 215–216
   theory of the will 265
   Trinitarian 190
   unattainability of ideas 221–224
   views about God 15, 121, 134, 137, 150, 170, 186, 268
   voluntarism 191, 242–246
Aquinas and Radical Orthodoxy (DeHart) 15
Arabic emanationism 227
Arabic metaphysicians 195
Aristotle 59, 197–198, 201, 206, 222, 226, 230
ascension 169–170
Athanasius (theologian) 86
Augustine (theologian) 157, 171, 195, 200–201, 212, 214, 226, 249
Avicennian bent of Albert 252
awareness 45, 50
   beatific 193
   divine 242
   God 44, 47, 51, 110, 192, 202, 225
   material realities 201

282 *Index*

precognitive 45
recollection 67
repetition 67
self 8, 45–47, 218, 234
selfhood 76
self-identity 45
world 47

Baillie, D. M. 86
Balthasar, H. U. von 128–134
Barth, K. 118–119, 180
Barthian theology of revelation 38
Battle of the Old and the New Soap-Cellars, The (Kierkegaard) 41
Bauerschmidt, F. 160
being and agency 76–81, 140
being and nonbeing 77
being and time 81
being-known 203
being-*qua*-being 26, 28
Blondel, M. 96
Bonaventure 201
Bonhoeffer, D. 164
Booth, E. 237
Bride of the Lamb (Bulgakov) 261
Bulgakov, S. 261–262
Burns, P. 15
Burrell, D. 1, 4

Caesar, J. 188
Cambridge History of Seventeenth-Century Philosophy (Marion) 33
Cartesian discourse of God 32, 34
Cartesian epistemology 27
Cartesian God 30–35
Cartesian infinite 38–39
Cartesian metaphysics 26, 36
Cartesian ontology 27
Cartesian subject 22
Cartesian theism 34, 37
categorical leap 238
Catholic Christian 212; *see also* Christian
Catholic orthodoxy 125
Chalcedonian orthodoxy 52
chaotic dynamics 239
Chapman, J. 16
Christ as God 161
Christendom 162, 173–174
Christ for humanity 160

Christian 1, 45, 64, 69–71, 79, 88, 92, 97, 113, 165, 232, 241
belief 2, 135, 173, 233
church 161, 166
claims 127, 159
community 44, 158–159, 164
confession 259
consciousness 43
cultural intervention 134, 176
discourse 87, 97, 134, 173–174
discovery of spirit 74
doctrine 37, 92, 110, 186
dogmatics 50, 76
eschatology 61
eschaton 152
faith 2, 46, 157, 172, 175
foundational 'myths' 165
gospel 105
metanarrative 181
metaphysical theism 105
mythos 175
ontology 167, 169
paradoxes 52, 74
persuasiveness 176
redemption 93
salvation 127
self-consistent 163
spirituality 228
theologian 3, 162, 219, 225, 261
theology 38, 42, 125, 161–162, 185, 195–196
tradition 97, 111, 259
truth 80, 160
vision 57–62
Christian Faith, The (Schleiermacher) 46
Christianity 1, 43, 62, 160, 181, 231
idolatry 72
pagan philosophy and 70
polarization 74
Christian Platonism 200, 202, 215, 264
Christological mystery 52
Christological Poetics, A (Milbank) 164
Christology 3, 50, 52, 82, 127, 166
creation and 86
ecclesiology 168
non-eschatological 167
theological role of 129
Christ the Key (Tanner) 85, 89
classical theism 3–4, 7

Index   283

"code-model" 235
collective consciousness 173; *see also* consciousness
commensurateness 62
Commentary on the Book of Wisdom (Eckhart) 229
common and usual course of justification 146
communion with God 143–144; *see also* God
comprehensores 170
Concept of Anxiety, The (Haufniensis) 42
Concluding Unscientific Postscript (Climacus) 46
consciousness 45, 78
  absolute dependence 47, 50
  active 51
  anti-Cartesian 34
  Christian 43
  collective 173
  God 44, 50
  human 48, 111
  immediate 45–46
  individual 76
  intermittent 112
  rational 8
  self 44, 46, 52, 83
"Constantin Constantius" 55, 57, 64, 69, 76–77, 80
continental metaphysics 255
contingency 43, 51, 134, 156, 190, 202, 216, 220, 239, 268–269
cosmic senescence 94
counter-ontology 159, 161
creation
  Christology and 86
  classical doctrine 1
  ex nihilo 1–2, 11, 14, 57, 67, 95, 105, 120, 186, 215–216, 219–220, 241, 265–267
  God and 195
  traditional 2
creational monotheism 1, 4–6
creational theism 4, 13
creative monotheism 2–4, 16
creator
  absolute 1, 23, 126
  Chalcedonian orthodoxy 52
  conceptuality 82
  ex nihilo 81, 114
  of heaven and earth 113
  intentions 58, 65, 81
  intimacy 87
  intimacy with 87
  monotheistic 241
  omnipotent 216, 233
  providential 233
  trace 171
  transcendent 1, 3, 58, 72
  unique 159
creatrix divinitatis 52
crucifixion 109
cultural anthropology 97

Dalferth, I. 5–6
Dasein 77, 81, 115
de Certeau, M. 173, 175
DeHart, P. 109
Deity 106
de la Mare, W. 225
de Lubac, H. 140, 144, 149, 152, 163, 180
demythologization 265
dependence *see* absolute dependence
de Saussure, F. 235, 268
Descartes, R. 23–29, 30–33, 35–38, 209, 254, 257–258
discourse, Christian 97
disintegration of divine being 30
Disputed Questions on Truth (Aquinas) 213, 243, 245, 248
dissolving unity of creative act 246–253
dissolving unity of creative agent 253–258
divine cognition 200
divine ideas as anti-Platonic ontology 241–269
  Aquinas, T. 242–246
  dissolving unity of creative act 246–253
  dissolving unity of creative agent 253–258
  voluntarism of creation 242–246
  world as God's inner life 258–261
divine ideas as anti-Platonic soteriology 219–240
  Aquinas, T. 221–231
  Eckhart, M. 227–231
  eschatology of existence 231–234
  individuality 236–240
  linguistic self as ontologically irreducible 234–236

pragmatic primacy of created existence 224–227
re-Platonizing double identity 227–231
unattainability of ideas 221–224
divine identity 108–109, 113, 116, 161, 259
divine infinity 5, 144
divine mind 195–218
  Aquinas, T. 196–200, 209–215
  Christian theology 195–196
  end of illumination 200–202
  ideas as objects 202–207
  ideas as the divine essence 202–207
  ideas as uncreated 207–209
  Marion's interpretation and question of Trinity 209–215
  Platonic ideas 195–196
  Platonism 207–209
  reconfiguration of idea theory 196–200
  Suarez, F. 209–215
divine names 36
divine self-creation 263
divine self-disclosure 112
divine self-gift 126
divine self-identification 116
divine self-objectification 112
divine self-utterance 121, 179
divine transcendence 32, 37–38, 58
divine Triunity 106, 117, 171
divine unity 117
dogmatics 43, 52
  Christian 50, 76
  philosophy and 41
  pure 42
  science 42
  speculative 42–45
doppelgänger 193
double onto-theo-logy 26
Dumont, M. 181
Duns Scotus, J. 5, 203–204, 206–208, 255–256
Duquoc, C. 117

ecclesiology, Christology 168
Eckhart, M. 220–221, 227–231
economic Trinity 113–114
Education of the Human Race, The (Lessing) 260
effacement of interiority 96–101
emanationism 227

Emery, G. 217
end of illumination 200–202
enjoyment without desire 94–96
epistemological revolution 22–29
Eriugena, J. 221
Ernst, C. 130, 166–167, 174
eschatology 62, 94, 98, 169, 176
  Christian 61
  of existence 231–234
esse distinctum 211
esse essentiae 207–208, 215
essence of repetition 72–76
essential existence 205
essentialism 208, 252, 259
esse objectivum 206, 208, 215
esthetic-metaphysical 42, 73
eternal self-mediation 117; *see also* self-mediation
eternal truths 31
European Christendom 173

Fabro, C. 83, 250, 253
false humility 132, 162–164
false modesty 36
Farrer, A. 4
Fear and Trembling (Kierkegaard) 69
feeling *(Gefühl)* 45–46
Fields, W. C. 268
Finite and Infinite (Farrer) 4
finite determinacy 2, 12
fittingness 217
formal existence 230
Franciscan 239, 254, 260
Francis of Meyronnes 207–208, 255
Frank, M. 179, 221, 235–240
freedom 46
  aggressive appropriation 46
  desire 9
  elusive 39
  eternal significance 68
  finite spirit 79
  human 1, 91, 96, 234
  immediate enjoyment 51
  from itself 51
  self-revealing 115
  subjective 234
  temporal 63
  theoretical refutation of 65
  transcendence 53

Freud, S. 100
Friedman, R. 256
Frissell, B. 192

Geiger, L. 250, 253
German idealism 4, 262, 265
German romanticism 4, 74
Gilson, E. 189, 225, 257
Glory of the Lord (Balthasar) 128
God 21–39
  absolute intellection 202
  absolute superiority 30
  act of being 144, 190, 196–197, 204, 240, 262–263
  attributes 107–108
  awareness 44, 47, 51, 110, 192, 202, 225
  causal agency 114
  in Christ 44, 51, 109, 111–112, 130
  cognition 227
  communion with 143–144
  creation 195, 239
  creative idea 193
  as creator 114, 199
  defined 5, 7, 21–23
  diversification by 221
  divine status 113
  in epistemological revolution 22–29
  essence/existence 24–25, 108, 119
  eternal ideas 222
  eternal identity 119
  eternal knowledge 220
  eternal life 113
  eternal self-apprehension 264
  eternal thoughts 195
  exemplary causality 264
  existence in 193
  externalization 262
  genuine gift 141
  governance of the world 139
  gracious act 168
  idea of God 207
  ideas of creatures 210
  identity 192, 262
  image in creation 6
  immutable vision of 171
  incarnate Word 178
  incarnation in Jesus Christ 86
  infinite 5, 13, 35–39, 79, 83, 111, 181, 187, 263, 268
  intellect 187, 264
  intelligence 214
  intelligibilities 238, 261
  internally self-generated 95
  invisibility 72
  of Israel 166
  knowing of creation 242
  knowledge 13, 170, 185, 206–207, 216, 221, 255
  lingering cultural death 111
  metaphysics 35–37
  mode of actuality 24
  multiplicity 12
  natural desire for 155
  natural love of 155
  nature and identity 107
  necessary self-willing 267
  of negative theology 107
  non-miraculous working of providence 146
  offer of communion 96
  omnipresence 72
  omniscience 197
  own identity 197
  perfection 255
  perfect knowledge 268
  philosophical legacy of Cartesian 30–35
  presence 107
  primal self-utterance 211
  providential vision 156
  as pure being 189
  pure benevolence 179
  reconciling presence 118
  relation to the world 2
  rich immensity 138
  salvation and 124
  saving grace 157
  self-bestowal 98
  self-comprehension 255
  self-contemplation 259
  self-disclosive 161, 166
  self-disclosure 130
  self-gift 95, 126–128, 178–180
  self-intelligibility 200
  self-knowing 216
  self-knowledge 100, 217, 248, 259–260
  self-regard 217
  self-relation 204
  self-understanding 255

self-willing 267
single act of self-understanding 205
speculative intellect 209
as spirit 260
theological ethics 92
transcendence 7
triune 94, 98, 143
triunity 112
ultimate Word 165
union with 144–145, 147
unsurpassable giving 147
unwarranted love 158
very act of being 215
vision of 144
willing act 267
world and 2
God as the Mystery of the World (Jüngel) 22–23, 34, 106, 110–111
God-ordinance 141–142
God-relations 50, 142
God-relationship 48, 71–72
God's Being Is in Becoming (Jüngel) 111, 120
Goris, H. 252
Gospel of John 230
Gouhier, H. 257
gray ontology 26–28
Greek
 anthropology 71
 Christian 63
 contemptus mundi 76
 pantheism of 72
Gregory of Nyssa 87, 91

habitual grace 146–147, 153–155
Hadewijch of Antwerp 228
Hayden, S. 15
Hebrews 1
Hegel, G. W. F. 5, 35, 41–42, 74–75, 112, 119, 160, 178, 231, 260
Hegelian idealism 41
Hegelianism 79, 231–232
Hegelian philosophy 73
Heidegger, M. 24, 26, 31, 82, 128
 analysis of *Dasein* 81
 conception of metaphysics 27
 distinction of Being and beings 135
 reading of metaphysics 27
Henrich, D. 235

Henry of Ghent 203–204, 206–208, 217, 252–253, 255
Hirsch, E. 82
Holl, K. 82
Holy Scripture 43
Holy Spirit 63, 95, 117
human being 208
human cognition 216
human community 165, 168
human consciousness 48, 111; *see also* consciousness
human culture 127
human desire 96, 98, 156
human freedom 91
human intellect 195
human intellection 98, 202, 206
human intellectual knowledge 201
human intelligence 156, 191
human knowledge 112, 196, 202–203
human nature 90–91, 145, 155, 157
human objectification 111
human psychodynamics 100
human psychology 100, 115
human self-experience 99
human transcendence 53
Humboldt, A. von 237

ideas as divine essence 202–207
ideas as objects 202–207
ideas as uncreated 207–209
identification 109, 112, 116, 160, 169–170, 206, 223–224, 227, 234, 263
illuminationism 200, 202
illuminationist epistemology 214
imago Dei 144, 146, 156, 171
imago trinitatis 177
immanent ontology 135
immediate consciousness 45–46; *see also* consciousness
immediate self-consciousness 46
incarnation and redemption 181
indeterminable by concept 36
individualism 93
individuality 236–240
infinite God 5, 13, 35–39, 79, 83, 111, 181, 187, 263, 268; *see also* God
infinite intelligibilities 249
infinite negative resolution 8, 46–47
infinite resignation 69

infinite space 83
inner infinity 74–75
intelligence 6
intelligibilities 201, 238, 249, 261
intentio intellecta 211, 213
internal alterity 211
internally self-generated 90, 95
intimacy with creator 87
intuitus originarius 188–189, 216, 238
inverse sublime 179
inwardness 46
Islam 1
Israel's God 113; *see also* God

Jauss, H. R. 263
Jesus, Humanity and the Trinity (Tanner) 85
Jesus as God 175
Jesus Christ 50–51, 90, 109, 129–130, 132, 168, 178, 214, 262–263
    ascension 169–170
    dispossession 176
    divine self-utterance 179
    humanity 86–87
    substantive meaning 167
    ultimacy 164
Jesus of Nazareth 6
Jewish monotheism 266
"Johannes Climacus" 21, 46, 79–80, 82
Jordan, M. 202, 216
Judaism 1, 163
Jüngel, E. 16, 22–24, 26, 29–31, 33–38, 105–121
    description of analogy 107–108
    discussion of God 115
    God as the Mystery of the World 22–23, 34, 106, 110–111
    God's Being Is in Becoming 111, 120

Kant, I. 31, 107–108, 187–188, 216, 265
Keller, C. 2
Kerr, F. 181
Kierkegaard, S. 21, 41–46, 50, 59–60, 65–66, 72–78, 80, 83, 106–110, 118, 176, 193, 221, 231–232; *see also* repetition
    anthropology of freedom 233
    Christian truth 80
    Christological mystery 52
    discussion of moment 69–70

divine transcendence 58
eschatology of existence 231–234
ethic of authentic subjectivity 82
Fear and Trembling 69
God-Man 52
infinite negative resolution 47
maximum intensification of subjectivity 51
modern-Christian epoch 79
ontology of agency 57, 81–82
ontology of *interesse* 76–81
pantheism of the Greeks 72
philosophical anthropology 237
philosophical/theological anthropology of repetition 68
protest of 117–121
repetition 63, 236
Repetition 55–56, 68
romanticism and idealism 57
theological anthropology 119, 234
vision of divine providence 49

Larmore, C. 53
Lash, N. 165
Lateran Council (1215) 110
lazy sophism 63–72, 76
Leibniz, G. W. 33, 55, 59–62, 64, 80–82, 188, 237, 256–260
    lazy sophism 63–72
    Theodicy 56–57, 60, 258
    views about repetition 57
Lessing, G. E. 259–260
Lévi-Strauss, C. 99–100
Lewis, C. S. 121, 123–124, 179
Lindbeck, G. 161, 178
linguistic self as ontologically irreducible 234–236
Løkke, H. 68
Lonergan, B. 143, 150, 189, 205, 214–215, 261
Lucinde (Schlegel) 74–75
Luther, M. 119–120
Lyotard, J.-F. 162

Marion, J.-L. 22–23, 26–27, 29, 31–37, 39, 209–215, 217, 253, 257
Martensen, H. L. 41
Marx, K. 93
Maurer, A. 209

McCabe, H. 1, 114, 171, 266
McCormack, B. 262
McFague, S. 2
McGinn, B. 229
Meditations (Descartes) 32
Mersenne, M. 32, 257
metanarrative 162–163, 166, 168, 173, 175, 178, 181
metaphysics 26–27, 34, 130, 139, 144, 154, 165, 221, 255
   God 35–37
   as onto-theo-logy 27, 29, 36
   process 2
Metaphysics and Phenomenology: A Relief for Theology (Marion) 37
Milbank, J. 123–181
   Christological Poetics, A 164
   cultural strategy 127
   Suspended Middle 148
   Theology and Social Theory 125, 129, 158–159, 163
   von Balthasar, H. U. 128–134
mind *see* divine mind
Mirandola, P. della 140
modernity 22, 34, 64, 79, 81–82, 107, 111, 118, 159, 162–163, 209
moment 70–71, 77, 82
monotheism 216, 266
most perfect being *(ens perfectissimum)* 35
movement of infinity 69
mutual other-relation 86–88

natural desire 145
nature grace 152–153, 155
Nature of Doctrine: Religion and Theology in a Postliberal Age, The (Lindbeck) 161
necessitarianism 227
negative theology 107, 110
New Testament 50, 62, 97, 109, 113, 116, 119
Nicene Creed 265
Nicholas of Cusa 190–191
Nietzsche, F. 35
nihilism 163
nonbeing and being 77
non-competitive 86

objective being 215
objectivism 215

occasionalist 112
omniscience 197
On Christian Theology (Williams) 14, 187
On Learned Ignorance (Nicholas of Cusa) 190
ontology; *see also* repetition
   of agency 57, 77, 79, 81–82
   immanent 135
   of *interesse* 76–81
   theological 135, 137, 139–140, 180
onto-theo-logy, metaphysics as 29, 36
Origen (scholar) 195, 215
original sin 93

pantheism 72, 227
paradigms *see* divine ideas as anti-Platonic ontology
Paradise Lost 115
paradox 44, 69, 187
   Christian 52, 74
   theology 149
   transcendent creator 72
pathos-filled transition 60
Patristic theology 219
Paul, J. 179
Peckham, J. 200
Pegis, A. 237, 252, 268
Peterson, E. 118, 173
Philo (philosopher) 215
Philosophical Fragments 43
Plato 209, 216, 218, 249, 264
Platonic dualism 226
Platonic epistemology 261
Platonic ideas 195–196
Platonism 191, 207–209, 219, 227, 254, 268
Pohier, J. 132
pragmatic primacy of created existence 224–227
predestination 153
principles of sufficient reason 33
Problem of Pain, The (Lewis) 121
process metaphysics 2
providence 137
Pseudo-Dionysius 36, 107–108, 171, 262
psychological analogy 212, 256
pure dogmatics 42; *see also* dogmatics
pure nature 154–155

radical orthodoxy 125
Rahner, K. 86
reconfiguration of idea theory 196–200
redemption and incarnation 181
repetition 55–84, 101, 236
   being and agency 76–81
   Christian vision 57–62
   defined 76
   essence of 72–76
   eternal identity 67
   lazy sophism 63–72
   ontology of *interesse* 76–81
   rescuing Kierkegaardian agent 81–84
   self confronts 57–62
   spirit 57–62
Repetition (Kierkegaard) 55–56, 68
re-Platonizing double identity 227–231
representationalism 215
resignation 69, 76
revelation 113, 265
romanticism 75
Ross, J. F. 189
Rückschluss 117
Rules for the Direction of the Mind
   (Descartes) 27

saving grace 146, 157
Schlegel, F. 72–76
Schleiermacher, F. 41–46, 49–50, 113, 121,
   179, 236–237
   aesthetic vision of harmonious unity 53
   basic predicament of sin 50
   Christian Faith, The 46
   God as non-metaphysical critical
     realism 48
   God in Christ 51
   Second Adam 52
   views about feeling 47
   work of Christ 51
Schmitt, C. 82, 173
Scholastics 206
school metaphysics 26
secularism 180
self-awareness 8, 45–47, 218, 234; *see also*
   awareness
self-concretion 264
self-consciousness 44, 46, 52, 83, 180; *see
   also* consciousness
self-construction 72, 234

self-creation 231
self-disclosure 112–113, 130
self-expression 73–74, 254
self-gift 126, 133
selfhood 64, 69, 98, 233–235
   conceptions of God 71
   deeper region 101
   inner infinity 75
   theology of 99
self-identification 112, 116
self-mediation 117
self-relation 116, 200, 211
Smith, J. Z. 174
social Trinitarianism 92
social Trinity 91–93
Socrates 60, 62, 68, 71, 80, 215
Sokolowski, R. 4, 86
Solger, K. W. F. 75
sophiology 261
soteriology 86, 91, 220, 230
speculative dogmatics 42–45
spirit 57–62, 73, 87, 145, 260
Spirit 99, 111, 126, 263
Stolina, R. 113
Suarez, F. 208, 209–215, 210, 215, 254, 257
subjectivity 15, 17, 29, 47–48, 51, 56, 58,
   70, 73, 79, 82, 87, 100, 145, 220,
   234–235
sublime 17
Summa Contra Gentiles (Aquinas) 15,
   211–213
supernatural 145, 147; *see also* God
supernatural charity 151, 154
supernatural gift 95
Supreme Being 188
Sur la prisme métaphysique de Descartes
   (Marion) 32, 35
Sur la théologie blanche de Descartes
   (Marion) 23, 27
Surnaturel (de Lubac) 149, 152
Suspended Middle (Milbank) 148

Tanner, K. 85–101
   algebra of redemption 88–91
   Christ the Key 85, 89
   effacement of interiority 96–101
   enjoyment without desire 94–96
   Jesus, Humanity and the Trinity 85
   L'automatisme de répétition 96–101

mutual other-relation 86–88
replicating pattern 86–88
social Trinity 91–93
theory of salvation 96
Trinitarian economics 91–93
temporalization of existence 31
te Velde, R. 189, 217, 237, 250–251
Theodicy (Leibniz) 56–57, 60, 82, 258
theologia crucis 4
theologians of glory 120
theological anthropology 88, 119, 147
theological ontology 135, 137, 139–140, 180
theological virtues 89
theology 42, 85, 125, 170
   brief systematic 86
   Christian 125, 161–162, 182
   negative 107, 110
   paradox 149
Theology and Social Theory (Milbank) 125, 129, 158–159, 163
Theology on the Way to Emmaus (Lash) 165
theorizing creation 266
trace, creator 171
traditional creation 2; *see also* creation
transcendence 159
   divine 58
   freedom 53
   of God 58
   human 53
Trinitarian/Trinitarianism 91, 97, 99
   analogy 100
   economics 91–93
   procession 256, 264
   teaching 92

theory 92
thinking 85, 113
Trinitarian Word 214
Trinity 121, 180, 212–213, 229, 256
   doctrine 112
   economic 113–114
   fecundity of 136
   of German idealism 259, 261
   givenness of being 140
   revelation and 113
   self-effacing character 101
   against Trinity 117
Triunity 156, 171
turn to consciousness 34

unattainability of ideas 221–224
universal instrumentality 143
universal intentionality 139

"Vigilius Haufniensis" 42–43
voluntarism 191, 238–239, 242–246

Waller, A. 68
Ward, G. 125
Whitehead, A. N. 2, 7, 177
white theology 26, 209
whole Christ 112
Williams, R. 1, 14, 125–127, 131, 133, 158–159, 161, 163–169, 175–176, 178, 187, 265
Williams Christology 132
Wippel, J. 252–253
Wood, C. 21
world as God's inner life 258–261

www.ingramcontent.com/pod-product-compliance
Lightning Source LLC
Chambersburg PA
CBHW072125290426
44111CB00012B/1775